Patterns in Post-Soviet Leadership

WITHDRAWN

The John M. Olin Critical Issues Series

Published in cooperation with
the Harvard University Russian Research Center

Patterns in Post-Soviet Leadership, edited by Timothy J. Colton and Robert C. Tucker

Central Asia in Historical Perspective, edited by Beatrice F. Manz

In Search of Pluralism: Soviet and Post-Soviet Politics, edited by Carol R. Saivetz and Anthony Jones

Soviet Social Problems, edited by Anthony Jones, Walter D. Connor, and David E. Powell

The Nationalities Factor in Soviet Politics and Society, edited by Lubomyr Hajda and Mark Beissinger

The Soviet Union in the Third World, edited by Carol Saivetz

Patterns in
Post-Soviet Leadership

EDITED BY

Timothy J. Colton
Robert C. Tucker

Westview Press

Boulder · San Francisco · Oxford

The John M. Olin Critical Issues Series

Copyright © 1995 by The Harvard University Russian Research Center

Published in 1995 in the United States of America by Westview Press, Inc., 5500 Central Avenue, Boulder, Colorado 80301-2877, and in the United Kingdom by Westview Press, 12 Hid's Copse Road, Cumnor Hill, Oxford OX2 9JJ

Library of Congress Cataloging-in-Publication Data
Patterns in post-Soviet leadership / edited by Timothy J. Colton,
    Robert C. Tucker
    p.   cm. — (The John M. Olin critical issues series)
    Includes index.
    ISBN 0-8133-2491-2 (HC : alk. paper). — ISBN 0-8133-2492-0 (PB :
alk. paper)
    1. Political leadership—Former Soviet republics.   2. Former
Soviet republics—Politics and government.   I. Colton, Timothy J.,
1947–   .   II. Tucker, Robert C.   III. Series.
JN6581.P38   1995
306.2'0947'09049—dc20   95-2368
                                                                                                 CIP

Printed and bound in the United States of America

The paper used in this publication meets the requirements
of the American National Standard for Permanence of Paper
for Printed Library Materials Z39.48-1984.

10   9   8   7   6   5   4   3   2   1

Contents

Tables and Figures

Tables

Figures

Introduction

Timothy J. Colton

The collapse of the Soviet regime, as one of the grand events of modern history, has rightly raised basic and vexing questions for scholarship. The assumptions and methodologies undergirding the study of the politics of the former Soviet Union and of the Russian Federation and the other successor states are open for scrutiny and debate as never before, as well as to research based on direct contact and observation.

There is a powerful trend in the transformed field of "post-Sovietology" toward working with large-scale variables. In the process, it is argued, we will focus on the most fundamental intellectual issues and will best engage in cross-national comparisons, especially with other countries undergoing transitions away from authoritarian rule. The variables that have drawn the most interest are threefold: the *state,* whose legitimacy and very existence have now been opened up as a subject of inquiry; *institutions,* prominent among them the post-Soviet institutions of political and economic governance that must be built if a robust new order is to be forged; and *society,* or *civil society,* the grass roots that were often perceived as of secondary concern in the Soviet dictatorship.

The interest in systemic variables is to be applauded and ought to bear much fruit as the field develops. But it is far from problem-free, especially at this early stage. Because post-Soviet politics have nowhere stabilized into a durable new constellation of power, it is not at all clear what system-level outcome we are being called upon to explain in these three dimensions. Consider only the Russian Federation, setting aside for the moment the variation across former Soviet republics. What feature of the postcommunist Russian state is most worthy of attention? Democratization, federalization, constitution building, and legislative-executive relations are some of the most obvious targets. But it must be observed that in each of these instances the provisional outcome in 1995 looks very different from the situation in, say, 1991, and it is no small task even to gauge how genuine the changes to date have been. The same is true for institutions and civil society: Today's promising organization may be tomorrow's dud (or a facade for yesterday's Soviet agency), and popular associations, movements, and political parties seem to rise and fall as the political winds shift.

An emphasis on the aforementioned variables may also be problematic if it breeds neglect of other political realities that should not be left out of the equation.

1

Indeed, concern about the possible inattention to one major variable—*leader-ship*—stimulated Robert Tucker and me to undertake this book.

Leadership was a principal component of traditional Sovietology—and for sound reasons that do not need elaborate explanation here. Given the degree of political centralization in the Soviet state, no exegesis of its affairs from 1917 to 1953 would have gotten very far without a consideration of the roles of Lenin and Stalin. After Stalin, from Khrushchev to Gorbachev, there was a marked diminution of the general secretary's unilateral power, but the leadership factor, broadly defined to take in the Politburo oligarchy and the higher echelons of the political elite, remained compelling for analysis.

Mikhail Gorbachev's accession to power in 1985 was followed shortly by epochal changes and, in 1991, by the breakup of the regime that he had intended to modernize by reformation from within. No less an authority than Boris Yeltsin, Gorbachev's nemesis and the first leader of postcommunist Russia, highlighted the importance of leadership in the genesis of perestroika. Gorbachev, Yeltsin wrote in his autobiography, could in all likelihood have gone on as Leonid Brezhnev did before him: "I estimate that the country's natural resources and the people's patience would have outlasted his lifetime, long enough for him to have lived the well-fed and happy life of the leader of a totalitarian state. He could have draped himself with orders and medals; the people would have hymned him in verse and song, which is always enjoyable. Yet Gorbachev chose to go another way."[1] A leader made a choice, with fateful consequences for his country and the world.

This is in no way to deny that systemic problems—economic stagnation, social malaise, frictions between the nationalities—were very real and pressing in 1985 and would have to be given all due weight in any comprehensive discussion of the origins of Soviet reform. Gorbachev defined the situation, taking these realities into account, as one that could not be allowed to go on; had he not done so, an enervated Soviet Union could have lingered for some years more. Nor are we attempting here to minimize the importance of nonleadership groups and forces—including politically mobilized elements of the population—in driving events subsequent to 1985, both before and after the watershed of 1991. If nothing else, democratization, imperfect and unconsolidated though it has been in the former Soviet Union, brings larger publics into the political process with some regularity. Without a doubt, responsible research on post-Soviet politics will have to be directed at a great many issues other than leadership.

Our premise is modest: Although leadership should in no way have the arena to itself, it ought to be considered a significant factor in the study of politics in the Soviet successor states. Leadership matters.

Patterns in Post-Soviet Leadership was at first conceived of as a collection of essays on individual leaders. It was understood that "post-Soviet" as a temporal category would encompass events dating from the eruption of destabilizing tendencies in the late 1980s, not just from the official dissolution of the Soviet Union. Our prospective authors were asked to look at post-Soviet leadership developmentally, as it emerged from the chrysalis of late-Soviet politics. Their instructions from the editors were to address four sets of questions.

The first and most elementary theme concerned *individual character and values.* How, we asked our contributors, has a Boris Yeltsin or a Zviad Gamsakhurdia dealt at a personal level with the transition from Soviet to post-Soviet reality? How has he related new perceptions and new opportunities for political action and success to old beliefs? How deep do changes in mentality run?

Our second envelope of questions was about *leadership roles and institutions.* Here our main interest was in how leadership authority is concretely exercised. Do post-Soviet leaders, in discharging their functions, operate more or less like their Soviet-era forerunners, or have they embraced new modalities? What organizational forms have they devised for embodying leadership—presidencies, executive establishments, collegial cabinets, political parties, or others? How effective have these arrangements been? How have they handled conflict with other institutions, for example, legislatures?

Third, we wanted to know about the *state and cultural framework* within which leadership is exercised. The essential question here is about differentiation among the post-Soviet countries and the relationship of current behavior to national traditions and legacies. Are we seeing the assertion or reassertion of, for example, a recognizably Russian or Lithuanian or Georgian style of leadership, as distinct from a shared post-Soviet syndrome? Do emerging patterns represent something as straightforward as degree and speed of evolution away from the Soviet archetype toward some universally defined alternative, or do they draw to any major extent on prior experiences or myths of statehood or political generalship?

Our fourth and broadest query was about an issue at the heart of almost all assessments and self-assessments of political leadership: *effectiveness.* How in a nutshell, we asked, have post-Soviet leaders coped with the existential problems—in particular, those of democratic development, economic reform, and preservation of the unity and integrity of the state—with which they have been confronted? Have they singly and collectively marshaled adequate answers to the questions posed, as Gorbachev several times said about perestroika, "by life itself"? How have they managed their political constituencies as these, too, have sized up objective problems?

As the project was fleshed out, we as editors decided to supplement the essays on individual leaders with contributions taking a somewhat different tack. Chapters were commissioned that take up the subject of *elite development:* the evolution of ruling strata, more broadly construed than biographical analysis. We further concluded that work touching on *mass and elite perceptions* of leadership would be valuable information. In a single edited collection, none of these issues can be treated exhaustively. Our hope has been to inform the reader about analytically significant pieces of the puzzle and to stimulate further work on the subject.

Chapter 1, by my coeditor, Robert C. Tucker, summarizes leadership and general political developments in the former Soviet Union since the onset of the reforms and serves to frame the chapters that follow.

In Chapter 2, David Lane uses the reputational method to trace changes in the structure of political influence in the twilight years of the Soviet regime and the opening phase of the postcommunist Russian Federation.

Chapters 3, 4, 5, 8, and 9 are organized by individual leader. I write on Boris Yeltsin in Chapter 3, emphasizing his mix of political strengths and incapacities. Yitzhak M. Brudny in Chapter 4 takes up two influential figures in the Russian transition, Ruslan Khasbulatov and Aleksandr Rutskoi, and traces their movement into political extremism and opposition. In Chapter 5, Alexander J. Motyl analyzes Leonid Kravchuk, the first head of state of independent Ukraine, presenting him as a "conceptual president" who was a natural phenomenon in the surrealistic environment of post-Soviet politics. In Chapter 8, Martha Brill Olcott provides a portrait of Nursultan Nazarbaev, the first president of post-Soviet Kazakhstan; she stresses his need to engage in a delicate balancing act between different ethnic communities. Islam Karimov of Uzbekistan is the subject of Chapter 9 by Donald S. Carlisle, who sees Karimov as an executor and to some extent a creator of an Uzbek political tradition.

Chapters 6, 7, and 10, by Alfred E. Senn, Ronald G. Suny, and Nancy Lubin, address elite trends more generally. Senn's study is of Lithuania, the first of the then Soviet republics to challenge Gorbachev and, several years later, the first former communist country to freely elect a reform-communist government. Suny writes simultaneously about the three Transcaucasus countries—Armenia, Azerbaijan, and Georgia—noting commonalities and differences in their experiences. And Lubin, in a comparative analysis of Uzbekistan and Kazakhstan, takes up the question of mass opinion about post-Soviet leadership, in this case in the relatively conservative Central Asian region.

Certain threads are integrated in Chapter 11 by Robert Tucker, who offers concluding theses and thoughts about future directions for study.

All of our authors have struggled to keep up with constantly unfolding events, as is the lot of anyone who labors on the affairs of Russia and the former Soviet Union. We are grateful to our colleagues for the diligence and good humor with which they absorbed and reported on history in the making.

Notes

1. Boris Yeltsin, *Against the Grain,* trans. Michael Glenny (New York: Summit Books, 1990), p. 139 (emphasis added). Yeltsin observed (p. 140) that Gorbachev "was practically alone" when the reforms were launched and that "at that all-important first moment of his reforming initiative, he operated with amazing finesse."

Post-Soviet Leadership and Change

Robert C. Tucker

The problems confronting leaders on the one-sixth of the earth's surface that for nearly seventy-five years was the USSR—and before that tsardom or the Russian Empire—are awesome in scope and complexity. In order to take their measure, it may be helpful to glance at the mid-1990s situation in historical perspective.

Troubled Times in Russia

Even before the Soviet order collapsed in 1991 and the fifteen "socialist republics" constituting the USSR became so many separate states, some Russians saw the advent of a new Time of Troubles (*smutnoe vremia* or *smuta*). The imperial Russian state had fallen apart twice before in its history, and now it was happening again.

The initial Time of Troubles came upon the Muscovite tsardom at the outset of the seventeenth century. The two previous centuries had seen the rapid expansion of the Muscovite principality as successor state to the rule of the Tatar-Mongolian khans. In 1547 Prince Ivan IV (better known as Ivan Grozny, or Ivan the Terrible) was crowned tsar of Moscow and All the Russias, and the Muscovite tsardom became more autocratic under his long and terroristic reign. Historians view Ivan's terror against the boyar aristocracy, along with the incessant expansionist wars waged by him and his predecessors, as underlying causes of the collapse of the tsardom not long after his death in 1584. An influential courtier, Boris Godunov, had become factual ruler during Ivan's final years, remained that during the reign of Ivan's feebleminded son Fyodor, and was elected tsar when Fyodor died childless in 1598, ending the Riurik dynasty. A famine and plague in 1601–1602 were followed by Boris's death, breakdown of state order, a succession of pretenders to the throne, civil war, and intervention by Poles and Swedes. Only after the installation of a new dynasty with the election of Mikhail Romanov to the throne in 1613 was anarchy ended and the tsardom restored.

The expansionist drive resumed under the Romanovs, and during the reign of Peter the Great in the first quarter of the eighteenth century, the now far larger tsardom became officially the Russian Empire. Internally the militarized state remained what it had become earlier, "a peculiar system of state socialism" based on the autocracy's claim to ownership of the land and on the binding of all strata of the people in compulsory service to the state.[1] The enserfed peasants were attached to their estates and under obligation to render service via the corvée or in produce. The nobles were obliged to render military or civilian service to the state, and the Table of Ranks introduced by Peter established a hierarchy of fourteen military and corresponding civilian ranks. The autocratic state thus created an administrative command system whereby the immense Russian Empire was governed from St. Petersburg by a uniformed officialdom. Not until 1762 was the nobility released by a later tsar's edict from obligatory state service. And not until 1861 did Tsar Alexander II introduce his Europeanizing reforms from above with an edict emancipating the peasantry from serfdom.

The abolition of serfdom, along with Alexander's judicial, military, and other reforms of the 1860s, went a long way toward emancipating Russian society from traditional subjugation to the centralized autocratic state and its ruling officialdom. The reforms also helped release oppositional forces from below and the Russian revolutionary movement of the late nineteenth century. Then, under the extreme stress of World War I, the tsardom collapsed after the abdication of Nicholas II in February 1917, and the provisional government that took over collapsed under the coup by Lenin and his Bolsheviks in October.

Again, the end of a dynasty was followed by the rise of anarchy. The events of 1917–1921, including the breakdown of the administrative command system, the disintegration of the Russian Empire as peripheral territories broke away, a civil war that cost millions of lives, and foreign intervention, went down in history books as the Russian Revolution. But some educated Russians who lived through that period called it, and justly, a new Time of Troubles.[2]

The Soviet order that emerged from the turmoil was by self-definition the antithesis of tsarism. There were indeed significant differences, yet certain fundamental features of the tsardom reappeared in new guise under Lenin and Stalin. The Bolsheviks' nationalization policies meant the resurgence in far more extreme form of that "peculiar system of state socialism," hypertrophy of the state, and bureaucratism. Their victory in the civil war against the Whites, in which they held most of the previous territories together, meant the revival of Russian Empire under the label Union of Soviet Socialist Republics. Lenin, the Bolsheviks' magnetic supreme leader, unwittingly became the founder of a new, this time ideological dynasty whose rulers, especially starting with Stalin, wielded monarchical power and professed allegiance to a new state religion called Marxism-Leninism, successor to the old regime's Russian Orthodoxy. Stalin's terroristic collectivization reimposed serfdom on the peasantry, and all strata of the people were again bound in compulsory service to a militarized, expansionist Russian state. The nominally ruling Communist Party of the Soviet Union (CPSU) was transformed by the Great Terror of 1934–1939 into the Stalin-dominated central mechanism of a renewed administrative command system whose again rank-ordered officialdom became informally known as *nomenklatura*. Like some tsars before him, in whom he found role models,[3] Stalin pursued, under his pact with Hitler and again during and after World War II, policies of aggrandizement that created an external Soviet empire in Eastern Europe and brought on the East-West confrontation that continued under his successors from Nikita Khrushchev to Konstantin Chernenko.

By 1985 the Soviet order was in profound crisis, and the Politburo chose its relatively youthful, well-educated, and energetic member, Mikhail Gorbachev, to be the new general secretary on the death of the old and ailing Chernenko. Gorbachev turned out to be, in aim and endeavor, a new reforming tsar. He preached the need for perestroika and sponsored glasnost—the openness that permitted people to speak up about past events, present problems, and directions of desirable change. In order to clear the way for radical domestic reform, it was imperative to end the Cold War. With this end in view, Gorbachev in January 1986 publicly proposed the abolition of nuclear weapons by 2,000, and at his meeting with President Reagan, in Reykjavik, Iceland, in October 1986, he proposed cutting in half the nuclear arsenals of the two superpowers. He went on to develop the principles of an international new thinking, one no longer bound by ideology, and he expounded the concept in an address to the United Nations General Assembly in 1988. Subsequently, his government made good on the promise of new thinking by peacefully surrendering Russia's East European empire, and the Cold War abated.

On the domestic front, the reform effort was a different story. Resistance to radical change from the twenty-million-strong officialdom, and especially the bulk of the party's higher echelon, confronted reform at every point. No more than small steps were taken toward the "socialist market economy" proclaimed as a goal, and Gorbachev backed away from the "500 Days" plan for systemic economic change developed by Stanislav Shatalin, Grigory Yavlinsky, and others. Democratizing political change went forward, however, with the creation of a Congress of People's Deputies partly based on contested elections, and with its approval Gorbachev acquired the newly instituted presidency of the USSR in 1989. By then glasnost in the media was providing an opening for radical currents of thought, and there emerged in the congress an oppositional movement led by anti-Communist deputies who called themselves and became known as the "democrats" (*demokraty*). As happened in the nineteenth century, reform from above led to the rise of movements for systemic change. Unlike some of their nineteenth-century predecessors, however, these were nonviolent movements. Nevertheless, by 1989–1990 the society was deeply divided and increasingly turbulent.

Some Soviet republics, Russia among them, were focal points of movements for radical change. Under the Soviet system, the constitutionally proclaimed independence of the fifteen union republics was fictional. Their organs of party and governmental authority were controlled at every step by the CPSU structures centered in Moscow. The Russian Soviet Federated Socialist Republic, whose capital was also in Moscow, was just as securely under Soviet Russian imperial control. But as central rule relaxed its grip owing to democratizing changes introduced under Gorbachev, some republic leaderships—in the three Baltic states, in the

Transcaucasus, in Ukraine, and in Russia—began to act on their own under pressure of awakening sociopolitical forces. Their previously fictional autonomy became increasingly real, particularly in the case of the Russian republic, which in 1992 adopted the name Russian Federation.

Many in its parliament were eager or willing to press harder for a break with the Communist past than was the Gorbachev regime. In 1990 its own recently elected Congress of People's Deputies chose as its chairman Boris N. Yeltsin, a former party apparatchik from the Urals industrial center of Sverdlovsk whom Gorbachev had brought to Moscow and who, having become estranged from his patron and the party-state, joined forces with the *demokraty*. In June 1991 he won a contested republic election for the newly instituted Russian presidency. The emergence of a second and rival Russian state in Moscow helped to precipitate the events of August 1991, when a group of Soviet leaders, acting without Gorbachev, sought and failed to reassert Soviet statehood by declaring a state of emergency. Afterward, Yeltsin issued edicts dissolving the CPSU and taking over its structures and resources.

To complete and formalize the victory of Russian over Soviet Russian statehood, it was necessary to abolish the USSR itself as a state formation. This Yeltsin managed by carrying off a nonviolent coup of his own together with Ukrainian president Leonid Kravchuk and the chairman of the Belarus parliament, Stanislav Shushkevich. In early December 1991 the three met near Minsk in Belarus and agreed to set up a Commonwealth of Independent States (CIS), which the other former Soviet republics were invited to join, as all but the Baltic states eventually did. On December 21 the defeated Gorbachev, who had fought desperately in his final period in office to hold the USSR together, had to turn over the seat of authority in the Kremlin to the new Russian president, thereby ending the Lenin dynasty and Soviet rule.

Once again, as in 1598 and 1917, the end of a dynasty in an imperial Russian state was followed by disintegration of empire, turmoil, and growing chaos. The new Time of Troubles foreseen in the late 1980s as imminent soon became apparent. Although leaders of the separate former Soviet republics would meet from time to time to discuss problems and seek agreements, the amorphous CIS did not become an effective authority structure. By 1992 civil war was raging in the Central Asian republic of Tajikistan. The Transcaucasian republics of Armenia and Azerbaijan remained at war over the latter's Armenian-populated enclave, Nagorno-Karabakh, and conditions in economically blockaded Armenia were described as worse than those experienced during World War II. The Georgian republic was locked in strife over separatism in its Abkhazian autonomous region. The Moldovan republic that Stalin had carved in part out of Bessarabia during his 1939–1941 collaboration with Hitler was politically divided between the main portion centered in the capital, Kishinev, and a separatist eastern Trans-Dniester area inhabited mainly by Russians and Ukrainians. Over 25 million Russians were living in non-Russian former Soviet republics now known as the "near abroad," and about 1.5 million Russians had sought refuge in a Russia unable adequately to provide for them.

It is not clear that Yeltsin and his supporters had fully grasped what the end of the CPSU and collapse of the party-state would mean for their country. Despite its continuing membership of many millions, the CPSU had long since ceased to be a political party in any normal sense of the term. It was a state authority structure, the core mechanism of the Soviet Russian administrative command system that had replaced and basically replicated the tsarist one. Its bureaucratic structures, from the Central Committee in Moscow to the republic and regional party committees across the country down to the town and district committees in the localities, were the real ruling bodies of what was nominally a "Soviet" state. Compliance with their instructions by people in state authority at all levels and in all fields of life was ensured by the ever present threat to take away their party membership cards and with them their elite status and privileges.

Although moves were made in 1992 to erect an edifice of Russian statehood in place of the fallen party-state edifice, no effective new administrative command system emerged, and some Russians described the situation as one of power paralysis (*bezvlaste*). Turmoil spread across much of the one-eighth of the earth's territory covered by the Russian Federation. Crime became rampant, official corruption grew epidemic, the armed forces were threatened by dissolution, extreme nationalist and fascist groups were active, armed violence spread to the Russian Federation's north Caucasian territories, and President Yeltsin was at loggerheads with the chairman of the Russian parliament, his one-time supporter Ruslan Khasbulatov.

In the midst of all this, a Russian historian observed that "the similarities between the *tragoedia moscovitica* A.D. 1598–1613 and the Soviet-Russian crisis of A.D. 1988–? are too obvious to be denied."[4]

Leadership and Systemic Change

The banning of the CPSU, the elimination of communism as a state creed, and the breakup of the USSR as an imperial formation marked in a deep sense the ending of the Soviet era. But in part because of the abruptness with which these events came about, much of the statist Soviet system and its political culture survived into the 1990s. New orders in the several successor states were slow to emerge in its place. Hence the period 1991–1993 brought no more than the beginnings of a sociopolitical, economic, and cultural transformation. Leadership and forces for systemic change collided with still formidable conservative forces possessing leadership of their own, as well as with extremist forces calling for another restoration of empire and autocracy.

In most of the successor states (the Baltic states were partial exceptions), Russo-Soviet etatism lived on institutionally in a multitude of state enterprises, state farms, and other bodies, including regional, town, and village soviets (councils) scattered across the vast territory, with a combined total of deputies running into the millions in Russia alone. Nor did any such sweeping turnover of elites as might be suggested by the word "revolution" take place as a result of August 1991. What happened, as an informed source put it, was the "dissolving" of the former CPSU apparatus into various executive, representative, public, economic, and commercial structures, in which many representatives of the former middle-range *nomenklatura* (such as plant directors, collective farm chairmen, and local officials) advanced to higher status.[5] Deputy Russian Premier Sergei Shakhrai, an influential adviser of Boris Yeltsin, observed that nearly all of Russia's executive, representative, regional, economic, and military structures remained in the same hands and said of these people: "Many of them have shed their communist apparel but have not, on that account, become different people."[6] A contemporary saying put it more simply: "Il'ich has gone out of the CPSU, but the CPSU has not gone out of Il'ich." The accepted ways of thinking and acting in standard situations, the patterns of culture acquired in the past, lingered on. Self-interested motivations, the desire to retain a relatively secure and privileged mode of life, made the older ways all the more tenacious among officialdom.

Given the survival of many old institutional structures and old ways of thinking and acting into the post-Soviet period, determined and effective leadership became a crucially important lever of transformative change. In few of the successor states did such leadership appear. In Ukraine and Belarus, leadership at top levels aimed at most to change things at a measured pace. President Nursultan Nazarbaev of Kazakhstan grappled with the tasks of developing that huge state's economy and trying to build a nation-state where none had existed before. In some successor states, leaders in power did little more than "shed their communist apparel," and leadership became a force for persistence of older ways. In the key Central Asian state of Uzbekistan, the one real power in the region, President Islam Karimov espoused the idea of a "strong state" with virtually unlimited presidential power. Uzbek human rights advocates were suppressed, the media were censored, an official Karimov personality cult was promoted, and the economy remained mostly under old ministries renamed "associations" and "concerns."[7] In the small but gas- and oil-rich Central Asian state of Turkmenistan, Saparmurat Niiazov, the republic's Communist leader since 1985, stayed on as an autocrat with the title of president and a personality cult reminiscent of Stalin's. In Tajikistan, the civil war—described by some Russian observers as an "intertribal" one—brought into office a harshly authoritarian regime totally dependent on Russian military support in warding off continuing armed opposition. War, civil war, and extremist separatism rendered leadership for reform a moot matter in the three Transcaucasian republics. Only in the three Baltic republics did changes go forward in peace.

In the Russian Federation, vigorous leadership for systemic change—for the transformation of Soviet Russia into a country with a free-market economy, a liberal polity, and a pro-Western foreign policy—found in 1992 a champion in Boris

Yeltsin and his administration. He set out to use the post-Soviet Russian presidency as a battering ram against the old order and a means of establishing something fundamentally different in its place. Gennadii Burbulis, a one-time Marxist-Leninist theory teacher in Yeltsin's Sverdlovsk, who became his close adviser in the early period of his presidency, later formulated Yeltsin's approach by saying that the Soviet system "is doomed and must end its existence as a whole. Reforms cannot be called reforms if they do not embrace the basic structures of society and the chief attributes of the state we inherited."[8]

Toward the end of his rule, Gorbachev moved in his thinking from communism in its reform version to social democracy, but he lacked the time, ability, and perhaps determination to mobilize a real constituency for such change by splitting away the amenable part of the CPSU from the fundamentally conservative larger part.[9] The coming of Yeltsin to power meant a deep change in leadership thinking from such a social democratic tendency to outright anticommunism. This was made clear in the hearings of July–November 1992 in the Russian Constitutional Court on the legality of Yeltsin's decrees of August and November 1991 disbanding the leadership structures of the CPSU and taking over its property. The Soviet Union, argued the president's lawyers, was not a "socialist democracy" but a "dictatorship of the organizational structures of the CPSU and its support stratum of about two million party *nomenklatura* officials and the many-million-strong bureaucratic apparatus serving them—such was the 'CPSU state.'" Moreover, the organization that called itself CPSU was not really a political party but a special sort of state mechanism, "a system of organs and institutions linked by hierarchical subordination and carrying out activities constituting a state monopoly."[10] During the protracted proceedings, the president's lawyers made public top-secret documents from closed Kremlin archives in order to show that the "CPSU state" was guilty of abuse of power and criminality on a grand scale, and no period of its existence, including Gorbachev's time of attempted reform, was exempted from this indictment.

In keeping with the anticommunism shown in the Constitutional Court's hearing, the Yeltsin regime initially sought speedy transformation of the statist Soviet economy into a free-market one as part of a veritable social revolution. Radical market reformism found leaders in the young economist Yegor Gaidar, appointed by Yeltsin as his acting premier, and the team of liberal economic reformers working with him. Most state price controls were lifted as of January 2, 1992. The central industrial ministries (such as those for the oil industry, coal, iron, and steel), which had directed the state enterprises, were eliminated, as was centralized distribution of state resources, state monopoly of foreign trade, and the practice of state purchase orders to industrial enterprises.

All this was designed to pressure the enterprises to operate according to free-market principles. It was understood that a period of inflation would ensue with the lifting of price controls, as it did. Yeltsin, however, publicly declared that 1992 would be the hardest year and that stabilization of the economy would begin before the end of it with incipient price reductions and the start of improvement in the people's standard of living.[11] This optimistic forecast was not borne out. The young liberal economists of the Gaidar team had not reckoned, it seems, with the resistance of the economy—and polity—to the new ways they wished to engender. Inflation raged throughout 1992 and beyond, living conditions for the majority grew harder, and the leadership was in political difficulty.

Confronted in December 1992 with a Congress of People's Deputies increasingly dominated by conservative forces of the old order's *nomenklatura,* Yeltsin was forced to let Gaidar go, and he appointed the industrialist Viktor Chernomyrdin as premier. Some saw in this the end of the "romantic phase" of Russian market reformism. But the situation was more complex, for in 1992, another attack on the statist Soviet economic order went forward in the form of privatization. By early 1993, about 60,000 small state enterprises had been transferred to private hands, and about 5,000 large plants were being transformed into joint-stock companies.[12] One of the latter was the huge Moscow ZIL automobile plant, which began selling off 35 percent of its assets for vouchers distributed to Russian citizens. Privatization proceeded more rapidly in regions where the leadership gave it a green light. One of these is the Nizhnii Novgorod region, whose young governor, Boris Nemtsov, stated in March 1993 that because small-scale privatization there was no longer in the hands of officials, it was irreversible. The privatizing of medium-sized enterprises was too far along to be stopped, he added, and the big fight would be waged over privatizing of large state concerns, with good chances for success if 1993 proved a "quiet" year.[13]

Privatizing in trade and industry went along with advances in private peasant farming in Russia and other successor states. The number of private farms in the CIS more than doubled in 1992 and came to about 470,000 by the outset of 1993, with a total of more than 12 million hectares of land involved. Of these the largest number by far were in the Russian Federation, where 220,000 farms were registered by March 1993, accounting for over 10 million hectares of land. At that time, approximately 10,000 new peasant farms were being registered every month.[14] The growth of private farming in Russia did not, however, involve in all cases the acquisition of private ownership of the land. Only about 40 percent of the privately farmed land was the property of the farmers; the remainder was held only in lifelong possession or by lease.[15] Pressure for unconditional legalizing of private ownership in land encountered resistance in the Congress of People's Deputies despite the success of activists of the Democratic Russia movement with a popular referendum that garnered 2 million votes in favor of such a reform. Parliamentary resistance to land being held unconditionally as private property found leadership in the agrarian lobby of collectives and state farms, for which legal restrictions on land ownership represented a way of maintaining the farm directors' "feudal-bureaucratic status."[16]

The spread of private entrepreneurship and private farming not only transfers state property to individuals and groups working on their own initiative. Over the longer run it can foster the formation of a middle class of property owners as a force for stability and the growth of civil society in Russia as well as other Soviet successor states. If successful, it will shift much of the burden of leadership for systemic change from political authorities to society itself.

But that assessment needs to be balanced by an account of the costs to society imposed by the Gaidar course of radical market reformism. A steady decline in gross industrial output ensued, reaching nearly 30 percent by early 1994. Emergent Russian capitalism took on the character of so-called *nomenklatura* capitalism as directors acquired financial interests in state enterprises under their command. Society became increasingly divided into a very small group of nouveau riche at one end and a large majority of the relatively or absolutely poor at the other end, with no widespread and steadily growing middle class, a situation that prompted St. Petersburg historian Dmitrii Likhachev to comment: "We are not moving toward capitalism in Russia. We are going to some kind of Arab or African system, where the money and power is in just a few hands."[17] Furthermore, the Yeltsin edict on freedom of trade, combined with continuing weak governance, opened the way to a surge of crime and the takeover of business enterprise by criminal gangs along with corruption among state officials linked with them. An estimated 3,000 to 4,000 criminal gangs were believed to be operative in Russia and other CIS states by 1993 with control over as much as 40 percent of the turnover of goods and service.[18]

Leadership and New Statehood

Under the CPSU administrative command system, Soviet statehood was unitary behind a facade of federalism comprising fifteen supposedly sovereign union republics and a larger number of supposedly autonomous republics within them. Not until late in the Gorbachev administration did some republic parliaments start to act on their own by declaring republican sovereignty or creating a republican presidency. Consequently, the end of union statehood in 1991 left the successor republics without such obvious attributes of real statehood as definite borders, national currencies, and national anthems. All their leaderships were confronted with a formidable challenge of building independent nation-states in a process that would go on for many years.

Various problems complicate this process and render uncertain the prospect that stable new forms of statehood will result. One such problem is a tendency in some republics with polyethnic populations to build ethnocratic nation-states. In two of the three small Baltic countries, Latvia and Estonia, radical nationalists want to address the situation created by large Russian-speaking populations by pressuring many Russians to emigrate and assimilating the rest or allowing them to stay only as low-paid labor without hope of advancement.[19] Below the level of the top leadership, ethnocratic tendencies have made themselves felt in Kazakhstan, where Russians account for 7 million of the 16 million population. Since most of the Russians live in compact areas in the north and east of Kazakhstan, bordering on Siberia, many have reacted to discriminatory moves (as in higher education) by favoring a change of borders that would bring them into Russia. Under President Nursultan Nazarbaev, the prevailing policy has been to make of Kazakhstan a multinational state albeit one in which all citizens master the Kazakh language.[20]

Republican Russian statehood arose with the Russian parliament's emergence as an independently acting body, of which Yeltsin became chairman in May 1990. He thereby became Russia's political first person as head of its 1,000-plus-member Congress of People's Deputies, the two-chamber standing Supreme Soviet (with 248 members), and the small Supreme Soviet Presidium. In June 1991, after running for and winning the Russian presidency with former military officer Aleksandr Rutskoi as his vice-presidential running mate, Yeltsin gave up the parliamentary chairmanship. With his approval it went to Ruslan I. Khasbulatov, a Moscow-based economist of Chechen ethnic background who, as a vice chairman of the parliament, had apparently impressed Yeltsin as an ardent supporter of his. After becoming the chairman (speaker), Khasbulatov set out to be a powerful political leader in his own right.

The erection of a new Russian system of governance in place of the old one was not chosen by the Yeltsin leadership as a first-priority task. That would have meant dismantling the two-tier legislature inherited from the Soviet period by calling new elections on the basis of a new constitution in place of the still extant 1978 one. This relic of the Soviet era proclaimed the Congress of People's Deputies to be the "supreme power" on all matters relating to the Russian Federation. The president, on the other hand, was described by a law on the presidency adopted shortly before the 1991 election simply as the "highest official" and the "head of executive power."

Some Russian observers believe that Yeltsin was in so strong a position in the aftermath of the August revolution that he could have proceeded with a restructuring of Russian statehood via the establishment of a normal two-chamber parliament. Instead, he and his advisers opted to proceed with systemic change in the economy. In November 1991 the Fifth Congress of People's Deputies gave him emergency powers, including the right to issue, for a one-year period, presidential decrees with the force of laws passed by parliament, the right to appoint ministers without parliamentary approval, and the right to appoint heads of local administrations (who soon began to be called governors) and presidential representatives in the regions to oversee the work of the administrations and local soviets, which remained in being as before. The system of presidential appointees in the provinces was far from constituting a new hierarchical setup in the Russian imperial and subsequent Soviet traditions. And given the rudimentary state of postcommunist Russian political parties, Yeltsin did not have (or initially seek) a broadly based political party as a mainstay of his presidential power.

In general, Western-type independent political parties failed to take shape in early post-Soviet Russia. What did emerge in 1992 were three main political tendencies represented by blocs or coalitions of relatively small groups lacking in strong organizational structures and mass membership. They have been characterized as "radical-democratic," "centrist," and "conservative."[21] The radical-democratic tendency had a sociopolitical base in what remained of the Democratic Russia movement, which assisted Yeltsin on his path to power in 1991, and was supported by the small Russian Movement for Democratic Reforms led by the mayor of St. Petersburg, Anatolii Sobchak, and the short-term mayor of Moscow, Gavriil Popov. Gennadii Burbulis was a major leading figure among the radical-democrats. They pushed for Russia's swiftest possible advance toward market reforms and a pluralist society on the Western model. Despite their proclaimed democratic position, however, the anticommunist radical-democrats were not averse to advocating authoritarian presidential rule in spring 1992 to stem resistance to radical market reforms.

The centrist tendency found political expression in the formation in June 1992 of Civic Union, a bloc of groups and small parties representing a moderately conservative opposition to the Gaidar line. The founding members included the People's Party of Free Russia, organized by Vice President Rutskoi, the Democratic Party of Russia, led by Nikolai Travkin, and the All-Russian Renewal Union, whose foremost leading figure was the influential lobbyist for state enterprises, Arkadii I. Volskii. The industrialist representatives grouped in Civic Union advocated strong Russian national statehood and its use to ensure an evolutionary shift to a market economy without such a steep drop in production as was occurring under Gaidar's policy of macroeconomic stabilization. For them the Western economic model was not an appropriate one for mechanical application to Russia. A career industrialist himself, Chernomyrdin emerged into governmental leadership as a representative of the industrial lobby, albeit also a supporter of moderate reform.

The conservative political tendency might also be described as radical-oppositionist. Its representatives became known as "patriots," "national-patriots," and "great-powerites." No unified organizational structure emerged. Among the groups associated with this tendency were the Russian National Assembly, formed in Moscow in June 1992 under a former KGB officer, Aleksandr Sterligov, who foresaw a monarchist future for Russia; the soon reborn Russian Communist Party under Gennadii Ziuganov; another successor party to the CPSU, the Russian Communist Workers' Party, headed by Viktor Anpilov; and the Russian Unity faction in the Supreme Soviet, led by deputies Sergei Baburin, Vladimir Isakov, and Nikolai Pavlov. Lastly, the radical-oppositionist tendency found leadership in a misnamed Liberal Democratic Party whose chief, Vladimir Volfovich Zhirinovsky, had come in third in the Russian presidential elections of 1991 with 7 percent of the vote. Prominent figures associated with the radical-oppositionist movement included the Russian nationalist writer Valentin Rasputin and the editor in chief of the newspaper *Den,* Aleksandr Prokhanov. The conservative oppositionists advocated the recreating of Russia within the borders of the former Soviet Union. They accused Gorbachev and Yeltsin of having acted as agents of world imperialism in bringing about the breakup of the USSR. Yeltsin's removal from office and the abandonment of policies aimed at Russia's Westernization became foremost elements of their program.[22]

The tumultuous Seventh Congress of People's Deputies in December 1992, at which Yeltsin faced strong opposition that a walkout by him failed to overcome, convinced him and those in his entourage that high priority should have been given earlier to establishing a thoroughly post-Soviet form of statehood through adoption of a new Russian constitution. In an interview shortly after, his adviser Burbulis, whom the congress had pressured Yeltsin into removing from the official post of state secretary, expressed regret over his failure earlier on to explain to Yeltsin that the presidency represented not the reality of power but only the possibility of it. Instead, he had encouraged Yeltsin to rely on the "imperial heritage" of investing the entire project of transformative change in the ruler's personal primacy. And now the president's reform course was confronted in the congress with an oppositionist majority that reflected "the huge negative resources of the Soviet type of governance and the worldview inherent in it."[23]

What Yeltsin and his aides failed to foresee was that the ingrained ways of thinking and acting under the Soviet system would reemerge in the parliamentary institutional complex. Article 104 of the constitution, a much amended version of the constitution adopted by the Soviet Russian republic under Brezhnev in 1978, legitimized this by giving the Congress of People's Deputies the right to consider and resolve "any question in the jurisdiction of the Russian Federation." Under an edict he issued August 21, 1992, Khasbulatov conferred on himself the power to give direction to the Supreme Soviet and on his deputies the power to give direction to its committees. Meanwhile, transplantation of Soviet political culture to the parliamentary system was facilitated by the provision of work in its staff of 1,500 functionaries for the great bulk of former officials of the departments of the CPSU Central Committee. Thus, especially from early 1992, the Congress of People's Deputies began acting as though it were a party congress, the Supreme Soviet as though its proceedings were plenums of the Central Committee, the Supreme Soviet committees as though they were Central Committee departments, the Supreme Soviet Presidium as though it were the Politburo, and Khasbulatov himself as though he were another general secretary.[24]

The parliamentary leadership sought to give guidance to the regional and other local soviets throughout Russia and in doing so to obstruct presidential power in the provinces. The earlier mass transfusion of regional party *nomenklatura* into corresponding levels of soviets, initiated by Gorbachev in 1988–1989 under the slogan of "All power to the soviets," brought into the soviets large numbers of former party officials with habits of mind and conduct favorable to the success of the parliamentary leadership's subsequent efforts. By spring 1993, according to one informed estimate, 64 percent of the local soviets had adopted a hostile position toward President Yeltsin.[25] Moreover, the posts of regional chiefs of administration (governors), earlier subject to presidential appointment, became in some cases elective with resultant drop in the president's influence on political life in the Russian provinces. A further move in this direction was the congress's attempt in March 1993 to abolish the institution of presidential representatives in the regions.

The conflict between president and parliament came to a first climax with two March 1993 sessions of the Congress of People's Deputies. The eighth session, held from March 10 to 13, stripped Yeltsin of many of the emergency powers granted him in late 1991 and rejected his proposal for a referendum on whether Russia should become a presidential republic under a new constitution. He then took the offensive by announcing on March 20 that he was issuing a decree on introduction of a "special mode of rule" to deal with the national crisis. In the resultant uproar, during which Yeltsin's declared (but then not fulfilled) intention was opposed not only by Khasbulatov but likewise by the head of Russia's Constitutional Court, Valerii Zorkin, and Vice President Rutskoi, the congress was again convened in extraordinary session and came within 72 votes of the necessary two-thirds for impeachment of the president. In the end, the Ninth Congress decided to hold a referendum on April 25, 1993, though not the referendum on a constitution desired by Yeltsin. The outcome, however, was a sufficiently positive popular vote of confidence in the president and of no confidence in the congress to encourage Yeltsin to embark on a fresh campaign for adoption of a new Russian constitution as the only way to end the impasse. As the second anniversary of the August revolution approached, Moscow was experiencing a condition of dual power that some found reminiscent of 1917 Petrograd. In appearance it was a clash between parliament and presidency; in actuality, it was a conflict between two different systems of power, one a persisting party-state kind of system in the parliamentary institutional setting, the other a still nascent presidential system. Academician Oleg Bogomolov summed up the situation by saying: "What we have is not a constitutional crisis but a most profound crisis of statehood. The state has become weak, it hardly exists: it cannot protect citizens from the crime wave, the regions are departing from subordination to the center, misdeeds by officials go unpunished, and market reforms are not legislatively reinforced."[26]

Leadership in Russia's Regions

If post-Soviet Russia comes out of the present Time of Troubles without a restoration of dictatorship, this will be due in part to events in Russia's provinces. Given the collapse of the administrative command system, the weakness of the vertical chain of command via governors in the provinces, and the paralysis of power resulting from the cold war between presidency and parliament, Russia's eighty-nine regions have become a proving ground for new ways in governmental administration and for change in the nature of Russian statehood. A leading political scientist said that "for the first time in Russia's whole history the fate of state power is being decided not alone in Moscow. Regional interests are becoming more and more actively involved in the process of its emergence."[27]

The development of statehood in Russian history showed an opposite pattern of subordinating regional interests to centralized power. The primacy of foreign policy underlay this pattern. The aim of Russian rulers was to build a unified Russian state under autocratic rule. The need for military power to support external defense and expansion dictated tsarist internal policy. This pattern was replicated under Soviet rule in the twentieth century, starting with the military-oriented five-year plan at the close of the 1920s. So extreme was the centralization of state power in Moscow that all the rest of the huge country became known colloquially as the "periphery." The secretaries of party committees in the republics and regions ruled them on behalf of the central Soviet regime more or less as appointed governor-generals ruled them before 1917 for the tsar.

Gorbachev's reform administration saw a momentous shift in the relation between foreign and domestic policy, a shift that has continued under Yeltsin. Instead of internal policy being harnessed to the needs of an external policy pitting Soviet Russia against the West in a never-ending confrontation, Gorbachev's international new thinking led to a subsiding of the Cold War for the sake of the needs of domestic reform. At the expense of its external East European empire, Russia gained the opportunity to concentrate on urgent internal tasks. The further breakdown of central power in 1991 liberated Russia's regions, within limits, to strike out on their own in political and economic affairs.

In some regions power struggles comparable to the one between the parliament and presidency in Moscow ensued. Some regional soviets tried to govern as party committees once did. One means of pursuing this aim was to draft local charters (regional constitutions) favoring local interests, which the amended Russian Federation constitution empowered them to do. Some drafted these charters in such a way as to confer on the local soviets all power, including administrative power.[28] In April 1993 the drive for regional dominance found expression in a decision by the conservative Supreme Soviet of the Russian Federation's Mordvinian Republic to abolish its presidency—a decision that had the advance imprimatur of Khasbulatov and fellow Moscow oppositionist leaders such as people's deputies Sergei Baburin and Vladimir Isakov.[29] On the other hand, the newly elected young businessman president of the Kalmyk Republic decided to replace its Supreme Soviet with a lesser formation and to abolish that republic's local soviets.

But not all the Russian regions became locked in power struggles similar to Moscow's. In some of them the administrations and regional soviets learned to work together in a process of leadership toward a new, decentralized Russian statehood. This process, if successful, will reverse the imperial Russian developmental pattern that took shape over past centuries. Instead of the autocratic centralized state dominating society and impressing the population into various forms of compulsory state service for imperial, expansionist needs, the emerging new process of regional leadership could foster a new kind of Russian statehood, initially on a local basis with certain territories emerging as what have been called "leader-regions."

A notable success story of this kind unfolded in the city and region of Nizhnii Novgorod on the Volga. Boris Nemtsov, who originally came to Yeltsin's attention as a deputy in the Russian congress and initially was appointed as his personal envoy in Nizhnii, proved to be a dynamic leader there for change as chief of administration, or governor. As mentioned earlier, the privatization process advanced rapidly in this region, and thousands of Nizhnii citizens became part owners of what had been state property. During this transition, Nemtsov worked in harmony with the chairman of the regional soviet and mayor of Nizhnii. The Nizhnii city soviet held a seminar on privatization for representatives of seventy other Russian cities. Governor Nemtsov and his fellow local leaders had the help of an able young Moscow economist, Grigory Yavlinsky. He spent three months working with local leaders in Nizhnii in early 1992. Still earlier, he arranged for a team of specialists from his Moscow think tank, Epitsentr, to work there for a full year on a report dealing both with local problems and prospects and with the larger subject of progress in the provinces toward a new Russia.

Published in September 1992, this report said that reforms in Russia traditionally were initiated from above and implemented by the central state power through its subordinate officialdom. By fall 1992, such reform had virtually exhausted itself, and now the country was moving in new directions. The old Russian paradigm of "reformism from above" was giving way to one of "self-development from below." This involved a reshaping of Russia into a new kind of state formation via changes proceeding, on the one hand, from the center out into the regions and, on the other, from the regions interacting with one another. Thus, Russian regions are now seeking, without help from the center, to resolve such problems as the payment of wages without money in cash form, the procurement of foodstuffs, and financial support for large enterprises. These matters require regional leadership because central state authority has proved impotent in them. Moreover, integration of Russian regions on a new foundation will bring into being the preconditions for a new kind of integration within the framework of the Commonwealth of Independent States.[30]

By moving out in these directions, the report went on, the Russian lands, represented by their governors (who should be elected locally, not appointed by the president) and their legislatures, would come to feel themselves fully empowered participants in the all-Russian political process. Moreover, should the Moscow center try to reinforce the old power hierarchy, the regions would respond with steps to liquidate or replace the existing federal state authority, and this would lead to social chaos. Ideally, the integrating of Russia should proceed both from the Russian lands and from the center simultaneously. Leader-regions would initiate the process by joining together in interregional economic associations, thereby influencing other regions to do likewise.[31]

Some developments in Siberia give support to this bold vision of a reintegrated Russia consisting of autonomously developing territories and territorial associations. Andrei Sobolevskii, a Siberian leader, confessed himself a "regionalist" and rejected the whole Russian historical precedent of creating, strengthening and expanding a centralized Russian state. He disagreed that defense considerations required a centralized Russian state, noting that every past act of Russian expansionism had been followed by a military defeat and that "the more aggressive a power is, the lower welfare becomes." The chief outcome of Russia's regionalization would be to bring local problems closer to solution, to create a stronger economy, and to overcome cultural provincialism.[32] In Moscow the regional idea found a visionary leader in an elder historian, the late Mikhail Gefter. As a member of Yeltsin's Presidential Council, Gefter argued that Moscow should welcome rather than resist the drive in the provinces for regional forms of development and identity, and he observed that provinces were opting for a Russia of regions in part out of concern to save themselves from ecological destruction.[33]

To its proponents, a "Russia of regions" would be a decentralized one based on the principle that the central government delegates maximum rights and powers to the regional and local levels and retains in its own competence only those matters (such as foreign policy and general developmental strategy) that cannot be decided at the regional level. A foremost Russian economist, Nikolai Shmelev, has advocated regionalization of Russia on economic as well as political grounds. It would mean the decentralization of Russian finances and the entire system of administration of the economy. More concretely, regionalization would mean a change in the ratio of tax revenues that go to Moscow and the regions. As matters stand, the ratio is 75 to 25 percent in Moscow's favor. If that ratio is not reversed in the very near future, Shmelev said, the regions themselves will do the reversing and Russia will cease to be a united federal state.[34]

Some Russians believe that early action toward the establishment of a Russia of regions is the only means of averting the Russian state's disintegration. Separatist tendencies of various kinds have already manifested themselves, especially among the twenty-one of the country's eighty-nine administrative-territorial units that have the special and superior status of republics with a non-Russian titular nationality. They have such attributes of statehood as constitutions, parliaments, and, in some cases, presidencies, whereas the nonnational administrative-territorial units (oblasts and krais) lack these. In twelve of the twenty-one national republics, ethnic Russians outnumber the indigenous population. In the Karelian Republic, for example, Russians account for 87 percent of the population.[35]

Two republics, Chechnia and Tatarstan, refrained from signing the Federal Treaty of April 1992 between the central government and the regions of Russia. Chechnia declared its full independence. Tatarstan adopted a constitution of its own that states it is only "associated" with the Russian Federation on the basis of an international treaty yet to be negotiated. Republics have rescinded legislative acts of the Russian parliament and ignored presidential decrees. Draft constitutions of Tuva, Kalmykia, Buriatia, and Bashkortostan proclaim the supremacy of their republic laws over all-Russian ones.[36] These developments have fueled demands by the leaderships of a number of Russian regions, especially in Siberia and the Far East, for rights and powers equal to those of republics. Thus the Krasnoyarsk region in Siberia has published a draft constitutional document in the form of a charter declaring this region to be "a member of the Russian Federation with rights, obligations and responsibility of a republic in Russia."[37]

To keep this "revolt of the provinces" (as it has been called) from becoming a force for Russia's disintegration, some Russians argue that Moscow should show leadership in espousing a decentralized form of Russian statehood that accords all the regions real autonomy on a par with the twenty-one republics. This, it is believed, would be a strong antidote to separatist tendencies. And some express the view that over the long run, say by 2005, the institution of constituent republics identified with a titular nationality should be dropped as a surviving relic of the Leninist nationality policy that sought to make of the USSR a model of a world Communist commonwealth on a sixth of the earth's surface.[38]

Should that vision come about, the Soviet tie between statehood and nationality at the regional level will be ended. What are now constituent republics with titular nationalities will become regions in which all nationalities enjoy full cultural autonomy. The Russian Federation itself will no more be a state of ethnic Russians than any territory of it is a state of some other ethnic group. Russia will evolve from a centralized empire with a hierarchy of ethnic groups into a union of free territories inhabited by citizens, perhaps with a name like Union of Eurasian States.[39]

The October Clash and After

In the spring and summer of 1993, conflict intensified between the Yeltsin administration and the Supreme Soviet under leadership by Khasbulatov and Rutskoi. Khasbulatov engineered the Supreme Soviet's adoption of a budget known to be unacceptable to the executive branch. His and Rutskoi's public pronouncements echoed the aggressive Russian nationalism of the radical-opposition. Yeltsin, for his part, sponsored a Constitutional Assembly with the aim of drafting—separately from the Supreme Soviet's constitutional commission that was created in 1990 to prepare a new constitution—a post-Soviet constitution for Russia. He opened the assembly on June 5, 1993, with a speech in which he declared that "the soviets and democracy are not compatible," whereupon Khasbulatov stormed out of the hall where the assembly was in session.[40]

These events presaged the final showdown that came on September 21, 1993, when Yeltsin issued decree no. 1400 ("On a Stage-by-Stage Constitutional Reform") in which he proclaimed the dissolution of Russia's Supreme Soviet and

Congress of People's Deputies. That evening the Russian Constitutional Court, chaired by Zorkin, ruled that the president had exceeded his constitutional authority and hence might be subject to removal from office. To this Yeltsin responded, after a time, with a decree suspending operation of the Constitutional Court.

Many members of parliament defied the decree on disbanding by remaining in the White House, as the parliament building was called. After several increasingly tense days, during which vain attempts were made to work out a compromise peace between the warring parties, the situation turned violent, and on October 2 Moscow became for several days the scene of civil war. When an unruly crowd of parliament supporters gathered by the White House on October 2, Rutskoi called on them to storm the mayor's office and the Ostankino television center, which they then set out to do. The next day Yeltsin declared that an armed uprising was in progress. On October 4 units of the Russian armed forces shelled the upper stories of the White House, forcing those remaining inside (and still unharmed) to leave the building and surrender. Rutskoi, Khasbulatov, General Albert Makashov and other leading figures in the Supreme Soviet resistance were taken into custody and imprisoned pending trial. How many persons suffered injury or death during the October clash was not officially announced.

Although civil war did not spread beyond Moscow, political confrontation did. Most of Russia's regional soviets came out in support of the Supreme Soviet, while nearly all the regional governors gave their support to the president. After the events in Moscow, Yeltsin reverted to his previously chosen role of battering ram against the Soviet order. On October 9 he issued a decree ordering the dissolution of the thousands of soviets at the city, urban-district, and village levels.[41] Without directly disbanding the regional soviets, he ordered elections in the regions to new standing bodies of fifteen to fifty deputies that would be called not soviets but dumas.

Yeltsin scheduled for December 12, 1993, a referendum on a new, post-Soviet Russian constitution and elections for a new two-chamber parliamentary body. The draft constitution put before voters—an outgrowth (with further post-October drafting) of the document that had been in preparation during summer 1993—provided for a two-chamber parliament to be called the Federal Assembly. Its upper house, the Federation Council, would have 178 representatives, two from each of the 89 subjects of the federation, one representing the legislative and one representing the executive organs of power. Its lower house, the State Duma, would have 450 deputies, half chosen by proportional representation of parties or blocs and the other half by a plurality of votes in single-member constituencies.

However, the post-Soviet Russia envisaged in this draft constitution would be a country with a strong (some Russians have said quasi-monarchical) presidency. The president would combine the roles of head of state, commander in chief of the armed forces, and chairman of the Security Council. He would propose the prime minister; approve ministerial appointments; appoint military commanders, diplomats, judges, and the chairman of the Central Bank; and set domestic and foreign policy guidelines. He would have power to dissolve the State Duma if it should block his choice of prime minister or pass two votes of no confidence in the government; to reject legislation passed by the State Duma; to declare a state of emergency with parliamentary consent; to pass decrees without reference to parliament; and to call parliamentary elections. Only 33.4 million out of 106 million eligible voters—a little over half of those who came to the polls—approved the draft constitution in the December referendum, which was thus adopted with support from far less than a majority of the population.

In the election for the Federation Council, 173 out of 497 registered candidates received seats, and 5 seats remained vacant. Many winning candidates were governors of Russian regions or presidents of national republics within the federation. Representatives of the central Yeltsin administration fared less well, but one winner was Deputy Premier Vladimir Shumeiko, who was subsequently elected chairman of the council. Although the pro-Yeltsin Russia's Choice bloc led by Gaidar received 50 seats in the council and could count on support from others, the election of over 50 oppositionists of one or another stripe to the council, along with the fact that many of the elected regional governors might be guided primarily by the interests of their regions, indicated that the Yeltsin administration could not always count on reliable support in the upper house.[42]

The outcome in the State Duma election was a serious political setback for the presidency. The decision to allocate half the seats to parties or blocs on the basis of proportional representation was presumably taken with a view to encouraging the emergence of a multiparty system and in confidence that democratic groups would garner a majority of the 225 seats to be filled on the basis of party lists as well as many seats in single-constituency elections. The results refuted that optimistic assumption. The Russia's Choice bloc gained only about 15 percent of the vote, and the democratic groups headed by Yavlinsky and Shakhrai gained little more than the minimal 5 percent needed for representation in the Duma. The Movement for Democratic Reform led by St. Petersburg's mayor, Anatolii Sobchak, and Moscow's former mayor, Gavriil Popov, did not cross the line with even 5 percent.

The big winner in the voting by party lists was Zhirinovsky's Liberal Democratic Party of Russia (LDPR), which gained 23 percent of the vote. Zyuganov's Communist Party received 11 percent, the conservative Agrarian Party 9 percent, and the Women of Russia bloc about 9 percent. When the Duma was convened following the election, the speakership went to a representative of Zyuganov's Communists, Ivan Rybkin. The Duma did not take long to manifest its oppositionist potential. Taking unexpected advantage of its amnesty-granting power under the new constitution, a Duma majority on February 23, 1994 brought the leaders of both the failed coup of August 1991 and the September–October 1993 standoff into what had been intended by the executive branch as a low-level amnesty. Khasbulatov, Rutskoi, and other leaders of the former anti-Yeltsin parliament emerged in freedom from Moscow's Lefortovo prison, and Rutskoi soon let it be known that he would be a contender in the new presidential elections due in June 1996.

The impressive strength shown by the conservative-to-radical opposition in the December elections seems to have been due in part to the appeal of Zhirinovsky's Russian nationalism, but that was not the primary factor. Any full explanation must take into account the widespread voter apathy shown in the low overall turnout; the negative attitude of many citizens toward a reform course that, along with some meaningful material improvements, brought extreme polarization of society between a tiny minority of the very wealthy and a poor to poverty-stricken large majority with no serious middle class in between; criminalization of the economy; growing unemployment or uncertain employment because of layoffs, forced vacations, and nonpayment of wages; and the lack of a positive vision and program for Russia's future as a stable, prosperous nation-state with a constructive role in world affairs. All this found reflection in the postelection emergence, with Yeltsin's blessing, of a basically centrist Chernomyrdin government minus the best-known market reformers, Gaidar and former finance minister Boris Fedorov.

Finally, a new contender for Russian leadership may have appeared on the political horizon in the person of the ultranationalist, xenophobic, and imperialist Zhirinovsky, whose Liberal-Democrats hold 64 seats in the Duma and can, by teaming up with an oppositionist majority (as in the February amnesty decision), seriously influence parliamentary decisionmaking. However, Zhirinovsky's temper tantrums, scandalous behavior abroad, extremist utterances, dictatorial ways with his own party (extending to physical violence against wayward associates), and manifestations of megalomania may bar a path to power for him.

The Outcome

As the third anniversary of the demise of Soviet power came at the end of 1994, the resulting turmoil was far from ended. Not only in the swath of lands now composing Russia's near abroad but in the Russian Federation too, firm new edifices of statehood had yet to be built, and progress in some areas was offset by regress in others.

The end of the Soviet internal empire posed the challenge of building independent functioning nation-states in what had been this empire's component parts, Russia included. Despite the continuity of political leadership in some, notably in Central Asia, and the return to key posts of individuals whose leadership capacities had been shown in Soviet times, including Eduard Shevardnadze in Georgia and Heidar Aliev in Azerbaijan, the obstacles to building stable new nation-states seemed discouragingly great.

The forced departure of reform leader Stanislav Shushkevich in Belarus and this state's subsequent entry into the ruble zone signaled a potential reunification of Belarus with Russia. The March–April 1994 parliamentary elections in

Ukraine, along with the somewhat earlier elections in the Crimea with their pro-Russian outcome, showed a Ukraine deeply divided between Ukrainian nationalists concentrated in the west and the Russia-oriented population in the east, with a weakened President Kravchuk presiding over a crisis-ridden economy and in the absence of a new younger leadership cohort committed to reform. Subsequently, Kravchuk lost the presidency in an election to a moderate reformer, the relatively pro-Russian Leonid Kuchma. In Moldova the leadership backed away from a course toward union with Romania but was still faced with the difficult problem of constructing a viable Moldovan nation-state including the separatist Trans-Dniester and Gaugaz regions in the east and southeast.

The three Transcaucasian republics were disaster zones, with Georgia unable to overcome Abkhazian separatism and with Armenia and Azerbaijan endlessly at war over Nagorno-Karabakh. Although the Tajik civil war ended in 1993, no secure peace came about between the warring parties, and the republic remained a Russian protectorate. Uzbekistan and Turkmenistan remained under dictatorships of their former Soviet leaders Karimov and Niiazov. Despite the efforts of President Nazarbaev to make a viable nation-state out of huge Kazakhstan, whose population of 16 million is divided more or less evenly between Kazakhs and national minorities (mostly Russians but also Ukrainians and Germans), the refusal of dual Kazakh and Russian citizenship for the Russians, the making of Kazakh into the state language, and the ongoing "Kazakhization" of official life have led large numbers of Russians and Germans to emigrate,[43] and a similar tendency is visible in small Kyrgyzstan under its well-meaning President Askar Akaev. Likewise, anti-Russian discriminatory policies are accompanying the rebuilding of independent nation-states in two of the three Baltic countries, Latvia and Estonia.

In Russia the new Time of Troubles has continued and in various ways worsened. The flamboyant Zhirinovsky conjures up memories of pretenders to the throne (*samozvantsy*) who surfaced during the first Time of Troubles. Notwithstanding the formal constitutional provisions for a strong presidential republic, the edifice of post-Soviet Russian statehood has remained weak. The spread and extent of organized crime are beyond the power of the state's law-enforcement agencies to control. Russians and others flood into the country from the outlying republics, and to these refugees must be added large numbers of others who make their way across porous borders into Russia from Asia and Africa. The new era finds Russians experiencing alienation from government and political life, disillusionment with forms of freedom gained by the collapse of order, and a loss of values, a situation noted by the president of the Russian Academic of Sciences, Yurii Osipov: "Before us burning bitter questions arise: What is happening in this country? Whence the decay of civic ethics, the outbursts of mass violence, the bloody ethnic clashes? Are there real ways to predict these things and deal with them? Or is this the windup to civilization as we've known it?"[44]

In the cyclical pattern of Russian history, each systemic breakdown has been followed by a restoration of the dynastic-imperial system with its authoritarian rule by a rank-ordered officialdom. Not surprisingly, restorationist tendencies manifest themselves in the present Time of Troubles. They make themselves felt, for example, in influential circles in the State Duma. Thus Vladimir Isakov, chairman of the key Duma Committee on Legislation and Judicial-Legal Reform, proposed at a plenary session on March 11, 1994, that in the future the presidency be subject to election not by the voters at large, as in 1991, but by a new Assembly of the Land (Zemskii Sobor) consisting of the members of the Federation Council and representatives of the territories. He might have added that this was how the first of the Romanovs was elected in 1613. *Izvestiia*'s commentator took the speech as a trial balloon to test receptiveness at higher levels to establishing a state system bereft of popular control, a dictatorship of the *nomenklatura*.

By early 1994 there was wide agreement among knowledgeable Russian observers of the scene that a trend toward reversion to previous Russian and Soviet systems of statehood was far advanced, that the "*nomenklatura* party" (or "bosses' party") was back in command, that officialdom was once again the dominant force in the country, and that the democratic reform process was stymied. As Lilia Shevtsova formulated this view, earlier assumptions regarding the demise of communism proved premature. The political culture of the Soviet era had persisted into the post-Soviet present.

What occurred, she wrote, was the transformation of Soviet officialdom, with some additions to it, into a new ruling class. The banning of the CPSU and closing down of its structures only facilitated the survival of pragmatic elements of the old elite who long ago had been prepared for a change of apparel and slogans. In this light, Yeltsin appeared not as the gravedigger of communism that he set out to be but as its savior, who helped the old ruling class exchange political for economic power; and now it was far along toward a recovery of political dominance as well.[45]

In closing, something needs to be said on the other side. In late 1994 Russia remained a country in transition, and the same could be said of the other successor republics. In Russia's case, there existed the threat of a totalitarian restoration in the event of economic chaos and collapse, with emergence of an ultranationalist or militarist dictatorship of strong imperial-expansionist complexion. However, no dictatorship, no administrative command system of either tsarist or communist character, had yet come about. A parliament of sorts was functioning. Elections were still taking place, locally and nationally. Although the press had fallen on hard times financially, censorship had not been restored, and people were still speaking out freely in print and in the normal other ways. A new, younger generation of potential Russian leaders was in the making. A stabilization of the situation and democratic development over time were not ruled out.

Such an outcome would be in the vital interest not only of the peoples of Russia and the whole former Soviet Union but also of the West and the world at large. In the face of the global turmoil that threatens humanity in the last years of the twentieth century and beyond, Russia's constructive participation with other major powers in leadership for civilization's survival is a sine qua non of such leadership's success.

Notes

1. George Vernadsky, *A History of Russia,* rev. ed. (New York: New Home Library, 1944), p. 56 and passim; and Vladimir Weidle, *Russia Absent and Present* (New York: J. Day, 1961), pp. 27–29.

2. For example, Yurii Gote in a diary much later published as *Time of Troubles: The Diary of Iurii Vladimirovich Got'e,* July 8, 1917, to July 23, 1922, trans. and ed. Terrence Emmons (Princeton: Princeton University Press, 1988). Gote was a professor of Russian history.

3. On this see Robert C. Tucker, *Stalin in Power: The Revolution from Above, 1928–1941* (New York: W. W. Norton & Co., 1990).

4. Evgenii Aleksandrov, "Iubilei samoderzhaviia: Za upakoi ili za zdravie?" *Nezavisimaia gazeta,* February 20, 1993.

5. Efrem Maiminas, "Traektoriia nashego dvizheniia," *Nezavisimaia gazeta,* February 4, 1993.

6. S. Shakhrai, "Ia mnogikh razdrazhal," *Literaturnaia gazeta,* August 26, 1992.

7. Semyon Novoprudskii, "My poidyem svoim putyem," *Nezavisimaia gazeta,* March 16, 1993; and Asal Azamova, "Vlast'—oppositsii: 'Vek svobody ne vidat,'" *Moskovskie novosti,* January 17, 1993.

8. Interview with Len Karpinskii, *Moskovskie novosti,* January 17, 1993.

9. Fyodor Burlatsky, "Model Litvy—budushchee Rossii?," *Nezavisimaia gazeta,* March 18, 1993. Burlatsky claimed that "several years ago" such an idea was proposed to Gorbachev but that he did not act on it.

10. M. Fedotov, A. Makarov, and S. Shakhrai, "'Delo KPSS' ili kakuyu organizatsiyu my poteriali," *Izvestiia,* July 2, 1992.

11. Interview in *Izvestiia,* June 11, 1992.

12. *Izvestiia,* April 3, 1993.

13. B. Nemtsov, "V Moskve net vlasti. Est' tol'ko bor' ba za nee," *Komsomolskaia pravda,* March 20, 1993.

14. *Izvestiia,* February 2, 1993; Evgenii Galkin, "Kazhdyi chetvertyi uzhe veteran," *Nezavisimaia gazeta,* April 1, 1993; and S. Vegran, "Trends in Russian Agrarian Reform," *RFE/RL Research Report,* March 26, 1993, p. 57.

15. *Izvestiia,* February 2, 1993.

16. Pyotr Filippov, "Feodaly protiv zemledel'tsev," *Izvestiia,* November 18, 1992.

17. A. Stanley, "In St. Petersburg, a Struggle for Room at the Top," *New York Times,* April 6, 1994.

18. Stephen Handelman, "The Russian 'Mafiya,'" *Foreign Affairs,* March-April 1994, p. 83. According to the former prosecutor general of the Russian Federation, Aleksei Kazannik, about 15,000 organized criminal groups were active in early 1994, a statistic based on information from the Ministry of Internal Affairs. *Nezavisimaia gazeta,* April 9, 1994, p. 1.

19. Otto Latsis, "Kak zhivut segodnia v Latvii," *Izvestiia,* April 14, 1993; Aleksandr Shegedin, "Utopisty u vlasti," *Rossiia,* March 24–30, 1993.

20. On Kazakh ethnocratic tendencies, see Vladimir Moiseev, "Sovremennaia istoriografiia Kazakhstana," *Nezavisimaia gazeta,* April 20, 1993; on Russians who favor a change of borders and on Nazarbaev's position, see Chapter 8.

21. A. V. Riabov, "Devianosto vtoroi god," *Kentavr,* no. 1, 1993, p. 8.

22. Ibid., pp. 11–13.

23. Burbulis interview with editor Len Karpinskii, *Moskovskie novosti,* January 17, 1993.

24. This comparison was made by various observers, among them Sergei Filatov, former vice chairman of the Supreme Soviet, in "Istoki termidora," *Rossiia,* January 13–19, 1993. On Khasbulatov's edict of August 1992, see B. Zolotukhin, "Post predsedatelia verkhovnogo soveta neobkhodimo uprazdnit'," *Izvestiia,* March 13, 1993. On finding work in the parliament for almost all former staff members of the Central Committee apparatus, see Sergei Chugaev, "Tret'e triumfal'noe shestvie sovetskoi vlasti," *Izvestiia,* March 20, 1993.

25. "Sergei Filatov obviniaet oppozitsii v provokatsiakh," *Izvestiia,* April 21, 1993.

26. "Na odin tank nel'zia vlezt' dvazhdy, ili vse na vybory," *Moskovskie novosti,* April 4, 1993.

27. Lilia Shevtsova, "Muki bezvlastiia," *Izvestiia,* November 3, 1992.

28. Sergei Alekseev, "Tikhii perekhvat vlasti," *Izvestiia,* November 19, 1992.

29. *Izvestiia,* April 9 and 10, 1993.

30. "Nizhegorodskii prolog," *Moskovskie novosti,* September 13, 1992.

31. Ibid.

32. Interview with Iakov Samokhin, *Literaturnaia gazeta,* September 2, 1992.

33. "V poiskakh novogo 'kuda?'" *Moskovskie novosti,* August 9, 1992. Gefter died in February 1995.

34. N. Shmelev, "Shansy dlia reformy," *Moskovskie novosti,* April 25, 1993.

35. Ann Sheehy, "Russia's Republics: A Threat to Its Territorial Integrity?" *RFE/RL Research Report,* May 14, 1993, p. 38; and Irina Buzygina, "'Rossiia regionov'— formirovanie novoi federatsii," *Nezavisimaia gazeta,* May 2, 1993.

36. V. Emelianenko, "Rossiia rukhnet esli budet poprezhnemu delit'sia na vassalov i siuzerenov," *Moskovskie novosti,* February 7, 1993.

37. A. Tarasov, "Obnarodovan proekt ustava Krasnoiarskogo kraia," *Izvestiia,* May 21, 1993.

38. Andrei Kibrik, "Protiv ellinov i iudeev v Rossii," *Moskovskie novosti,* May 9, 1993; and Busygina, "'Rossiia regionov.'"

39. Andrei Kibrik, "Zavetam Lenina verny," *Moskovskie novosti,* May 23, 1993.

40. "A Second October Revolution: Yel'tsin Disbands Soviets," *Radio Free Europe/Radio Liberty Research Bulletin,* November 16, 1993.

41. Ibid.

42. Mikhail Petrachev, "Senat i senatory," *Nezavisimaia gazeta,* April 7, 1994.

43. Boris Lysenko, "Nemtsy pakuiut chemodany i uezhaiut iz Kazakhstana," *Izvestiia,* April 12, 1994.

44. Kim Smirnov, "Akademikom u nas stat' ne legche, chem v S.Sh.A. prezidentom," *Izvestiia,* March 30, 1994.

45. Lilia Shevtsova, "My umudrilis' otvratit' narod ot demokratii eshche do togo, kak ona nastupila," *Literaturnaia gazeta,* December 29, 1993.

CHAPTER 2

Political Elites Under Gorbachev and Yeltsin in the Early Period of Transition: A Reputational and Analytical Study

David Lane

The closed nature of political decisionmaking created enormous problems for researchers in the Soviet period, but the collapse of the old order has led to problems in the definition and analysis of leadership of a novel kind. In periods of rapid political change, there may be a shifting set of political actors and institutions. Political power may have no consistent pattern, and the occupants of defined political positions may lack authority.

In the transitional environment, the *positional approach* to political power, which was dominant in the study of Soviet politics, has become of limited use.[1] Moving constellations or coalitions of people, groups, and institutions may be captured in the first instance by the insight of informed people given by the *reputational method.* The student of politics may find wisdom in the anthropologist's technique of asking an unknown tribesman to "tell me who are your leaders." Its advantage, if properly applied, is that it takes account of the views of political insiders who may have insights and knowledge of which people are influential.

Such an approach has some drawbacks and should be used with caution. Subjective evaluations of who has influence may reflect the preferences of the respondents, whose opinions may be based on hearsay evidence or on no evidence at all. Indeed, reputational analysis uncovers variation among different people's perceptions of the powerful: Not all can be unambiguously correct. But in the absence of access to documents and observation of the decisionmaking process, this approach can provide important insight and may indicate which groups of people form the political elite—though their influence within it is indeterminate. The findings of such surveys may act as a basis for further research and a source of hypothesis creation. Finally, reputational analysis may reveal a great deal about informed public opinion: in this case, about who people think are political agents and about which institutions and social forces are believed to be playing a formative political role. The extent of such differences of perception of the ruling elite and the ways they change over time are also important components of the political culture.

The reputational approach may be particularly appropriate as a method in societies with centralized and fused political and economic institutions and a political leadership operating in relatively few political networks—as probably was the case in Russia under Mikhail Gorbachev and Boris Yeltsin in 1991 and 1992.[2]

This study is a reputational one concerned with the opinions of people having some expert knowledge of politics in the USSR under Gorbachev and in Russia under Yeltsin. Forty-eight persons, drawn from three different constituencies, were interviewed in October and November 1992. Their composition was as follows: leading deputies of the Russian Supreme Soviet (N = 16); academics and advisers (N = 16); executives of government (N = 16). All the respondents were interviewed in Moscow by Russian interviewers.

The respondents were selected evenly from people who had knowledge and experience of the Gorbachev and Yeltsin periods of leadership. The interviews reported here were conducted by telephone by interviewers from the Institute of Sociology in the Russian Academy of Sciences.[3] The questions were devised to define groups of people having influence at the top level under Gorbachev (from the period he took office as general secretary of the party to the attempted coup in August 1991) and Yeltsin from the coup to mid-1992. The study was also designed to gain information on different institutions and social and political forces that may have been instrumental in policy formation during these periods.

There were seven pairs of questions, three of which were related to the Gorbachev era and four to the Yeltsin period (see Table 2.1). For the Gorbachev period, I defined three topics, each having two parts: the first concerned with the persons whom the respondents believed to have influence, the second with the institutions or forces (sily) believed to have been powerful. In an effort to uncover different elements of the political elite, interviewers asked questions covering different areas of decisionmaking: internal politics, economic policy, and relations with other states. Questions were asked on an internal security topic—the Union Treaty (questions 1 and 2), on an economic issue—the introduction of cooperatives, or quasi-private enterprise (3 and 4), and international relations—the withdrawal of Soviet troops from Eastern Europe (5 and 6). The strategy was similar for the Yeltsin period: There were questions on internal politics—the banning of the Communist Party (7 and 8); on the introduction of market reforms (9 and 10); and on the breakup of the USSR (11 and 12). In addition, one pair of questions (13 and 14) addressed to the respondents probed their views on the people or forces they thought in general were the most influential in Russia at the time of the interview. To each of these questions, the respondents were asked to give five responses. These were open-ended questions, and the respondents were not prompted about any persons or groups and institutions. (However, interviewees were asked not to mention in their answers Yeltsin and Gorbachev in questions referring to them.)

TABLE 2.1   Survey Questions About the Gorbachev and Yeltsin Periods

1. Who, in your opinion, had decisive influence on Gorbachev in the formation of the Union Treaty? Give five names.
2. Which sociopolitical forces influenced the taking of this decision [on the formation of the Union Treaty]? Name five forces.
3. Cooperatives began to operate for the first time under Gorbachev. Who, in your opinion, had the most decisive influence on the taking of this decision? Give five names.
4. Which sociopolitical forces supported cooperatives? Name five.
5. Under Gorbachev the USSR withdrew its military forces from Eastern Europe. Who, in your opinion, played the most decisive role in the making of this decision? Give five names.
6. Which sociopolitical forces influenced the taking of this decision [to withdraw Soviet military forces from Eastern Europe]? Name five.
7. Under Yeltsin the Communist Party was decreed to be illegal. Who, in your opinion, had the most decisive influence in making this decision? Give five names.
8. Under Yeltsin the Communist Party was decreed to be illegal. What sociopolitical forces influenced the taking of this decision? Give up to five responses.
9. Who, in your opinion, most actively supports the widening of market reforms? Give five names.
10. Which sociopolitical groups support the extension of market reforms?
11. Under Yeltsin the USSR was dissolved, which led to the formation of a group of independent states. Who, in your opinion, was more influential in making this decision? Give five names.
12. Under Yeltsin the USSR was dissolved, which led to the formation of a group of independent states. Which sociopolitical powers influenced the taking of this decision? Give up to five responses.
13. Who (excluding Yel'tsin) do you think are the five most influential people in Russia? Give five names.
14. Which are the five most influential sociopolitical forces in present-day [late 1992] Russia?

Influential People Under Gorbachev

Table 2.2 gives the distribution of people cited by all forty-eight respondents as having had influence under Gorbachev on three crucial issues. Because the questions were open-ended, a wide range of people were cited among the total of sixty-six; only the top sixteen are listed in the table (most of the others would be unknown to the nonspecialist Western reader). These people included not only those internal to the incumbent political elite but also those seeking to influence it from outside the Soviet Union (such as foreign leaders).

Examination of the frequency of names cited gives some indication of the political influences at work. These necessarily refer to different persons at different periods of Gorbachev's time in office. In question 1 (on the proposed Union Treaty), the responses show that in the sphere of internal relations among the republics, Gorbachev was already strongly believed to have been under the influence of people outside his chosen elite at the center of the USSR: The republican leaders Nursultan Nazarbaev, Boris Yeltsin, and Leonid Kravchuk made up three of the top four. The answers to question 3 (on private trade) confirm Aleksandr Yakovlev

TABLE 2.2   Gorbachev's Reputational Political Elite

	Question			
	1	*3*	*5*	*Total*
Yakovlev	19	18	35	72
Shevardnadze	11	5	34	50
Nazarbaev	29	0	0	29
Yeltsin	23	0	0	23
Abalkin	0	16	1	17
Kravchuk	14	0	0	14
Ryzhkov	0	13	0	13
Shakhnazarov	7	2	4	13
Kohl	0	0	12	12
Bush	1	0	10	11
Aganbegian	0	9	0	9
Shatalin[a]	2	6	0	8
Bakatin[a]	2	1	4	7
Cherniaev[a]	2	2	3	7
Reagan[a]	0	0	7	7
Thatcher	1	0	6	7
Others (50 named persons)	44	46	22	114

[a]Not shown in Figure 2.1.

(previously Soviet ambassador to Canada from 1973 to 1983, then from 1987 full Politburo member and close associate of Gorbachev) as the single most important immediate influence on Gorbachev.

Study of other responses shows a different pattern from that found on the Union Treaty. In the economic sphere, economists Leonid Abalkin (previously head of the Institute of Economics of the Academy of Sciences), Nikolai Ryzhkov (who had had a career in Gosplan until 1982, when he became chief of the Economic Department of the Central Committee, and who in 1985 became chairman of the Council of Ministers of the USSR), Academician Abel Aganbegian (director of the Institute for Production Forces and National Resources), and Academician Stanislav Shatalin (previously dean of economics at Moscow University) were much more frequently reputed to have played a more important role, whereas in the discussion of the Union Treaty, politicians were predominant. On question 5 (on the decision of the Soviet Union to withdraw military forces from Eastern Europe), yet another important constituency in its influence on the Gorbachev leadership becomes prominent. After Aleksandr Yakovlev and Eduard Shevardnadze, both top Politburo members in the communist leadership, come four foreign politicians: Chancellor Helmut Kohl of Germany, U.S. presidents George Bush and Ronald Reagan, and Prime Minister Margaret Thatcher. Their summed score comes to thirty-five—the same as for Yakovlev individually. Vadim Bakatin, who was minister of the interior and chief of the KGB until 1990 and 1991, managed to muster only five mentions on this question. Clearly, an understanding of policymaking must take account of international interests and pressures.

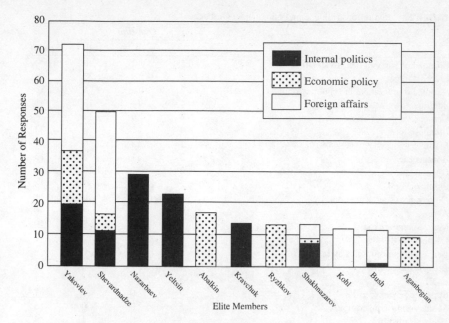

FIGURE 2.1   Gorbachev's Reputational Elite by Area of Influence

On the basis of these three sets of evaluations, it is possible to develop a consolidated list of influential people under Gorbachev forming the political elite (column 4 of Table 2.2). The top leaders (those having nine or more mentions) are shown in Figure 2.1, which also plots the areas in which their influence was attributed. Notable is the dominance of the Communist Party leadership: Yakovlev and Shevardnadze (the latter a member of the Politburo from 1978, a full member from 1985, and minister of foreign affairs) and two men with a regional base—Leonid Kravchuk, president of Ukraine, and Nursultan Nazarbaev, president of Kazakhstan. Also prominent are foreign statesmen Kohl and Bush and advisers Abalkin, Georgii Shakhnazarov (a longtime official in the Central Committee apparatus and vice president of the International Political Science Association), Abel Aganbegian, and Anatolii Cherniaev (previously deputy chief of the International Department of the Central Committee and Gorbachev's main aide on foreign policy after 1986). Later in the chapter I compare the political constituencies of the people cited here with those cited for the Yeltsin period.

Influential Institutions and Forces Under Gorbachev

One of the mysteries about the collapse of the Soviet Union has been which institutions contributed the policies that undid the country and led to the disbanding of the Communist Party. The set of questions on institutions sought to cast some light on the problem.

34

TABLE 2.3   Institutions Influencing Policy Under Gorbachev

	Question			
	2	4	6	Total
Communist Party of the Soviet Union	22	12	6	40
External forces	7	3	28	38
Nationalist movement in republics/regions	27	0	5	32
Intelligentsia	4	14	13	31
Democrats	8	6	14	28
Nomenklatura	8	7	5	20
Mafia	1	15	0	16
Bourgeoisie	3	11	1	15
General laws	2	1	10	13
Public opinion	2	9	2	13
Government sector of economy	1	10	0	11
Army	6	0	4	10
Mass communications	1	6	3	10
Democratic Russia	5	2	2	9
Leaders of the republics and regions	9	0	0	9
Bureaucracy, center	1	7	0	8
KGB	5	1	1	7
Supreme Soviet (central)	7	0	0	7
Military-industrial complex	5	0	0	5
Higher leadership	3	0	1	4
Administration (Russia)	3	0	0	3
Deputies	3	0	0	3
Diplomats	0	0	3	3
Yeltsin's circle	3	0	0	3
Gorbachev's circle	1	0	2	3
Government	1	0	2	3
Komsomol	0	3	0	3
Bureaucracy, regions	2	0	0	2
Central leaders of parties	2	0	0	2
Liberals	0	0	2	2
Opposition	1	1	0	2
Supreme Soviets (republics)	2	0	0	2
Agrarians	0	1	0	1
Democratic Party of Russia	1	0	0	1
Yakovlev's people	1	0	0	1
Movement for Democratic Reform	1	0	0	1
Neo-Communists	1	0	0	1
Peasant movement	0	1	0	1
People's Party of Free Russia	1	0	0	1
Trade unions	0	1	0	1
Workers' collectives	0	1	0	1
Youth	0	1	0	1

Table 2.3 presents the results for question 2 on which sociopolitical forces had influence in the decision on the Union Treaty; question 4 on sociopolitical forces backing Gorbachev on the formation of cooperatives; and question 6 on the sociopolitical forces having influence over the decision to withdraw Soviet forces from Eastern Europe. The final column shows the totals.

The responses to question 2 identify influential groups that were outside the Gorbachev elite as defined in the earlier questions, which focused on individuals. The nationalist movement in the republics figures highly in the responses (twenty-seven), more so than the Communist Party of the Soviet Union (twenty-two). In this area, the democrats had a relatively low index (eight). These results would indicate that Gorbachev was pushed by the nationalist forces in his policy on the Union Treaty.

On the question about influences on the introduction of private enterprise, there is a predominance of economic forces outside of the established apparatus of political power. The total for the mafia (a term often used to refer to various types of traders and people in business generally, as well as speculators) and the bourgeoisie is well in excess of the next nearest group (the intelligentsia). The intelligentsia category also included professionals, such as physicians, who were able to sell their services on the market. Cooperatives seem to be favored by a range of institutions, including sections of the Communist Party and the government sector of the economy (to which also belonged the responses referring to the central bureaucracy and the *nomenklatura*).

Finally, in the international sphere, rather surprisingly perhaps, external forces are by far given the highest rank, followed by quite general social forces (democrats and the intelligentsia). The CPSU and the *nomenklatura* were not attributed very much influence here. Internal institutions, as contrasted with general social forces, were given little weight in determining this policy. Foreign policy appears to be largely decided by the political elite in Gorbachev's immediate circle.

These results are analyzed in more detail, after discussion of responses to similar interview questions concerning political power after the rise of Yeltsin to the helm. I then compare differences in the composition of the political elites in the two periods.

Influential People Under Yeltsin

A similar interview procedure was adopted to discover leadership influence under Yeltsin. Results of the questions are shown in Table 2.4 . From responses to question 7 about the banning of the CPSU, the most frequently cited persons would indicate that significant influence was exercised on Yeltsin by close political associates. These included Gennadii Burbulis, who was state secretary attached to the president of the Russian Federation until November 26, 1992, when he became head of the Group of Advisers to the president; Sergei Shakhrai, deputy prime

TABLE 2.4   People Having Influence Under Yeltsin

	Question				
	7	11	9	13	Total
Burbulis	34	22	12	34	102
Gaidar	0	4	33	30	67
Kravchuk	1	39	0	0	40
Shakhrai	23	10	0	2	35
Khasbulatov	4	2	0	28	34
Rutskoi	3	0	4	24	31
Volskii	0	0	4	20	24
Poltoranin	10	5	2	5	22
Popov	11	2	4	3	20
Shushkevich	0	20	0	0	20
Chubais	0	0	17	2	19
Skokov	0	0	1	16	17
Shokhin	0	0	12	2	14
Petrov	0	0	1	12	13
Gorbachev[a]	4	4	0	2	10
Nazarbaev	0	10	0	0	10
Others (64 named persons)	48	49	69	28	19

[a]Not shown in Figure 2.2.

minister with responsibility for legal questions until November 5, 1992, when he became responsible for nationality questions and chairman of the State Committee for Interethnic Policy; Gavriil Popov, the head of the Russian branch of the Movement for Democratic Reform and until June 1992 mayor of Moscow; and Mikhail Poltoranin, who, after being minister of the press and information and deputy prime minister of the Russian Federation, was appointed head of the Federal Information Center in November 1992.

Question 11 focused on the dissolution of the USSR. Respondents cited important influences from outside Russia, particularly Leonid Kravchuk (president of Ukraine), Nursultan Nazarbaev (president of Kazakhstan), and Stanislav Shushkevich (head of state in Belarus). This suggests that the leadership was responding to the elites outside the Russian Federation. There is little evidence here to suggest that this measure could primarily be attributed to the political faction led by Yeltsin.

Question 9 was designed to tap the constituencies influencing economic decisions. In addition to Gennadii Burbulis, the top four included Yegor Gaidar, at the time of the interviews the acting chairman of the Russian government; Anatolii Chubais, formerly deputy chairman of the Leningrad soviet and lately deputy prime minister responsible for privatization; and Aleksandr Shokhin, deputy prime minister for social and foreign economic issues. All three are economists by training, which indicates that the economic intelligentsia played a leading role in this area of policymaking.

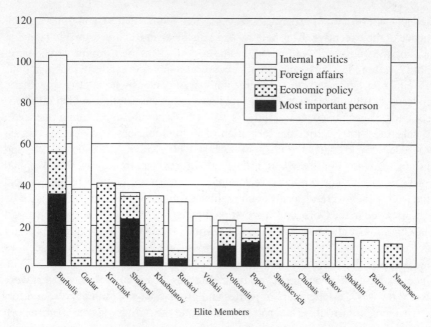

FIGURE 2.2   Yeltsin's Reputational Elite by Area of Influence

These questions cover important topics, but they do not exhaust the areas of political controversy, and the answers may exclude people with influence in other areas and with potential for political activity. Hence interviewees were asked question 13 about who they thought was the most influential overall. I discuss later the
institutional background of these people, but here it is important to note that of the
top six persons cited, four had positions in the executive branch of the Russian
government: Gennadii Burbulis; Vice President Aleksandr Rutskoi, who was also
chairman of the People's Party of Free Russia and cochairman of the Civic Union
political coalition; Yegor Gaidar; and Yurii Skokov, the secretary of the Security
Council. But Ruslan Khasbulatov, speaker of the Russian Congress of People's
Deputies, and Arkadii Volskii, as president of the Russian Union of Industrialists
and Entrepreneurs and cochairman of Civic Union, represented countervailing
forces to the Yeltsin leadership.

To form a composite Yeltsin-era political elite, I have aggregated the four sets
of responses in the last column of Table 2.4.

Figure 2.2 indicates the areas in which these individuals were believed to have
had influence. Among the most influential leaders are three major interests that
can be used to divide them into main groupings and thereby form a segmented political elite: first, members of the government executive and advisers to President
Yeltsin (Burbulis, Gaidar, Rutskoi, Poltoranin, Shakhrai, Chubais, and Popov),

second, leaders of other republics (Kravchuk and Shushkevich); and third, a group outside of the executive, Khasbulatov and Volskii, with Rutskoi arguably being, at the time the questions were posed, in this as well as the first group. As shown in Table 2.4, there is a very long tail of persons with low scores; these rankings indicate either a fragmented elite or a large number of persons who interacted with the top leaders. What is also striking from Figure 2.2 is the extent to which influence seems to be specialized. Only Burbulis was seen as having significant influence in all spheres. Clearly, after the formation of individual post-Soviet states, which proceeded quickly after the crisis of August 1991, Kravchuk, Shushkevich, and Nazarbaev were eliminated as influential figures within Russia. Rutskoi and Volskii, however, come into the reckoning as members of factions of the political elite from which were to spring counterelites to challenge Yeltsin.

Compared to the Gorbachev reputational elites, there have been many changes. The Communist elite has gone. The low number of citations to this group is partly accounted for by the reference to previous members of the elite (such as Gorbachev) whose activity was believed to have precipitated action by Yeltsin. Under Yeltsin, the government executive elite was clearly predominant; next were elected leaders. Top members of parties and groups played a minor role, and foreign leaders, industrialists and entrepreneurs, and the military appear to have been very minor actors.

Sociopolitical Forces in Support of Yeltsin

As previously noted, discussion of the background of the leaders cannot take account of the shifting allegiances of people, and leaders may not always respond to the institutions or groups they are ostensibly leading or may be deemed to represent. Therefore, a complementary set of questions to those posed on individuals asked what forces influenced the same policy options. The respondents found these questions more difficult to answer because they assumed a more abstract understanding of politics.

The results are shown in Table 2.5 . Answers to question 8 about sociopolitical forces having decisive influence on banning the Communist Party appear in the first column. The major political forces cited here are the democratic opposition under the Gorbachev leadership. Numerous respondents answered in terms of the party and its elite bringing about their own downfall (some mentioned the State Committee for the State of Emergency and the CPSU). In this table there are few references to national patriots and to republic-level and regional forces.

In the second column are responses to question 12 about the sociopolitical forces having influence on the breakup of the USSR into sovereign states. The responses emphasize quite different forces from those responsible for the banning of the CPSU—in particular, movements in the republics and regions, supported by democratic forces.

Responses to question 10 about the sociopolitical forces supporting the introduction of market reforms again have a different balance. The bourgeoisie was at

TABLE 2.5   Sociopolitical Forces in Support of Yeltsin

	Question				Total
	8	12	10	14	
Bourgeoisie	4	5	32	8	49
Democratic Russia	15	6	10	15	46
Democrats	18	9	10	7	44
Nationalist movement in republics	1	33	0	7	41
Civic Union	0	0	3	23	26
Government sector of economy	0	0	7	14	21
Nomenklatura	6	6	4	4	20
National patriots	2	3	1	14	20
Intelligentsia	4	3	10	1	18
Mass communications	4	3	2	6	15
External forces	1	6	6	1	14
CPSU	6	3	0	4	13
Public opinion	3	2	6	2	13
Mafia	3	1	5	4	13
Yeltsin's circle	4	3	0	5	12
Deputies	2	1	1	8	12
Administration (Russia)	2	2	5	2	11
Leaders of republics/regions	0	4	0	5	9
Opposition	0	1	0	6	7
Agrarians	0	0	4	3	7
State Committee of Emergency	6	0	0	0	6
Bureaucracy, center	1	3	1	1	6
Military-industrial complex	0	0	0	6	6
Party of Economic Freedom	0	0	5	1	6
Army	0	0	0	5	5
Government	0	0	2	3	5
Parties in the republics	0	0	4	1	5
People's Party of Free Russia	0	0	4	1	5
Russian People's Assembly	0	0	0	5	5
Trade unions	0	0	1	4	5
Neo-Communists	2	0	0	2	4
Business lobby	1	0	2	1	4
Democratic Party of Russia	0	0	3	1	4
Supreme Soviet (central)	0	0	2	2	4
Workers' movement	2	0	0	1	3
General laws	1	2	0	0	3
Central leaders of parties	0	0	1	2	3
Workers' collectives	0	0	0	3	3
Parties	2	0	0	0	2
Higher bureaucratic employees	0	0	2	0	2
Movement for Democratic Reform	0	0	0	2	2
Peasant movement	0	0	0	2	2
Anti-Communists	1	0	0	0	1
Clergy	1	0	0	0	1
KGB	1	0	0	0	1
Bureaucracy, regions	0	1	0	0	1
Higher leadership	0	1	0	0	1
Gaidar's people	0	0	1	0	1
Komsomol	0	0	1	0	1
Liberals	0	0	0	1	1
Russian Christian Democratic Movement	0	0	1	0	1
Socialist Party	0	0	0	1	1
Youth	0	0	1	0	1

the forefront of the consciousness of respondents; next were democratic forces and the intelligentsia.

Finally, for reasons mentioned earlier, there was a general question (number 14) about the most influential sociopolitical forces in Russia in October and November 1992. The answers shown in the fourth column of Table 2.5 cover a much wider range of alternatives. At the top are three different constituencies: the Civic Union (twenty-three) and national patriots (fourteen), the Democratic Russia movement (fifteen), and the government sector of the economy (fourteen). Democratic Russia, Yeltsin's major political support in his rise to power, is not supreme, and it may be noted that the political elites are composed of quite distinct constituencies, which will become clearer in the analysis that follows.

Rather surprisingly, perhaps, the largest group seen to be influential under Yeltsin is the bourgeoisie (to which should be added the reference to the mafia); second is Democratic Russia. The nationalist movement is much more prominent here than it was under Gorbachev. The institutions and forces of Soviet Russia have suffered a severe decline—the CPSU, KGB, and army have very low rankings. Notable also is the low frequency of mentions given to social groups: peasants, workers, and clergy.

Comparisons Between Elites in Support of Gorbachev and Yeltsin

I have used the respondents' answers to generalize about the political groups sustaining the political elite. In comparing the elite support of the Gorbachev and Yeltsin periods, I have constructed two comparative scales. The first is based on the backgrounds of the persons named in the responses (Tables 2.2 and 2.4) and the second on the institutions named by the respondents (Tables 2.3 and 2.5).

Although the biographies of the top influential figures named are of interest to the specialist on Soviet and Russian affairs, they do not exhaust the catalogue of individuals cited by the respondents. Moreover, further analysis is needed so as to generalize about the political constituencies from which they originate and which they may represent. In the analysis that follows, I have compared the institutional background of the political elites under Yeltsin and Gorbachev. Each person mentioned in answers to questions 1, 3, and 5 (see Table 2.2) and questions 7, 9, 11, and 13 (Table 2.4) has been allocated to a specific political group or constituency as illustrated in Table 2.6 and Figure 2.3. Under conditions of rapid political flux and mobility, it is impossible to allocate a person unambiguously to a single constituency. Here I have chosen to assign an individual to the most high-status position occupied or to the one for which the person is most well known.[4] This evaluation will be supplemented later when I consider specifically the social and political forces identified by respondents.

The following sixteen divisions were used: (1) Communist Party elite (CPE), persons who had held a leading position in the CPSU under Gorbachev and did not leave the party; (2) elected political elite (ELE), people in major electoral posi-

TABLE 2.6   Constituencies of Named Members of the Political Elite: Gorbachev and Yeltsin Eras Compared

Code	Constituency	Gorbachev	Yeltsin
CPE	Communist Party elite	104	17
ELE	Elected legislative elite	77	177
GEM	Government executive elite	72	257
FL	Foreign leaders	40	2
ADV	Advisers	37	80
AC	Academics	17	8
PAL	Leaders of political parties/groups	8	73
CPF	Communist Party functionaries	7	0
ELR	Elected representatives (deputies)	6	1
K	Kin of leaders	5	0
W	Writers and pundits	5	0
RL	Republican leaders	4	6
ICE	Industrialists/entrepreneurs	2	8
MC	Mass communications	2	1
M	Military (or previous military)	1	0

Note: Chi square = 188.25 with 9 degrees of freedom, p value = 0.001. Significant at the 0.1 percent level. Two entries—mass communications 2 and 1 and military 1 and 0—were omitted to obtain these figures.

tions under the Yeltsin leadership (such as mayors and presidents); (3) government executive elite (GEM), for members of the government; (4) foreign leaders (FL) outside the area of the former Soviet Union; (5) advisers (ADV); (6) academics (AC) having policy interests; (7) leaders of political parties/groups (PAL); (8) Communist Party functionaries (CPF) (lower-level apparatchiks); (9) elected representatives (ELR) (deputies to Supreme Soviets); (10) kin of leaders (K); (11) writers and pundits (W); (12) republican leaders (RL), not elected to a presidential post; (13) industrialists and entrepreneurs (ICE); (14) executives in mass communication (MC) (press, television, and radio); (15) military (M) (or previously military); and (16) a residual category (Others).

This procedure has the advantage of indicating the distribution of all the reputational elite, not just those at the top who are well known. It also gives some notion of the institutions and forces behind the reputational leaders that were influential in the latter period of Gorbachev's leadership and of how they differed under Yeltsin. Table 2.6 then gives an indication of the political constituencies of the total political elite.

It is possible to hazard a number of conclusions about the political constituencies shaping elite politics under Gorbachev and Yeltsin. There can be no doubt that the political constituencies changed decisively from the first to the second period; the chi-squared test indicates a significant statistical difference between the two constituencies. The people influencing Gorbachev were drawn from within the established political elites, overwhelmingly from the Communist Party leadership followed by government leaders and top elected leaders. These groups could be

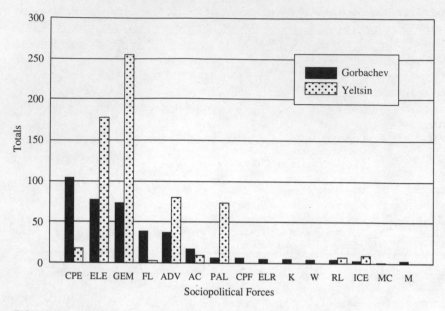

FIGURE 2.3   Political Elite Background: Gorbachev and Yeltsin Eras Compared

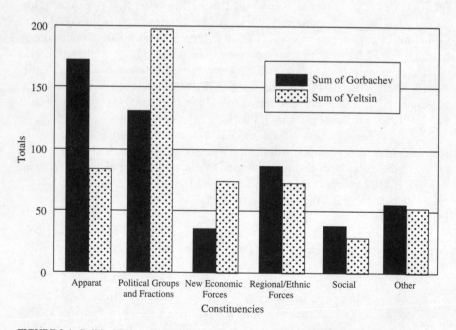

FIGURE 2.4   Political Forces Compared, Gorbachev and Yeltsin

said to originate from a single political constituency. Nearly all those with high scores were persons with positions within the Communist elite (Yakovlev, Shevardnadze, Nazarbaev, Kravchuk) and could be said to be Gorbachev supporters. The only exception is Yeltsin, who was a leading opponent and representative of the elected representative elite. Foreign leaders received notably high rankings because of their supposed influence over foreign affairs. Various kinds of advisers, academics, journalists, and others outside the political establishment had much lower rankings.

Under Yeltsin, the Communist elite has gone. The low number of responses (seventeen) is partly accounted for by the reference to previous members of the elite (particularly Gorbachev) whose earlier activities had influenced Yeltsin or who may have been held responsible for the insurgents' actions. Under Yeltsin, the government executive elite is clearly predominant; next are elected leaders and advisers. Leaders of parties and groups have a significant level of representation. Foreign leaders, industrialists and entrepreneurs, and the military appear to be very minor players. There is no named leader associated with a trade union or the industrial working-class constituencies. The number of foreign leaders falls dramatically, whereas the leaders of parties and groups rise significantly. Women had very few mentions, as they did under Gorbachev.[5]

The second comparative scale considers social forces. Here I have attempted to generalize about the various groups and social players, on the one hand, underpinning Gorbachev's rise and fall from power and, on the other, sustaining or opposing Yeltsin. On the basis of the responses listed in Tables 2.3 and 2.5, I have divided the various institutions and forces into six categories:

1. The apparat
2. Political groups and factions
3. New economic forces
4. Regional and ethnic forces
5. Social groups
6. Others (a residual category)

The totals are illustrated in Figure 2.4 and Table 2.7.

Here, again, there was a highly significant statistical difference between the frequencies with which the various constituencies were mentioned. Under Gorbachev, the apparat is the largest single group (172 mentions). Under political groups and factions, a political counterelite can be distinguished (external forces, democrats, and Democratic Russia). Personal groupings (e.g., Yakovlev's people) indicative of cliques in the early stages of party formation had made an appearance but were relatively small. National forces based on the republics and regions occupy an important place (85). On the other hand, new economic interests had very few mentions (36). Social groups were given a low total rating (38); only the intelligentsia received a significant score (31). Workers' collectives (1), trade unions

TABLE 2.7   Political Institutions and Forces Compared, Gorbachev and Yeltsin Political Elites

Total Constituency	Gorbachev	Yeltsin
Apparat	172	83
Political groups/factions	130	197
New economic forces	36	73
Regional and ethnic forces	85	76
Social groups	38	28
Others	56	53

Note: Chi square = 59.41 with 5 degrees of freedom, p = 0.001. Chance occurrence less than 1 in 1000.

(1), and the peasant movement (1) all had a conspicuously low ranking. Nor were public opinion (13) and mass communications (10) considered particularly crucial.

Under Yeltsin, the new elites had a different basis. This analysis revealed the following six most frequently named forces: the bourgeoisie (49), Democratic Russia (46), democratic forces (44), nationalist movements in the republics and regions (41), Civic Union (26), and the government sector of the economy (21). The largest group is composed of political associations and factions, first Democratic Russia, democrats, and Civic Union, then a string of small parties. Moreover, the nationalist movement and national patriots combined have 61 references. The other important development is the high rating given to the new economic forces: The business lobby and the mafia receive 66 mentions in all. This is much larger than for the institutions forming the apparat: The government sector had only 21 and the *nomenklatura* 20. The army and KGB had remarkably low rankings. Social groups, such as the clergy, youth, workers' collectives, the peasant movement, and trade unions, were perceived to have had very little influence. The conclusion from this is that there was a low level of interest articulation by such groups and little mass mobilization, both in the postcoup situation in 1992 and in the period before it.

Conclusion

A reputational study is but one approach to the analysis of elites and underlying political forces, and it must be supplemented and checked by other methodologies. But in periods of intense and revolutionary change, it is one of the most promising sources of information in defining the persons and institutions constituting the political leadership.

The analysis presented here confirms a number of general points about the political orientation taken by the reform movement under Gorbachev. Influence varied by type of decision: Regional interests appeared to be more decisive in the formation of the Union Treaty; economic advisers were more influential on the introduction of the market. The most important political institutions and persons to influence policy appear to have been leaders of the Communist Party and the apparat in various forms. Yeltsin was the only internal nonestablishment leader given any significant role as a leader of the counterelite. Gorbachev was confronted by other groups and institutions to which he reacted in making his policy. The forces in the republics and regions and the democratic movement were of major importance, and their influence was divided by sphere of interest: The democrats backed economic and political reform, whereas interest groups in the republics were most concerned with the redivision of power between the center and the regions. External forces in the form of leaders of foreign governments were reputed to have been a major influence on foreign policy issues under Gorbachev. The politics of transition cannot be understood independently of the international political system.[6]

Reputational analysis of the Yeltsin leadership has revealed that both the elite structure and its composition have changed significantly. Such systemic changes have undoubtedly contributed to a lack of integration of political elites. This is surely a portent for regime instability. Decisions determining constitutional arrangements, the economy, and relations with other states of the former Soviet Union are perceived to be influenced by different constellations of people and political forces. Three kinds of interests appear to be dominant. First, the bourgeoisie and democratic forces desire a political system based on markets, civil society, and pluralism. Second is a group of national and patriotic forces emphasizing solidarity on national and traditional values. Third are elements within the government administration that may include interests linked to the previous economic and political order. It is beyond the scope of this chapter to consider ideology, but it should be noted that these interests have different preferences for the type of political system they seek to promote. The respondents' answers serve as a reminder that class forces in the form of the nascent bourgeoisie are present in the first category, whereas administrative, traditional (including those of the Communist system), and national values typify the other two groups.

The responses also indicate which groups and forces lack influence. The political parties (with the possible exception of Democratic Russia in the terminal period of Gorbachev) do not aggregate interests and are perceived to be of minimal influence. The party system has remained in an embryonic form, as self-styled parties are tiny, loose associations of people with no clearly articulated policies, membership, or mass following. Clearly, the role of workers, peasants, and trade unions was minor; and that of the former pillars of the political order, particularly the KGB and the army, appeared negligible. This lack of influence may be interpreted in two ways. It may indicate the lack of mass mobilization and therefore the absence of any threat to the incumbent political elites. Or it may indicate a lack of integration and participation in the regime and presage a more significant regime change. An obvious scenario here would be some kind of alliance with the Russian nationalist segment of the political elite.

Study of social forces leads to the inference that the main agents of political change anticipated by Marxist theory—new economic forces and the working class—played a very minor role in driving the reform movement in the terminal period of the USSR. If this was a revolution, it was a political one, led from the top and encouraged by two different kinds of internal counterelites—the nationalists and the democrats—and, at a distance, by the overwhelmingly conservative leaders of the leading Western nations. In the post-Communist regime, survey respondents were beginning to sense that the bourgeoisie was an incipient political force. In the case of the transition away from CPSU rule, rather than classes propelling the reform process through the agency of political elites, the reverse would appear to hold true: Political elites were driving the process of change and attempting to create a class structure on which its future could rest.

The implication is that in the early transition period of political change, the sources of political conflicts and the dynamics of social change are to be found not in the mobilization of the nonelites but in contradictions of goals and interests among the elites.

Studies of elites in the process of transition have important implications for policy formation. The basis of any regime's stability rests on the solidarity of its elites.[7] National elites that lack consensus produce unstable regimes alternating between authoritarianism and formal democracy. In contemporary Russia, the political forces favoring markets, political pluralism, and democracy in the sense of competing political parties and negotiated settlements are relatively weakly supported. To enhance the possibilities of political stability, the Yeltsin political executive must form an alliance with one of the other groups—the nationalists or administrative elites. Unless some kind of pact or compromise is made, elite disunity will continue and will exacerbate the breakdown in government and further the impotence of the regime. However, a pact with either of these groups will enfeeble aspects of the reform movement in its quest for marketization.

The elite fragmentation I found here would seem to suggest that Western governments should be wary of backing one set of forces or leaders rather than another in the hope that they will introduce democracy and strengthen reform. Such a policy is likely to intensify rather than eliminate the causes of instability that will certainly undermine reform. In contemporary Russia, a rapid movement from a command economy and unconditional support for marketization and the emergent bourgeoisie may aggravate conditions of social disunity. Western governments may be faced not with a choice between "democracy and reform" or authoritarian rule, but between authoritarian rule defining markets and an emerging bourgeoisie, on the one hand, or an elite settlement that may ensure regime stability with limitations on the development of a Western market system, on the other hand. Neither pattern will entail stability based on elite settlements and consensual electoral democratic choice, a combination that has evolved in countries like the United States and Britain over a period of centuries. Such countries are exceptional in their regime structures, and it would be utopian to expect the transitional societies of Eastern Europe and Russia to join them without a long period of bitter political adjustment among the elites. The absence of articulate leaders for the major mass forces (particularly the working classes) before October 1992 precluded mobilization against the new ruling elite under Yeltsin and has also minimized participation within it. A heightening of mass discontent may have uncontrolled and uncontrollable consequences. Policy should be directed to support the strengthening of interest articulation and the formation of coalitions and to advocate the prospects for compromise between these fledgling elites on which regime stability and eventually democracy can rest.[8]

Notes

I acknowledge the support of the British Economic and Social Research Council in financing the survey reported in this research under the East-West initiative and of the Russian Research Center of Harvard University that enabled me to do the writing at Harvard.

1. *Positional* considers the occupants of authoritative posts; *reputational* refers to opinions about who wields power or influence. Two other methodologies may be used in the analysis of political power: the *decisional,* which is based on the study of actual decisions, and the *distributional,* which considers the effects of decisions (who benefits or gains).

2. Since January 1993, the paper *Nezavisimaia* has printed every month a list of the top one hundred politicians based on the assessment of a list of names by fifty experts drawn from the media and political research centers. These results are not strictly comparable with this research, as the respondents are not asked to specify on what issues the cited politicians have influence.

3. Dr. Olga Kryshtanovskaya and another twenty-nine specialists were contacted but were unable or unwilling to complete the interviews. Two interviews were incomplete and were replaced by interviews of persons having similar status.

4. President Nazarbaev, for example, is included as a member of the elected political elite rather than as a Communist Party leader.

5. Only six women were mentioned by respondents for the Gorbachev period; the top two were Margaret Thatcher and Raisa Gorbachev. Two were mentioned for the Yeltsin period. Women are not shown on Table 2.6.

6. Peter Gourevitch in the late 1970s produced an influential article drawing attention to the ways that exogenous forces influence domestic policy. See "The Second Image Reversed: The International Sources of Domestic Politics." *International Organization,* Autumn 1978, pp. 881–912.

7. See the discussion in John Higley and Michael G. Burton, "The Elite Variable in Democratic Transitions and Breakdowns," *American Sociological Review,* vol. 54, 1989, pp. 17–32.

8. Text written April 1994.

CHAPTER 3

Boris Yeltsin, Russia's All-Thumbs Democrat

Timothy J. Colton

It is not easy to pinpoint where Boris Nikolaevich Yeltsin's odyssey picks up and the main sweep of the political development of Russia and the former USSR leaves off. At every bend in the road since 1985, Yeltsin has been there. No one has been more of a player in the breakup of the Soviet state and the inauguration of a post-Soviet reality. He, in turn, has been shaped as few have by the very history he helped make, events far larger than himself.

Crisp thinking about Yeltsin is not helped by confusion about categories coming out of the recent and distant Russian past. Observers used to wonder whether Mikhail Gorbachev should be typecast as a "reformer" or a "revolutionary," as if that would settle everything else. About Yeltsin, Gorbachev's nemesis, they have mostly asked whether he is a bona fide "democrat" who has forsaken Russia's autocratic heritage or, as a cut-and-dried alternative, is a "demagogue" or a "Bolshevik."[1] The view that Yeltsin's democratic credentials are genuine, an inference generally drawn abroad after the watershed of 1991, is now the cornerstone of Western policy toward the post-Soviet lands.

In the lexicon of Soviet Marxism, "democrat" and "democracy"—mantras applied to phenomena at odds with their commonsense meaning—had little concrete content. Gorbachev's call for *demokratizatsiia,* which was really for liberalized, enlightened control by the Communist Party, began to change that. The pace was quickened by meaningful elections, the relaxation of curbs on communication and organization, and the exploitation of the opening by societal groups. When the upshot was a legitimacy crisis for the CPSU, "democrat" was in essence a synonym for anyone opposed to single-party rule, and from almost any ideological angle.[2]

By that yardstick, Yeltsin, the first national figure to spurn the party and then the issuer of the decree that obliterated it, rated as a democrat at the turn of the 1990s. But so did all manner of others whose behavior since betrays no understanding of, let alone commitment to, democratic values. Yeltsin's paeans to democracy tell us little, for the terminology is being debased in the new Russia almost as shamelessly as it was in the old.

A scholarly definition of democracy, after conceding its multiplicity of specific forms, would hold that generically it is "a system of governance in which rulers are held accountable for their actions in the public realm by citizens, acting indirectly through the competition and cooperation of their elected representatives."[3] There assuredly is ample room for Yeltsin under this tent. As Kremlin maverick, de facto head of the opposition, and then freely elected president, he has done more than anyone to expand the public domain in Russia and to empower passive subjects as citizens.

Giving credit where credit is due should not blind us to Yeltsin's limitations. A parallel with Soviet-type planning in economics is instructive. The trouble with central planning, to use a metaphor of Charles Lindblom's, was that in contradistinction to its "strong thumbs," which were well suited to simple and direct tasks, it had "no fingers," none of the dexterity needed in an intricate, advanced economy.[4] Thus, after a fashion, it has been with Yeltsin in political affairs. He has made his niche in history by applying muscular thumbs and, one has to say, fists, to ram causes forward and brush aside obstacles. He has been much less of a virtuoso at the fingertip coordination, through bounded competition and flexible cooperation, that is the stuff of a stable democracy. Russia and the world had better hope that the defects in his handiwork do not overwhelm the merits.

Ordinary Apparatchik

Yeltsin reminisced in his 1990 autobiography, the only extensive guide we have to his formative years, that he had gone through not one but "three different lives." The first, "though tense and difficult," was, he asserted, "much like other people's lives—study, work, family, career."[5] And so it was, up to a point.

Born in February 1931 in the village of Butko in Sverdlovsk oblast, deep in the Urals, Yeltsin grew up there and in Berezniki, a factory town in adjacent Perm oblast. We know from a journal published in 1994 that the Yeltsins were moderately prosperous peasants—they owned a threshing machine and about ten horses and cows and hired several field hands—and this was enough for them to be branded "kulaks," wealthy farmers, and forced into a collective farm. His grandfather, Ignatii, went into hiding, and in 1934 his father, Nikolai, and uncle, Andrian, were arrested in Kazan, Tatarstan, where they had found work in construction. Nikolai served a three-year sentence on trumped-up charges of sabotage. The incident was not mentioned in Boris Yeltsin's autobiography and seems not to have left much of a mark on him, perhaps because he was a preschooler when it happened and his father imposed absolute silence on the subject in the home.[6]

What Yeltsin paints as a "joyless" childhood was not terribly different from how millions of youngsters were reared under Stalinism and the privations of the war and postwar recovery. After his divorce from the CPSU, he was to assert that all along he had been "a rebel by nature."[7] He certainly was no rebel against the

Soviet regime, his father's mistreatment notwithstanding. The early chapters of his autobiography depict, at most, a succession of small eruptions: a rambunctious country lad seeking relief from hardship and boredom by engaging in athletics (he excelled at volleyball), pranks, and mild acts of defiance in classroom and neighborhood.

Close perusal of these same pages uncovers a darker range of responses to adversity, too, among them flashes of the obstinacy, moodiness, and self-righteousness not far below the surface of his adult persona. Some of the meanest features of his environment, Yeltsin testifies, found reinforcement around the family hearth: "My father's character, like my grandfather's before him, was rough. No doubt they handed this on to me. ... My father's chief tool for teaching lessons was the strap, and he punished me roundly for any misbehavior." Years anon, Yeltsin conceded to a journalist that he smiles rarely, and mostly "inside myself." "I have not been trained in Hollywood," he said with clumsy irony. "I am indeed a rather hard man."[8]

Like many smart, rural-born Russians of his generation, Yeltsin in 1950 packed his bags for a big city, to earn a postsecondary diploma in a nuts-and-bolts specialty that the government deemed useful to its industrialization effort. In his case, the move was to the regional center, Sverdlovsk, to attend the building division of the Urals Polytechnic Institute. He felt in his element with the technical curriculum; only in later life would he be thin-skinned about not having a humanistic education. Any inborn rebelliousness was put on ice at the institute and remained suspended as he began his career; after Yeltsin's graduation in 1955, he worked contentedly as a construction foreman and organizer for thirteen years. In interviews decades afterward, he would tag himself "primarily a man from the production sector" and take testy exception to any hint that he was "half-civilized."[9]

Far from handicapping him politically, Yeltsin's narrow professional profile put him smack in the mold of the engineers who dominated the Soviet establishment from the Great Purge of the 1930s to the 1980s. He portrayed his entry into the party in 1961 as motivated by a sincere faith "in the ideals of justice the party espoused" and preceded by "careful study" of its program and the writings of Marx and Lenin. In all probability it was, but it also would have been a normal careerist step even if he had stuck with economic management. The suggestion, again, is that any insubordinate streak was in abeyance. Yeltsin "was not surprised" to be recruited to the staff of the Sverdlovsk *obkom* (oblast committee of the CPSU) in 1968 as head of its building section, since he had been been "constantly" doing volunteer party work, a token of conformism and ambition. He threw himself "into a party career as I had once thrown myself into spiking a volleyball."[10] It took him only eight years and two promotions to become first secretary of the *obkom,* a position that automatically placed him on the Central Committee at Leonid Brezhnev's last party congress in 1981.

As of the accession of Gorbachev, therefore, Yeltsin, prosaic as some of his experience had been, was in select company. He ranked among the several hundred top power brokers in the USSR and, in his words, was infallible "god, tsar, and lord" in a province of 4.5 million people. He made no bones in his memoir about having been "steeped in the administrative-command methods" of his milieu. Whether he was chairing a meeting or signing a directive, "everything came out as threats, straining, and pressure."[11]

Perestroika and Disgrace

In April 1985 Yeltsin was one of the first provincial viceroys enlisted to lend a hand with perestroika. He was feeling tremors of doubt about the effectiveness of the Soviet system of rule, as Gorbachev was, yet had by no means given up on it. When the invitation to Moscow was tendered by Gorbachev's right-hand man, Yegor Ligachev,[12] Yeltsin's only cavil was that the post offered, department head in the Central Committee Secretariat, was too junior in status. Designation as a full secretary in July 1985 he "considered to be a natural progression of events."[13] There was a like feeling of traveling a well-signposted highway when he was transferred in December 1985 to first secretary of the Moscow *gorkom* (city CPSU committee), supplanting Viktor Grishin, the Brezhnevite who had been the party old guard's stalking horse against Gorbachev. As was the office's due, Yeltsin was elevated to alternate member of the Politburo in February 1986.

The twenty-three months as Moscow boss thrust Yeltsin into the limelight and into conflict with Ligachev and then Gorbachev. It is revealing and not inaccurate that he later subsumed this period into his first, Soviet existence.

Yeltsin lived out to a fault the watchword of the early Gorbachev administration: acceleration (*uskorenie*). He was all for accelerating everything worthwhile in Moscow, from construction of housing to macaroni production; for a bevy of subgoals, he and his city party bureau drafted otiose "programs" crammed with quotas and deadlines. Later he would fault Gorbachev, aptly, for pursuing a pet project (the antialcohol policy of 1985–1986) "with the methods of a cavalry charge."[14] The remark could be applied, and more consistently, to his own kinetic behavior. Yeltsin was in many regards the consummate Soviet campaigner, moving each mission along with a barrage of scoldings, invocations of "discipline," and firings. He did not spare himself, he told his associates, as he was laboring "flat out," eighteen hours a day, in order "to reach the turning point" in perestroika.[15]

None of this is to deny that Yeltsin displayed an innovative and proto-democratic stripe in Moscow or that inch by inch it was distancing him from his erstwhile sponsors. His subway tours and chats with ordinary Muscovites were a foretaste of his vaunted "populism." Biting words in the same vein about the hidden privileges of the *nomenklatura* earned him Ligachev's enmity. Yeltsin warmed fast to the potential of glasnost, although his tendency was to treat freer flow of information as a galvanizer of mass opinion rather than as an end in itself. His irreverent talk and shattering of taboos occupy an honored place in the subversion of the "equilibrium of lies" undergirding the dictatorship.[16] Equally notable is his tolerance, if not avid support, of the discussion clubs springing up in Moscow, some of them welcoming former dissidents and political prisoners amnestied from Siberia. Underlings of his loaned a meeting hall in August 1987 to the first Soviet symposium of unofficial political groups.

Yeltsin was not ready, however, to jettison all he had sworn by in his first life. Repeatedly in his rhetoric he saluted characteristics, real and imagined, of Soviet communism's founding fathers, namely, their utopianism, flexibility, and taste for "social justice." When he urged candor about the USSR's problems in a vinegary address to the Twenty-seventh CPSU Congress in 1986, he said this would be "as Vladimir Il'ich Lenin advised," and he patted himself on the back for speaking the "Bolshevik truth." Pushing the next year for more vigorous pursuit of perestroika, Yeltsin also went out of his way to counsel moderation:

> I keep on hearing ... polar points of view, all the way from radical ones ("Liquidate," "Abolish," "Introduce tomorrow") to cautious, skeptical ones ("Aren't we turning too sharply?" "You get further if you go quietly"). In my opinion, such a diversity of views is normal and is a lot more valuable than mute contemplation.
>
> The pioneering ... decisions we have taken and are preparing to take have naturally given rise to great expectations, burning impatience, a desire to eliminate as quickly as possible all elements of stagnation and social corrosion. In human terms, it is understandable why people would want to make a sharp, qualitative step in the development of society and to receive the fruits of renewal right away. But the originality and scale of the transformations that we have begun require, not emotions or a wholesale denial of our past experience, but sober analysis of the causes of our mistakes and a consistent, unwavering creation of the new. ... Those who dramatize a passing lack of success and fall into panic about the absence of instant benefits are as politically immature as people who ... put things off indefinitely.[17]

These words were spoken in April 1987. How odd it was, then, that only a half year later Yeltsin, in his celebrated speech to the plenary session of the Central Committee on reassessments of Soviet history, voiced the "burning impatience" he had earlier denigrated, and in so doing broke with Gorbachev and the Politburo majority.

It was arguably only a matter of time before Gorbachev, the gradualist reformer, would be outflanked by some person or group in more of a hurry than he. There was upheaval throughout the series of democratizations in many parts of the world in the 1970s and 1980s: "Liberal reformers who succeeded standpatter leaders usually turned out to be transition figures with brief stays in power," in that they incited militant demands for more far-reaching changes and thus sparked either a democratic breakthrough or an antidemocratic reaction.[18]

To appreciate the portent of Yeltsin's dissent, one need not overdraw its coherence. Yeltsin did not take the rostrum at the plenum of October 1987 to lay out a lucid countervision to Gorbachev's. His intent was to withdraw—to resign from an unbearable work situation—and as he did so to take a parting shot at Ligachev, the overpraise of Gorbachev, and reform "half measures." His rambling philippic expressed a mood, not a program. It was mute about democracy and popular participation, made only glancing mention of the Stalin issue that was the nub of intellectual controversy in 1987, and for justification blandly invoked "Leninist norms" of intraparty procedure. Pressed by Gorbachev to explain the purpose of his intervention, Yeltsin said it would be "sacrilegious" if he disrupted party unity.[19]

Nonetheless, the outburst put a stop to Yeltsin's first life, as he realized it would: "I knew what would come next. I would be slaughtered in a methodical, organized manner, almost with a sense of satisfaction and enjoyment."[20] The only point on which he and Gorbachev sparred was how his departure would be staged.

Why did it fall to Yeltsin and not someone else to speak up? The answer must lie in no small measure in psychology and in the personal chemistry between him and Gorbachev. If not a lifelong rebel, as he has at times averred, he was obviously a restless and inquisitive man and was fast shedding some of his taught inhibitions. The same qualities of mind that led Yeltsin to fling himself into perestroika were conducive to rapid disillusionment once it ran into obstructions. He sensed that cautious reforms were rendering "command methods" obsolete without fashioning new levers that would govern and modernize Soviet society better. In sum, he was profoundly frustrated with the contradictions of his assigned role, several years before a like perception surged through the entire *nomenklatura*. His discomfort was worsened by the high visibility of his capital-city post, which impelled him to try harder than any of Gorbachev's lieutenants to make a go of it and simultaneously limited his ability to act independently.

Yeltsin's démarche violated unwritten rules about the primacy of the general secretary, as Gorbachev's bitter rejoinder at the plenum and his extraction of a degrading confession from Yeltsin in front of the *gorkom* proved. "You are not happy," Gorbachev blustered, "to have Moscow alone revolve around your person. Now you want the Central Committee, too, to devote itself to you!"[21] The norms of Soviet power politics gave Gorbachev no choice but to erase the threat; Yeltsin still had none but to submit.

Leader of the Opposition

In his autobiography, sent to press in late 1989, Yeltsin wrote that since October 1987 he had passed through a second life, "the existence of a political outcast, surrounded by a vacuum," and, with his coming in from the cold as a winning candidate for the USSR parliament in March 1989, had commenced a third existence.[22] Both lives were at root oppositional, the former informal and covert, the latter formalized and overt. Together they lasted about four years, until the collapse of the central government and his confirmation as uncontested leader of post-Soviet Russia.

The interval in the political wilderness was one of physical and mental torment for Yeltsin. For months after the bruising showdown with Gorbachev, he was heavily medicated and prone to despondency and insomnia. His plight would have been far grimmer if Gorbachev, after some vacillation, had not thrown a lifeline by giving him a ministerial sinecure (first deputy chairman of Gosstroi, the State Construction Committee) and declining to oust him from the Central Committee.

The reasons for Gorbachev's forbearance—a colossal blunder, in hindsight—remain somewhat of an enigma. But the most plausible explanation to date is the conjecture by Yeltsin that Gorbachev wanted to set up a political balancing act with himself at the fulcrum: "If Gorbachev had not had a Yeltsin, he would have had to make one up. ... He understood that he needed to keep such a person—sharp-edged, prickly, refusing to let the bureaucratized party apparatus live in peace—close at hand." Gorbachev, in Yeltsin's reading, scripted a "real-life drama" in which he was the revisionist foil to relative hard-liners like Ligachev, leaving Gorbachev as "the wise, omniscient hero" in the middle.[23]

This external drama was mirrored by an internal one. Barely less shocking for Yeltsin than adjustment to his disgrace was the dawning of a realization that not all was irretrievably lost. Editors, students, and club organizers began gingerly to seek him out as the Gorbachev thaw proceeded. Invitations to be heard multiplied after Yeltsin was permitted to speak at the Nineteenth CPSU Conference in July 1988. Torn to and fro, he went through "a real struggle within myself ... an analysis of my every deed, word, and principle, of my views of past, present, and future."[24] His Gosstroi chief of staff, Lev Sukhanov, fittingly drew him at this juncture as a dual personality:

> It was as if there were still two Yeltsins. One was the party leader, used to power and homage, and at a loss when all these things were taken away. The second was Yeltsin the mutineer (*buntar'*), rejecting or, to be more accurate, beginning to reject the rules of the game woven into the system. These two Yeltsins fought it out. And I would not be far wrong if I said that the tussle was a savage one and victory came with far from lightning speed. ... He would fall to mocking himself when he recalled his confusion during his first minutes off of the party Olympus. He hated it, yet was still invisibly shackled to it.[25]

Remaining fetters were severed one by one, in a private emancipation intimately tied to the public unraveling of coercive and ideological controls pushed by Gorbachev and his confederates. Often, if not always, Yeltsin was a step ahead, though he was not much better at foreseeing where it all would end. Typical of those caught up in the ferment of the late Soviet period, he regularly made pronouncements that sounded audacious when delivered yet paled before what he was saying but a few months afterward.

Yeltsin's theses at the Nineteenth Conference, for example, are almost quaint in retrospect. He rebutted the charge that he had made improper remarks to foreign correspondents yet did not dispute the party's right to interrogate him about them. Curt about its failings in one breath, he affirmed "pride in socialism" in the next. Making a brief for greater political contestation, he employed Gorbachev's constrained formula of "socialist pluralism" and could see no benefit in a multi-party system. His closing plea was for his "rehabilitation" back into the CPSU fold. As late as March 1990, weeks before bolting the party, he described as "not correct" the theory that he had abandoned Marxism-Leninism: "I only reject some dogmas, such as the principle of democratic centralism." Although democratic centralism—subordination to the leadership—was no minor point, the fact that Yeltsin at the eleventh hour found anything kind to say about Soviet doctrine shows his difficulty in making a clean break with his past.[26]

The Electoral Chariot

The catalyst of Yeltsin's swift maturation was the same factor that precipitated the fracturing of the Soviet order at large: the authentic elections Gorbachev sold the CPSU on at the 1988 conference. The first multicandidate election since the early 1920s was held to choose a USSR Congress of People's Deputies in spring 1989. Although Communists captured the bulk of the seats and Gorbachev was enthroned as congress chairman, enough CPSU stalwarts were humiliated for it to fit the pattern of "stunning elections" emblematic of democratizing countries.[27] Voting for legislatures in the union republics in 1990 deepened the trend, returning radically oriented pluralities or majorities in two-thirds of them, including the RSFSR (Russian republic).

The 1989 election was a godsend for Yeltsin. Coinciding with his return to health, it provided a sterling chance at vindication and a pulpit for preaching "mutiny" against the old ways. The CPSU oligarchy played into his hands. Had it instructed him on pain of expulsion to keep his hat out of the ring, or had Gorbachev headed a progressive slate and asked him to join, it is possible that he would have complied. Instead, the Politburo got the worst of all worlds: (1) Harassed but not excluded, Yeltsin ran on its doorstep, in the all-Moscow district; (2) Gorbachev, looking cowardly by comparison, declined to stand in a popular contest, preferring to be seconded to the congress by his Central Committee, and the CPSU in effect waged no campaign; and (3) Yeltsin was the butt of inept press attacks and dirty tricks that, he said gleefully, "backfired and gave me all the more support from the people."[28] If stunning elections are all about "sending a message," nothing could have sent a louder and clearer one than Yeltsin's 90 percent of the Moscow votes.

His presence in the USSR congress, the standing Supreme Soviet, and their joint presidium (as chairman of the committee on construction) gave Yeltsin the soapbox he wanted, uninhibited by a government or party office. It also brought him into contact with representatives of the liberal intelligentsia, many of whom had considered him a ruffian since his days as Moscow first secretary. The Interregional Deputies' Group, the first organized parliamentary caucus, recognized his stature by making him the only nonintellectual on its five-member board. Interaction with the group, with mentors like Andrei Sakharov and Gavriil Popov, and with gifted younger members of parliament such as Gennadii Burbulis of Sverdlovsk helped Yeltsin iron out inconsistencies in his ideas and come around to the need to amend Article VI of the USSR constitution and introduce multiparty democracy.[29]

It was in his capacity as a parliamentarian that Yeltsin made a timely visit to the United States in September 1989. His worldview had been sufficiently unhinged that the trip had an enormous impact. Thunderstruck that a Houston supermarket's assortment of foods was richer than that available to Politburo members, he proclaimed to his aides that the sight of the delicacy-laden shelves punctured forever the "fairy tales" about socialism and capitalism he had accepted since his youth. Lev Sukhanov expressed a belief that the tour was Yeltsin's philosophical point of no return, and that it was on the homebound flight that he decided to quit the CPSU.[30]

For all the excitement his arrival had generated, Yeltsin did not stand out in the all-star USSR congress. Nor was he or the Interregional Deputies' Group sanguine that this assembly, its center of gravity to Gorbachev's right and its term fixed to 1994, would legislate thorough economic and social reform. Fortunately for Yeltsin, the preset election timetable offered another occasion for advancement of his influence and agenda in the RSFSR in 1990.

Yeltsin mulled taking revenge on the Moscow apparatus by trying to take over the municipal council there. Only upon reflection did he fasten on the republic legislature. His hope was to make "some kind of a breakthrough in the matter of the national, economic, and cultural renaissance of Russia" and to kick off a chain reaction above: "The center may be compelled to change its policy [by] the radicalization of Russia."[31] He won in a cakewalk in Sverdlovsk oblast and was the headliner of the 5,000 candidates backed by Democratic Russia, an insurrectionary "electoral alliance" thrown together after nominations closed.

What with his aura and the disarray of the Communist Party, Yeltsin could not have been kept out of Russia's deputies' congress and supreme soviet. But he might conceivably have been deprived of the chairmanship of the soviet, the highest political office in the RSFSR. In a ragged sequence of events, Gorbachev endorsed, then pulled the rug out from under, two CPSU loyalists. On May 29, 1990, Yeltsin, snagging the votes of the Democratic Russia caucus and of wavering deputies, won the prize by a wafer-thin margin. Six weeks later he handed in his Communist Party card, saying a parliamentary chairman had to be nonpartisan.

That position was a stepping-stone to the one Yeltsin was really after—president of Russia. He had advocated mass-franchise election of republic and USSR heads of state since 1989, criticizing Gorbachev for accepting the office of president of the Soviet Union from the congress, without recourse to the population, in March 1990. On June 12, 1991, Russians gave him 57 percent of the 74 million votes cast for six presidential candidates and his most dazzling ballot-box triumph. Discord within the CPSU was again a boon, as various factions, with Gorbachev hovering behind the scenes, let him get a congressional majority for instituting an elected presidency and then split the anti-Yeltsin vote at the polls.[32]

Yeltsin was far from the only ranking member of the late-Soviet elite to find his legs in emerging post-Soviet politics. Other former apparatchiks discussed in this book came center stage and in a variety of ways: in the parliamentary setting (Leonid Kravchuk), in interparty competition and negotiations with Moscow (Algirdas Brazauskas), as insurance against civil disorder (Eduard Shevardnadze and Heidar Aliev), or as preservationist of a national tradition (Islam Karimov), to mention only some.

Boris Yeltsin was unique in three respects. One was the elementary matter of timing: He was the first party boss to make a break, albeit a messy one, with the Soviet status quo.[33] His prophetic protest, the Politburo's egregious mishandling of it, and his theatrical and earthy style gave rise to a second difference, in political constituency: Yeltsin was an irresistible magnet from the start for the popular disaffection being uncorked by liberalization. From this flowed a third hallmark: his early and unflinching reliance on electoral mobilization. Yeltsin was the only former CPSU secretary to capitalize on mass alienation in the opening rounds of contested voting in 1989 and 1990 and to ride this chariot to the summit.

Vexed Breakthrough

On July 10, 1991, at an ornate ceremony in the Kremlin, a glowing Yeltsin took the oath of office as Russia's first president. In casting its lot with him, he exulted, the country had "chosen not only a personality ... but above all a road down which our Russia is to go ... the road of democracy, reforms, and rebirth of the worth of the individual."[34]

This rosy prognosis was ostensibly borne out by three occurrences in the next five months. During the August 19–21, 1991, crisis, Yeltsin's sure-footedness and fortitude were vital to the blunting of the reactionary coup attempt by the State Committee for the State of Emergency. His fiery speech atop an army tank, the iconic image of resistance, will be indelibly associated with him in the history books.[35] On November 6, Yeltsin drove the last nail into the coffin of the CPSU, the party of Lenin and Stalin, by decreeing its dismantlement on Russian soil. And on December 8, 1991, in the wake of the Ukrainian independence referendum, he joined President Kravchuk and Stanislav Shushkevich of Belarus to put ink to the Minsk agreement that liquidated the USSR, recognized the statehood of the fifteen republics, and hatched the feeble Commonwealth of Independent States. Gorbachev's acquiescence and retirement seemed to be the final confirmation of Yeltsin's paramountcy.

These epochal events were a crowning moment for Yeltsin. They propelled him, to use the multiple-lives imagery of his autobiography, from his third into a fourth life.[36] The role flip of 1987 was now to be reversed: He was going from opposition back to governance.

The 180-degree turn of events carried with it dilemmas as well as pleasures. For one thing, Yeltsin had become comfortable in his oppositional robes. Asked by an interviewer whether he had to "become a different Yeltsin" than he had been lately, he agreed but confided that it would take some effort: "It would be easier to criticize, and it is considerably harder to be creative." After years as critic in chief, he was striving to be constructive "to the best of my ability."[37]

Yeltsin's estimate of the nature of the change Russia was ripe for was also in flux. Although, like Gorbachev, he had once mused about perestroika being a "revolutionary" process, recent tumult and the roiling street scenes of August 1991 awoke in him a visceral fear of violence. In a commemorative essay on the anniversary of the putsch, his proudest boast was that he had spared Russia a repeat of its "catastrophic" revolution of 1917: "Our people knows all too well what a revolution is, how great are its temptations and how tragic its results. ... We have chosen the way of reforms and not of revolutionary jolts."[38] Still seeking a systemic change that would be revolutionary in its overall scope and effect, he accepted that the means to that end had to be evolutionary and, above all, that the transformation needed to be accomplished without giving rise to uncontrollable disorder.

Yeltsin took pains to get across that the reforms he would promulgate would be "radical," "decisive," "deep," "resolute"—qualitatively superior to those tried and found wanting during perestroika. The defeat of the 1991 coup convinced him that the time had come to strike. "The period of progress by small steps is over," he informed the Russian people in a televised address to the Russian Congress of People's Deputies on October 28, 1991. "The minefield hampering reforms has been cleared. A *large-scale reformist breakthrough* is needed."[39]

And yet, when it came to mapping the breakthrough, as distinct from telegraphing its urgency, Yeltsin was at a disadvantage. For the most part, his mode of ascent to power had not required him to put forward a program soberly addressing the substantive questions of the day. It had usually sufficed to stake out a global position to the left of Gorbachev. This radical contrarianism had widened his following at a time of welling and inchoate mass discontent, while deterring Gorbachev from getting too close to right-wing forces. Whenever possible, Yeltsin dichotomized the ideological and policy options, casting them as choices between "the system" and "the people." In his pivotal election races, his pledges and assurances were riddled with omissions and inconsistencies. He declined, supposedly on principle, to comment on other candidates by name or to take part in candidate roundtables. His presidential campaign manager, Burbulis, confessed that many voters "did not go for a thought-out program of reforms but for a savior. ... That is, this was a purely religious form of protest and hope."[40]

Yeltsin was at his wooliest on the megaquestions of relations with the other republics and economic reform. On the first, he was a latecomer, having taken up expressly Russian issues only on the eve of the 1990 election, and mainly as a cudgel for pounding at the Soviet center. His headline proposal then was that Russia "stop handing out raw materials dirt cheap,"[41] an axiom enshrined in the RSFSR's declaration of political and economic "sovereignty" in June 1990. A fulsome advocate of more power for the republics, Yeltsin was altogether unclear on how the consequent conflicts were to be resolved to Russia's satisfaction, and until Minsk he remained in favor of supplanting the ersatz Soviet federation with a negotiated "union" around a "strong center." The CIS formula, improvised by staff adjutants and hastily ratified by the Russian deputies' congress, fell far short of this and planted the seeds of future disharmony.

Yeltsin's economic program was, if anything, more amorphous. Its only un-equivocal note was that he wanted speedier movement toward a "civilized econ-omy." In the 1990 republic election, he touted a slender plan for "economic stabi-lization in three years." That summer, while still chairman of the RSFSR parliament, he reached a preliminary accord with Gorbachev on a "500 Days" sketch that would have made a start on marketization and privatization under con-joint Soviet-Russian auspices. This auspicious initiative died when Gorbachev backed out and Yeltsin concluded that Russia could not go it alone.

From the burial of 500 Days until mid-1991, Yeltsin confined himself to snip-ing at USSR policy. His perspective was populist and conveyed the impression that he could mend the economy without lowering living standards. When the So-viet cabinet hiked retail prices in spring 1991, he lashed out in indignation: "They ought not to have begun economic reform by suddenly laying all the hardships on the shoulders of the population."[42] On the presidential hustings, he lavished promises on the electorate—indexation of minimum wages, pensions, and student stipends at 50 percent above the USSR average, more vacation time, and a shorter workweek—while stonewalling requests to divulge how they would be paid for. In his last days in opposition, Yeltsin could still afford to grandstand. Once his vic-tory over Gorbachev and the old regime was in the bag, he had to move from words to action and face up to nasty realities.

The Political Mismanagement of Economic Reform

The crux of Yeltsin's "reformist breakthrough" was economic transformation. His premise was that political change had become self-sustaining in Russia, whereas economic renovation had gotten nowhere and vital signs were going from bad to worse. "We have won political freedom," he said in his address to parliament and nation in October 1991. "Now we have to get back our economic freedom." Yeltsin portrayed Russia's ailment as being within the realm of curable "economic diseases" from which many foreign countries had recovered: "There is no cause for panic. ... The only things needed are an accurate diagnosis, strict rules of behavior, and coordinated, competent actions." Yeltsin's tonic had two main ingredients: macroeconomic stabilization, achievable through the unfreezing of retail and most wholesale prices, monetary restraint, and tight credit; and privatization, "the creation of a healthy mixed economy with a strong private sector" via the selling off and giving away of state assets and the stimulation of new businesses.

Given license to issue reform decrees for one year by parliamentary resolutions in fall 1991, Yeltsin instructed a new cabinet under the youthful Moscow economist, Yegor Gaidar, to render the rudiments of the plan into executive directives. The first of them went into effect in January 1992. They were a bold departure from decades of statist inertia, incomparably more ambitious than Gorbachev's failed schemes. There were prompt salutary effects, led by a steep reduction in consumer queueing, a dampening of inflation, and the acquisition of equity in thousands of Russian firms by employees and investors.

At the same time, the program had its shortcomings. The professional conversation among Western and Russian economists over its technical virtues and vices is beyond the scope of this chapter. It is the political dimension that is taken up here.

Admirers and detractors agree that the program was hamstrung by political factors. Yeltsin felt compelled four months into it to concede that it needed refining, to bring industrialists skeptical of it into his government, and to accept the dilution of several provisions. The most serious dent in its integrity was the loss of rigor on loans and monetary emission, which rekindled inflation and all but precluded the winnowing out of inefficient firms. Unappeased, the parliament of the Russian Federation (as the RSFSR was renamed in December 1991) went from coolness toward the reform to opposition and, as the one-year grace period expired in autumn 1992, to trench warfare against it. Ruslan Khasbulatov, the parliamentary speaker, shared generalship in the campaign with Yeltsin's vice president, Aleksandr Rutskoi, from whom Yeltsin had been estranged since fall 1991. The hostilities were only slightly muffled when Gaidar was replaced in December 1992 by Viktor Chernomyrdin, the former head of the Soviet natural gas ministry.

Managing the politics of the "shock therapy" aspect of the reform, in particular, would have been arduous on the cheeriest assumptions. Untoward circumstances, his own passion for change, and his previous, loudly stated positions on economic reform dealt Yeltsin a staggeringly difficult hand. It could have been played to a win only with flawless execution.

Yeltsin went through the game, however, with anything but perfect skill. The striking thing about the battle over economic transformation is the near absence of what had been his trump suit time and again during his march to power: the harnessing of mass support.

The most straightforward course—and the one many reformers regret to this day was not taken—would have been for Yeltsin to appeal directly to the populace before launching the reform. He would have had to amend and explain away some of his prior verbiage (on price controls, say), but this was not beyond him, and overall blame for the economic mess could still have been loaded onto the CPSU.

Russians would have had to be told more or less frankly how long radical therapy would take, who would gain, and who would lose.

The best bet procedurally, though not without risk, would have been to fit the consultation into the form Yeltsin had mastered: an election. The election would have been of a new Russian parliament, combined if necessary with a presidential rerun. Yeltsin would have been obliged to postpone the kickoff of the economic program for several months, perhaps until early in 1992, and to take personal charge of the radical forces as leader of a progovernment bloc or party. My own guess, and that of quite a few Moscow specialists, is that in a snap election within a half year of the euphoria of August 1991, he would have gleaned a mandate for economic reform and a legislative majority to enact it into law.

But this was not Yeltsin's scenario. After pondering a climactic national debate and election, he decided not to hazard it. Partly this was in the belief that it would be difficult to line up voluntary legislative support for fresh elections. He was reluctant to threaten involuntary dissolution and abrogation of the RSFSR constitution, as he had just handed over the parliament's helm to Khasbulatov and, until December 1991, wanted its support against Gorbachev.[43]

Rightly or wrongly, Yeltsin was also uncertain about the electoral outcome and concerned that a close-fought campaign might be social dynamite. This anxiety extended to the subnational level. On the heels of appointing "presidential representatives" as overseers in the regions of Russia in summer 1991, he highhandedly installed chief executives in those localities whose leaders had backed the August coup. Congress was willing in November to cede him the right to do so in all regions until late 1992 and to postpone the scheduled elections of mayors and governors—which Yeltsin hitherto avidly approved—until then.

Of the greatest weight in Yeltsin's calculations, I suspect, was something else: a weariness with mass politics and the desire of an engineer and functionary to get on with the job at hand. It was as if the balance between the "two Yeltsins" Sukhanov identified in the late 1980s had tipped away from Yeltsin the mutineer toward Yeltsin the boss, "used to power and homage" and convinced that power was rightfully his to use in society's best interests. The itch to produce results without further delay and ado comes through in pronouncements of Yeltsin's such as the following from October 1991:

Now we need action, action, and more action. Now we are going to have fewer political debates. They must be reduced to a minimum. The most important thing now is reform and the drafting of the relevant laws and decrees connected with reform and implementation of reform. There must be responsibility for implementation from top to bottom because this vertical line of executive authority is now being reconstructed. ... It had been destroyed and chopped up into pieces. It will now be fully built up.[44]

At some ultimate level, the defenders of the economic program are surely correct to say that it differed from the reformations "from above" that punctuate Russian history in that it aimed to deed significant power to nonstate actors, in this case profit-making businesses and consumers. At the level of practical action, however, Yeltsin sought to attain this liberal end largely by illiberal means that operated, as he put it, "from top to bottom." It is hard not to catch here echoes of the Soviet "command methods" he had ostensibly renounced and, not too fancifully, of the modernizing monarchs of presocialist Russia.[45]

A pair of techniques used in presenting the reform to the public also harked back to Yeltsin's "first life." One was the short-term time horizon and the conviction that a single furious offensive would bring relief. Severe deprivation would last only about six months, he declared at the outset. "By the autumn of 1992 ... the economy will have stabilized and people's lives will gradually get better."[46]

The other old habit was the conceptualization of the social interests involved in unitary terms. Neither in the winter of 1991–1992 nor later did Yeltsin forecast who would be the winners and who the losers in the reform game. Thoughtful Russians had been arguing since the late 1980s the need to build a propertied middle class as a social foundation for modernity and a dynamic economy. Yeltsin evoked, by contrast, a homogeneous society not parsed into strata or segments. His oratory cited three analogies for the approaching ordeal: (1) the Great Patriotic War against Nazi Germany, (2) the "August days" of 1991, and (3) a journey to safety by a frightened band of mountaineers "along the most narrow path possible" at the brink of a ravine.[47] The moral in each tableau was the same: that the solidarity of the whole, not the selfish urges of any part, would be determinative.

Yeltsin's presumptions proved untenable once the reform caravan set out. His timetable was so unrealistic that he has to be suspected of either naïveté or dissembling in propounding it in the first place. Even with a brilliant start, Russia's voyage to economic normalcy would require many times the six to nine months Yeltsin vowed would suffice for "stabilization." The plain fact is that the Russian economy shrank by the month in 1992 and 1993, and the Russian people in the aggregate grew poorer.

More disabling still was his failure to develop a strategy for manufacturing popular consent. Blinkered by his unitary concept of society, Yeltsin had no focused vision of either the actual or the potential bases of support. He built no bridges to the likely winners—making no mention, so far as I can find, of a putative bourgeoisie or salaried, possessive middle class—and prepared no hedges for neutralizing the likely losers. Indeed, with the passage of time he spared less and less effort for public relations. Forays into the provinces became rare in 1992 and 1993, and televised appearances were often delayed, wooden, and unconvincing.

The problem worsened as Yeltsin was progressively more embroiled with the Congress of People's Deputies. Western onlookers, not unfairly, have often taken the deputies to task for putting their personal and corporate welfare above their voters'. But they have not often enough recognized what an astute Russian scholar, Liliia Shevtsova, wrote in *Izvestiia* in 1992:

> Our political institutions are oriented only toward themselves and concentrate on their own survival. This conclusion is eloquently confirmed by what goes on in the Russian parliament. ... [It] long ago lost ties with society and turned itself into something self-sufficient.
>
> *The presidential camp has also been incapable of sustaining constant communication with society. And so it has not created a mass base for its political course.* It has not managed to find even a narrower foothold for itself in the form of a steady dialogue, with appropriate mutual obligations taken on by the participants, with so much as a few of our political groupings. ...
>
> Once again society finds itself at a crossroads. The attempt to define a way forward now has to be carried out under conditions of a crisis of the democratic movement and deepening attitudes of despair and fatigue on the part of the masses. Many trials lie before us.[48]

Nowhere was this more a liability than in the interinstitutional and constitutional confrontation that absorbed Yeltsin. His diffident posture gave resourceful elites, like the factory managers and their friends in parliament, the opportunity to fight him to a draw, and even to inflict defeats, on terrain of their choosing. More than once—as when managers pleaded that their workers would be angered if termination of subsidies jeopardized their jobs—unelected bureaucrats were better than an elected president at knitting together vertical alliances with common people. Yeltsin was caught, as Yegor Gaidar lamented, in "a vicious sociopolitical circle": (1) His government's disconnectedness from the grassroots and from even the potential beneficiaries of its policy "lowered [its] resistance to the demands of bureaucratic lobbyists," and (2) the resultant retreats and their economic symptoms (inflation, in particular) "beat on" and further estranged its fragile constituency.[49]

The "communication" and "dialogue" Shevtsova looked for would not have happened with the flick of a switch. There were no switches mainly because there was no preexisting, noncoercive wiring plugging the state into society. Yeltsin at the peak of his powers could have done something about closing the gap in one of two ways.

First, he could have created organizational circuitry of his own, logically a political party or movement to wage an impending or eventual election campaign and to hold those elected to a common policy. To do so he would have had to set time and energy aside for the task and overcome the revulsion against "the party," the monopoly CPSU, that he shared with many Russians. This never happened. Yeltsin hinted in 1990 that he might want to head up a "new Russian party," and in November 1992 endorsed the initiation of "a party or movement of supporters of reforms," which he would be willing to join if not lead. Nothing came of either idea.

If Yeltsin had no stomach for building a party, a second option would have been to assemble a coalition with associations put together by other democrats. Democratic Russia, the electoral alliance that boosted many radicals into the Russian parliament, might have been the core of such a grouping, but Yeltsin, perhaps reluctant to be overshadowed, pulled back from it after the 1990 election. Once ensconced as parliamentary chairman, "he did not want to identify with DR, acknowledge his dependence upon it, or accept any formal obligation to it."[50]

Yeltsin seemed to change heart on the issue when he unveiled his economic reform the next year. He suggested in October 1991 that political parties well inclined toward the reform package establish "a single political bloc," saying this was "necessary to mobilize mass support for the policy of transformations and to ensure political stability in the republic." He would be prepared to engage in "systematic dialogue" with the proreform alliance and to consult it on government decisions. "This bloc of political parties, having concluded a strategic union with the president, would become a major source of ideas, suggestions, and plans for implementing reforms."[51]

This tantalizing possibility, too, withered on the vine. Twice, in December 1991 and May 1992, Yeltsin met with the leaders of sympathetic parties; presidential advisers and government ministers conferred with the parties more often. But by summer 1992, all the encounters had assumed a "random character" and Yeltsin was holding aloof.[52] They petered off into desultory conversations with parliamentary factions of all hues. In short, no "strategic union" of the left or left-center was consummated or seriously broached.

A Half-Built House

Yeltsin's political career until 1991 had been wholly in the Communist Party machine and in legislatures. The presidency was his first post in the executive arm of government. He entered it bent on overhauling archaic policymaking and administrative structures that counted for little when the CPSU was in charge but, with the party on the way out, badly needed rationalization. Western commentary on Yeltsin in the institutional sphere has been sparse and has dwelt on his tortured relations with parliament. I shall go light on that subject, which is considered in some detail by Yitzhak Brudny in Chapter 4, and say more about the neglected matter of reform of the executive branch.

Yeltsin's sole institutional innovation prior to the 1991 presidential election was to attach a sounding board, a grandly titled Supreme Consultative and Coordinating Council, to him as chairman of the RSFSR Supreme Soviet. The panel, seating twenty-two luminaries from the arts and sciences, was an unsubtle device for wooing intellectuals away from Gorbachev. It had scant say on policy and did no coordinating to speak of, but discussions in and around it spurred Yeltsin—and especially his most intimate adviser, Gennadii Burbulis, the council's deputy chairman—to ponder governmental reform in earnest.[53]

Yeltsin's first step upon being elected was to establish an obedient and well-provisioned Presidential Chancery (Administratsiia Prezidenta). An enlargement of the Business Office previously under the Council of Ministers, it was lodged after August 1991 in the former Central Committee headquarters on Moscow's Staraia Ploshchad and headed by a onetime CPSU apparatchik from Sverdlovsk, Yurii Petrov. The chancery prepared documents for the president and supervised staffing throughout the government. It also dispensed petty patronage such as access to state dachas and medical clinics—perquisites that, his earlier fulminations about illicit privilege aside, Yeltsin was now glad to enjoy and dispose of.[54]

Further changes were made in the Council of Ministers, the disjointed cabinet whose role in the past was to watch over the myriad branches of the planned economy and leave big decisions to the party organs. Yeltsin announced that the cabinet would report to him as president and be chaired by him "when necessary." The number of portfolios was halved to twenty-three. Whereas ministers used to "spend most of their time arguing with each other," his "streamlined" version was "a team that understands each other" and would push in unison for reform.[55]

The novel aspect of the reorganization was a trio of collegial bodies under the president designed to integrate the governmental machine and be the kernel of what Burbulis, whose brainchild the scheme was, dubbed a "constructive state." The first two—the Council for Federation and Territorial Affairs, a liaison with Russia's regional authorities, and the Security Council, for national security—had passably clear mandates. But the horizon of the third—the State Council—was panoramic. Burbulis conceived of it as a supercabinet that would "help the president work out a distinct state and political strategy,"[56] vetting draft decrees and laws and keeping tabs on the bureaucracy. It comprised "state counselors" for six or seven policy areas and several cabinet ministers and was chaired by Burbulis as "state secretary." Some pundits were frightened that the council would be as all-powerful as the defunct Politburo; others countered that the counselors were democrats (they were by and large intellectuals seasoned in radical politics) and that they answered to a legitimate head of state, not a CPSU chieftain.[57]

The restructuring immediately hit rough water. The parliamentary leadership was the source of some of it, successfully objecting that the Council for Federation and Territorial Affairs unconstitutionally infringed on its turf. That body never got off the drawing boards.

But much of the trouble originated within the executive branch, where Yeltsin's word should have been law. It transpired that personal, ideological, and bureau rivalries seethed among his "team" members, that his new governmental house was half-finished, and that he could not or would not set it aright.

Nowhere in the organizational blueprint was there room for Aleksandr Rutskoi, Yeltsin's running mate in June 1991. His exclusion helped estrange Rutskoi from the president and turn him into a sworn enemy within the executive establishment.

The very first daggers were thrown at the Federation Council not by the legislature but by Ivan Silaev, Yeltsin's prime minister from June 1990 to September 1991, and by Burbulis, of all people. Yurii Skokov, a defense industrialist and deputy premier whom Yeltsin had asked to start up the Federation Council—after breaking a promise to give him Silaev's job, according to Skokov—was left in the lurch and reassigned by Yeltsin in early 1992 to be secretary of the Security Council. Meanwhile, a fierce and semipublic fight broke out over a replacement for Silaev. Burbulis expressed support one time or another for both Gaidar, whose acquaintance he had just made, and for his townsman Oleg Lobov, who had been Yeltsin's second secretary in the Sverdlovsk *obkom* in the early 1980s. When Yeltsin opted for Gaidar as head of the cabinet, Burbulis's wings were clipped by the transfer of State Council jurisdiction over the "power ministries" (military, police, and foreign affairs) to Skokov and the Security Council.[58]

The State Council never did establish itself as a credible strategist and gatekeeper for Yeltsin. Ministers and smaller fry soon discovered that they could approach the president independently of it with petitions and draft regulations and decrees for his signature.[59] If Yeltsin found this chaos a problem, he did not say so, and the council drifted. He bridled at Burbulis's prickly personality and at his "infantile division of people into 'ours' and 'theirs'—those on 'our team' and those on the 'other team'"—to put it differently, at Burbulis's insistence upon imposing a consistent cleavage structure on the executive establishment, beginning with the president's entourage.[60] In May 1992 Yeltsin allowed the Cabinet of Ministers to scupper the State Council, which left only separate advisers writing weekly memoranda to him. Burbulis, already deprived of most of his titles and of Yeltsin's ear, resigned from the administration in November.

Yurii Skokov, who proved an adroit infighter, for a while supplanted Burbulis in Yeltsin's favor. A presidential directive about the Security Council in June 1992, one month after it began to meet regularly, gave it leeway to consider an extraordinary gamut of issues, including "economic security" and "the achievement of stability and good order" in Russia. That edict, Skokov's rapport with Yeltsin, and several cryptic utterances of his convinced some analysts that his creature was going to be a "ministry of politics," a latter-day State Council.[61]

The parallel was misleading. The Security Council, unlike the State Council, was populated entirely by state functionaries, and Skokov's personal politics were markedly more conservative than Burbulis's. Although Skokov picked up several more powers in late 1992,[62] his fuzzy mandate turned out to be as much a hindrance as a help. His dealings with Yeltsin became strained, and the council made few real inroads in the broader reaches of domestic policy. Skokov resigned in April 1993 after disagreeing with Yeltsin over how to treat parliament.

A similarly tattered story unfolded in the regular government cabinet. The reorganization of 1991 was followed by a second one a year later. The name changed both times (to Cabinet of Ministers in November 1991 and back to Council of

Ministers in December 1992), but little of substance did. Periodic reductions of bureaucratic clutter were cosmetic only. Agencies mushroomed after the pruning of 1991, so that a cut two years later would merely reduce the ministers to the same number (twenty-three) that Yeltsin began with. Despite the brave words about "teamwork," Yeltsin's first cabinet was put together "eclectically ... out of personal considerations, to deal with particular situations, because a position had to be found for someone who 'helped in the struggle.'" To compensate for disunity, interdepartmental commissions, ancillary boards, and advisory panels were piled on, "all according to Parkinson's Law."[63]

The appointment of the centrist Chernomyrdin as prime minister in December 1992, a move forced by an anti-Gaidar majority in parliament, clouded rather than clarified the picture. Yeltsin moved off blithely in different directions, handing senior portfolios to conservatives with clientelist links to him (notably Oleg Lobov from Sverdlovsk, the first deputy premier for industrial policy from April 1993) while at the same time shielding the remaining radical marketizers from a purge. The result was not a coalition based on manifest compromises and reciprocity but a conglomeration of individuals whose only unifying thread was personal rapport with the president. As ministers attacked their cabinet colleagues in the mass media and leaked innuendo about them, information and publicity departments proliferated. In a bizarre extension of press freedom, journalists were admitted to not only the ceremonial quarterly sessions of the full Council of Ministers but also the weekly working meetings of its presidium (inner cabinet); their readers were then regaled with verbatim quotations from ministers' sallies against one another.

Predictably, public policy mirrored the half-built quality of the structures making it. "The government has neither a clear economic strategy nor tactics," one columnist wrote in summer 1993. "Today it undertakes one thing, tomorrow another." Every vice premier and minister, he continued, "has to get through to Yeltsin" and get him to sign the latest decree percolating up from his agency, because otherwise a rival would hound the president into striking off on another tangent.[64] It was a manic situation that could not have persisted, not even in Russia.

Boxed In

The fourth life that Boris Yeltsin took up in 1991 underwent a quantum change two years later, so much so that we may speak of him as transiting into a sort of fifth life. If the preceding one revolved around the attempt, at best partially efficacious, to orchestrate a "large-scale reformist breakthrough," his latest and maybe last political existence is characterized by less ambition, fewer possibilities, and fewer illusions. Today's Yeltsin is in a holding pattern, to all intents and purposes boxed in by the consequences of his past actions and by changes in the Russian context for which he must take a large share of responsibility.

The crossing of this threshold was triggered by the Russian constitutional crisis of September–October 1993, a collision that reflects glory on neither side. In the nearly one year that the standoff was brewing, Vice President Rutskoi, Speaker Khasbulatov, and the anti-Yeltsin forces arrayed in the Congress of People's Deputies and Supreme Soviet followed a bellicose and progressively more reckless line vis-à-vis the president. Yeltsin, for his part, made periodic retreats and concessions on economic policy and the composition of his cabinet, but never ventured upon the painstaking, explicit bargaining and transinstitutional coalition-building that might hypothetically have underpinned stability. In those instances when he did cultivate ties with parliamentary influentials, most of them associates of his from 1990–1991, as often as not he negated the political benefit by recruiting them into his executive branch, hence diminishing his rump of adherents in the congress.[65]

Disaster ensued when both groups of gladiators arrogantly overplayed their hands. Although a national referendum in April 1993 produced majority shows of support for the president and his reform program, the opposition continued to profess that economic recession meant the tide was running their way. They also believed that Yeltsin would most likely refrain from the use of force against them and, if he did not, that the military would balk. Yeltsin erred by gambling that his foes would back down when faced with presidential resolve. More grievously, he misread the referendum and his landslide victory of 1991 as evidence that the people would be with him and a reform course no matter how the options were laid before them.

The outcome of this zero-sum politics is there for all to see. On September 21, 1993, Yeltsin—after "tortured" soul-searching, he says[66]—carried out a nonviolent presidential coup. He disbanded the congress and ordered election of a new parliament that would enact economic reforms and adopt a constitution for the post-Soviet "presidential republic" he had been seeking since 1990. A quorum of the deputies refused to bow to his will and resolved to impeach him and make Rutskoi president. On October 4, after a day of mayhem and bloodshed in downtown Moscow, tank crews obedient to Yeltsin shelled the congress into submission. The official body count in the "October events" was 145 with 733 wounded; Rutskoi and Khasbulatov were bustled off to Lefortovo prison in handcuffs.

Buoyed by the rout, Yeltsin incorporated into the election a referendum on a draft constitution prepared by a commission aligned with him. Fifty-eight percent of the Russian citizens who voted December 12 approved the draft, many out of the not unreasonable conviction that it was the best bet to stave off further strife.

This, however, was the only good that came out of the ballot for Yeltsin. The populist whose string of election victories helped seal the fate of the Soviet regime grossly misjudged the public mood and underestimated the rage engendered by Russia's economic collapse. Nothing would convince him to place his own office on the line. Intervening in the constitutional referendum only, he cut pro-government candidates off from his political coattails. And he paid a heavy price for having failed to organize a supportive political party or movement. The banner of marketizing reform was carried by Russia's Choice, a quasi-party concocted in October 1993 and led by Yegor Gaidar, who had not a whit of campaign experience and seemed bewildered by the task. In the best barometer of public opinion, the party preference voting for the State Duma (the lower house of the Federal Assembly), Russia's Choice harvested only 15.4 percent of the votes. The far-right Liberal Democratic Party of Vladimir Zhirinovsky received 22.8 percent, and two neocommunist parties 20.3 percent.

The 1993 constitution gives Yeltsin abundant prerogatives. The Presidential Chancery, now estimated to have 3,500 employees, is a formidable resource, and Russia's regional bureaucracy remains under presidential control.

These realities do not, though, make him a dictator. In any future crisis of state, the loyalty of the army officer corps—which kept Yeltsin in suspense in October 1993 before obeying his order to shoot—cannot be presumed, and Yeltsin may well find himself bidding for it even at normal times. More pressingly, he must reckon with a legislative branch that retains not inconsiderable powers, has a much fresher electoral mandate, and, contrary to his expectations, is at least as hostile to him as the old congress was. One early indicator of its attitude was the Duma's decision in February 1994 to amnesty Rutskoi, Khasbulatov, and the others arrested in October 1993 and the leaders of the putsch of August 1991.

Boris Yeltsin, well into his sixties and not in the best of health, is thus left with a most uncertain and quite possibly an abbreviated political future. His all-thumbs approach has been distinguished by a propensity for polarization, frontal blows at entrenched adversaries, reliance on undifferentiated, antiestablishment mass opinion, and inattention to administrative detail and organizational structure. With this operational mode, he has moved mountains since 1985, but it seems unlikely to take him or Russia much further in the near future.

"In emergency situations, I'm strong," Yeltsin wrote in his autobiography. "In ordinary situations, I'm sometimes too passive."[67] What would be extraordinary in most parts of the world has become ordinary in post-Soviet Russia. So far as political democracy and market economics are concerned, Russians will be lucky for the present if they see the "progress by small steps" that Yeltsin disdained in 1991. Bringing these gains about at all will require the "finger" skills—ones that emphasize consensus and ambiguity, maneuver and coalition-building, appeals to specific social groups, and the construction of dependable organizational tissue— that are conspicuously underdeveloped in Boris Yeltsin's repertoire. He has learned new tricks before. This time, the challenge may elude him.

Notes

1. The most nuanced discussion in this vein, and the best by far of the several biographies written by Western journalists, is John Morrison, *Boris Yeltsin: From Bolshevik to Democrat* (New York: Dutton, 1991).

2. "In the polarization and subsequent conditions of multiple sovereignty which unfolded in Russia, a 'democrat' was synonymous with 'anti-Communist'—nothing more,

nothing less—as long as the communist regime held power." Michael McFaul, "Party Formation After Revolutionary Transitions," in Alexander Dallin, ed., *Political Parties in Russia* (Berkeley: University of California, 1993), p. 16.

3. Philippe C. Schmitter and Terry Lynn Karl, "What Democracy Is ... and Is Not," *Journal of Democracy,* vol. 2 (Summer 1991), p. 76.

4. Charles E. Lindblom, *Politics and Markets: The World's Political-Economic Systems* (New York: Basic Books, 1977), ch. 5.

5. Boris Yeltsin, *Ispoved' na zadannuiu temu* [Confession on an assigned theme] (Moscow: PIK, 1990), p. 169. The book is available in English as Boris Yeltsin, *Against the Grain: An Autobiography,* trans. Michael Glenny (New York: Summit Books, 1990). It was drafted by the Moscow journalist Valentin Iumashev but is based on long conversations with Yeltsin and was closely edited by him.

6. His father's persecution is not mentioned in his autobiography, even though in 1989, when he composed it, it would have been natural enough to include it. It is described in Boris Yeltsin, *The Struggle for Russia,* trans. Catherine A. Fitzpatrick (New York: Random House, 1994), pp. 94–98. Yeltsin said in that account that he remembered the night of his father's arrest and especially the tears shed by his mother, but he learned the details only from a police file provided him when he was president of Russia. "Perhaps," he said, "my life would have taken a different turn if I had been able to see my father's file earlier: If I could have been convinced without a doubt of what ordinary, banal horror our industry, our powerful Soviet reality was steeped in." It is not clear how long the grandfather stayed in hiding; Yeltsin in his autobiography described him building stoves in Butko in 1935.

7. FBIS-SOV-91-104, May 30, 1991, p. 61.

8. Yeltsin, *Ispoved'*, p. 20, and FBIS-SOV-91-106, June 3, 1991, p. 81.

9. FBIS-SOV-90-049, March 13, 1990, p. 76, and FBIS-SOV-91-110, June 7, 1991, p. 64. In *Struggle,* p. 162, Yeltsin portrayed his student days as a period of "happy and slightly frantic romanticism that now seems simply impossible to imagine," mentioning space exploration, "communism," and Nikita Khrushchev's Virgin Lands agricultural program as issues that caught his attention. He also referred to his first years at work and of marriage to Naina Yeltsin as "the happiest period of my life." Ibid., p. 163.

10. Quotations from Yeltsin, *Ispoved'*, pp. 40, 44, and *Struggle,* p. 163.

11. Yeltsin, *Ispoved'*, pp. 55, 64.

12. Ligachev, who was soon to become an enemy of Yeltsin's, took the initiative in the appointment. See his rueful statement in *XIX Vsesoiuznaia konferentsiia Kommunisticheskoi partii Sovetskogo Soiuza, 28 iiunia–1 iiulia 1988 goda: Stenograficheskii otchet,* 2 vols. (Moscow: Politizdat, 1988), vol. 2, p. 82.

13. Yeltsin, *Ispoved'*, pp. 68, 76.

14. Ibid., p. 96.

15. "Vypiska iz vystupleniia t. Yel'tsina B. N. 11 aprelia s. g. pered propagandistami g. Moskvy," Radio Free Europe/Radio Liberty, *Materialy samizdata,* no. 23/86, July 18, 1986, p. 9. For a full analysis of Yeltsin as Moscow leader, see Timothy J. Colton, *Moscow: Governing the Socialist Metropolis* (forthcoming 1995 from Harvard University Press), ch. 7.

16. I have borrowed the phrase from Adam Przeworski, who elaborated: "In regimes of ritualized speech, where everyone goes through the motions of uttering words they do not believe and do not expect anyone else to believe, fresh words are subversive. Once the king is announced to be naked, the equilibrium is destroyed instantaneously." Adam

72   TIMOTHY J. COLTON

Przeworski, *Democracy and the Market: Political and Economic Reforms in Eastern Europe and Latin America* (Cambridge: Cambridge University Press, 1991), p. 58.

17. *Moskovskaia pravda,* April 14, 1987, p. 1. Yeltsin rounded out his comment with two quotations from Lenin.

18. Samuel P. Huntington, *The Third Wave: Democratization in the Late Twentieth Century* (Norman: University of Oklahoma Press, 1991), pp. 131, 134.

19. "Plenum TsK KPSS—oktiabr' 1987 goda," *Izvestiia TsK KPSS,* no. 2, February 1989, pp. 239–241, 279–280.

20. Yeltsin, *Ispoved',* p. 133.

21. "Plenum TsK KPSS," p. 241.

22. Yeltsin, *Ispoved',* p. 169.

23. Ibid., p. 141. Yeltsin speculated that another reason for his lenient treatment was that Gorbachev, after learning about a wave of pro-Yeltsin letters reaching *Pravda* and other newspapers, decided that harsh punishment would alienate public opinion. This explanation is quite implausible. Manifestations of public support would more likely have increased Gorbachev's fear of Yeltsin and inclined him toward harsh treatment.

24. Ibid., p. 142.

25. Lev Sukhanov, *Tri goda s Yel'tsinym: Zapiski pervogo pomoshchnika* (Riga: Vaga, 1992), pp. 40–41.

26. Quotations from *XIX Vsesoiuznaia konferentsiia,* vol. II, pp. 55–62; and FBIS-SOV-90-049, March 13, 1990, p. 76.

27. See Huntington, *The Third Wave,* pp. 174–192.

28. Yeltsin, *Ispoved',* p. 6.

29. Sukhanov wrote that Sakharov, the conscience of the group and a cochairman until his death in December 1989, had a large influence on Yeltsin. Sukhanov, *Tri goda s Yel'tsinym,* p. 337. Sakharov, however, was less admiring of Yeltsin. He wrote in a memoir published posthumously that although he respected Yeltsin, he considered him a figure "of completely different scale" from Gorbachev. In one vignette, Sakharov described being boorishly upstaged by Yeltsin at a public rally in Moscow. Andrei Sakharov, *Gor'kii, Moskva, dalee vezde* (New York: Izdatelstvo imeni Chekhova, 1990), pp. 168–171.

30. Sukhanov, *Tri goda s Yel'tsinym,* pp. 142–150. Yeltsin gave slightly different timing in *Struggle* (p. 137), where he said that his epiphany was during a steam bath organized by Sukhanov and other aides upon his return to Moscow. There was a political discussion in the bath, interlarded with the customary Russian beating of the naked bathers' backs with birch twigs: "That moment in the [bath] was when I changed my world view, when I realized that I was a Communist by historical Soviet tradition, by inertia, by education, but not by conviction."

31. FBIS-SOV-90-045, March 7, 1990, p. 77.

32. Accounts differ on Gorbachev's role in the turning points of both 1990 and 1991. Aleksandr Vlasov, the first candidate for the congress chairmanship whom he supported in May 1990, remained on good terms with him and worked for the next year in the Central Committee apparatus. But the second, Ivan Polozkov, later claimed convincingly in interviews that Gorbachev, despite public words of support, undercut him behind the scenes. In spring 1991 Yeltsin pushed through a constitutional amendment creating the presidency only when a parliamentary splinter group called Communists for Democracy, headed by his future vice president, Aleksandr Rutskoi, swung to his side. Polozkov again accused Gorbachev of going along with Yeltsin and paving the way for his popular election.

33. A number of CPSU officials later to retool as "democrats" joined in the attack on Yeltsin in 1987. At the October Central Committee plenum, for example, Shevardnadze castigated Yeltsin for "slander," "irresponsibility," and "primitivism" and heaped praise on Ligachev. "Plenum TsK KPSS," pp. 265–267.

34. *Izvestiia,* July 10, 1991 (evening edition), p. 1.

35. Divisions within the military and KGB ruled out violent suppression of resistance, so the issue was decisively fought out on the television screens of the nation, "where scripts, images and styles offered viewers starkly opposed versions of the past, present and future." Yeltsin's oratory and decrees were central to the version of events that gained credibility with viewers. Victoria E. Bonnell and Gregory Freidin, "*Televorot:* The Role of Television Coverage in Russia's August 1991 Coup," *Slavic Review,* vol. 52 (Winter 1993), p. 831.

36. The best symbolic division point is Yeltsin's speech on the tank on August 19. He recounted (*Struggle,* p. 69) that he "was already a completely different person" when he returned from the square to his office.

37. FBIS-SOV-91-202, October 18, 1991, p. 57.

38. *Rossiiskaia gazeta,* August 20, 1992, p. 1. Yeltsin had always rated the chances of mass disorder higher than those of a right-wing coup. Asked in March 1990 what would happen if perestroika were to fail, he predicted that "the people would take to the streets and would take their fate into their own hands, as the people in Eastern Europe have done." FBIS-SOV-90-049, March 13, 1990, p. 74.

39. All quotations from the speech are taken from FBIS-SOV-91-209, October 29, 1991, pp. 46–55; my emphasis.

40. *Izvestiia,* October 26, 1991, p. 2.

41. FBIS-SOV-90-045, March 7, 1990, p. 77.

42. FBIS-SOV-91-110, June 7, 1991, pp. 64–65.

43. Yeltsin later wrote that "the most important opportunity missed after the coup was the radical restructuring of the parliamentary system" (*Struggle,* p. 120), but he provided few details of his thinking.

44. FBIS-SOV-91-202, October 18, 1991, p. 59.

45. Yeltsin has several times expressed his admiration for Peter the Great, the autocratic emperor of the early eighteenth century. Asked by a reporter in 1992 which Russian ruler he most admired and given a list including Alexander II, the liberal reformer of the 1860s and 1870s, Yeltsin replied: "Peter I, of course. I consider him a creator, though not without tsarist excesses." *Komsomol'skaia pravda,* May 27, 1992, p. 2.

46. Speech of October 28, 1991.

47. FBIS-SOV-91-225, November 21, 1991, p. 58.

48. *Izvestiia,* November 3, 1992, p. 3; emphasis added.

49. Ibid., February 10, 1994, p. 4.

50. Yitzhak M. Brudny, "The Dynamics of 'Democratic Russia,' 1990–1993," *Post-Soviet Affairs,* vol. 9 (April-June 1993), p. 146.

51. FBIS-SOV-91-209, October 29, 1991, pp. 53–54. Yeltsin told a German correspondent shortly after the speech that he hoped the bloc would be in place within six months.

52. *Rossiiskie vesti,* September 8, 1992, p. 2.

53. See Elizabeth Teague, "Boris El'tsin Introduces His Brain Trust," RL/RFE, *Report on the USSR,* April 12, 1991, pp. 14–15, and the comments by Burbulis in *Izvestiia,* October 26, 1991, p. 2.

54. A smaller secretariat within the chancery, directly tied to Yeltsin's needs, was headed by another former CPSU official from Sverdlovsk, Viktor Iliushin.

55. FBIS-SOV-91-225, November 21, 1991, p. 56.

56. *Izvestiia,* October 26, 1991, p. 2.

57. See Mikhail Leont'ev in *Nezavisimaia gazeta,* August 13, 1991, p. 2, and Alexander Rahr, "El'tsin Sets Up New System for Governing Russia," RL/RFE, *Report on the USSR,* August 23, 1991, pp. 9–12.

58. I draw heavily here on Yeltsin's account in *Struggle,* pp. 150–160, and materials in *Rossiiskaia gazeta,* August 22, 1992, p. 2, and *Nezavisimaia gazeta,* October 5, 1991, p. 2, April 9, 1993, p. 2, and June 10, 1993, p. 5. The last is an interview with Skokov.

59. See the remarkable accounts of officials plying Yeltsin with requests in *Nezavisimaia gazeta,* September 18, 1991, p. 2, and September 19, 1991, p. 3.

60. *Struggle,* p. 158.

61. See in particular Sergei Parkhomenko in *Nezavisimaia gazeta,* July 31, 1992, pp. 1–2, and August 4, 1992, p. 2, and also *Rossiiskie vesti,* January 30, 1993, p. 2.

62. Skokov's council was the staff organ for the Council of Heads of Republics, an advisory group to Yeltsin, when the second body was created in October 1992. In December 1992 the Security Council was given a subcommission with the right to investigate all foreign policy issues.

63. Vice Premier Vladimir Shumeiko in *Nezavisimaia gazeta,* October 6, 1992, p. 2. Committees advisory to Yeltsin himself multiplied. The original Supreme Consultative and Coordinating Council was reborn as the Presidential Council in February 1993.

64. Vitalii Marsov in ibid., July 7, 1993, p. 1.

65. For example, of Khasbulatov's several deputy chairmen at the start of 1992, two (Vladimir Shumeiko and Yurii Yarov) had become deputy premiers by the end of the year, and a third (Sergei Filatov) was named head of the Presidential Chancery in January 1993.

66. Yeltsin, *Struggle,* p. 242.

67. Ibid., p. 205.

CHAPTER 4

Ruslan Khasbulatov, Aleksandr Rutskoi, and Intraelite Conflict in Postcommunist Russia, 1991–1994

Yitzhak M. Brudny

In no other communist country was the collapse of the regime followed by so intense, prolonged, and ultimately violent a conflict within the "regime founding coalition" as in Russia.[1] At its heart was a bitter power struggle involving Boris Yeltsin, on the one hand, and Ruslan Khasbulatov and Aleksandr Rutskoi, on the other.

The crisis was generated by two main factors: strategic choices made by Khasbulatov and Rutskoi, and Russia's institutional setup during this period. The alliance of leaders who came to power in the aftermath of the August 1991 coup attempt and the subsequent dismantling of the USSR disintegrated when Khasbulatov and Rutskoi adopted positions increasingly incompatible with Yeltsin on the key issues of economic reform, the constitution, and the boundaries of the Russian state. Their positions flowed from previously held views and from strategic calculations concerning political allies. After beginning as centrists primarily disenchanted with the government's economic policy, Khasbulatov and Rutskoi ended up in league with a hard-line communist-nationalist opposition bent not only on opposing the government's policies but on overthrowing it. This alliance ruled out any possibility of compromise with Yeltsin and precipitated the crisis of September–October 1993.

The personal views and politics of Khasbulatov and Rutskoi acquired enormous importance because of their support by a solid parliamentary majority. The presence of this majority reflected growing opposition to the government's approach to radical economic reform. Since Yeltsin's government refused to relent, the parliament sought to take control of economic decisionmaking. The Russian governmental system, based on dual popular legitimacy of the legislative and the executive branches, made parliament a natural oppositional vehicle and one conducive to promoting the political agendas of Khasbulatov and Rutskoi.

The Rise and Fall of the Regime Founding Coalition

In social background and early career, Khasbulatov and Rutskoi were typical of many coming members of the new Russian political elite. A mid-level academic and a middle-rank army officer without prior governmental experience, the two entered political life in 1989, attempting to win seats in the Soviet parliament, and gained elite status by getting elected to the Russian legislature in 1990. Their subsequent rise to leadership positions was meteoric: In less than two years, Khasbulatov was head of the Russian Supreme Soviet, and Rutskoi was vice president. Neither started out as a radical reformer, and both in fact owed their electoral victories to the support of the CPSU's provincial apparatus. Their swift rise to prominence in the pro-Yeltsin alliance was due to their desertion of the CPSU loyalist camp at a critical moment for Yeltsin. They played crucial roles during the putsch of August 1991 and the ratification of the December 1991 Minsk accords dismantling the USSR.

Entry into Politics

Ruslan Khasbulatov was born in 1942 in Groznyi, Chechnia, the son of a deputy director of the local metallurgical plant. Two years later, his family, along with the rest of the Chechen nation, was exiled to Kazakhstan, where he stayed even after the Chechens were permitted to return to their homeland in the 1950s. He enrolled in Kazakh State University in Alma-Ata in 1962 and two years later transferred to Moscow State University, from which he graduated in 1967 with a major in economics. He went on to graduate studies and in 1970 defended his dissertation on the public sector of the Canadian economy.

Khasbulatov's political ambitions first appeared during his student years. From 1965 to 1967, he was a secretary of the Komsomol committee of Moscow State University. Three years later, he joined the Agitation and Propaganda Department of the Central Committee of the Komsomol but apparently chose not to pursue this career path further. In 1972, he returned to academia and in 1979 took a post at the Plekhanov Institute of National Economy, where he worked for eleven years, ultimately becoming head of the department of international economics.[2]

In the early years of perestroika, Khasbulatov's published works were critical of the command economy and of the Stalinist legacy in ethnic relations. He was careful, however, not to go beyond Gorbachev's line at the time. It was probably his loyalty that earned him a position on the USSR Council of Ministers' Committee on Social Development, which drafted the law on the lease of state property.[3]

Although Rutskoi's early career was somewhat different, he, too, was not part of the *nomenklatura* system, and his upward path was a direct result of Gorbachev's political reforms. Born in 1947 in the city of Kursk in south Russia, Rutskoi followed in the steps of his father, a retired lieutenant colonel, by becoming a career army officer. He graduated in 1971 from the aviators school in the Siberian city of Barnaul and for the next fifteen years climbed the military career ladder, reaching the rank of air force colonel.[4]

In 1985–1986 and again in 1988, Rutskoi served in Afghanistan, where he became a national celebrity after *Pravda* published a report on his battle valor.[5] In August 1988, he was shot down and captured by Pakistani troops who several days later exchanged him for a Pakistani intelligence officer. Upon his return, Rutskoi received a hero's welcome: He was awarded the highest military decoration of the USSR, Hero of the Soviet Union, profiled in two articles in *Pravda,* and sent to attend the General Staff Academy.[6]

We do not know the effect of the Afghan experience on Rutskoi's personality or political views. We do know that he returned a fervent Russian nationalist. In spring 1989, he helped found Otechestvo, a nationalist association that brought together nationalist and communist intellectuals and antiperestroika army officers, and became its deputy chairman.[7]

Both Khasbulatov and Rutskoi were beneficiaries of the competitive elections introduced by Gorbachev in 1989, even though their first attempts at candidacy flopped. In 1989, Khasbulatov sought to contest a seat in the USSR Congress of People's Deputies in his native Chechen-Ingush republic. But the local party organization, suspicious of his reformist views, forced an electoral committee to deny him registration.

Rutskoi did succeed in getting a nomination and ran in the Kuntsevo district of Moscow. He was one of seven candidates, including such well-known public figures as playwright Mikhail Shatrov and journalist Valentin Logunov. Rutskoi campaigned as an unabashed Russian nationalist: He justified the Soviet invasion of Afghanistan, condemned new private enterprises, and called for the restoration of preperestroika "social justice." He was endorsed by the Moscow party committee, whose newspaper, *Moskovskaia pravda,* printed a laudatory profile of him four days before the ballot. He did well in the first round, getting 30 percent of the vote while no other candidate received more than 20 percent, but was defeated in the second round (65 to 35 percent) by Logunov, who was endorsed by Yeltsin and strongly supported by grassroots democratic organizations.[8]

The experience of 1989 was educational for both Khasbulatov and Rutskoi and helped them to win election in 1990. Also favorable to their victories was the backing of the local party organs. Khasbulatov ran again in 1990 in Groznyi, this time for the RSFSR Congress of People's Deputies. Conditions in the republic were more favorable primarily because he enjoyed the support of the new republican party secretary, Doku Zavgaev. Khasbulatov's electoral platform aimed both to affirm his credentials as a Gorbachev loyalist and to appeal to the growing nationalist sentiments of the Chechens.

The combination of Zavgaev's support, a program that attracted a wide audience, and vigorous campaigning—Khasbulatov claimed to have made 220 public appearances—brought victory. He was the leading candidate in the first round with 32.6 percent of the vote and won in the second round with 52.6 percent.[9]

Like Khasbulatov, Rutskoi decided to run for a seat in the RSFSR congress not in Moscow, where his chances were slim, but in his home town of Kursk, where the democratic organizations were very weak and the regional party apparatus had little difficulty in electing its candidates to the USSR parliament.

Rutskoi's 1990 electoral platform was a contradictory mix of his 1989 criticism of perestroika and a newfound support for radical economic and military reforms probably aimed at broadening his appeal to voters of all persuasions. He criticized perestroika for creating an atmosphere of permissiveness, irresponsibility, and loss of respect for Soviet symbols; portrayed democrats as striving to "destroy the party and the military, open the borders, set the economy adrift, and discard morality"; and called for strengthening the nation's "love of the Motherland ... and belief that its toil, deprivation, and sacrifices were not in vain." In the same breath, he urged the government to grant full freedom of economic activity to firms and individuals, close down unprofitable enterprises, create more joint ventures, privatize land, and reduce the size of the military by 70 percent.[10]

Despite his national name recognition, Rutskoi did rather poorly in the first round, finishing second with 12.8 percent of the vote, well behind the local parish priest, Father Nikodim Yevmolaty, who received 33 percent. In the two weeks before the runoff, the oblast party apparatus committed all its resources in the effort to assure Rutskoi's victory.

This effort culminated in the publication one day before the second round of voting of a long article by Rutskoi in *Kurskaia pravda,* the daily oblast newspaper. The essay reveals that Rutskoi had decided to defeat his opponent by adopting a fervent nationalist stand calling for the creation of a Russian Communist Party and for the introduction of a law that would make the principle of proportional ethnic representation the basis for filling posts in political, social, economic, and cultural organizations. In order to gain votes on the collective and state farms, Rutskoi also reversed support of the privatization of land and stressed the primacy of collectively held property. These program adjustments, combined with the massive support of the local party apparatus, helped Rutskoi to defeat Yevmolaty in the second round with 51.3 against 44.1 percent of the vote.[11]

Formation of the Political Alliance

Khasbulatov's and Rutskoi's ascent to leadership positions was a direct consequence of a shift in their political loyalty to Yeltsin at a crucial moment in Russian politics. For Khasbulatov that moment was the First Congress of RSFSR People's Deputies in May 1990; for Rutskoi it was the Third Congress in March–April 1991. From the time the shift was made until the fall of 1991, both men were viscerally involved in the Yeltsin-led alliance that battled Gorbachev and the CPSU over the right to rule Russia.

At the First Congress, Khasbulatov was expected to vote for Aleksandr Vlasov, Russia's prime minister and Gorbachev's candidate for the position of chairman of the RSFSR Supreme Soviet, but he voted for Yeltsin instead.[12] This decision was vital to his subsequent election to the first deputy chairmanship of the soviet. There was a consensus among the deputies that the position should go to a representative of one of Russia's minority nationalities. Democratic deputies did not have a strong nominee of their own but were determined to deny Gorbachev's candidate, Ramazan Abdulatipov, the majority he needed. After several rounds of voting, when it became clear that Abdulatipov was unelectable, Khasbulatov was proposed as a compromise candidate. His vote for Yeltsin swayed democratic deputies, and he was elected with 604 votes in his favor.

Between June 1990 and August 1991, Khasbulatov was one of the key members of the pro-Yeltsin alliance. He ran the parliament on a day-to-day basis, as Yeltsin largely focused his energy on the executive branch of the government. He quickly understood the power of his office and wielded it skillfully to help Yeltsin in his struggles against his main parliamentary opposition, the Communists of Russia faction. In particular, Khasbulatov played a crucial role in the crisis of March 1991 when Yeltsin was threatened with impeachment.

Through backroom deals, Khasbulatov was able to convince many independent deputies to vote for the postponement of the emergency meeting of the Congress of People's Deputies from March 4 to March 28, 1991. The delay was of major significance because it postponed the discussion of Yeltsin's impeachment until after the March 17 referendum, in which more than 70 percent of the electorate supported Yeltsin's proposal to introduce the post of popularly elected president of Russia. The referendum result was one of the main factors that forced the Communists of Russia to abandon its effort to impeach him.

In addition to allowing him to run the parliament, Yeltsin entrusted Khasbulatov with the important task of negotiating the new Union Treaty with the Gorbachev government. In this capacity, Khasbulatov was an outspoken proponent of expanding Russia's power at the expense of the center. He reiterated Yeltsin's charge that the USSR was trying to prevent Russia from realizing its sovereignty and to undermine its territorial integrity by pitting its autonomous republics against it. He had particularly harsh words for the communists and Russian nationalists, whom he accused of betraying Russia in favor of the Union.

Finally, Khasbulatov also was one of Yeltsin's main spokesmen on economic matters, using every opportunity to condemn the command economy and Gorbachev's unwillingness to carry out radical reform. He ardently supported the "500 Days" program for a fast transition to the market, arguing that Russia should implement it unilaterally if need be.

Election as an RSFSR deputy was also Rutskoi's ticket into the political stratosphere. In May 1990, at the First Congress of People's Deputies, he was chosen as chairman of the Supreme Soviet Committee for the Affairs of Invalids, War and Labor Veterans, and the Social Defense of Servicemen and their Families, a post that made him a member of the Presidium of the Supreme Soviet. In September 1990, he was elected to the Central Committee of the newly created Russian Communist Party(RCP).

Yet in fall 1990, Rutskoi's status was hardly a dominant one. His seat on the 272-member Central Committee of the RCP gave him a certain visibility but no significant power. At the same time, he was not a skilled parliamentarian, like Khasbulatov, who could use the institution to promote himself.

Rutskoi had two immediate options for advancement: to become a leading figure in the anti-Yeltsin Communists of Russia faction in the Supreme Soviet or to break with it and ally himself with Yeltsin and his group. Rutskoi chose the second path.

His emergence as a sworn democrat and Yeltsin ally began during the Second Congress of RSFSR People's Deputies in December 1990. Even though he was a member of Communists of Russia, he effectively joined the pro-Yeltsin Democratic Russia bloc; out of twenty-one major ballots in which he participated, he voted with Democratic Russia on nineteen occasions and with the Communists of Russia only twice.[13]

On January 21, 1991, before the Supreme Soviet, Rutskoi expressed his support for Yeltsin's condemnation of the government's attack on the Vilnius television tower.[14] This was the first indication of the role he had decided to play in the confrontation between Yeltsin and the CPSU at the Third Congress of People's Deputies, which was convened by the Communists of Russia faction in order to remove Yeltsin from office. On April 2, Rutskoi announced to the congress that 170 deputies had formed the Communists for Democracy faction, which would act as a counterbalance to the Communists of Russia in the parliament. The new faction pledged support for Yeltsin and his policies.[15] Even though Rutskoi's new faction hardly affected the balance of forces—its membership was not 170 members, as claimed, but only 95, of whom only 11 were former members of Communists of Russia—it was a bombshell to the Communists of Russia and helped derail their plans to eliminate Yeltsin from office.

Sensing that his action had been well received by rank-and-file members of the party, Rutskoi called for the formation of Communists for Democracy chapters in regional and local soviets, neighborhoods, workplaces, and party organizations as the first step in the formation of a new party. At the same time, he borrowed a page from Yeltsin's populist handbook by sharply attacking the CPSU for its indifference to the harsh realities of daily life, its vast property and privileges, its refusal to introduce market economics, and its readiness to sacrifice Russia's interests in favor of the Soviet Union.[16]

In less than a month after his congressional démarche, Rutskoi had acquired the reputation of a rising star in Russian politics, and newspapers began to view him as a potential presidential contender. His increasing public exposure was no doubt a factor in Yeltsin's invitation to him to run as his running mate in the presidential elections of June 12, 1991. Yeltsin also wanted him at his side because his chief rival, Nikolai Ryzhkov, the former Soviet prime minister, had chosen General Boris Gromov, the last commander of the Soviet troops in Afghanistan, as his vice-presidential candidate.[17]

Yeltsin's and Rutskoi's convincing victory June 12 greatly enhanced Rutskoi's status and added momentum to his efforts to split the CPSU. On July 18, he issued a manifesto of principles for a new Democratic Party of Russian Communists. On August 2, the new party held its organizing conference. Four days later Rutskoi was expelled from the CPSU.[18]

The high point of the Yeltsin-Khasbulatov-Rutskoi alliance, and probably of the political careers of Khasbulatov and Rutskoi, came during the coup episode of August 1991. During the three days of the coup, Khasbulatov rallied the parliament in support of Yeltsin. He also cosigned with Yeltsin and Prime Minister Ivan Silaev an appeal to the people of Russia calling upon them to resist the coup.[19] Rutskoi, for his part, organized the defense of the White House and flew to the Crimea to free Gorbachev. In a symbolic recognition of his effort to foil the coup, Yeltsin promoted Rutskoi to the rank of major general.

Beginning of the End

Shortly after the failed coup and the ensuing ban of the CPSU, the first signs of dissension within the Yeltsin-Khasbulatov-Rutskoi alliance appeared. By January 1992, the coalition had fallen apart completely. It collapsed because although the primary goals uniting its participants—to remove Gorbachev, destroy the CPSU, and abolish the Union structure—were fulfilled, a consensus on new goals, such as the nature of the new constitution or the strategy for pursuing economic reform, could not be reached. Another critical issue was the allies' individual roles in the new Russian state. Both Khasbulatov and Rutskoi expected that they and their offices would be assigned prominent places, but Yeltsin was not willing to grant them this concession.

Even before August, there were signs of Khasbulatov's forthcoming conflict with Yeltsin and his radical supporters in the parliament. Khasbulatov supported Yeltsin's drive to introduce an executive presidency, but he emphasized that this should not result in the weakening of the legislature. And although he continued to talk about radical economic reform, he strongly opposed reforms emphasizing price liberalization, which would be a key component of the Gaidar program.[20]

These differences did not ripen until 1992, but conflict over Khasbulatov's use of his office broke dramatically into the open soon after Yeltsin was elected president. A special session of the Congress of People's Deputies was convened in July 1991 in order to elect a new chairman of the Supreme Soviet. Khasbulatov, the acting chairman, secured Yeltsin's endorsement and saw himself as the front-runner. However, approximately 150 pro-Yeltsin deputies refused to support him, accusing him of attempting to concentrate too much power in his hands and of using it against parliamentarians who disagreed with him. This nearly produced Khasbulatov's defeat. In each of six rounds of voting, he came second after Sergei Baburin, a Russian nationalist deputy supported by the Communists of Russia. Baburin, however, failed to gain the 531 votes needed for victory, and this allowed Khasbulatov to continue as acting chairman until the next session of congress in October 1991.[21]

One can reasonably assume that if the August 1991 putsch had not occurred, Khasbulatov's career would have been stalled. The coup allowed him to demonstrate his loyalty to Yeltsin and the democratic cause and thus significantly weakened the resistance of many democratic deputies to his candidacy for parliamentary speaker. Yeltsin, at this time at the peak of his popularity, strongly endorsed Khasbulatov's candidacy, and this helped further. In late October 1991, at the Fifth Congress of People's Deputies, Khasbulatov was elected chairman of the Russian Supreme Soviet, receiving 559 votes to Baburin's 274.

Despite Yeltsin's assistance, relations between the two men began to sour in mid-October. The bone of contention was the division of power between parliament and president. The Supreme Soviet, with Khasbulatov's tacit encouragement, insisted on the public election of the heads of regional administration and set the election date for December 8, 1991. Yeltsin was vehemently opposed and demanded the right to fill the posts by presidential appointment, vetoing the parliament's decree.

The legislature decided not to challenge Yeltsin head-to-head on this issue, but it quickly demonstrated that it was not willing to cede him control of economic policy. Shortly after the Fifth Congress, the Supreme Soviet, at Khasbulatov's initiative, rejected the government's attempt to subordinate Russia's Central Bank and affirmed parliamentary control of it. This time confrontation was avoided because Yeltsin decided not to challenge the parliament.

The sharp break between Yeltsin and Khasbulatov took place in the wake of the launch of the program of liberalizing economic reform on January 2, 1992. On January 13, Khasbulatov sharply attacked the emancipation of most prices and demanded changes in the composition of the government, threatening parliamentary intervention if Yeltsin did not comply.[22]

As with Khasbulatov, Rutskoi's original disagreements with Yeltsin were not ideological but concerned the sharing of power between the two executive positions. Yeltsin never discussed the scope of Rutskoi's role as vice president. He assumed that Rutskoi would behave more or less as a U.S. vice president does and took Rutskoi's "officer's word of honor" never to oppose him. Rutskoi, on the other hand, was convinced that he would be given wide administrative powers.[23]

Rutskoi's first major disappointment after the coup occurred when he expressed the desire to play a part in the design and implementation of economic reforms and to have a sizable staff to monitor compliance. Instead, he was given six assistants and given the job of troubleshooter for the administration. His first major assignment was to settle an internal conflict in the Chechen-Ingush republic, which by early October was on the verge of civil war. He flew to Groznyi and met with the leader of the opposition, Dzhakhar Dudaev, threatening to use force if Dudaev did not back down. This strategy proved disastrous, as it elevated Dudaev to the status of national champion and facilitated his election as president of the republic. On November 7, Yeltsin on Rutskoi's recommendation signed a decree declaring martial law. Dudaev counterattacked with mobilization of the local population and threatened to turn the republic into a second Afghanistan. On November 13, fearing bloodshed, the Russian parliament lifted martial law and ordered Russian troops to withdraw. The result was the effective secession of the Chechen republic from Russia.[24]

The debacle strained relations between Rutskoi and Yeltsin. Rutskoi was bitter that Yeltsin had not backed him to the end and allowed the Supreme Soviet to humiliate him. Yeltsin, on the other hand, no longer trusted Rutskoi to undertake any serious mission on his behalf. The outcome was the relegation of Rutskoi to coordinator of the work of six minor committees. More important, he was denied any input into the course of economic reform. Having no say in the selection of Yegor Gaidar and his program, he felt no obligation to support it, even though he had advocated an immediate transition to free-market prices and an end to subsidies as recently as October 1991.[25]

In late November 1991, Rutskoi went on a tour of Siberian military-industrial enterprises, blasting the concept of price liberalization and making derogatory remarks about Gaidar and his ministers at every stop. In mid-December, Yeltsin retaliated by stripping Rutskoi of all assigned duties. This, in turn, provoked Rutskoi to give a series of interviews in which he criticized the entire reform project, asserting that, if implemented, it would undermine the Russian military, push the majority of the population below the poverty line, and destroy law and order.[26]

With these disagreements in the background, Yeltsin excluded both Khasbulatov and Rutskoi from any significant part in negotiations about the future of the Soviet federation. However, common interest in the removal of central structures led to a last gasp of cooperation among the three leaders. Khasbulatov came out enthusiastically in favor of the formation of the Commonwealth of Independent States (CIS), presumably because it eliminated the Soviet parliament. Since the Russian constitution placed the RSFSR in the USSR, a change in the republic's status ought to have been subject to a vote by the Congress of People's Deputies, whose attitude was uncertain. Khasbulatov correctly calculated that the Minsk accords would be confirmed by the Supreme Soviet, which, indeed, voted 188 to 6 to approve the dissolution of the USSR and thereby to make Russia's parliament supreme. Rutskoi's role in the drama was less crucial but important nevertheless, as he called upon parliament to go along. His only misgivings concerned the ambiguities of the accords and the haste with which they were drawn up.[27]

Intraelite Confrontation

The Institutional Dimension

Dissolution of the CPSU and the USSR removed two of the common goals that had held Yeltsin, Khasbulatov, and Rutskoi together. The policy of liberalizing economic reform, put into effect by the Gaidar cabinet in January 1992, provided the source of discord that wrecked the alliance completely. Opposition to the government's economic policy became the basis of a new alliance bringing together Rutskoi, Khasbulatov, and the parliamentary majority. In 1992, the goals of this alliance were largely confined to changing government economic policy and its architects. In 1993, they expanded to overhauling Russia's constitutional structure with the aim of transforming it into an unambiguously parliamentary republic. This goal expansion was a consequence of the decision of Khasbulatov and Rutskoi to ally themselves with the communist-nationalist opposition that strove to overthrow Yeltsin. The parliamentary majority supported this shift because it suited the parliament's interest in preserving the power and privileges of the deputies as long as possible.

It is hardly surprising that the economic policies of price liberalization and restricted credit, which brought about a significant decline in industrial production and the wholesale impoverishment of the Russian population, greatly fueled the intraelite struggle. As Adam Przeworski convincingly argued, both the strategy and the policy style necessary to implement a neoliberal economic reform program in newly democratizing countries were bound to cause a major political crisis:

> Since the neo-liberal "cure" is a painful one, with significant social costs, reforms tend to be initiated from above and launched by surprise, independently of public opinion and without participation of organized political forces. ... The political style of implementation tends toward rule by decree. ... Legislatures are given the impression that they have no role to play in the elaboration of policy; nascent political parties, trade unions, and other organizations learn that their voices do not count.[28]

The main difference between the Russian case and the Latin American and East European cases that were the base for Przeworski's argument was the existence in these other countries of a larger and more durable elite consensus concerning the introduction and continuation of such policies. In Poland, for example, the Tadeusz Mazowiecki cabinet enjoyed significant support within the top echelons of the political establishment during the first eight months of "shock therapy." In comparison, Rutskoi began publicly attacking the Russian program even before its introduction, and Khasbulatov joined the attack only days after it was implemented.

As in the case of the political leadership, the Russian parliament shifted its position from supporting the reforms to strongly opposing them much more quickly than the Polish Sejm. In October 1991, at the Fifth Congress of People's Deputies, Gaidar's prospective program was approved with an overwhelming majority of 876 to 16; only six months later, at the Sixth Congress of People's Deputies, only 231 deputies expressed support for government policy while 632 opposed it.

The emergence of this solid parliamentary bloc against continuation of neoliberal reforms meant that from April 1992 on, such reforms could be carried out only by means of presidential edicts bypassing the parliament. In December 1992, the parliament responded with an attempt to take control of economic policy through a series of constitutional amendments aimed at stripping Yeltsin of his control of government. At this point, the goals of the parliamentary majority began to coincide with Khasbulatov's and Rutskoi's increasingly open drive for power.

The transformation of the Russian Supreme Soviet from the institutional mainstay of Yeltsin's power to that of his opponents was the decisive factor in the development of the intraelite struggle. As described previously, the introduction of a neoliberal program of economic reform played a significant role in the shift of the political orientation of the parliamentary majority. However, the constitutional structure of postcommunist Russia itself facilitated the consolidation of this majority and the expansion of its political goals.

As of June 1991, Russia was, loosely speaking, a presidential republic and therefore was prone to confrontation between the executive and legislative branches of government. As noted by Juan Linz, in the presidential system, the president makes a "strong claim to democratic, even plebiscitarian legitimacy." The parliamentarians, however, can make their own claim for democratic legitimacy since they are also elected by the people. This situation can provoke a serious conflict. What makes this conflict worse is the fact that "there is no democratic principle on the basis of which it could be resolved, and the mechanisms the constitution might provide are likely to prove too complicated and aridly legalistic to be of much force in the eyes of the electorate." A compromise between president and legislature over policy is also difficult to achieve because the president tends to "define his policies as expressions of the popular will and those of his opponents as the selfish designs of narrow interests."[29] This statement accurately describes the Russian situation in which both Yeltsin and the parliament justified their actions by the respective popular legitimacy they received.

Three main features of the Russian constitutional structure made the conflict between the president and the parliament virtually impossible to resolve. First, the Russian presidential system, as it was established in 1991, clearly belonged to the "president-parliamentary" type. In this system, both the parliament and the president enjoy some control over the cabinet of ministers, but the precise division of power between the two is not defined clearly. As Matthew Shugart pointed out, the president-parliamentary constitutional design "has bred instability wherever it has been used."[30]

To make matters worse, the law on the presidency failed to distinguish sufficiently between the prerogatives of the president and the chairman of the Supreme Soviet. It gave the president the right to issue direct orders to government ministries and agencies. However, the chairman of the Supreme Soviet retained the same right. In 1992, Khasbulatov issued 66 such orders and in the first six months of 1993 more than 630.[31] Thus, the law on the presidency effectively created two competing heads of state, the president and the chairman of the Supreme Soviet.

Second, the Russian law on the presidency failed to provide a mechanism for resolving conflicts between the two branches of government. Fearful of an all-powerful executive, the Russian parliamentarians denied the president the right to call referenda or new parliamentary or presidential elections, preferring to keep these rights as their exclusive prerogative. Moreover, although Russian legislators paid substantial attention to the office of the president, they paid hardly any to the vice presidency. They merely copied the Soviet law, which gave the vice president no specific functions beyond the stipulation that he would succeed in the case of the president's death, resignation, impeachment, or disability.[32] As both Soviet and Russian experiences have demonstrated, in the absence of an established traditional role for the vice president, such a formulation tempts him to try to usurp presidential powers.

Finally, the Russian Supreme Soviet itself was a parliament of a particular kind. It was an institution whose members developed a strong corporate identity with interests that transcended all political cleavages. Russian parliamentarians began to develop this corporate identity during the struggle with the CPSU and the USSR government over the power to rule Russia.[33] This process greatly accelerated during the confrontation with Yeltsin over the same issue. The corporate interest was especially strong among the 347 most active deputies (the members of the Supreme Soviet and the deputies who worked full-time in the committees or the apparatus of the Supreme Soviet), who therefore were the beneficiaries of the political power and economic benefits at the disposal of the parliament.[34] Moreover, since most of these deputies neither belonged to any political party nor wished to join one, they were well aware that their power and privileges would end after the next election. Thus, the majority of active deputies had a common interest in postponing the elections for as long as possible while devising a scheme that would perpetuate their hold on power. The only way to do this as conflict with Yeltsin intensified was to support Khasbulatov's effort to eliminate the presidency as a competing institution of power.[35]

In the light of the pivotal role played by the Supreme Soviet, the question arises whether the worsening of the intraelite conflict was dictated by parliament rather than Khasbulatov and Rutskoi. Relations between parliament and the Khasbulatov-Rutskoi duo were very complex. Suffice it to say that in 1992 Khasbulatov's political behavior was a consequence largely of his acute sense of the mood of parliament and his ability to adapt his own politics accordingly. However, the post of parliamentary speaker enabled him over time to increase his power within and control over the institution, and this in turn significantly improved his ability to steer the legislature in the direction he desired. Thus, in 1993, more often than not he was able to impose his priorities on the parliament. This control of the Supreme Soviet made Khasbulatov the actual leader of the anti-Yeltsin opposition.

Relations between Rutskoi and the parliamentary majority were dictated by mutual need. Only the parliament could elevate Rutskoi to the position of Russia's president without an election. This constitutional reality explains why he sided with parliament against Yeltsin when curtailment of presidential powers was at stake. At the same time, whereas the ratings of the parliament and Khasbulatov in public opinion polls were extremely low, Rutskoi was one of the most popular Russian politicians.[36] Moreover, he was the main leader of the Civic Union, the strongest political alliance outside the parliament in 1992 and into 1993. All this made his support for the parliament and Khasbulatov politically invaluable since he conferred upon their actions much needed popular legitimacy.

Rutskoi's open backing of the parliament during the moments of crisis in December 1992 and March 1993 was crucial in strengthening the will of its majority to continue the confrontation. Moreover, he himself was often a catalyst of the conflict by making policy statements, not cleared with Yeltsin or the government, that greatly complicated Russia's relations with neighboring states and by making inflammatory speeches and accusations against government ministers and Yeltsin himself. Finally, in the September–October 1993 crisis, it was Rutskoi who made the key decisions that led to the armed uprising and bloodshed.

The Choices of Political Actors, 1992

The emergence of the parliament as the institutional bulwark of opposition to Yeltsin's economic reform—a factor Khasbulatov ably exploited to expand the scope of parliamentary control over the government—fully manifested itself at the Sixth Congress of People's Deputies in April 1992. Sensing the growing unhappiness with the neoliberal economic reforms, Khasbulatov skillfully manipulated the congress's proceedings. They culminated in a resolution that harshly condemned the Gaidar government and demanded that Yeltsin submit a significantly altered program of economic reform within one month.

Khasbulatov linked the demand for change in economic policy with an attempt to subordinate the government to the Supreme Soviet. The resolution on economic policy demanded that Yeltsin relinquish the prime minister's post and submit a candidate for approval by the Supreme Soviet, and that a law "On the Council of Ministers of the Russian Federation," subordinating the government to parliament, be passed within three months.[37]

The resolution triggered a major showdown when Gaidar's government reacted to the resolution by collectively resigning, whereupon Yeltsin's closest advisers openly threatened to dissolve the congress. Worried deputies pressured

Khasbulatov to compromise. He agreed, temporarily abandoning the confrontation and negotiating a compromise solution in the form of a new resolution that called for a correction of the reform policy in accordance with "developing social and economic conditions." The demand that Yeltsin relinquish the post of prime minister and the threat to enact a law on the subordination of the government within three months were also omitted from the resolution.[38]

This was the first of three compromise agreements that Khasbulatov struck with Yeltsin. None led to a lasting settlement, and the collapse of each was followed by heightened confrontation. The differences in approach to economic reform and especially to the constitution became irreconcilable as Khasbulatov sought to undermine the presidency and transfer real decision power to the Supreme Soviet and ultimately to himself. This determination was only strengthened by his growing unpopularity, which eliminated any possibility of a successful presidential bid.[39]

Khasbulatov's actions in the months following the Sixth Congress escalated the confrontation. In summer 1992, he began tightening the screws on institutions subordinate to the Supreme Soviet. First, he established strict parliamentary control over the Russian Central Bank, forcing the resignation of its head, Georgy Matiukhin, who had cooperated with Gaidar on issues of monetary emission and credit policy. From that time until October 1993, the Central Bank sabotaged the policies set by the Yeltsin government.

Second, Khasbulatov took personal control over the operation of the Supreme Soviet Presidium and began exercising sole authority concerning the budget and personnel of the Supreme Soviet. In addition, he created a mechanism that gave him the ability to decide first how the soviet would respond to Yeltsin's decrees, with a minimum of consultation with his deputy chairmen. Finally, he established control over the work of the Constitutional Commission of the Russian Federation and effectively used it to delay indefinitely the adoption of a new constitution.[40]

Third, Khasbulatov attempted to improve the image of the Supreme Soviet and of himself in the mass media, which by and large had sided with Yeltsin in the unfolding conflict. The first victim was *Rossiiskaia gazeta,* the newspaper of the Supreme Soviet. Previously strongly pro-Yeltsin, it in the spring of 1992 became the mouthpiece of Khasbulatov, defending his policies and dutifully publishing his numerous speeches and essays in a manner reminiscent of Soviet days.

Against newspapers not subordinate to the parliament, Khasbulatov had at his disposal a Sixth Congress resolution, prepared on his specific instructions, stipulating that criminal proceedings could be initiated against organizations or individuals who "discredit institutions of state power through the spread of false information." In the second half of 1992, he repeatedly threatened to use the resolution to close down publications critical of the parliament.[41] Specifically, he sought to subordinate *Izvestiia,* the newspaper most critical of his actions, to the Supreme Soviet.

On October 14, *Izvestiia* disclosed the existence of a 5,000-member armed parliamentary guard subordinate to Khasbulatov alone. This, plus other revelations, led Khasbulatov to order the guard to seize *Izvestiia*. However, Yeltsin was ready neither to lose his most supportive publication nor to tolerate an armed formation under Khasbulatov's personal control. On the same day that Khasbulatov issued his command (October 26), Yeltsin issued a decree subordinating the parliamentary guard to the Ministry of Interior.[42]

Khasbulatov did not challenge Yeltsin's decree, since this might have led to an armed confrontation that he had little chance of winning. He also agreed that the *Izvestiia* dispute be settled by the Constitutional Court, something he previously had opposed. Soon after the incident, however, he began preparing the forthcoming Seventh Congress of People's Deputies, where he planned to strip Yeltsin of his power to control the government.

To legitimate his attack on Yeltsin, he portrayed himself as defending the constitutional rights of the parliament. On the eve of the congress, he published a seventy-page pamphlet and two programmatic essays in which he argued that the constitution made the legislature, rather than the presidency, the institution responsible for determining policy, and proclaimed that the parliament "must certainly regain the leading role in shaping, approving, and monitoring the government's implementation of socioeconomic policy."[43]

To this end, he succeeded in blocking renewal of Yeltsin's emergency powers and proposed seven constitutional amendments that would have transferred control of the cabinet from the president to the Supreme Soviet. He received the necessary 695 votes for three relatively minor amendments, but failed to pass the four main amendments that would have granted the parliament the right to confirm appointment and dismissal of the prime minister, his deputies, and ten key ministers, as well as the right to confirm the creation and dissolution of government ministries and agencies.

After failing to get his way through changes in the basic law, Khasbulatov tried replacement of Gaidar with an official ready to carry out economic policies advocated by the parliamentary majority. The December 1992 congress indeed failed to confirm Gaidar as prime minister and, after many maneuvers, approved Viktor Chernomyrdin for the position. Its rejection of Gaidar precipitated a walkout by Yeltsin, who began rallying public support for a referendum on the basic provisions of a new constitution. Taken by surprise by Yeltsin's move and fearing the forcible dissolution of the congress, Khasbulatov quickly negotiated a compromise. He agreed to Yeltsin's demand for the referendum in exchange for sacrificing Gaidar and granting the Supreme Soviet the right to confirm the appointment of the ministers of defense, security, interior, and foreign affairs.

The Seventh Congress also marked the first open cooperation between Rutskoi and Khasbulatov and the parliamentary majority. On December 10, after Yeltsin stormed out of the parliament building, Rutskoi rushed to provide his personal support for the political course of the parliament. In a flashy speech, he condemned Yeltsin's call for the referendum, endorsed the congress's demand for a change in economic line, and called for the prosecution of Yeltsin advisers who had supported confrontation with the parliament.[44]

Rutskoi's emergence as an ally of Khasbulatov and the parliament was most likely a consequence of his greatly increased political ambitions. In late 1991, there was still no organized force positioned between the pro-Yeltsin democratic forces and the communist-nationalist opposition. In early 1992, Rutskoi articulated the ideological tenets of centrism in three programmatic essays offering nationalism, democracy, and social protection of the population as the foundational principles of a future centrist alliance. Nationalism was presented as a belief in the unitary nature of Russia and active protection of ethnic Russians in the former Soviet republics; democracy was defined as the freedom of political competition but with a very strong emphasis on law and order; the social protection of the population was formulated as a criticism of the government's economic policies.[45]

Nationalism was clearly the most important of the trio. To demonstrate this, Rutskoi went on a tour of the separatist Trans-Dniester region of Moldova, declaring throughout that the Russian military ought to defend ethnic Russians in all former Soviet republics. These statements were not coordinated with Yeltsin and created major tensions between Russia and Moldova as well as other former Soviet republics.

After unsuccessfully trying to organize the centrist bloc around the cause of Russian nationalism, Rutskoi switched the emphasis of the new alliance to opposition to Gaidar's economic policies. This strategy proved successful and led to the formation in June 1992 of the Civic Union, an alliance joining Rutskoi's People's Party of Free Russia, the Democratic Party of Russia, the Russian Union of Industrialists and Entrepreneurs, the Federation of Russian Trade Unions, and five parliamentary factions. This gathering of major institutional players around a program carefully balancing a rejection of the government's economic policies, defense of the rights of the Russians in the former Soviet republics, and a commitment to democratic principles not only gave Rutskoi a more solid organizational base but also contributed to the growth of his personal popularity. By late summer, he eclipsed Yeltsin as the most popular politician in Russia.[46]

All this only intensified the conflict with Yeltsin. In autumn 1992, Rutskoi's antigovernment rhetoric became much more inflammatory. He began demanding the ouster of Yeltsin's leading ministers and advisers. This was a combination of personal vendetta for his removal from the presidential decisionmaking circle and a general Civic Union strategy aimed at wrestling control of the economy from Yeltsin.[47] Thus, Rutskoi's emergence as an ally of Khasbulatov at the Seventh Congress was the culmination of his growing confrontation with Yeltsin and his government throughout 1992.

The Choices of Political Actors, 1993

The escalation of the intraelite crisis beyond the point of no return resulted from a critical determination made by Khasbulatov and Rutskoi in January 1993. They abandoned the December agreement with Yeltsin, which had allowed parliament to choose the prime minister in exchange for a referendum on April 11, 1993. By engaging in this gambit, Khasbulatov and Rutskoi effectively abandoned the compromise-oriented center of the political spectrum, greatly damaging it in the process, and joined the confrontation-oriented communist-nationalist opposition.[48]

Khasbulatov's gamble was that Yeltsin would not dare dissolve the parliament and therefore that he could push unimpeded toward a decisive confrontation with Yeltsin that would result in his impeachment. On January 9 and 10, Khasbulatov published two lengthy essays in which he argued that the December agreement was unconstitutional and agreed to under duress. Moreover, the referendum, he warned, would only destabilize Russian politics and even lead to the disintegration of the state. Finally, the referendum would have to be followed by new elections, which would discredit representative institutions. The last argument was a clear message to the deputies: Either they had to stand up to Yeltsin, or they would see their political careers ended through defeat at the polls.[49]

Throughout January, he reiterated this argument on every possible occasion, while behind the scenes he helped collect the signatures of the 321 deputies needed to convene an emergency congress to repeal the December agreement. In February, after the signatures had been gathered, Khasbulatov went to Novosibirsk to drum up support from the leaders of the provincial soviets. At his insistence, they adopted a resolution calling for an emergency congressional session to cancel the referendum. He, in turn, used this resolution back in Moscow to convince still-reluctant deputies that the provinces would back the parliament in its confrontation with Yeltsin.[50]

Rutskoi initially endorsed the December compromise. But by February, seeing that Chernomyrdin was continuing the economic policies of his predecessor and fearing that the referendum would only strengthen Yeltsin, Rutskoi joined Khasbulatov in calling for abandonment of the December agreement. Since cancellation of the referendum meant an inescapable confrontation with the president, Rutskoi was indicating clearly that he would renounce the compromise-oriented Civic Union position in favor of the nationalist-communist approach that advocated a showdown with Yeltsin.[51]

The Eighth Congress in early March 1993 followed the script carefully prepared by Khasbulatov: The December agreement was revoked, and Yeltsin's power to rule was curtailed by a resolution that allowed the Supreme Soviet to repeal his decrees by a simple majority vote. Moreover, in anticipation of an attempt by Yeltsin to dissolve the parliament, the congress passed a constitutional amendment mandating the automatic impeachment of the president if he were to attempt such an act. Khasbulatov calculated that Rutskoi would support him if Yeltsin decided to challenge the parliament. This turned out to be correct: After Yeltsin declared "special rule" on March 20 and set a new referendum date of April 25, Rutskoi refused to cosign Yeltsin's decree and sided with the parliamentary majority, evidently in the hope that Yeltsin would be impeached and power transferred to him.

Khasbulatov also assumed that Civic Union deputies would vote against Yeltsin, as they had at the Seventh and Eighth Congresses. This presumption, however, turned out to be wrong when the issue of impeachment arose. After Khasbulatov convened the Ninth Congress to consider impeachment, he discovered that the Civic Union faction was split on the issue and that he lacked the two-thirds majority needed to force impeachment. Stymied, Khasbulatov negotiated yet another compromise that canceled the referendum in exchange for presidential and parliamentary elections in November 1993. However, this time he badly misjudged the mood of the parliamentary majority. It was so infuriated by the prospect of new elections that it rejected the proposal and passed a motion to vote on impeachment of the president and the removal of the speaker.

Khasbulatov survived the vote to remove him but did not dare resubmit the compromise proposal to the congress. Forced to accept Yeltsin's referendum demand, he nevertheless wanted reassurance that its results could be used to his advantage. This explains his insertion of the second question on the referendum, which asked Russians whether they supported the president's socioeconomic policies. Khasbulatov clearly hoped that a negative response would provide the necessary legitimation for the drastic curtailment of presidential power.

On the eve of the referendum, Rutskoi politically reinvented himself once again. He discarded the image of a centrist leader seeking political compromise in favor of the leadership of the communist-nationalist opposition. As before, his latest political reincarnation was marked by a programmatic publication, this time defending his and the Supreme Soviet's stand in terms of the urgent need to save Russia from economic collapse and curb Yeltsin's attempts to impose "one-man dictatorship reflecting the interests of the newfound millionaires."[52]

As in March 1991, the most important act of political reinvention was a dramatic appearance in the Supreme Soviet. On April 16, speaking as the head of an interdepartmental commission on crime, Rutskoi made sweeping accusations of corruption against past and present leaders of Yeltsin's cabinet. He appeared as a courageous corruption fighter analogous to Yeltsin's 1989–1990 image of a fighter against party privileges. The timing of the announcement was clearly calculated to destroy the credibility of Yeltsin and his government on the eve of the referendum. However, it had far-reaching consequences, because by threatening criminal prosecution of his opponents, Rutskoi linked political survival to freedom from arrest, something not known in Russia since the Stalin era. In retaliation, the government leveled its own corruption charges against Rutskoi.[53]

Rutskoi's confrontational strategy and his unconditional backing of parliament came at a heavy political price. His charges not only failed to persuade Russians to vote against government economic policies and for early presidential elections, as he urged them to do, but also damaged his personal popularity.[54]

More important, his course of action triggered a split within the Civic Union and the disintegration of the political center. This process began at the Ninth Congress of People's Deputies, where more than half of the Civic Union faction voted against Yeltsin's impeachment.[55] It greatly accelerated after the referendum, when Nikolai Travkin resigned from the parliament and pulled his Democratic Party of Russia out of the Civic Union. The split reached the ranks of Rutskoi's own party, as leading members and provincial chapters began demanding disassociation from the politics of their chairman. By mid-summer 1993, Civic Union practically ceased to exist as a major political force; its dismal showing in the December 1993 elections confirmed this.

Yeltsin's victory in the referendum of April 25, 1993, dealt a major blow to Khasbulatov's plans and compelled him to choose between a new pact with Yeltsin or alliance with the communist-nationalist opposition and a continuation of the confrontation. The first option promised to bring Russia a new constitution and multiparty elections but would have rendered Khasbulatov politically irrelevant since he had no political base outside of the existing Supreme Soviet; the second preserved the Supreme Soviet and gave him some hope of besting Yeltsin in the end. He chose the second option, refusing to cooperate with Yeltsin on a new constitution, reiterating his position that it ought to be adopted gradually through amendment of the existing document, and rejecting Yeltsin's efforts to move the elections to the fall of 1993.

Thus, by early summer 1993, Khasbulatov, like Rutskoi, had reinvented himself as a leading member of the communist-nationalist opposition. He and his confederates now portrayed the soviets that they were defending as both traditional Russian representative institutions with roots in the medieval town meetings (*veche*) and Land Assemblies (*Zemskie Sobory*) and as defenders of Russia against attempts by the West to transform it "into a colonial enclave region which performs the role of a mere source of strategic raw materials for the world economy and a dumping ground for [its] obsolete technologies." Moreover, he began denouncing the Minsk accords as an anticonstitutional plot that had destroyed Russia as a great power, and he made pronouncements calling for the reconstitution of the USSR.[56]

Khasbulatov's alliance with the extreme opposition and his determination to continue the confrontation were manifested during the summer 1993 session of the Supreme Soviet, where he sought to shatter two pillars of the government's economic policy: tight budget constraints and voucher privatization. With Khasbulatov's active involvement, the parliament passed a budget with a mammoth 22 trillion ruble deficit and issued a series of resolutions that suspended

voucher privatization and removed most of the powers of the State Property Committee, the agency responsible for the privatization program. At the same time, he prepared a series of constitutional amendments, to be adopted at the forthcoming Congress of People's Deputies, that were designed, among other things, to abrogate the president's right to head the Security Council and to sign international treaties.[57]

The most plausible purpose of this strategy was to provoke Yeltsin into dissolving the parliament. In accordance with the aforementioned constitutional amendment, this action would result in automatic impeachment of the president. Khasbulatov clearly expected to win this confrontation, believing that the armed forces would not side with Yeltsin, and that in any event, he would hesitate to use them against the parliament.

Speaking on September 18, Khasbulatov barely disguised his strategy. He argued that Yeltsin could not continue to be head of state because his judgment was impaired by alcoholism and that he was attempting to impose a "dictatorial, plutocratic regime." He also warned Yeltsin that any attempt to dissolve the parliament would immediately result in his ouster and urged the army to remain loyal to the constitution.[58]

Defeat in the referendum and loss of personal popularity made Rutskoi more determined than ever to bring Yeltsin down. The disintegration of Civic Union and turmoil within his own party eliminated any hesitancy on his part to become a leader of the forces seeking a showdown with the president. He adopted all of Khasbulatov's key positions as well as those of the communist-nationalist opposition. He also launched personal attacks on Yeltsin, which hitherto he had avoided, calling on him to resign for transforming Russia from a superpower into a source of raw materials for the West and for allowing widespread corruption within his government.[59]

By September 1993, Rutskoi's activity had eliminated any possible accommodation with Yeltsin. In a speech given on the eve of Yeltsin's dissolution of the parliament, he explicitly ruled out any compromise and demanded Yeltsin's unconditional surrender.[60]

The roles of Khasbulatov and Rutskoi in the clash of September–October 1993 deserve special attention because they illustrate the crucial importance of the strategic choices made by individual leaders. According to Yeltsin, information about the forthcoming presidential decree dissolving the parliament was leaked to Khasbulatov and Rutskoi in advance.[61] It is clear that both saw it as an opportunity to come to power through a reenactment of the 1991 defense of the White House. They accordingly refused to accept a compromise, negotiated by the chairmen of the two Supreme Soviet chambers with Yeltsin, that proposed simultaneous elections for the parliament and the presidency.

Moreover, Rutskoi, who was declared by the parliament to be Russia's acting president, made a decisive step toward armed confrontation by issuing arms to the most militant elements of the communist-nationalist opposition, including members of the neo-nazi Russian National Unity movement, who came to defend the building. By doing so, Rutskoi and his troops took control of events away from Khasbulatov and the deputies who had chosen to remain with him in the parliament building.

Rutskoi's behavior was of vital importance for the direction the conflict took on October 3. Addressing the militant demonstrators who had swept away the militia cordons surrounding the White House, he exhorted them to storm the Moscow mayor's office and the Ostankino broadcasting center. This appeal effectively transformed a violent demonstration into an armed uprising that included the ransacking of the mayor's building and the vicious battle over the Ostankino television tower.

Rutskoi evidently surmised that the uprising would succeed because the military would either refuse to intervene or would switch its loyalty to him. This expectation was not completely groundless: As Yeltsin described in his memoirs, even after the battle at Ostankino had begun, the army was extremely reluctant to move troops into the city, and it took a great effort to convince the high command to suppress the uprising. Moreover, once the order to attack the parliament building was issued, the elite troops assigned to the task initially refused to obey.[62]

The military's decision to intervene, combined with the failure of the uprising to spread into the provinces, doomed it. Rutskoi was extremely slow to appreciate this outcome. Video footage taken during the assault on the parliamentary tower showed Rutskoi desperately appealing to the army units to come to his aid. He surrendered only after troops penetrated the building and showed no signs of readiness to join his cause.

In sum, the conflict between Yeltsin and his two erstwhile allies escalated largely because of the choices of strategy and allies made by the latter. Cancellation of the December 1992 agreement and the alliance with the hard-line communist-nationalist opposition made the crisis unavoidable.

After October 1993

The failure of the insurrection and the arrest of Khasbulatov and Rutskoi allowed Yeltsin to reshape the Russian constitutional structure that had helped perpetuate the intraelite conflict. The new constitution approved by voters on December 12, 1993, muffled the power struggle between the executive and legislative branches by greatly enhancing the powers of the former at the expense of the latter. Nonetheless, it did not eliminate the other critical sources of intraelite conflict—namely, the course of economic reform and the extent of the territorial boundaries of the Russian state.

The December 1993 parliamentary elections heralded the emergence of a new powerful nationalist leader: Vladimir Zhirinovsky, the head of the hitherto marginal Liberal Democratic Party, who campaigned on a platform of expansion of Russia's borders to those of the former USSR, defense of ethnic Russians in the former Soviet republics, amnesty of participants in the October uprising, and an end to economic reform. Zhirinovsky came in first in the party-preference voting for the new lower house, the State Duma, with almost one-quarter of the vote. The removal of Khasbulatov and Rutskoi from the political scene thus in a sense paved the way for the ascendance of an extremist who promoted essentially the same set of ideas.

In late February 1994, the new Duma voted 252 to 67 to grant amnesty to Khasbulatov, Rutskoi, and all other participants in the October 1993 insurrection. In principle, the comeback road is open to both men. And yet, new political and institutional realities make a successful political comeback very unlikely for Khasbulatov and difficult at best for Rutskoi.

The dissolution of the Congress of People's Deputies took away the locus of Khasbulatov's power. Although his return to parliament after future elections cannot be ruled out, it is improbable that he will ever again exercise much influence. The reason is simple: Contrary to its predecessor, the current legislature is an institution led by the heads of the electoral parties and blocs. Khasbulatov does not belong to any of these parties or blocs and is not likely to join them. His tour of Chechnia shortly after his release from Lefortovo prison suggests that if Khasbulatov harbors ambitions to return to politics, it will be through regional leadership.

Rutskoi left prison with no regrets about the past, and his desire to replace Yeltsin has now acquired an additional justification: to avenge the humiliation of October 1993.[63] His political orientation has not changed, either; he has reiterated his allegiance to the communist-nationalist opposition by calling for Yeltsin's overthrow and the extension of Russia's borders to those of the former USSR.

It is clear from Rutskoi's recent activities that he is preparing himself for the presidential elections scheduled for 1996. In March 1994, he joined other lions of the communist-nationalist opposition in creating an umbrella organization, Accord in the Name of Russia, and in May 1994 he was reelected chairman of his party, now purged of his opponents and renamed the Russian Social Democratic People's Party. Both the coalition and the party are projected as the organizational bases of his forthcoming presidential bid.[64]

However, Rutskoi faces major barriers to the realization of his ambitions. First, the present Duma seeks compromise rather than confrontation with the president and is unlikely to become a springboard for his ambitions, unlike the former Supreme Soviet. Second, his popularity rating is still very low; according to a poll in mid-May 1994, only 5 percent of urban Russians would support his candidacy for the presidency.[65] Third, even though Zhirinovsky campaigned for Rutskoi's release, he is not ready to abandon his own presidential aspirations in order to accommodate Rutskoi. The two will most likely compete for the same electorate, thus splitting the opposition vote. In fact, Zhirinovsky has already provided a glimpse of his future strategy by accusing Rutskoi of having Russian blood on his hands. Rutskoi's role in the October 1993 uprising may become one major political liability among others during any future electoral campaign.

Conclusions

Khasbulatov and Rutskoi were among the principal leaders of the new elite that took power in Russia in the early 1990s. A consensus on two issues—removal of the CPSU from power and the desirability of ruling Russia without interference of the USSR government—kept this group together in an uneasy alliance. This consensus provided sufficient basis for an intraelite alliance that showed its strength by defeating the August 1991 coup attempt.

After these goals were achieved, the winners found themselves deeply divided over the issues of the structure of government, the program of economic reform, and the extent of the borders of the Russian state. These divisions issued in a fast unraveling of the alliance and a fierce intraelite conflict fueled by political ambitions and irreconcilable policy differences.

I have argued here that the conflict and its bloody denouement were a consequence of the peculiar constitutional design that existed in Russia after the fall of communism and of the strategic choices made by Khasbulatov and Rutskoi. The Russian Supreme Soviet turned out to fuel intraelite conflict instead of mediating it. In fact, the desire of most deputies to block neoliberal economic policies, combined with their determination to perpetuate their own power and privilege, induced them to support the power strivings of Khasbulatov and Rutskoi until virtually the very end. With key institutions unable and unwilling to mediate conflict, the political choices of leaders acquired crucial importance. Cancellation of the December 1992 agreement on a referendum, followed by the decision of Khasbulatov and Rutskoi to abandon the political center in favor of a hard line, helped escalate the crisis and move it toward the bloody battle on the streets of Moscow.

Finally, it is important to consider the conflict's long-term effects. One was the rise of Zhirinovsky to fill the political vacuum created by the incarceration of Khasbulatov and Rutskoi. Another was the creation of an overbearing presidency specifically designed to prevent a recurrence of the intraelite conflict Russia experienced in 1992 and 1993. Sad to say, an institution with such sweeping powers might not only be ill-suited to resolve different types of political conflict but might also provide the means whereby a Zhirinovsky or a Rutskoi might in future install a dictatorial regime.

Notes

1. For the concept "regime founding coalition," see Juan J. Linz, *Crisis, Breakdown, and Reequilibration* (Baltimore: Johns Hopkins University Press, 1978).

2. Account of Khasbulatov's early career based on *Politicheskaia Rossiia segodnia: Predstavitel'naia vlast'* (Moscow: Moskovskii rabochii, 1993), pp. 302–304; *Kto est kto v Rossii i v blizhaishem zarubezh'e* (Moscow: Novoe vremia, 1993), pp. 689–690; Alexander Rahr, "The Rise and Fall of Ruslan Khasbulatov," *RFE/RL Research Report,* vol. 2, no. 24 (June 11, 1993), pp. 12–16.

3. See, for example, his writings "Chto vidno v zerkale tseny," *Pravda,* June 15, 1986, p. 2; "Natsional'nyi vopros," *Komsomolskaia pravda,* June 17, 1988, p. 2; and *Biurokratiia—tozhe nash vrag* (Moscow: Politizdat, 1989).

4. Account of early stages of Rutskoi's career based upon *Politicheskaia Rossiia segodnia: Ispolnitel'naia vlast* (Moscow: Moskovskii rabochii, 1993), pp. 302–304; and *Kto est kto,* pp. 559–560.

5. V. Izgarshev, "161 vzlet razreshaiu," *Pravda,* February 14, 1988, p. 6.

6. A. Gorokhov and V. Izgarshev, "Samolet vzorvalsia," *Pravda,* August 18, 1988, p. 6; A. Gorokhov and V. Izgarshev, "Vernulsia domoi," *Pravda,* August 22, 1988, pp. 1, 8.

7. On Otechestvo, see *Rossiia: Partii, assotsiatsii, soiuzy, kluby,* vol. 5 (Moscow: RAU-Press, 1992), pp. 59–64.

8. Yurii Shabanov, "Chetvertoe rozhdenie," *Moskovskaia pravda,* May 11, 1989, p. 3. Account of Rutskoi's electoral campaign based on Ilia Kudriavtsev, "Vybornaia kampaniia polkovnika Rutskogo," in *Vybory-1989* (Moscow: Panorama, 1993), pp. 50–55.

9. *Groznenskii rabochii,* March 12, 1990, p. 3, and March 24, 1990, p. 1.

10. A. V. Rutskoi, "Ne razrushat' a sozidat'!" *Kurskaia pravda,* January 12, 1990, p. 1.

11. A. V. Rutskoi, "Nuzhny energichnye mery," *Kurskaia pravda,* March 17, 1990, p. 3.

12. Ruslan Khasbulatov, *The Struggle for Russia* (London: Routledge, 1993), p. 36.

13. The information on Rutskoi's votes at the Second Congress was kindly provided to me by Regina Smyth of Duke University.

14. A. Rutskoi, "Da spaset nas Rossiia!" *Argumenty i fakty,* no. 4, 1991, p. 2.

15. *Tretii (vneocherednoi) S''ezd narodnykh deputatov RSFSR,* bulletin no. 11 (evening session), pp. 13–14.

16. See, for example, Aleksandr Rutskoi, "Ne nado byt' sobakoi na sene," *Argumenty i fakty,* no. 17, 1991, p. 2; "Vystuplenie na Plenume TsK KP RSFSR A. V. Rutskogo," *Sovetskaia Rossiia,* May 15, 1991, p. 5.

17. Boris Yeltsin, *The Struggle for Russia* (New York: Random House, 1994), p. 31.

18. "Za sozdanie demokraticheskoi partii kommunistov Rossii!" *Rossiiskaia gazeta,* July 18, 1991, pp. 1–2; ibid., August 3, 1991, p. 1.

19. B. N. Yeltsin, I. S. Silaev, R. I. Khasbulatov, "K grazhdanam Rossii," *Kuranty,* August 20, 1991 (spetsvypusk no. 2), p. 1.

20. For a sample of Khasbulatov's writings on these issues, see the following articles: "Praviashchaia oppozitsiia," *Moskovskie novosti,* July 15, 1990, p. 5; "Kakim byt' soiuznomu dogovoru?" *Argumenty i fakty,* no. 28, 1990, p. 2, and no. 30, 1990, p. 4; "RSFSR: Nashe videnie federativnogo dogovora," *Moskovskie novosti,* September 2, 1990, p. 8; "Tsel' soiuznogo dogovora—razval Rossii," *Kuranty,* March 22, 1991, p. 5; "Odin iz professorskoi volny," *Moskovskie novosti,* April 28, 1991, p. 16; "Rossii inogo puti ne dano," *Literaturnaia gazeta,* June 5, 1991, pp. 1, 2; "Pochem funt vlasti," *Ogonek,* no. 28, 1991, pp. 1–3.

21. In the six rounds of voting, Baburin received between 412 and 485 votes, and Khasbulatov received between 342 and 409 votes.

22. Sergei Parkhomenko, "Novyi vitok konfrontatsii mezhdu ispolniteliami i zakonodateliami," *Nezavisimaia gazeta,* January 15, 1992, p. 1.

23. Yeltsin, *The Struggle for Russia,* p. 32; Ol'ga Bychkova, "Polkovnik bez strakha i upreka," *Moskovskie novosti,* June 2, 1991, p. 7.

24. Rutskoi gave his account of the events in several television, radio, and newspaper interviews: FBIS-SOV-91-198, October 11, 1991, pp. 40–43; FBIS-SOV-91-218, November 12, 1991, pp. 44–45; *Komsomolskaia pravda,* November 14, 1991, p. 1. Dudaev's version of his meeting with Rutskoi is in *Argumenty i fakty,* no. 45, 1991, p. 2.

25. A. V. Rutskoi, "Sotsial'no-ekonomicheskoe polozhenie v RSFSR i zadachi partii," *Materialy Pervogo S''ezda DPKR—Narodnoi partii Svobodnaia Rossiia* (Moscow: Narodnaia partiia Svobodnaia Rossiia, 1992), p. 45.

26. See, for example, A. V. Rutskoi, "V Rossii net ni vlasti ni demokratii," *Nezavisimaia gazeta,* December 18, 1991, pp. 1–2, and "Ubezhden v pravote svoikh vzgliadov," *Pravda,* December 27, 1991, pp. 1–2.

27. For Rutskoi's views on the CIS, see FBIS-SOV-91-240, December 13, 1991, pp. 51–52.

28. Adam Przeworski, "The Neo-Liberal Fallacy," *Journal of Democracy,* vol. 3 (July 1992), p. 56.

29. Juan J. Linz, "On the Perils of Presidentialism," *Journal of Democracy,* vol. 1 (January 1990), pp. 53, 57.

30. Matthew S. Shugart, "Of Presidents and Parliaments," *East European Constitutional Review,* vol. 2 (Winter 1993), p. 32.

31. Domenic Gualtieri, "Russia's New War of Laws," *RFE/RL Research Report,* vol. 2, no. 35 (September 3, 1993), pp. 14–15.

32. See *Sbornik zakonodatel'nykh aktov o Prezidente RSFSR, o vyborakh Prezidenta RSFSR* (Moscow: Verkhovnyi Sovet RSFSR, 1991).

33. This was expressed in the overwhelming support for the declaration of the RSFSR's sovereignty at the First Congress of People's Deputies in June 1990, the firm backing of Yeltsin during the coup of August 1991, and the easy ratification of the Minsk accords by the Russian Supreme Soviet in December 1991.

34. The figure of 347 deputies is based upon *Rossiiskii parlament: Spravochnyi material k sedmomu s''ezdu* (Moscow: Press-tsentr Verkhovnogo Soveta Rossii, 1992), p. 3.

35. In fact, the deputies did not want to hold even the scheduled parliamentary elections in spring 1995 and were devising schemes to postpone them. One such scheme proposed the abolition of the Congress of People's Deputies and the transfer of its powers to the Supreme Soviet, which would be reelected in two stages. The first 50 percent of the deputies would be chosen in fall 1994 and the rest only in 1996. FBIS-SOV-93-141, July 26, 1993, p. 25.

36. In June 1993, only 6 percent of Russians named the congress as the political institution they trusted (the lowest positive rating), and 49 percent viewed it as untrustworthy (the highest negative rating). Oleg Savelyev, "Komu v Rossii doveriaiut bol'she," *Kuranty,* June 18, 1993, p. 2.

37. "O khode ekonomicheskoi reformy v Rossiiskoi Federatsii," *Shestoi S''ezd narodnykh deputatov Rossiiskoi Federatsii* (hereafter, *Shestoi S''ezd*) (Moscow: Respublika, 1992), pp. 29–34.

38. "O podderzhke ekonomicheskoi reformy v Rossiiskoi Federatsii," *Shestoi S''ezd,* pp. 35–36.

100   YITZHAK M. BRUDNY

39. In 1992–1993, Khasbulatov's popularity rating stood around 10 to 12 percent. In the same period, however, his negative rating almost doubled. A November 1992 poll found that his positive rating was 10 percent and the negative one was 37 percent; in March 1993, the ratings were 11 percent positive, 60 percent negative. See *Konstitutsionnyi vestnik*, no. 13, 1992, p. 219, and FBIS-SOV-93-071, April 15, 1993, p. 34.

40. *DR-Press*, no. 408 (September 3, 1992), p. 1; no. 413 (September 8, 1992), p. 2.

41. "O zashchite konstitutsionnykh organov vlasti," *Shestoi S''ezd*, pp. 85–86.

42. Sergei Mostovshchikov, "V Moskve deistvuet krupnoe vooruzhennoe formirovanie s neiasnymi polnomochiiami," *Izvestiia*, October 14, 1992, pp. 1–2; Sergei Chugaev, "Volna skandalov zakhlestyvaet Rossiiskii parlament," ibid., October 22, 1992, pp. 1–2; Sergei Mostovshchikov, "Prezident Rossii likvidiruet nezakonnoe vooruzhennoe formirovanie," ibid., October 27, 1992, p. 1.

43. Ruslan Khasbulatov, *Vlast': Razmyshleniia spikera* (Moscow: Tsentr delovoi informatsii, Yezhenedel'nik Ekonomika i zhizn, 1992); "Sovershenstvovanie parlamentarizma—put k demokratii," *Rossiiskaia gazeta*, November 7, 1992, pp. 1, 5; "Novoi diktatury strana ne perezhivet," *Nezavisimaia gazeta*, November 24, 1992, pp. 1, 3.

44. "Vystuplenie vitse-prezidenta A. V. Rutskogo," *Rossiiskaia gazeta*, December 11, 1992, pp. 1, 5.

45. Aleksandr Rutskoi, "V zashchite Rossii," *Pravda*, January 30, 1992, pp. 1, 3; "Yest' li vykhod iz krizisa?" *Pravda*, February 8, 1992, pp. 3–4; "Sil'naia vlast—dlia demokratii," *Nezavisimaia gazeta*, February 13, 1992, p. 5.

46. A poll conducted in July found that Rutskoi was fully trusted by 28 percent of the population, partially trusted by 36 percent, and not trusted by a mere 19 percent; Yeltsin was fully trusted by 24 percent, partially trusted by 33 percent, and not trusted by 32 percent. Leontii Byzov, "Aleksandr Rutskoi vykhodit na pervoe mesto," *Nezavisimaia gazeta*, July 29, 1992, p. 2.

47. For a typical example of Rutskoi's statements from this period, see Aleksandr Rutskoi, "Ia za rasshirenie prav byvshikh avtonomii," *Rossiiskaia gazeta*, October 29, 1992, p. 2.

48. Rutskoi's former press secretary suggested a psychological interpretation of Rutskoi's rejection of Civic Union's policy of compromise. He pointed to Rutskoi's impulsiveness and preference for clear-cut decisions and argued that he never felt comfortable with the role of centrist leader. Nikolai Gulbinskii, "Tsentrizm v Rossii—menshe, chem tsentrizm," *Novoe vremia*, no. 33, 1993, pp. 7–10, and "Vzlet i posadka," *Moskovskie novosti*, November 21, 1993, p. 11A.

49. Ruslan Khasbulatov, "S''ezd narodnykh deputatov i konstitutsionnaia reforma," *Rossiiskaia gazeta*, January 9, 1993, pp. 1, 5, and "S''ezd narodnykh deputatov i refendum," ibid., January 10, 1993, p. 2.

50. *Rossiiskaia gazeta*, ibid., February 20, 1993, pp. 1, 4; Sergei Chugaev, "R. Khasbulatov preduprezhdaet ob opasnosti diktatury demokratov i prezyvaet mestnye sovety vziat pod kontrol' pravokhranitelnye organy," *Izvestiia*, February 23, 1993, pp. 1–2; Ivan Rodin, "Referendum ili zhizn'," *Nezavisimaia gazeta*, February 26, 1993, p. 1.

51. Rutskoi's opposition to the referendum was articulated in essays and interviews. See Aleksandr Rutskoi, "Yest' eshche shans priniat' pravil'noe reshenie," *Rossiiskaia gazeta*, February 9, 1993, p. 1; "Plan Aleksandra Rutskogo," *Nezavisimaia gazeta*, March 3, 1991, p. 1.

52. Aleksandr Rutskoi, "Rossiiane, sdelaite svoi vybor," *Rossiiskaia gazeta,* April 17, 1993, p. 6.

53. See Aleksandr Rutskoi, "Rossiia, skazhi mafii net," *Pravda,* April 17, 1993, pp. 1, 3.

54. In a nationwide exit poll conducted during the referendum, 45 percent of respondents said they would vote for Yeltsin if the presidential election were held the next week; only 13 percent named Rutskoi. Amy Corning, "Russian Referendum: An Analysis of Exit Poll," *RFE/RL Research Report,* vol. 2, no. 19 (May 7, 1993), p. 9.

55. *Rossiiskie vesti,* April 10, 1993, p. 2.

56. His speeches, essays, and interviews from April to June 1993 are reprinted in Ruslan Khasbulatov, *Vybor sud'by* (Moscow: Respublika, 1993), pp. 85–288 (quote from p. 119); and Ruslan Khasbulatov, "Ne shutite s gosudarstvom," *Den,* no. 35, 1993, pp. 1–2.

57. *Nezavisimaia gazeta,* August 11, 1993, p. 2; *Kommersant-Daily,* August 13, 1993, p. 2.

58. Ruslan Khasbulatov, "Tol'ko v usloviiakh demokratii vozmozhny reformy dlia naroda," *Rossiiskaia gazeta,* September 21, 1993, pp. 3–4.

59. See, for example, Aleksandr Rutskoi, "Vitse prezident nastaivaet na svoem," *Nezavisimaia gazeta,* May 8, 1993, pp. 1–2, and "Kakuiu primem Konstitutsiiu, takuiu vyberem sud'bu," *Rossiiskaia gazeta,* May 13, 1993, p. 3.

60. Aleksandr Rutskoi, "Zashchitim Konstitutsiiu—sokhranim Rossiiu," *Rossiiskaia gazeta,* September 18, 1993, p. 5.

61. Yeltsin, *The Struggle for Russia,* p. 250.

62. Ibid., pp. 11–14, 271–280.

63. See Aleksandr Rutskoi, "A zhivym—very i nadezhdy," *Pravda,* April 4, 1994, pp. 1, 4.

64. The movement's initial statement is in "Ob''edinit' patriotov—spasti Rossiiu," *Zavtra,* no. 11, 1994, p. 1.

65. The same poll revealed that Yeltsin enjoyed 14 percent support, Yavlinsky 8 percent, and Zhirinovsky 7 percent. *Segodnia,* May 26, 1994, p. 2.

CHAPTER 5

The Conceptual President: Leonid Kravchuk and the Politics of Surrealism

Alexander J. Motyl

The artistic movement known as surrealism glorified the casual juxtaposition of objects that in real life do not belong together. We know that clocks do not resemble molten wax, but in the paintings of Salvador Dali they do. We also know, *pace* René Magritte, that boulders do not float in thin air, that evening streets do not go together with afternoon skies, and that shoes do not have living toes. Politics, too, can be surreal, if it involves a similar juxtaposition of things that do not go together. Ukrainian independence—like Russian or Lithuanian or Uzbek independence—is just such a surreal political condition. After December 1, 1991, Ukraine unquestionably became independent in the formal sense of the term. But like Magritte's floating boulder, Ukrainian independence involved the juxtaposition of two contradictory notions. Sovereignty, which presupposes a nation and a state, confronted entities that, being as insubstantial as the air on which surrealist boulders rest, barely resembled nations and states. Independence floated on the canvas of Ukraine.

Ukrainian independence was surreal because of the unexpectedness with which that quality of political existence descended upon the territorial-administrative entity called the Ukrainian Soviet Socialist Republic. Mikhail Gorbachev's haphazard collection of reforms known as perestroika destroyed the Soviet system; the August 1991 putsch then destroyed the putschists and Gorbachev. After the dust settled, all the republics suddenly realized that they were free, not because they necessarily wanted to be so but because the collapse of the old order forced them to be free. Unlike many Third World colonies, almost none of the republics could point to a "national liberation struggle" preceding independence. The high point of the Ukrainian "struggle" proved to be a well-orchestrated and utterly unromantic referendum.

A comparison with Russia is worth pursuing. Although Ukraine's northern neighbor experienced far more turmoil—starting with the August 1991 putsch and continuing through Boris Yeltsin's coup d'état of October 1993—it, too, awoke to independence. Yeltsin, in his power struggle with Gorbachev, may have aspired to a looser Soviet Union, but he certainly never hoped for the USSR's collapse and Russia's humiliating loss of empire. Russia's post-Soviet political condition is therefore doubly surreal. Russia was forced to be free, and it has been forced to be free of its colonies. The distance between Russia's supposed independence and posttotalitarian reality on the one hand and between its former imperial grandeur and current pitiable plight on the other thus represents an especially formidable obstacle to its rapid transformation into a "normal" state. Sadly, President Yeltsin has been oblivious to these confining conditions, believing instead that revolutionary determination could suffice to bring about a breakthrough. His bloody conflict with the parliamentary opposition and the subsequent emergence of Vladimir Zhirinovsky as a formidable political force are the price myopic post-Soviet leaders—and their equally myopic Western advisers—must pay for failing to recognize the complex and possibly intractable nature of their political environment.[1]

Compared to the revolutionary élan of Yeltsin, Leonid Kravchuk's presidential style came across as tame, even unimaginative. There was more to Kravchuk than met the eye, however. As the following citation suggests, Kravchuk was aware that moderation also required enormous political will: "It is not accidental that one would refer to a first president as a kamikaze. There is some exaggeration in this comparison, but it does make sense. Hard though it is to adopt an unpopular centrist position in this difficult transitional period, I will not allow the state to be dragged into conflict from the left or from the right."[2] Kravchuk evidently believed that because centrism was the appropriate response to the confining conditions of difficult transitions, it would perforce provoke the opposition of radicals determined to bring about the president's downfall. Seen in this light, Kravchuk's political style appears to have been rather more like Yeltsin's than we might at first have imagined. Where they differed sharply was in the policies they adopted and in their appropriateness, the second criterion being of course central. Although Kravchuk's policies obviously were far less spectacular than Yeltsin's, they were also, I argue in this chapter, willy-nilly far more appropriate to the needs of a post-Soviet republic.

Nation, Elite, and State in Post-Soviet Ukraine

Independence met Ukraine in so unprepared a condition for several reasons. One was that the last time Ukraine had a genuine political class, a state administration, and something resembling a coherent society may have been in the mid-seventeenth century, when the Khmelnytskyi rebellion revived the Cossack elite, generated the Hetmanate state, and galvanized a sense of popular cohesiveness that resembled modern national identity. The elite adopted Russian cultural norms by the mideighteenth century, the Hetmanate became an autonomous province soon after the 1654 treaty at Pereiaslav, and what might have become a nation was transformed by decades of war and harsh colonial rule into a mass of ignorant peasantry.

The revolution of 1917 produced a Ukrainian nationalist movement that failed ignominiously at state building but succeeded in generating a nationalist protoelite and a Ukrainian protonation. Both were then crushed in the 1930s under Stalin. Even so, Soviet rule, for all its vicissitudes, did endow Ukraine with a linguistically coherent population that resembled a nation, a set of political activists who resembled an elite, and an administration that resembled a state. Postmodernist claims notwithstanding, resemblances are obviously not reality—or at least not all of it.

Three-fourths of Ukraine's 52 million inhabitants are identified as "Ukrainian" and about one-fifth as "Russian." Almost 90 percent of registered Ukrainians consider Ukrainian to be their native tongue, and virtually all registered Russians consider Russian to be theirs. Although the statistics suggest that ethnic Ukrainians dominate Ukraine, the reality is far more complex, as most urban residents speak Russian at work, on the streets, and often even at home. The population of Ukraine thus consists of three major groupings—Ukrainian-speaking Ukrainians, Russian-speaking Ukrainians, and Russian-speaking Russians—and a variety of small ones such as Jews, Poles, Ruthenians, Hungarians, Bulgarians, and Belarusans. Although many modern nations are multilingual and multiethnic (and multiconfessional, a characteristic that applies in particular to Ukraine with its primary cleavage into Orthodox and Uniate Christians), it is premature to proclaim all the inhabitants of Ukraine a nation. Even if one overlooks the many divisions within the ethnic Ukrainian population, ethnic Russian loyalties to Ukrainian "nationhood" are tenuous, as may be those of Ruthenians, Jews, and others. It was not, therefore, *the* Ukrainian nation that voted for independence in December 1991 but the inhabitants of Ukraine who may, in time, come to constitute a genuine nation.

Similarly tentative conclusions apply to the Ukrainian elite. Although there are many individuals active in politics in today's Ukraine, only one group, the former Communist apparatchiks, resembles a genuine elite—if that is defined as a more or less coherent and more or less institutionalized set of political activists. The apparatchiks still occupy positions of influence in the center and especially in the localities; they have retained an esprit de corps; they share certain normative inclinations; and they tend to be organized within the revived Communist Party of Ukraine and the weaker Socialist Party of Ukraine. In contrast, the democrats and nationalists are only in the process of acquiring such a corporate identity. Small wonder that the Communists emerged as the strongest party in the parliamentary elections of spring 1994.

The source of the imbalance is obvious. The apparatchiks are heirs to seventy years of unchallenged rule. The oppositionists-turned-policymakers are the products of a totalitarian system within which institutionalized patterns of social and nonstate political behavior never existed and are only now in the process of formation. Ukraine's political parties are a case in point. Although there are scores of self-styled political associations, they are not yet "real" parties with actual ties to social constituencies but are instead debating clubs of intellectuals, writers, would-be leaders, and rabble-rousers. As these parties represent for the most part only themselves, parliamentary deputies are not really deputized by anyone, and the parliament inevitably comes to resemble a debating society as well. Under conditions such as these, politics of the who-gets-what-and-when variety becomes well-nigh impossible because parliamentarians are free to adopt extremist, unyielding, and unrealistic positions at little cost to themselves.

The Ukrainian state may, without excessive exaggeration, also be viewed as a glorified debating club—a characterization that, in comparison to strife-ridden Russia, Georgia, Tajikistan, and Moldova, almost sounds like praise. Although formally designated a state, the political entity that goes by that name in Ukraine is anything but a coherent set of administrative, coercive, and extractive institutions with exclusive control over some territory. The sources of these failings are also found in Soviet times, when republican bureaucracies, like central ones, were shapeless organizations run by Communist Party bosses. After the Communist Party of Ukraine (CPU) was suspended and its apparatus nudged aside, the locus of decisionmaking shifted to a state administration that was not only unprepared but also unstructured, understaffed, inexperienced, and lacking in the elementary tools of administration to deal with the demands of the times.

The turbulent years of perestroika enhanced the profile of the pseudonation, the pseudoelites, and the pseudostate, but only minimally. Had perestroika involved a popular upheaval, had the collapse of the system been the work of mass-driven liberation struggles, nations, elites, and states might have begun to crystallize in the course of the fight, as they to some degree did in the Baltic states or in many Third World revolutionary countries such as Vietnam, Algeria, and Cuba. Protracted struggles compel populations to engage in self-organization for the sake of self-defense; as a result, elites and identities can form, and rudimentary militaries and administrative apparatuses can emerge, too. But in Ukraine, as in most of the other republics, perestroika was something that happened to the system. Restructuring was not an initiative of the people but an imposition on the people.

The starting point of the process was Gorbachev's decision to rein in the secret police, the KGB. Once repression of political dissent was eased, the public expression of critical opinions became possible. For reasons that do not concern us here, glasnost spun out of control, destroying Soviet ideology and the illusion of unity in values. No less important, Gorbachev's assault on the Communist Party bureaucracy, which was the major obstacle to reform and to the consolidation of his power, weakened and ultimately undermined the linchpin of the system, and his economic measures threw the command economy into chaos. Finally, the loosening of the central party's control over its republican branches left the non-Russian Communist elites defenseless against attacks from below, thus forcing them to be responsive to their ethnic constituencies, to adopt increasingly nationalist positions, and to forge partnerships with popular fronts against the center. The CPU's de facto adoption of the Rukh platform was the classic instance of such a fusion of interests.[3]

Independence Comes to Ukraine

Gorbachev's destruction of the Soviet Union served as the backdrop to Ukraine's uncertain move toward independence. Although the Chernobyl disaster contributed to anti-Soviet sentiments, the leading nationalist organization, the Ukrainian Popular Front in Support of Perestroika (Rukh) emerged only three years later, in 1989. Until then, nationalist activity in Ukraine had been small in scale, involving the renewal of some of the dissident organizations crushed in the 1970s, the formation of several others, and the agitation of patriotically minded Ukrainian writers.

The months following Rukh's appearance on the political stage witnessed several events that greatly facilitated the growth of a proindependence movement. Foremost was the removal in late 1989 of Volodymyr Shcherbytskyi, who had personified the ultraloyal colonial administrator since becoming CPU first secretary in 1972.[4] Several months later, in March 1990, elections to the Ukrainian Supreme Soviet resulted in the democratic opposition's winning nearly a third of the seats. Finally, Russia declared sovereignty on June 12, 1990, thereby giving Ukraine the green light to follow suit in July. Not surprisingly, Rukh ended its first year of existence by condemning the Communist Party of the Soviet Union (CPSU) and expressly supporting Ukrainian independence.

The tug-and-pull surrounding Gorbachev's many versions of a new Union Treaty occupied much of 1991. In the referendum of March 17, 1991, 70.2 percent of Ukraine's population came out in support of a proposition concerning an unrealistically idealized union, and 80.2 percent supported "Ukrainian sovereignty." In April, the "nine-plus-one" agreement appeared to herald a compromise acceptable to all: Russia, Ukraine, Belarus, the Central Asian republics, and Azerbaijan agreed with Gorbachev on a significant devolution of authority. One day before the new treaty was to have been signed, however, conservatives staged the abortive coup that, in the eyes of the West, transformed Boris Yeltsin overnight from a maverick Communist into an unimpeachable democrat. Within days virtually all of the republics declared independence and suspended their communist parties. Ukraine's own proclamation was issued August 24; soon thereafter its party took its richly deserved place on what Soviet propagandists liked to call the final destination of capitalism—"the ash heap of history."

Three tense months later, Ukraine's independence was confirmed in the referendum of December 1. Even the nationalists did not expect such an overwhelming vote of support; indeed, many feared that the population might vote against independence. But their fears were unwarranted, as Kravchuk and his comrades in the party machine also supported independence. After several months of "agitation and propaganda," *nezalezhnist* (independence) became the only imaginable option. Over 90 percent of the voters supported the government's initiative; over 60 percent made Kravchuk independent Ukraine's first president.

The Transformation of Kravchuk

Leonid Makarovych Kravchuk's uninspiring biography contains no hint of the dramatic role he was to play in 1991. The son of Ukrainian peasants, Kravchuk was born in the Volhynian village of Velykyi Zhytyn near Rivne, then part of Poland, on January 9, 1934. Volhynia, it may bear noting, was an economically undeveloped region with large numbers of poor and landless peasants; it was also home to two Ukrainian revolutionary movements, the Communist Party of Western Ukraine and the Organization of Ukrainian Nationalists.[5] Kravchuk's wartime experiences may have been traumatic, as Volhynia came under the brutal rule of Erich Koch, a Reichskommissar determined to treat Ukraine as a colony and its population as *Untermenschen*.[6] Leonid's father, who had also served in the Polish armed forces at one time, died on the front as a Red Army soldier in 1944.

After the war, Kravchuk attended the cooperative technical school in Rivne. In 1958 he received an advanced degree in political economy from Kiev State University and studied at the CPSU Academy of Social Sciences in Moscow. After joining the CPU that same year, Kravchuk began his party career as an instructor in political economy at the financial technical school in Chernivtsi (which had been annexed to Soviet Ukraine from Romania in 1940). In 1960 he entered the oblast party apparatus, where he worked in and eventually came to head the ideology department. Kravchuk was promoted to the Central Committee apparatus in Kiev in 1970. He became head of the Department of Agitation and Propaganda in 1980 and was appointed Central Committee secretary in charge of ideology and a candidate member of the Ukrainian party's Politburo in September 1989. He became CPU second secretary on June 23, 1990, and chairman of the Ukrainian Supreme Soviet on July 23.[7]

Kravchuk underwent a breathtaking political metamorphosis in the period 1989–1991: from Volhynia's leading counterpropagandist to Ukraine's leading statesman, from enemy of Ukrainian nationalism to Ukrainian nationalist par excellence. Although Kravchuk's conversion to independence was surely motivated by a healthy dose of political expedience, there is much more to the story than mere opportunism. His rethinking of communism and of Ukraine's position within the USSR appears to have been sincere. Unlike Ukraine's acquisition of independence, Kravchuk's conversion to independence was not a bolt from the blue but the result of several years' realignment.

Things were different before perestroika. In 1984, for instance, Kravchuk loyally hewed to the party line and could, without any evident embarrassment, laud the establishment of "political discotheques," take pride in the fact that more than 135,000 people attended courses on "Developed Socialism: Problems of Theory and Practice," and betray his aesthetic tastes as unabashedly Brezhnevite: "Literature, the cinema, and theater that expose imperialism and accurately depict the bourgeois way of life play an exceptionally important role in political education.

Vitaly Korotich's novel *The Face of Hatred* occupies a special place among literary works of this type. ... It would be good if our writers wrote many more books like this one."[8]

By 1988 Kravchuk had changed, even if he, like the adaptable Korotich (who had since moved to Moscow, where he edited the proreform magazine *Ogoniek*), had done so by marching in step with Gorbachev. In comments reflecting the contradictions in Gorbachev's own thinking, Kravchuk recommended that the party "democratize its own agitation and propaganda" and thereby "raise people's social activity" and help resolve the "tasks facing the country at this critical juncture." Communists should "learn democracy," Kravchuk admonished in a reference to Soviet-style surrealism, and "remove the gap between the social ideal created by our means of mass information and reality." Kravchuk also supported the party's endorsement of the "development of the independence [*nezalezhnist*] of union republics" as part of their "responsibility for the consolidation and development of our multinational state and for the step-by-step perfection of the Soviet federation on the basis of democratic principles."[9]

As different as his sentiments had become, Kravchuk's turgid style shows that he was changing within officially sanctioned parameters. Even his willingness to address the founding congress of Rukh was in line with Gorbachev's opening to political opposition. Kravchuk's conciliatory speech was striking less for its substance—he underlined his opposition to political independence—than for its having been made while Shcherbytskyi was still in power. Kravchuk's presentation may thus have reflected a rift within the CPU between Shcherbytskyi diehards and perestroika supporters. This was seemingly confirmed later in September when a party plenum replaced Shcherbytskyi with Volodymyr Ivashko, the party second secretary responsible for organizational and cadre questions and a relative moderate on policy issues.

The year 1990 was a turning point for Kravchuk. On June 4, Ivashko was also appointed chairman of the Ukrainian Supreme Soviet; later in the month, he stepped down as CPU chief and was replaced by a hard-liner, Stanislav Hurenko. Then in July, at the Twenty-eighth Congress of the CPSU in Moscow, Ivashko abandoned Soviet Ukraine's quasipresidency for a job as Gorbachev's second-in-command in the all-union party. His timing could not have been worse. Rukh was acquiring momentum, the March 1990 elections to the Supreme Soviet gave the democrats an official voice, Lithuania had declared independence, and Russia, whose lead most Ukrainian Communists were used to following, had already proclaimed sovereignty. So obvious a slap in the face as Ivashko's abandonment of Kiev infuriated even the Communist-dominated Ukrainian legislature, which proclaimed Ukraine sovereign on July 16.

After replacing Ivashko as chairman one week later, Kravchuk amazed the world by remaining an unconditional supporter of Ukrainian sovereignty. Whatever the connotations of the concept, it was sufficiently meaningful for him to sign a treaty on November 19 with Russian President Yeltsin, which recognized Ukraine and Russia as sovereign states. That Kravchuk was beginning to think of sovereignty in almost nationalist terms became even clearer in the course of 1991, when he repeatedly insisted that a renewed union give priority to the republics and thus be a confederation in everything but name.

Opportunism does not adequately explain the shift. Kravchuk paid at least lip service to perestroika because, as chief of ideology, he had to follow the Moscow line. By 1989 at the latest, however, he appeared to have become a genuine supporter of Gorbachev's new course. Then, in 1990, he was catapulted to the Ukrainian Supreme Soviet chairmanship, a position that, in combination with Ukraine's evolving real sovereignty, moved Kravchuk toward nationalism. Where Kravchuk was sitting more or less determined where he stood. In this sense, the August 1991 coup may have been an unwelcome disruption of his routine, but it is implausible to argue that Kravchuk could have hoped for its success. If nothing else, that would have meant rolling back all the authority and prestige he had personally accumulated since 1990.

Explaining Kravchuk's Success

Kravchuk's success in appropriating the nationalist agenda was a function of his many years as counterpropaganda strategist and, perhaps, of his Volhynian roots. A master of Soviet ideology—of, dare I say, Soviet "discourse"—Kravchuk was unusually qualified to understand the complexities created by perestroika's devastating impact on the communist way of life. Perestroika had destroyed Soviet language, the system of coherent symbols, concepts, and signs that had given meaning to Soviet reality. At a time of terminological confusion, Kravchuk's expertise in staging communist verbal pyrotechnics guided him through the political maze that had developed since 1987. As one who had spent most of his life constructing that system and in developing ripostes to its critics, Kravchuk was well equipped to cope with the consequences of its collapse and to build a new set of meanings that would be more responsive to postindependence conditions. Kravchuk knew the agenda of nationalism as well as the nationalists, but his nationalist and communist opponents (and for that matter Gorbachev) had only one conceptual map to go by—their own.

It surely matters that Kravchuk was born and raised in northwestern Ukraine, which witnessed a massive anti-German nationalist revolt in 1943–1945 and an anti-Soviet underground that persisted into the late 1940s. Unlike someone from the Sovietized parts of the country, Kravchuk was well aware of the armed struggle led by the Organization of Ukrainian Nationalists and the Ukrainian Insurgent Army and of the "insurgent republics" that served as pockets of sovereignty in the forests of Volhynia; he may well have known their language and arguments and understood their mentality.[10] Unlike Gorbachev, who grew up in the ethnic mosaic of the north Caucasus but never experienced firsthand a nationalist movement with a coherent agenda and mass popularity, Kravchuk must have known that nationalism was a potent force, one capable of leaving its mark even on the Communist Party of Western Ukraine, dissolved by Stalin in 1938.[11]

When independence finally came, Kravchuk was prepared to accept its challenges. As a counterpropagandist, he could understand the arguments and logic of Ukrainian nationalism; as chairman of the Supreme Soviet, he could translate his views into political results. Neither administrative skill nor talent for backroom politicking was the secret to Kravchuk's success. Having spent all his professional life juggling concepts, he could not claim unusual expertise in these fields. Rather, his ability to lead the ideological struggle *against* "Ukrainian bourgeois nationalism" permitted him to lead the struggle *for* it as well. In return, his position as chairman of the Supreme Soviet permitted him to lead it successfully.

But why did a majority of the population believe a former Communist ideologist? Why did such dissidents as Vyacheslav Chornovil and Levko Lukianenko, who had consistently supported independence for most of their adult lives, fare less well in the presidential elections of 1991? The answer to both questions lies in the surreal quality of the nation to which all three were making their appeals. If the *narod* (people) of Ukraine had been a full-fledged Ukrainian *natsiia* (nation), Chornovil and Lukianenko would have been the more attractive candidates by far. But the inhabitants of Ukraine were (and still are) anything but a nation. The conceptual confusion characteristic of post-Soviet society was mirrored by the cultural-linguistic confusion within Ukrainian society.

Just as the chaos without permitted Kravchuk to paint himself as a nationalist, so the chaos within enabled him to appeal to substantial segments of the three groups comprising the *narod*—Ukrainian-speaking Ukrainians, Russian-speaking Ukrainians, and Russian-speaking Russians. The first group could see in Kravchuk a defender of the nation; the second, a champion of moderation; the third, a supporter of continuity. It was not that Kravchuk said different things to different audiences but rather that his knowledge of nationalism, his understanding of the Russifying effects of Soviet nationality policy, and his training as a Communist combined to create a multidimensional political personality that could appeal to, resonate with, and seem familiar to diverse audiences. In contrast, Chornovil and Lukianenko could appeal to one group only—the ethnic Ukrainians, and especially those with a decisively nationalist bent. The electoral results bore out this hypothesis. Kravchuk did more or less uniformly well in much of the country except the most nationalistically inclined western oblasts; Chornovil and Lukianenko did comparatively well only in the west.[12] Most impressive perhaps was Kravchuk's credibility with Ukrainian émigrés, whose almost visceral hatred of all things Soviet turned into a genuine appreciation of his statesmanlike skills in the course of 1991 and 1992. When Kravchuk's critics joked that he could walk between raindrops, they had in mind just this capacity to communicate with different audiences. Not surprisingly, after two and a half years in office, Kravchuk came to be associated with the policies he most vigorously promoted—nation building and state building—thereby losing both the capacity to be all things to all audiences and the presidential elections of mid-1994.

Confining Conditions and Post-Soviet Priorities

Despite the fanfare surrounding the dissolution of the Soviet Union, Kravchuk's office was almost as imaginary as Ukrainian independence. He possessed the title but not the authority, just as he was chief executive of a paper entity and not a bona fide country. The world he entered was one of smoke and mirrors, where reality and appearance had very little to do with each other. To his credit, Kravchuk both managed to survive political surrealism and succeeded in closing much of the gap between appearance and reality. Contrary to Western theory and Yeltsin's practice Kravchuk must have realized that his primary task was not to reform the economy—that, as I argue at greater length later, could not have been done immediately anyway—but, to pursue the artistic metaphor, to develop a "realist" Ukrainian political style, to create conceptual coherence within the political system.

Kravchuk assumed "conceptual power" in a territorial space inhabited by people who were not yet a nation and administered by bureaucrats who did not constitute a state. And he did so with the support or against the wishes of political activists who were only a half-elite. At a minimum, Ukraine could be a meaningful term only if its inhabitants were Ukrainian citizens and its activists were genuine elites. In turn, independence could be a meaningful synonym for sovereignty only if there were a state capable of exercising effective decisionmaking authority. Kravchuk's overriding goal, therefore, had to be to create all three—a nation, a state, and an elite—while enhancing his own authority by filling the presidency with presidential content. His good fortune lay in the mutually supportive relationship between nation building and state building, on the one hand, and authority building on the other. His bad luck lay in the incompatibility between the pursuit of these goals and elite incompleteness.

Wittingly or not, Kravchuk accepted the limits of the possible, the confining conditions of postindependence reality, and pursued first things first. He focused on defining the concepts that underpin independence and on associating them with their supposed referents in the political system. A statement made at a gathering in honor of Ukraine's national poet, Taras Shevchenko, suggests that Kravchuk was at least implicitly aware of the connection between conceptual frameworks and institution building: "We are a people, we are a nation, we are the great family of the people of Ukraine. And, according to the testament of our great bard [Shevchenko], we live in peace and harmony, we live in a new and fraternal family. We acquired the independence of our Ukraine, and we are building our state according to the testament of the great bard."[13] It is almost as if Kravchuk were saying that one's definition of nation—a "great family"—determines whether the institutions of the state will promote "peace and harmony" or not.

Kravchuk was most successful in defining nation and state and least successful in coping with the elite. Nation building may be interpreted as a prolonged exercise in conceptual construction, resting mainly (though far from exclusively) on the development or elaboration of myths, traditions, customs, and meanings. Indeed, a nation exists when a group of people accepts a set of beliefs regarding its past, present, and future.[14] State building resembles nation building inasmuch as it, too, involves assigning conceptual meaning to symbols, signs, and other accoutrements of statehood as well as semantic coherence to otherwise unconnected offices, agencies, and people.[15] In contrast, elites are living *persons*—existing, to be sure, within certain conceptual boundaries but possessing, in the final analysis, all the strengths and weaknesses of individuals. Elites thus are least susceptible to symbolic manipulation; cadres, like administrative competence and technical skills, cannot be "constructed" or "invented."

In a world of self-styled nation-states, nation building and state building necessarily overlap. Because the symbolism that attaches to the one often works just as well for the other, they are mutually supportive processes. The conceptual elements present in both also feed into the process by which new leaders in nascent nation-states can enhance their authority, especially under posttotalitarian conditions. Since, to put the case somewhat starkly, posttotalitarianism is defined by the absence of authoritative institutions—be they nations, states, or presidencies (a fact of which Yeltsin failed to take heed)—the symbolic manipulations involved in building any one "from scratch" can facilitate the construction of the others. Building authority in stable political environments often means dispensing favors and courting elites; building authority in surreal conditions necessitates overcoming surrealism and creating the elements of a more or less stable political environment. The presidents of stable systems have only the elites to worry about; the presidents of nonexistent systems must first construct them before they can even begin worrying about elites.

The daunting problem facing all post-Soviet leaders, however, is that they cannot act as if they were Rousseauian lawgivers confronting no competition and capable of overcoming all opposition. They cannot, for better or for worse, ignore the pseudoelites populating the political system, as there is, after all, no one else to work with. And yet, although leaders must take existing elites into account, they dare not become beholden to them. As representatives (the neocommunists) or products (the nationalists and democrats) of the Soviet past, they are generally of little use in fashioning viable posttotalitarian states, nations, and economies. The neocommunists are experienced enough to resist change; the democrats are too inexperienced to bring it about.

Economic Reform and Sequencing

Economic reform, especially of the kind demanded by supporters of big bangs, shock therapies, great leaps forward, and permanent revolutions, must therefore take a back seat under posttotalitarian conditions. In addition to the imperative of conceptual construction and the obstacle of elite incompleteness, there is another, far more important reason for viewing this proposition as true. The collapse of the Soviet totalitarian state—and of its capacity extensively and intensively to supervise political, social, economic, and cultural life[16]—meant that all the republics lacked the institutions that totalitarianism had never permitted to arise. Markets, civil societies, rule of law, democracies, nations, elites, and states, if all viewed as sets of institutions, as coherent relations, rules, and procedures and not mere agglomerations of people, were missing. Black marketeering, dissent, the Brezhnev constitution, intraelite struggles, Soviet nationality policy, the Communist Party, and the republican bureaucracies may have laid the foundations for markets, civil societies, and the rest, but they were no substitute for them.

Naturally, all post-Soviet republics aspire to create these institutional sets as quickly as possible. As I have argued elsewhere, simultaneity of creation is impossible, as some institutional sets are preconditions of others.[17] For instance, an effective rule-of-law state is the precondition of democracy, which is a regime characteristic of already existing and minimally self-regulating states. Markets, as opposed to marketplaces, may also presuppose states, which act as the political-legal framework within which complex economic interactions take place. And elites, obviously, are indispensable to states, markets, perhaps nations, and certainly to reform efforts. In turn, some sets of institutions, though not preconditions of others, may be facilitating conditions. Thus, nations and markets are logically independent of each other, but it is reasonable to suppose that a strong sense of national identity, as in postcommunist Poland, facilitates marketization by increasing the tolerance level of a population in times of unusual hardship. In sum, it makes sense to suggest that in the historically unique circumstances of posttotalitarian ruin, elites and states *must* precede markets, and nations *should* precede markets. Those post-Soviet leaders, such as Kravchuk, who have recommended go-slow change appear to be at least intuitively aware of the complexities of the reform process and of the necessity of some kind of sequencing. Others, such as Yeltsin, evince the typical revolutionary's inclination for voluntaristic solutions.

The argument for sequencing means not that no economic reforms may be pursued before elites and states are in place—reducing state subsidies, freeing most prices, abolishing restrictive legislation and practices, and privatizing certain branches of the economy are all possible—but that hurried attempts to create full-fledged markets will fail if the initial conditions of marketization are absent. Kravchuk thus sinned by failing vigorously to promote any kind of serious economic reform; Yeltsin erred by permitting *nomenklatura* privatization and organized crime to hijack the protomarket. Still, economic stagnation is preferable to market deformations. The former can be corrected with reform policies—such as those to which Kravchuk's successor, Leonid Kuchma, has committed himself—but the latter may be irreversible.

Building a Nation

In light of the obsession many Ukrainians have with Russia, it was no surprise that Kravchuk quickly identified Russia as "the other" against whom the inhabitants of Ukraine might define themselves as Ukrainian. Kiev's conflict with Moscow over the troops stationed in Ukraine, the Black Sea Fleet, the Crimea, foreign assets, and many other things, though above all a clash of two postimperial sovereignties, provided ideal opportunities for such nation building. In mid-January 1992, for instance, when the dispute over ownership of the Black Sea Fleet first erupted, Kravchuk offered the *narod* a simple syllogism: "There is a Ukrainian state. There is a people of Ukraine. And they must be defended."[18] The twofold premise—state and nation—was anything but obvious, as the former CPU counterpropagandist no doubt knew. In coupling them with an equally nonexistent naval capacity, however, Kravchuk in effect suggested that attaining the third, which seemed more within Kiev's immediate grasp, was tantamount to constructing the first two. However questionable its foundations, there was something to be said for such logic, as a navy could become a symbol of statehood and nationhood and, as such, might rally both about itself.

That Kravchuk was engaged in willful nation-building seems clear from his unusual sensitivity to the danger that "the other" might become not Russia but ethnic Russians. Accordingly, official terminology spoke of the "people of Ukraine," not the "Ukrainian people," as being sovereign in the country. Russia and the "Muscovites" were publicly criticized, but not the Russians and especially not the Russians of Ukraine. Kiev's language policies were also eminently sensible. While attempting to enhance the woeful status of Ukrainian, policymakers prudently accepted the legitimacy and reality of Russian as the language spoken in most of Ukraine's cities, including Kiev, and in much of Ukraine's media.

Second on Kravchuk's list of nation-building measures was his involvement as president in the elaboration of national rites, rituals, and symbols. His speechmaking schedule suggests that Kravchuk purposefully hoped to give his personal imprimatur to virtually every gathering of civic-minded Ukrainians, on the rationale, apparently shared by many political leaders, that authoritatively sanctioned public displays of national solidarity would help create both a national elite and a national mythology. Kravchuk also used the authority of his office to legitimate— as well as to draw succor from—the symbols of nationhood in Ukraine. Among other things, he officially endorsed the Ukrainian Autocephalous Orthodox Church, wholeheartedly adopted the formerly nationalist symbols—the blue and yellow flag, the trident, and the hymn "Shche ne vmerla Ukraina" (Ukraine has not yet died)—and associated himself, especially in photo opportunities, with images of Ukrainian history and everyday rural life.

Finally, Kravchuk successfully portrayed himself as the defender of the "people of Ukraine," the wise and calm patriarch able to heal wounds, unite the people, and provide some sense of purpose. Not surprisingly, he also attempted to transform himself into a symbol, perhaps the central symbol, of Ukraine. A collection of his interviews, speeches, and commentaries, *There Is Such a State—Ukraine,* nicely illustrates the strategy. In the photograph on the front cover he is gazing upward—at the handwritten title and, presumably, into the future. The first of the photographs in the appendix shows Kravchuk proudly holding a *bulava,* the mace that symbolized the authority of the Cossack Hetmans. The back cover shows him grinning amid a group of traditionally costumed Ukrainians while wearing a blue Adidas windbreaker.[19] The statesmanlike man of vision, the proud man of authority, and the modern man of the people—they are all Kravchuk and he is unquestionably Ukrainian.

Paradoxically, Kravchuk's symbolic maneuverings resulted in the presidency's becoming an office with greater legitimacy and authority at the same time as the president lost popularity—coming to enjoy the "absolute mistrust" of almost half the population by early 1994—and, one assumes, authority as well.[20] The paradox melts away upon closer examination. The nation-building strategies pursued by Kravchuk surrounded his office with a mystique, whereas the state-building strategies invested it with some substance. But the price of this achievement was that the conceptual president and his policies came to be judged by higher and different standards. Naturally enough, Kravchuk was held responsible for Ukraine's overall condition, sociopolitical and economic, and he was held responsible not as a former ideology secretary or supreme Soviet chairman but as the Ukrainian president of Ukraine. Consider in this light the results of the presidential elections of mid-1994. In a complete reversal of his performance in 1991, Kravchuk swept the western oblasts and lost resoundingly in the eastern ones, garnering 45.1 percent of the total vote.[21] Evidently, his earlier nationalist detractors, the Ukrainian-speaking Ukrainians, were impressed with the manner in which his presidential qualities promoted their agenda. His earlier supporters, the Russian-speaking Ukrainians and Russians, punished him for betraying their expectations by failing to transform the Ukrainian presidency he successfully constructed into an engine of economic growth.

To be sure, the governmental stalemate of 1992–1994, when the president, a divided parliament, and three prime ministers were incapable of producing a coherent reform package, was not the sole fault of Kravchuk. But because Kravchuk, as president, had to take responsibility for Ukraine's economic plight, his loss to Leonid Kuchma should not, perhaps, have come as a surprise. In the final analysis, Kravchuk's loss was the price he had to pay for ameliorating Ukraine's surreal condition with the conceptual skills at his disposal. He was, in other words, hoisted by his own petard. Seen in this light, Kuchma's victory marked the end of the conceptual presidency and signaled Ukraine's possible entry into the postconceptual stage of reform.

Building a State

Kravchuk's first state-building strategy—some of his critics called it a diversion—was his incessant search for international recognition. Kravchuk's forays into the international arena were intended, on the one hand, to provide Ukraine with a modicum of security from the threatening behavior of its northern neighbor and, on the other, to infuse Ukrainian statehood with some positive content. Symbols of international recognition, like glossy postage stamps, national airlines, and prestige projects, are supposed to suggest that there is more to the state than actually meets the eye. By encouraging international actors to treat Ukraine as a bona fide state, Kravchuk no doubt hoped to facilitate the transformation of Ukraine's bureaucrats into something worthy of the name of *derzhava* or state.

By the same token, Kravchuk consciously played Ukraine's only international trump card—atomic weapons—for all that it was worth. He hemmed and hawed his way toward acquiescing in the withdrawal of tactical weapons, continually reminding whoever cared to listen that Ukrainian statehood might be endangered by too rash a removal. More important, however, were Kravchuk's maneuverings with regard to strategic weapons. Fully cognizant of the fact that only they made Ukraine worthy of attention to Western policymakers, Kravchuk succeeded both in raising Ukraine's international profile and in forcing the West to consider exchanging something tangible for Ukraine's acceptance of the Strategic Arms Reduction Treaty (START I). Kravchuk appears to have understood that START II's being contingent on Ukraine's ratification of START I actually worked in Ukraine's favor. Its threats notwithstanding, Washington could not compel Kiev to sign because it had no credible negative sanctions to impose. Having given Ukraine nothing, Washington could withdraw nothing; having failed to help even the Russians, whom Washington claimed to favor, the United States was in no position to threaten not to supply Ukraine with vast sums of largesse. Kiev had little or nothing to lose by not signing, because, by late 1993, it had nothing and expected to gain nothing from the West. Kravchuk thus maneuvered the United States into the position where it had first to offer something concrete to Ukraine for START II to get off the ground. That something was the Tripartite Agreement of early 1994 among the United States, Russia, and Ukraine, which officially transformed Ukraine from an obstacle to denuclearization into a genuine interlocutor of the United States and Russia—one worthy of membership in the Partnership for Peace and of substantially greater U.S. aid.[22]

Although Kravchuk's international ventures helped alleviate the Ukrainian state's surreal condition, at home, where it mattered most, the state remained woefully incomplete. Two and one-half years of independence brought virtually no improvement in its ability to act as a genuine state—to administer a territory, police it, collect taxes, and maintain the public sphere—in large measure because of Kravchuk's inability to extend state authority into the provinces in general and Crimea in particular. In a conscious imitation of France and Yeltsin's Russia, Kravchuk appointed "presidential representatives" at both province and district levels in 1992. The move made sense in terms of state building and authority building but it could but fail given the lack of competent local administrators, the shapelessness of regional bureaucracies, and his own reliance on apparatchiks. Yeltsin's quandary was, of course, identical—which fact goes to show that their difficulties with imposing central authority on recalcitrant or secessionist oblasts were structural legacies of Soviet rule and not personal dilemmas.

Involving institutions and not just symbols, Kravchuk's creation of a Ukrainian army was his greatest state-building success but only because the army was above all the side effect of his redefinition of the Soviet military presence in Ukraine. Since an immediate withdrawal seemed unlikely in early 1992, and since Ukraine claimed part of the armed forces as its own, Ukrainizing the units—that is, labeling them Ukrainian—proved to be the most logical way of engaging in simultaneous de-Sovietization and state building. Direct lineage with the Soviet army worked to the advantage of the Ukrainian army and Ukraine. Even so, the deployment patterns and force structure mandated by the Treaty on Conventional Forces in Europe, a woefully incomplete armaments production capacity, the sporadic quality of the army's equipment, and the untested loyalties of its mostly Russian or Russified officers mean that its capacity to act as a real Ukrainian army, and not a conceptual surrogate for one, is still unclear.[23]

Finding an Elite

In view of the continued elite status of the apparatchiks and the pseudoelite status of the nationalist democrats, Kravchuk was forced to rely extensively on the former and, at best, to attempt to incorporate elements of the latter into his governing coalition. Kravchuk could not ignore the former Communists, as they represented the only genuine political class in the country. By the same token, he could not embrace the democrats, even if he had wanted to, because there was no one there to be embraced. Kravchuk's three prime ministers—the impotent Vitold Fokin, the reform-minded Leonid Kuchma, and the conservative Yukhym Zviahilskyi—illustrate the limits of presidential authority. Kravchuk could not govern without the support or noninterference of established elites—and that meant, in the first place, the former apparatchiks and "red directors" who prolonged Fokin's political life, disrupted Kuchma's, and propeled Zviahilskyi's—but he also could not govern easily with them. The results were double-edged. Thanks to presidential moderation and elite consensus, the presidency, cabinet of ministers, and parliament became more institutionalized. For the same reasons, however, reform measures were not adopted, and Ukraine continued to stagnate.

Once again, a comparison with Russia is illuminating. Yeltsin's unwillingness to reach a compromise with the former Communists led inexorably to the violent confrontation of October 1993. Their removal from the political scene, however, heralded not the end but the beginning of his troubles. The Russian democrats were anything but a coherent and competent elite able to execute Yeltsin's grandiose schemes. Indeed, the weakening of his opponents and the weakness of the democrats had the contrary effect of promoting political deinstitutionalization, facilitating the emergence of demagogues such as Zhirinovsky and making Yeltsin dependent on the military and the former KGB. Clearly, Yeltsin's elite strategies have had serious costs.

Kravchuk's approach likewise took a toll. The following example illustrates this point as it relates to Kravchuk's policies toward Russia. Although Kravchuk surely contributed to the overall deterioration in Ukraine's relations with Russia, he as a rule went out of his way to accommodate Russian interests. The reasons for Russo-Ukrainian tensions must therefore have lain outside Kravchuk. The inability of many Russian elites to take Ukraine seriously was perhaps one such reason. More to the point for our purposes were the consequences of Kravchuk's approach to post-Soviet politics—a conceptual presidency committed to nation and state building on the basis of a partnership with the pseudoelite. Under such conditions, the elite's opinions perforce mattered and affected policy. A Yeltsinite approach might have resolved this problem but, as noted, at the cost of creating others.

Seen in this light, the difficulties Kravchuk encountered after his negotiations with Yeltsin at Massandra appear quite understandable. Kravchuk's willingness to exchange Ukraine's share of the Black Sea Fleet for its debt to Russia (the exact details of the stillborn deal in Massandra in September 1993 need not concern us) was a masterstroke. Kravchuk had first been able to convince Yeltsin to part in principle with half of the fleet in summer 1992; then, although Ukraine's possession of the antiquated fleet was theoretical only, Kravchuk was again able to persuade Yeltsin that it made sense for Russia to take back what in reality was its and to forgive all or part of Ukraine's debt in exchange. This was clearly an instance of Ukraine's getting something, indeed quite a lot, for nothing. And yet the Ukrainian elite, and especially the democrats and nationalists, responded to Kravchuk's coup with howls of protest, threatening to impeach him for treason and rejecting the Massandra agreement in toto. The savage irony was, of course, that Massandra so neatly highlighted the surrealism of independent Ukraine. Kravchuk had bargained away the nonexistent navy of a nonexistent state, but the nonexistent elite claimed that this maneuver was a slap in the face of the nonexistent nation whose honor had been violated by a scheming president!

Not surprisingly, Kravchuk attempted to alleviate elite incompleteness by directing his attention to that part of the elite under his jurisdiction if not his control—the state apparatus. Retraining existing bureaucrats, although a lengthy process, was begun, and the training of competent civil servants became the expressed goal of three Kiev-based educational institutions officially supported by Kravchuk. Removing incompetents was more difficult, as Kravchuk's dependence on the apparatchiks meant that there were limits to what he could do about depriving them of positions of authority.

Problems did not dissolve with Kravchuk's election loss. Corruption in particular will remain an intractable problem as long as bureaucrats control scarce resources, and attracting talented individuals to public service will be difficult as long as so little prestige is attached to the state and so much money can be made outside of it. Despite his anticorruption rhetoric, President Kuchma is unlikely to be more successful than Kravchuk or Yeltsin in uprooting what is a systemic problem and not a policy failing.

The Future of Ukraine

Ukraine became less surreal after several years of Kravchuk, but its movement toward greater realism, as in a painting by Goya, also highlighted the desperate straits of a country struggling to overcome the legacies of posttotalitarian rule and to construct, more or less simultaneously, a nation, an elite, a state, and an effective economy. The task is far from finished. The difficulties facing Ukraine are and will remain enormous. After two years of Kravchuk's nation- and state-building efforts, however, Kuchma's reform program may actually succeed in transforming Ukraine's economy without unduly disrupting the society and state.

There are, as I have argued in this chapter, no quick fixes to Ukraine's—or Russia's—mountainous problems. If this proposition is true, then good statecraft must be defined as doing what is possible and not attempting to do what is impossible, at least in given circumstances. If sequencing is necessary and simultaneity of reform is the surest road to disaster, then conceptual presidencies of the kind that Leonid Makarovych Kravchuk exercised—however mediocre they may seem to observers impatient for change—may be the best that post-Soviet states can hope for in the immediate aftermath of independence. Laying the symbolic foundations for nations and states and building the foundations of presidential authority are ways, even if unspectacular ones, of establishing nations and states and, hence, of permitting genuine markets to take root. President Kuchma is, as a result, in an excellent position to do what President Kravchuk wisely refrained from doing—to move Ukraine vigorously toward a market economy. Seen in this light, Kravchuk's greatest achievement may be that he made Kuchma possible.

Notes

I thank the editors and Mark von Hagen for their comments on earlier drafts of this chapter, which was first presented at Harvard University on February 24, 1993. Several sections have been drawn, in substantially rewritten and updated form, from my *Dilemmas of Independence: Ukraine After Totalitarianism* (New York: Council on Foreign Relations, 1993).

1. For a detailed argument on the complexities of postcommunist change, see Alexander J. Motyl, "Reform, Transition, or Revolution: The Limits to Change in the Postcommunist States," *Contention,* vol. 4, no. 1 (Fall 1994), pp. 141–160.

2. FBIS-SOV-92-169, August 31, 1992, p. 33.

3. I discuss Gorbachev's impact on the Soviet system in *Sovietology, Rationality, Nationality: Coming to Grips with Nationalism in the USSR* (New York: Columbia University Press, 1990).

4. For a revisionist view of Shcherbytskyi, see Vitalii Vrublevskii, *Vladimir Shcherbitskii: Pravda i vymysly* (Kiev: Dovira, 1993).

5. Alexander J. Motyl, "The Rural Origins of the Communist and Nationalist Movements in Wolyn *Województwo,* 1921–1939," *Slavic Review,* vol. 37, no. 3 (September 1978), pp. 412–420.

6. On Nazi policies in Eastern Europe, see Alexander Dallin, *German Rule in Russia, 1941–1945* (London: Macmillan, 1957).

7. These biographical details were taken from my forthcoming biographic article about Kravchuk in *Collier's Encyclopedia.*

8. *Focus on Ukraine,* vol. 1, no. 1 (February 1985), p. 30.

9. L. M. Kravchuk, "Ateisticheskaia rabota v novykh usloviiakh," *Pod znamenem leninzma,* no. 6 (March 1988), p. 14; "Zmitsniuiuchy demokratychni zasady," *Komunist Ukrainy,* no. 4 (April 1988), p. 38; "Deiaki metodolohichni aspekty vykhovannia v umovakh perebudovy," *Ukrainskyi istorychnyi zhurnal,* no. 12 (December 1988), pp. 10, 14, 16.

10. Interview with Kravchuk, January 17, 1995. On the Ukrainian nationalist movement, see John Armstrong, *Ukrainian Nationalism,* 2d ed. (Littleton, Colo.: Ukrainian Academic Press, 1980).

11. On Gorbachev's views of the national question, see my "The Sobering of Gorbachev," in Seweryn Bialer, ed., *Politics, Society, and Nationality Inside Gorbachev's Russia* (Boulder, Colo.: Westview, 1989).

12. A statistical breakdown of the vote is in *The Ukrainian Weekly,* December 9, 1991, p. 5.

13. Leonid Kravchuk, *Ie taka derzhava—Ukraina* (Kiev: Hlobus, 1992), p. 189.

14. For a critical analysis of the constructivist literature, see my "Inventing Invention: The Limits of National Identity Formation," unpublished manuscript.

15. The quintessential symbolic state is, of course, that discussed by Clifford Geertz in *Negara: The Theatre State in Nineteenth-Century Bali* (Princeton: Princeton University Press, 1980).

16. I discuss the totalitarian state in "The End of Sovietology: From Soviet Studies to Post-Soviet Studies," in Alexander J. Motyl, ed., *The Post-Soviet Nations* (New York: Columbia University Press, 1992), pp. 302–316.

17. See Alexander J. Motyl, *Dilemmas of Independence: Ukraine After Totalitarianism* (New York: Council on Foreign Relations, 1993), pp. 51–70.

18. Ukrainian television broadcast of January 9, 1992.

19. *Ie taka derzhava—Ukraina.* The photograph of Kravchuk with the *bulava* is on p. 225.

20. *Ukrainian Weekly,* March 20, 1994, p. 3.

21. Dominique Arel and Andrew Wilson, "Ukraine Under Kuchma: Back to 'Eurasia'?" *RFE/RL Research Report,* vol. 3, no. 32, August 19, 1994, p. 10.

22. See Taras Kuzio, *Ukraine: The Unfinished Revolution* (London: Institute for European Defence and Strategic Studies, 1992); Stephen J. Blank, *Russia, Ukraine, and European Security* (Carlisle Barracks, Pa: U.S. Army War College, 1993).

23. On the Ukrainian military, see John Jaworsky, *The Military-Strategic Significance of Recent Developments in Ukraine* (Ottawa: Department of National Defence, 1993).

CHAPTER 6

Post-Soviet Political Leadership in Lithuania

Alfred Erich Senn

Since 1988 the political pendulum in Lithuania has swung from one extreme to the other and then back again. In 1988 and 1989, after almost a half century of running Lithuania as a satrapy of Moscow, the Lithuanian Communist Party (LCP), seeing its control of Lithuania slipping away, broke with Moscow and sought a new constituency in a multiparty system. In March 1990 the anti-Communist forces, having taken the leadership of the national movement, Sajudis (Lithuanian Movement for Perestroika), took power through parliamentary elections, and the newly independent LCP went into the opposition. In fall 1992 the Lithuanian Democratic Labor Party (LDLP), the successor of the LCP, regained control of the parliament, becoming the first Communist or former Communist Party in the former Soviet Union to regain power through parliamentary means after first losing it.

The new political leadership of Lithuania arose from three wellsprings: the LCP, the nonparty intelligentsia, and forces that had remained aloof from and even opposed to the Soviet system. It also reflected a fundamental clash of political outlooks: Was there anything to be saved from the Soviet order? One current of thought said yes and wanted to reform the existing structure; the contrary current called the Soviet order an occupation regime and demanded the construction of a new order based on a healthy national consciousness. The resulting disputes made the development of stable political institutions very difficult. Much of the story is common to post-Soviet Eastern Europe; some of it is uniquely Lithuanian.

The Apostasy of the Lithuanian Communist Party

The Lithuanian Communist Party's challenge to Moscow in 1988 and 1989 constituted a natural development in the history of the party in Lithuania. Begun as a tool for Moscow, the party sought to sink roots in the republic, and as an unexpected result, it began to absorb unorthodox and even heretical thoughts. The leadership could keep this out of sight so long as Moscow propped it up, but in 1988, when Moscow relaxed its grip, the party leadership in Lithuania succumbed to new forces within its own ranks.

The LCP first took power in 1940 and 1941 when the Soviet Union annexed the republic, and after World War II it returned as Moscow's administrative tool. Lest the LCP leaders not understand their function, Moscow sent specialists to guide them. In 1940 V. G. Dekanozov, whom Joseph Stalin's successors purged in 1953, steered the republic into the USSR, and in the immediate postwar years Mikhail Suslov, later the ideological specialist of the Politburo, supervised the party's work.[1]

Over the years the first secretary of the LCP was always an ethnic Lithuanian: Antanas Sniečkus, 1940–1974; Petras Griškevičius, 1974–1987; Ringaudas Songaila, 1987–1988; and Algirdas Brazauskas, 1988–1990. Sniečkus was at times something of a maverick, but he served Soviet leaders from Stalin to Brezhnev; Griškevičius and Songaila made no trouble for the central authorities; Brazauskas eventually led the party and Lithuania into the new age.

Moscow watched the Lithuanians up close and also from afar. As its eye in Lithuania, the Central Committee of the Communist Party of the Soviet Union would designate the second secretary of the LCP, responsible to Moscow and removable only by Moscow; in 1988 Nikolai Mitkin held this position. The CPSU's Party Organizational Department maintained its own apparatus, reporting to the Central Committee secretary for personnel matters (Georgii Razumovskii in the middle and late 1980s). Razumovskii's aide, V. Babichev, supervised the Baltic area from Belorussia to Leningrad; Babichev's assistant, Yevgenii Trofimov, supervised Lithuania; another specialist, Nikolai Leonov, had the job "to know everything about Lithuania."[2]

When Soviet forces arrived after World War II, most ethnic Lithuanians refused to collaborate with this occupation regime, and armed resistance continued into the early 1950s. The makeup of the LCP in those years testified to the opposition of the Lithuanians: On January 1, 1945, the LCP claimed 3,536 members, of whom 1,127 were Lithuanians and 1,901 Russians; in 1946, of 8,060 members, 1,962 were Lithuanians and 4,537 Russians; and in 1949 the party had 5,056 Lithuanian members and 13,851 Russian members. (Brazauskas has spoken of the party in those days as being made up of *chinovniki,* petty officials, from Moscow.) Only in 1954, after Stalin's death, did the Lithuanians outnumber the Russians in the party, 14,250 to 13,983. It was several more years before they constituted the majority of party members.[3]

The LCP nevertheless maintained a disproportionately high ratio of Russians in its membership and a low ratio of Lithuanians. On January 1, 1990, the LCP numbered 197,673 members plus another 2,244 candidate members. Of these, 34,726 were Russians and 140,533 were Lithuanians. The proportion of Russians in the party was almost twice their proportion of the population (9 percent), and the proportion of the Lithuanians was 12 or 13 percent below their proportion of the population (80 percent).[4]

Eventually, however, the influx of Lithuanians affected the party's work. The changes began in the Khrushchev period, and by the 1960s, as a new generation passed through higher education and chose careers, more Lithuanians were joining the party. As Aleksandras Shtromas (Štromas) put it in 1977: "Ending active resistance to the occupiers, the nation followed a feeling of its own purely political realism, which dictated that it was imperative somehow to make peace with the conditions of occupation so that the nation would be able to remain a living nation organism until better times, especially since those better times could not be realized just by our own efforts." An émigré leader, Vaclovas Alksninis, even dared to suggest that a person could be a party member and still be an honest person.[5]

Not all Lithuanians approved of the compromises implicit in the act of joining the party. In response to Shtromas's argument, the poet Tomas Venclova asserted, "One could work within the system under three conditions: (1) that this be done carefully, (2) that it be done sensibly, and (3) that it be done without surrendering to demoralization." A decade later he argued that any cooperation with the regime was immoral.[6] It came down to a question of what compromises an individual could make while still maintaining his or her integrity.

The heterodox elements in the party grew rapidly. As V. Stanley Vardys noted, "Membership was now considered a ladder for personal career advancement which could also help to protect Lithuanian interests." Shtromas characterized 10 percent of party members as destructive to the national interests of the Lithuanians and the other 90 percent "conservationists." According to Vytautas Skuodis, half of the members of the LCP had joined because "they thought they could be more useful to Lithuania and to the Lithuanian people"; another 40 percent were "materialists" seeking the benefits of party membership; 5 percent sought power and privilege; this left only 5 percent as "internationalist" true believers. Although these analyses lacked objective data, they pointed to a clear lack of ideological conviction within the party.[7]

In his election campaign in 1992, Brazauskas was to put special emphasis on this unorthodoxy, insisting that the LCP had constituted "in essence a still, quiet resistance, struggling to do what it could for Lithuania." He estimated the "fanatics" in the party at no more than "some 5 percent," and he argued that the party constituted an imposed part of life in Lithuania.[8] Brazauskas of course had a vested interest in claiming that the Lithuanian Communist Party had protected the interests of the Lithuanian nation.

Critics scorn efforts to cast the party in a heroic or martyr's mold. Whatever the inner reservations that party leaders held, when Moscow insisted, they publicly jumped—at least until the autumn of 1988.[9] From the outside, Moscow's policies appeared successful. Many Western Sovietologists considered the nationality question in Lithuania and elsewhere in the Soviet Union to have been "resolved."

When party discipline crumbled in 1988, the unorthodox, heretical, and even apostate elements in the party provided leadership for the reform movement. In June they made up almost half of the Sajudis Initiative Group; in October they contributed greatly to Brazauskas's election as LCP first secretary. In 1989 these elements fueled the drive to establish the party's institutional independence of

Moscow, and in December 1989, after the restructuring of the LCP, they moved into its Central Committee and the Bureau of the Central Committee, where they supported the idea of Lithuanian independence. The fact that many of them subsequently resigned from the party points up their ideological indifference.

Splitting the Communist Party

The political turmoil in 1988 left the party leaders most obedient to Moscow the most confused. When Gorbachev began to tinker with the system, the LCP's leadership felt abandoned. As one reformer put it, "Then, in the winter of 1987–1988, the authorities of the republic were paralyzed with fear and uncertainty, but we could not believe this, and until the end of spring we fought among ourselves."[10]

The key developments of 1988 that determined the LCP's fate were (1) Mikhail Gorbachev's extension of his struggle for control of the CPSU into the provinces, (2) the formation of the Lithuanian Movement for Perestroika, better known as Sajudis, and (3) the endorsement of Sajudis as a democratic reform movement by Aleksandr Yakovlev, Gorbachev's lieutenant for ideological affairs.[11]

After Yakovlev had given Sajudis his blessing during his visit to Lithuania in August 1988, reform elements in the party ousted Songaila and elected Brazauskas. To say, however, as Hedrick Smith did, that Brazauskas was "installed by Gorbachev" is to misrepresent the situation.[12] Brazauskas insisted in a 1993 interview that he traveled to Moscow October 19–20, 1988, not to seek approval but only "to become acquainted": Gorbachev "did not know me"; there was "no decision" to be made.[13] Brazauskas was the LCP's own candidate for first secretary, and at the same time the LCP replaced Mitkin as second secretary with Vladimir Beriozovas, a Lithuanian Russian. Brazauskas's accession to power represented Lithuania's first formal step into the post-Soviet era.

During the winter of 1988–1989, Brazauskas set his course cautiously—in his words, "step by step." He insisted that he was under no pressure from Moscow: "The fundamental pressure came after, in June [1989], [the LCP had] taken the decision to call an extraordinary party congress."[14] He nevertheless challenged Moscow by issuing policy statements without first clearing them with Moscow, endorsing a new draft constitution for Lithuania, and, after the LCP's disastrous showing in the elections to the USSR Congress of People's Deputies in March and April 1989, opting for positions more responsive to the demands of his Lithuanian constituents. Over Moscow's protests, he directed the LCP's reformation, and as a result, in December 1989 and January 1990, after it had formally broken with the CPSU, the LCP enjoyed a genuine, albeit short-lived, popularity unprecedented in its history.[15]

Although Gorbachev reacted slowly, other Moscow agencies responded immediately to the events in Lithuania. According to Vadim Bakatin, Gorbachev's last chief of the KGB, the KGB fostered the formation of "international fronts" as points of support in the Baltic states.[16] Gorbachev eventually yielded to the conservatives in Moscow and abandoned Brazauskas, choosing instead to deal with a splinter group, which refused to follow Brazauskas's lead and called itself the LCP on the Program of the CPSU (LCP/CPSU).

Moscow thought that its LCP/CPSU loyalties constituted a significant force in Lithuania. In summer 1990 Gorbachev rewarded its leader, Mykolas Buro-kevičius, with a position in the restructured CPSU Politburo. The party's second secretary, Vladyslav Shved, a Russian who spoke Lithuanian, was considered by many to be the real leader of the group, and Juozas Jermalavičius, like Burokevičius a professor of "scientific Marxism," became the major spokesman of the group. To give the group some muscle, Moscow transferred a Lithuanian general, Algimantes Naudžiunas, from the space center in Baikonur to Vilnius, where he became a Central Committee secretary.[17]

The LCP/CPSU actually had little future in Lithuania and was even dangerous for Gorbachev himself. Although its leadership was ostensibly Lithuanian, the majority of the party's Central Committee probably were officers associated with the Soviet troops in the Baltic areas.[18] The party's leadership, moreover, tended to criticize Gorbachev as too lenient and hesitant toward the Lithuanians. Buro-kevičius, who as late as 1972 had praised Stalin's *Short Course* in the history of the CPSU,[19] is said to have voted frequently against Gorbachev in the CPSU Polit-buro in 1990 and 1991.

The LCP leadership of the late 1980s would have little to do with the LCP/CPSU. Songaila, the former first secretary, reportedly joined the independent LCP. In January 1991, when Soviet troops ravaged Vilnius, Vytautas Sakalauskas, the former prime minister of Soviet Lithuania, refused KGB chief Vladimir Kriuchkov's invitation to head a new government. According to rumor, in spring 1991 pro-Gorbachev forces were planning a coup within the LCP/CPSU so as to bring it into the post-Stalin era.[20] In any case, the Burokevičius-Jermalavičius group epitomized the bankruptcy of Gorbachev's policies in Lithuania.

The Rise of Sajudis

The growing force in Lithuanian politics in 1988 and 1989 was Sajudis. Sajudis arose from the intelligentsia, and its Initiative Group, formed in June 3, 1988, brought together at least three major groupings of intellectuals: Representatives of the Lithuanian Academy of Sciences gave the group political clout in dealing with the LCP; members of the creative unions, well-known artists and writers, gave it public visibility; and the younger members were ready to take risks that the more established figures shied away from. In addition, almost half of the Initiative Group were members of the Communist Party, unorthodox elements as described previously, not party bosses but nevertheless able to provide access to the powerful.

The Initiative Group at first had no single leader; instead, a different member chaired every meeting. Nevertheless, it needed a secretary, a treasurer, and an editor for its newsletter. The treasurer, Julius Juzeliunas, and the editor, Arvydas Juozaitis, became well known, but they built no personal power bases. The secretariat, on the other hand, became a significant mechanism for political power in the hands of Virgilijus Čepaitis, a professional translator.

Vytautas Landsbergis, a musicologist, emerged as the group's leader in autumn 1988 when Sajudis became more directly involved in politics. In the early meetings of the Sajudis Initiative Group, he distinguished himself by his knack for words; the others frequently turned to him to formulate a position for them. At the Sajudis constituent congress in October, he and Romualdas Ozolas, a philosopher, directed the business meeting that considered the group's resolutions on current questions, and in November 1988 when Sajudis began to organize political protests, Landsbergis became a special target for Moscow's wrath.

Landsbergis rode a wave of growing radicalism. The Sajudis Initiative Group was made up of Vilnius intellectuals who were in fact part of the Soviet establishment, and it at first maintained a certain distance from the radicals, or "extremists" as they were called in the summer of 1988. It opened its doors to the radicals, however, when it declared that it would remain a "movement" and be open to anyone who joined a support group. The radicals joined and demanded that Sajudis be more aggressive. The Sajudis Seimas, elected by the constituent congress, became the forum in which the radicals' voices rang the loudest, and this group, which represented openly anti-Soviet elements in the society, elected Landsbergis its chairman, in effect the leader of Sajudis.[21]

The vanguard of the new forces in Lithuanian politics came from three major sources: dissidents, the underground, and former political prisoners. The dissidents, those who before 1988 had publicly raised their voices against Soviet rule, were few in number: One had to sacrifice a great deal to challenge the Soviet system, and few were ready to pay the price. The open opposition to the regime before 1988 focused on support for the Catholic Church; even individuals indifferent to religious beliefs supported the church in the conviction that religious rights constituted an integral part of general human and political rights.[22] In 1988 the Lithuanian Freedom League (LFL) emerged as the leading group of dissidents.

The underground, which was secretly producing and distributing publications like *The Chronicle of the Catholic Church,* was more numerous than the dissidents. Participants—workers, students, and even university professors—were risking their futures; they faced the loss of position and privilege if exposed. Like the dissidents, they supported the church as a fundamental national institution. Once an underground worker felt he or she had been uncovered, the person might become a public dissident in that brief period before arrest in the hope of warning off others.

The former prisoners, deportees and exiles of the 1940s and 1950s and even their children born in Siberia, had for the most part remained sullenly silent since their return. They lived as second-class citizens with limited rights, but in 1988, unleashed by glasnost, they rediscovered their voices.[23] The public granted them considerable moral authority in recognition of their suffering, and they became a significant force on the new political stage.

Radical opponents of Soviet rule also emerged from other sources—ranging from individuals who had remained aloof from public life in the past to individuals who had in various ways "collaborated" with the Soviet regime. Many prominent radical leaders in Sajudis in 1990 and 1991 had party or at least Komsomol links in their backgrounds, but a "patriotic" attitude could go far in "rehabilitating" an individual who had a record of having "collaborated."

The radicals pressed for stronger statements and action in favor of Lithuanian independence, and they denounced the Soviet order as an occupation. They rejected Soviet political institutions as illegitimate; Antanas Terleckas, the head of the LFL, refused even to participate in the electoral process of 1989 and 1990. Sajudis nevertheless engaged itself in the Soviet political system from which it had arisen.

Forming a Political Spectrum

The new and old political outlooks, Sajudis and the LCP, began to interact institutionally at the beginning of 1989. In January several Sajudis representatives won seats in by-elections for the Lithuanian Supreme Soviet. In the elections to the USSR Congress of People's Deputies in March and April 1989, Sajudis sponsored candidates for every available seat, but then, fearing Moscow's still heavy hand, its leaders decided not to oppose Brazauskas or Beriozovas. In the two rounds of voting, the Sajudis grassroots machine overwhelmed the party, eventually winning 37 of the 42 available seats.

When the Lithuanian deputies traveled to Moscow, they put forth a united front, LCP and Sajudis together, demanding political sovereignty for their republic, republican economic self-sufficiency, and an official investigation of the provisions of the Molotov-Ribbentrop pact of 1939 whereby the Germans had recognized the Baltic as part of the Soviet sphere of influence. The deputies arrived in Moscow as an isolated provincial delegation, but there they won worldwide publicity. This strengthened their resolve in the confrontation with Gorbachev, not to mention Gorbachev's frustration in dealing with them.

In a way the Lithuanians typified the problems inherent in Gorbachev's efforts to use the USSR Congress of People's Deputies. They took advantage of his every reform, thereby forcing him to retreat. He had provided for elections with multiple candidates, and the Lithuanians were among the first to implement the reform. Gorbachev, however, was not ready to give up the party's role in directing Soviet society. Angered by the results in Lithuania, the Soviet leader eventually tried to reverse the process, and he thereby contributed heavily to his own political demise.

The development of the multiparty system cost Gorbachev control of the Lithuanian Communist Party. Brazauskas drew the obvious conclusions from the elections of March and April, and in an effort to win popular support he drew closer to the Sajudis line. (As he described it to me, he had to work with a more radical constituency than Gorbachev did.) In June the LCP leadership decided to convene an extraordinary party congress to consider reorganizing as a Lithuanian political party independent of Moscow. CPSU leaders denounced the thought and dropped Brazauskas from the distribution list for major party documents,[24] but they could not remove him from office.

By the fall of 1989, as Moscow's role in Lithuanian politics waned, Lithuania had embarked on a domestic struggle for power. Brazauskas's supporters put forth the idea of a formal, strong presidency; Sajudis leaders, wary of Brazauskas's personal popularity and ever distrustful of the party, strongly opposed the establishment of a presidency. The radical wing of Sajudis professed not to believe that Brazauskas had any dispute with Moscow at all.

When the Twentieth Congress of the LCP announced its break with the CPSU in December 1989, it elected a new Central Committee and a new Bureau. Over half of the Central Committee were said to be of "Sajudis orientation," and the party bureau included four former members of the Sajudis Initiative Group. The question "Is the party 'sajudicizing' or is Sajudis 'partifying'?"[25] disturbed Sajudis leaders and Moscow alike.

Sajudis leaders who did not belong to the party put their colleagues in the new party hierarchy on notice: Sajudis would support the LCP's move toward independence, but it would oppose the party in Lithuania's domestic affairs. The members of Sajudis in the party hierarchy would have to choose sides. When Gorbachev visited Lithuania in January 1990, Sajudis ostentatiously greeted him as the political leader of a foreign state, not as the leader of the CPSU. This angered Gorbachev and caused some embarrassment for Brazauskas, but the leaders of Sajudis welcomed both these results.

In February 1990 the Central Committee of the CPSU formally recognized Burokevičius's "nighttime" party as the Communist Party of Lithuania, and Brazauskas, who in January had taken the post of chairman of the Supreme Soviet, lost the major source of his power and prestige—namely, the creative tension of the Moscow-Vilnius axis. After March 1990 he found himself in the opposition on the left side of the new Lithuanian political stage. Brazauskas personally remained a popular political figure, but his independent LCP/LDLP—the party changed its name in December 1990—drifted rather aimlessly for quite a while, compromised by its past.

In the elections of February and March 1990, Sajudis claimed 94 to 98 of the 141 seats in the Lithuanian Supreme Council (Supreme Soviet),[26] and the Sajudis deputies proclaimed the reestablishment of Lithuanian independence. They did not claim to secede from the Soviet Union; they announced that the Soviet Union had illegally occupied Lithuania in 1940 and that they were restoring the Lithuanian state as it had existed at that time. By this act, Sajudis leaders denounced the institutions of the Soviet order in Lithuania and of course all the people that had served in them, especially in the Lithuanian Communist Party.

Landsbergis became chairman of the Presidium of the Supreme Council, essentially the head of the state,[27] and he owed this position to the work of Virgilijus Čepaitis, the secretary of Sajudis, who directed the work of the Sajudis Deputies Club. (Čepaitis took as his model the organization of the Solidarity bloc in the Polish parliament.) Čepaitis forged a coalition of deputies coming from outside Vilnius, and the Sajudis Deputies Club chose Landsbergis over Romualdas Ozolas.[28] In the parliament the Sajudis deputies then voted as a bloc: Landsbergis triumphed over Brazauskas by a vote of ninety-one to thirty-eight.

Lithuania now had a single political spectrum in which Sajudis became the right and the socialists constituted the left. (In the political confusion of the day, the LCP/CPSU represented the reactionary left.) Some members of Sajudis thought that the organization should now either itself become a party or at least spawn a political party, but the thought prevailed that the organization should remain a movement. At its second congress in April 1990, Sajudis shed many of its intellectuals—some retired from politics, others went into government—and in its new form, known as Second Sajudis, it undertook to mobilize the nation in support of the government.

The Catholic Church, once the stronghold of intellectual resistance to the Soviet order, had by then generally withdrawn from politics. In August 1990 Vincentas Cardinal Sladkevičius told me that he considered the task of the church to be "the spiritual rebirth of Lithuania" (*Lietuvos dvasinis atgimimas*). Individual protests entered the political arena in their own names—Monsignor Alfonsas Svarinskas would be a notable example—but the church basically pursued its own mission, at the same time supporting all expressions and institutions of Lithuanian independence.

The New Politics

Landsbergis transformed his office into a strong executive. As an intellectual from Vilnius, he of course began with a certain handicap in the eyes of radicals, but he quickly took an aggressive, uncompromising position. He named his deputy chairman, Bronius Kuzmickas, as his successor should he be incapacitated,[29] and he named Kazimiera Prunskiene Lithuania's prime minister. Prunskiene, one of the founding members of Sajudis, had served as deputy premier since summer 1989, and although she resigned her membership in the LCP, the Sajudis majority in the Supreme Council claimed not to trust her. When Landsbergis and Prunskiene clashed, Landsbergis had the support of most Sajudis deputies in the parliament.

Sajudis's control of the political stage began to crack during Gorbachev's economic blockade of Lithuania in spring 1990. Gorbachev had expected the Lithuanians to collapse quickly under the pressure, and when the people resisted, the Soviet leader himself looked for a way out of the tangle. The Lithuanians split among themselves as to whether to agree to some compromise, and the left insisted that compromise was essential. A Center Faction formed consisting of Sajudis deputies who hoped to convince Landsbergis that he could move his base of support away from the right and into the center of the political spectrum.[30]

The formation of the Center Faction catalyzed the development of other political parties in the Supreme Council. Out-of-town deputies, housed in the Draugyste Hotel, had begun to meet each afternoon for tea, and out of this "tea party" (*arbatele*) arose several right-wing parties. Čepaitis organized the March 11 Party, which later changed its name to the Independence Party, and other groupings included the revival of the two prewar political names: the Lithuanian Christian Democratic Party (LCDP) and the Nationalists (Tautininkai).[31]

The political situation was complicated by a clash of personalities between Landsbergis and Prunskiene. Landsbergis wanted to control foreign policy, but Prunskiene, particularly in her trip through Western capitals in May 1990, enjoyed considerable international attention and praise. The two then disagreed in their attitudes toward negotiating with Gorbachev. Prunskiene, supported by the Center Faction, believed that it was a good time to reach a settlement, but the radical right wanted Landsbergis to continue the confrontation to a final decision on independence.[32]

Landsbergis eventually accepted the support of the center and agreed to a compromise solution, but he showed no interest in negotiating with Moscow for a lasting settlement. Prunskiene subsequently argued that Lithuania had missed an opportunity to win a profitable arrangement with Gorbachev, but Landsbergis, rejoining the right, placed his bet on the victory of Boris Yeltsin, and in the subsequent months Gorbachev's mounting campaign against Lithuania strengthened Landsbergis's position. Moscow's support of Burokevičius and the LCP/CPSU, together with the Soviet assault in January 1991, evoked a spirit of national unity in Vilnius, and Landsbergis exploited the situation to force Prunskiene's resignation as prime minister.[33]

After January 1991 Lithuania lay frozen in a state of suspended animation that ended only with the failed Moscow putsch in August. Soviet troops controlled the streets, carrying out arbitrary and willful actions, but the Lithuanian people generally refused to recognize Moscow's authority. The failed August putsch broke the deadlock in Lithuania: Moscow withdrew, and Gorbachev recognized Lithuanian independence. Landsbergis's bet on Yeltsin seemed to have paid off.

The Politics of Independence

Formal, recognized independence brought Lithuanian political life into a new era. The Sajudis majority in parliament had been eroding for some time, and it now collapsed. The opposition eventually constituted a small majority, but it did not have the will and power to unseat Landsbergis or Prime Minister Gediminas Vagnorius. The deputies in turn showed little inclination to convene a constituent assembly or even to call for new elections.

As politics sank into a deadlock, Landsbergis demanded enhanced powers, and when parliament refused, he turned back to Sajudis for support. By the end of 1991, however, Sajudis was only a shadow of its former self; it now had a much narrower social and political base, much further to the right, than it had in 1988. It was able to get enough signatures on a petition in favor of more presidential power to force the Supreme Council to schedule a referendum, but it no longer had the power to assure Landsbergis of victory.

Landsbergis and Sajudis, moreover, suffered a major blow in November 1991 with the revelation that Čepaitis had been a KGB informant.[34] Playing on the hatred that many Lithuanians had felt for the Communist system, Čepaitis had led the campaign to de-Sovietize Lithuania and to root out KGB agents. Many observers, especially foreign journalists, considered him the person closest to Landsbergis. The scandal forced Čepaitis out of public life, stimulated intense arguments about who else might have been agents of the KGB, and, of course, brought chaos into Landsbergis's camp.

Deprived of Čepaitis's advice, Landsbergis saw his position progressively disintegrate in the course of 1992. Fearing that his referendum on presidential power might fail for lack of voter turnout, Landsbergis proposed a second referendum, this one requiring that Soviet troops leave the country by the end of the year. Lithuanians would surely turn out to support such a referendum, but the parliament foiled Landsbergis by separating the two questions, scheduling the presidential referendum for May 23 and the vote on Soviet troops for June 14, the anniversary of the mass deportations carried out by the Soviets in 1941.

Landsbergis lost in his bid for more power when the voters failed to accept his referendum. He won 69.4 percent of the vote, but since less than 60 percent of the voters had turned out, he failed to win the required absolute majority of registered voters. (The referendum demanding the withdrawal of Soviet troops passed easily.) Reaching deeply into his reserves of sarcastic imagery, Landsbergis lashed out at his critics, warned of a "creeping coup," and scornfully noted that the referendum would have passed in the West where less was expected in terms of voter turnout. Although the parliamentary term had several years yet to run, he then called for new elections in the fall. Despite the referendum's failure, he calculated that the masses would support him in an election; he was mistaken.

The Return of the Old Guard

The elections of 1992 confronted the Lithuanian people with the fundamental problems of post-Soviet life. The economy was in shambles; inflation was eating up savings. Should the voters return the leaders descended from the old regime, or should they support the so-called "patriotic" forces? The old leaders had contacts and know-how. The "patriotic" forces lacked experience but they insisted that they were anti-Communist crusaders. Political figures occupying a middle ground had trouble making themselves heard.

Relations with Russia and the Commonwealth of Independent States constituted a major issue in the election. Russia was holding back energy supplies; Lithuania had little gasoline and oil. Landsbergis had shown his strength in confrontation, but although he signed an agreement on the withdrawal of Soviet forces, he had not distinguished himself as a negotiator. Brazauskas had a strong record as an economic specialist in Soviet Lithuania, and he symbolized the hope for better economic relations with Moscow. The LDLP seemed to hold out the hope of improving that relationship.

The elections resulted in victory for Brazauskas's party, the LDLP, which won an absolute majority of the seats in the new parliament, the Seimas, at least 73 seats of 141. Most Lithuanians seemed to expect a result similar to the one in Poland: a multiplicity of small groups in the parliament. Although Western commentators tended to interpret the LDLP victory as a return of the Communists, neither communism nor Moscow presented the same face as in 1988 or 1989. Despite considerable confusion concerning the party's role in the new Lithuania, Brazauskas had succeeded in maintaining it as the largest political grouping—the party claimed some 30,000 members—and had constructed an effective grassroots election organization.

For Landsbergis and for Sajudis the elections constituted a stunning defeat. Many Lithuanians attributed Sajudis's failure to the fact that it had organized its campaign as an anti-Communist crusade rather than around a program. Sitting among the ruins of his regime, Landsbergis complained that the Russians had influenced the election by restricting energy supplies, but he admitted that he had probably erred in calling for elections. He also conceded that he had concentrated on Lithuania's foreign relations, and the domestic economy had deteriorated out of control.[35] He now retired to the post of leader of the opposition.

Evaluation of Landsbergis's historical role in the period from 1988 to 1992 is difficult. He aroused admiration for his confrontation with Moscow, and his supporters insisted that his greatest achievements lay in foreign policy. In foreign affairs he far overshadowed Lithuania's official foreign minister, Algirdas Saudargas, and he certainly represented Lithuania forcefully.

Critics argue that he provided little leadership in terms of moving the country into the future. His speeches played to emotions rather than to reason. His foreign policy lacked specificity: He did publicize Lithuania's name by his travels to the far corners of the globe, but his other achievements in this area remained vague. His repeated emphasis on Lithuania as a victim entitled to reparations quickly wore thin, and Lithuania generally failed to capitalize on the sympathy that it had at one time enjoyed.

Landsbergis's tenure also contributed little to the development of political institutions. He made the office of chairman of the Supreme Council into a strong executive, and he had a leading role in expanding the powers of the parliament vis-à-vis the cabinet of ministers. Yet in 1992, frustrated in his bid for greater presidential powers, he likened the deputies to a pack of dogs; his sarcastic denunciations of his opponents were destructive to political discourse. In fall 1992 his supporters prepared a draft constitution with a strong presidency only to watch aghast as Brazauskas took the office.

In evaluating Landsbergis's tenure in office, one must also factor in Mikhail Gorbachev's policies; Landsbergis's policy of confrontation might not have been so successful had he not had Gorbachev as his partner. Gorbachev's choice of Burokevičius as his viceroy in Lithuania guaranteed disaster, and the Soviet leader then tried to destroy Lithuania in order to "save" it. In an interview with *Der Spiegel* at the beginning of 1993, Gorbachev insisted that his conscience rested easy on the question of Lithuania; there can probably be no greater proof of the bankruptcy of his policies vis-à-vis not only the Lithuanians but also the other nationalities of the Soviet Union.

Another significant result of the 1992 elections in Lithuania was the failure of the center. Despite sympathizers' urging that they form larger coalitions,[36] center groups entered the election fractionalized and failed to gain even the 4 percent of the vote necessary to win a seat in the Seimas. Sajudis leaders, to be sure, welcomed polarization, insisting that there was no middle ground between Sajudis and the LDLP,[37] but centrist leaders tried to explain their defeat by saying that Lithuanian society had not yet developed to the point of understanding them.[38]

Upon assuming power in December 1992, Brazauskas assembled a team that promised to struggle with the economy. He himself had been an economic specialist in the LCP; as prime minister he chose Bronius Lubys, a member of the Liberal Union, who had headed a major Lithuanian business with foreign sales in the millions of rubles; the new foreign minister, Povilas Gylys, for the last two years had been heading the department of international economics at the University of Vilnius. (Adolfas Šleževičius replaced Lubys in March 1993.) They all paid verbal tribute to the free market, but market principles were not clearly discernible in their economic policies or in practice.

In accordance with the new constitution approved on October 25, 1992, the Lithuanians had to elect a president, and the electoral campaign spotlighted another political problem: the role of the émigrés abroad in the new Lithuania. Stasys Lozoraitis, the Lithuanian ambassador to the United States but for most of his life an émigré, presented himself as an independent candidate for the presidency, and although he quickly won the support of almost all political groupings from the Social Democrats on the left to Sajudis on the right, the fact that he was an émigré made him vulnerable. In the vote on February 14, 1993, Brazauskas won handily, receiving 60 percent of the vote to Lozoraitis's 38 percent.

Brazauskas's victory held the promise that relations among the main political institutions of Lithuania—presidency, parliament, and cabinet—could now develop in more orderly fashion. (Some Lithuanians had feared that if elected,

Lozoraitis would dissolve the parliament, thereby prolonging political crisis indefinitely.) After the elections in fall 1992, Brazauskas had emphasized his determination to bring conciliation into Lithuanian politics, but it remained to be seen whether he would pursue this as president or whether other prominent political figures would agree to cooperate.

The political institutions of Lithuania still lack stability. Groups on the right give ample sign that they consider Brazauskas's election to have compromised the political system. In April 1993 some Seimas deputies sought to embarrass Brazauskas by complaining about him to the British House of Commons; Landsbergis explained that this was how dissidents had had to act under the Soviet regime.[39] Until all major political groupings recognize the legitimacy of institutions as independent of the individuals momentarily controlling them, the system has to be considered not yet firm.

Conclusion

The LDLP emerged from the elections of 1992 as the largest and strongest party in Lithuania. It won because of its grassroots organization. Former LCP members who had drifted away came back for the electoral campaign and after the LDLP's victory and brought with them considerable economic resources—their ranks included many captains of industry from the old days. As a result, the LDLP finds itself financially stable.

The LDLP's victory does not, however, mean the reincarnation of LCP rule in the years before 1988. The party does not control the instruments of power the way it did in the old days, and it does not have the powers of internal discipline that it once had. The party may well split into conservative and reformist wings.

The LDLP's success dictates that its opponents organize stronger political parties. Up to the elections of 1992, Lithuanian politics seemed to remain highly personalized, focused on individuals.[40] In 1993 conservatives reorganized themselves as a political party, the Union of the Fatherland. Leaders of opposition groups and parties must nevertheless yet prove that they are not generals without armies.

The new capitalists of Lithuania may hold the key to the political development of the republic. As noted, the LDLP enjoys the support of the old captains of industry, but the new entrepreneurs are yet to be heard from, although some argue their influence behind the political stage is growing. Businesspeople are prominent in the Liberal Union, but other parties in the center and on the right are also looking for economic support. Since there is considerable competition among groups of entrepreneurs, one can expect them to come out in support of different political groupings.

The émigrés have proved to be only a minor force in politics so far. Some may find a place with domestic groups, as Kazys Bobelis has with the LDLP, but

Vytautas Landsbergis enjoyed strong political support and considerable financial backing from émigrés in his disastrous campaign in fall 1992.

The minorities of Lithuania have yet to establish their places in the system. Lithuanians constitute 80 percent of the population, Russians about 8.7 percent, and Poles 7.1 percent. The Russians and Poles seem to have supported the LDLP in fall 1992, and their sympathies will probably continue to stay on the left side of the Lithuanian political spectrum.

Many Western commentators have noted how the Lithuanians' political path has differed from that of the Estonians or the Latvians. The demographic situation in Lithuania, with its preponderance of the eponymous people, is undoubtedly a major reason for this difference: The Lithuanians could afford to take a less confrontational position toward the Russians at home and abroad once the fact of independence had been established. In addition, the LDLP's history of having challenged Moscow in the past and the clash of personalities between Brazauskas and Landsbergis seem to have no equal in Latvia or Estonia.[41]

In conclusion, one should note the absence of violence in Lithuanian politics. In 1991 and 1992, right-wing thugs attacked leftist organizations, but as yet there is no organized violence between political camps or national groups. (At the same time, one should note that there is considerable violence between economic camps.) The peaceful nature of Lithuanian politics up to this point bodes well for the growth and development of a parliamentary system once the contending parties respect institutions as distinct from the individuals directing them.

Notes

1. On Suslov's role in Lithuania, see Roy Medvedev, "Emissar Stalina (M. A. Suslov v Litve, 1944–1946 gody)," in *Komsomolskaia pravda* (Vilnius, the Russian version of *Komjaunimo tiesa*), August 11, 1989.

2. Algirdas Brazauskas, interview with the author, January 11, 1993. See also his *Lietuviškos skyrybos* (Vilnius: Politika, 1992), pp. 18–19.

3. For membership statistics, see *Lietuvos Komunistų Partija skaičiais* (Vilnius: Mintis, 1976), pp. 120–123. Brazauskas made his comment in his interview with the author, January 11, 1993.

4. See *Izvestiia TsK KPSS*, 1990/5: p. 60.

5. Aleksandras Štromas, *Politinė samonė Lietuvoje* (London: Nida, 1980), p. 21. Vaclovas Alksninis made his statement at a meeting of VLIK (Supreme Committee for the Liberation of Lithuania), December 6–7, 1969; manuscript in possession of his sons.

6. Venclova's response to Shtromas in Štromas, *Politinė samonė Lietuvoje*, p. 87; see also T. Venclova, "Nepriklausomybè ir atsakomybè," *Gimtasis Kraštas,* 1990, no. 33.

7. V. Stanley Vardys, "Lithuanians," in Graham Smith, ed., *The Nationalities Question in the Soviet Union* (London and New York: Longman, 1990), p. 77; Vytautas Skuodis, "Lietuvių tautos diferenciacija pavergtoje Lietuvoje," *I laisvę,* vol. 102, pp. 13–14. Skuodis, a former university lecturer, argued that his classification of party members, together with the estimates, was valid for the whole Soviet Union, as confirmed by "the years

spent by the author in Mordovia camp Nr. 3, where I socialized with prisoners from various nationalities. Of them a good third were former Comparty members." For a pro-Moscow account that characterized Lithuanian Communists as naive careerists, see Philip Bonosy, *Devils in Amber: The Baltics* (New York: International Publishers, 1992).

8. Brazauskas, *Lietuviškos skyrybos,* pp. 117–119; see also pp. 73–74.

9. See ibid., pp. 115–116. On the functioning of controls, see Arvydas Sabonis and Stasys Sabonis, eds., *Rašytojas ir cenzura* (Vilnius: Vaga, 1992); also the critical account of Brazauskas's political career in Vytautas Tininis, "Algirdo Brazausko karjera: Kelias tarp istorijos išraustų duobių," *Lietuvos rytas,* December 22, 1992. For a well-balanced account of Lithuanian history in the postwar years, see Romuald J. Misiunas and Rein Taagepera, *The Baltic States: Years of Dependence, 1940–1980* (Berkeley: University of California Press, 1983), pp. 196–197.

10. Georgii Yefremov, *My liudi drug drugu. Litva: budni svobody 1988–1989* (Moscow: Progress, 1990), p. 17.

11. On the events of 1988 in Lithuania, see Alfred Erich Senn, *Lithuania Awakening* (Berkeley: University of California Press, 1990).

12. See Hedrick Smith, *The New Russians* (New York: Random House, 1990), p. 360.

13. Interview with the author, January 11, 1993.

14. Ibid.

15. See Alfred Erich Senn, "Toward Lithuanian Independence: Algirdas Brazauskas and the CPL," *Problems of Communism,* March-April 1990, pp. 21–28.

16. Vadim Bakatin, *Izbavlenie ot KGB* (Moscow, 1992), p. 49.

17. Brazauskas insisted to me that Naudžiunas was not a major player in the work of the LCP/CPSU, but there is considerable evidence affirming his significance. According to Brazauskas, Jermalavičius was the major figure in the LCP/CPSU. Interview, January 11, 1993.

18. I have not been able to identify the members of the LCP/CPSU Central Committee, and I base my estimate of the role of the military on the mass of uniforms I saw in the television coverage of the Central Committee session in August 1990.

19. See Mykolas Burokevičius, *Lietuvos KP ideologinis darbas su inteligentija 1940–1965 m.* (Vilnius: Mintis, 1972), p. 89.

20. See Vedas Rechlavičius's study of the intrigue in the LCP in *Lietuvos rytas,* June 13, 1991, and Burokevičius's interview in *Rakurs* (Tomsk), reprinted in *Lietuvos aidas,* June 28, 1991.

21. On the constituent congress of Sajudis, see Lietuvos Persitvarkymo Sajudis, *Steigiamasis suvažiavimas* (Vilnius: Mintis, 1990); Senn, *Lithuania Awakening,* pp. 217–236.

22. Monsignor Alfonsas Svarinskas, a noted frequent political prisoner of the Soviet regime, admitted to me that he would have trouble distinguishing the religious and the national elements in his activity that evoked the wrath of the Soviet authorities. Interview, August 20, 1990.

23. For an example of the type of memory that the exiles and deportees contributed to the Lithuanian national consciousness, see Onutė Garbsteinė, *Hell on Ice* (Vilnius: Ethnos '91, 1992), a diary of exile in Siberia, 1941–1957.

24. Brazauskas interview, January 11, 1993.

25. See Senn, *Lithuania Awakening,* p. 254.

26. The official records, to be sure, did not record the Sajudis victory, because as a movement rather than a party, it had no place in the official returns. According to the legislature's Mandates Commission, 7 deputies were nonparty, 63 belonged to parties, and 8 seats remained unfilled. Of the party members, 40 belonged to the LCP, 9 to the Lithuanian Social Democratic Party, and 2 to the Lithuanian Christian Democratic Party. *Lietuvos Respublikos Aukščiausiosios Tarybos (pirmojo šaukimo) pirmoji sesija. Stenogramos* (Vilnius: Lietuvos Respublikos Aukščiausioji Taryba, 1990), vol. 1, p. 20.

27. Landsbergis subsequently insisted that he should be called "president" abroad. The Lithuanians also made a determined effort to change the English translation of Aukščiausoji Taryba from "Supreme Soviet" to "Supreme Council." When in August 1990 I gave Brazauskas a copy of my article about him in *Problems of Communism* (March-April 1990), his first question was why the caption on p. 23 spoke of "Supreme Soviet."

28. See the account in Andrius Ažubalis, "Vienybės kaina," *Atgimimas,* 1990, no. 12.

29. See *Akiračiai,* 1992, no. 6. For a more detailed account of Landsbergis's rhetorical style, see Alfred Erich Senn, "Metmenys politinei biografijai," *Akiračiai,* 1991, no. 8. See also Anatol Lieven's evaluation of Landsbergis's turn rightward in his *The Baltic Revolution: Estonia, Latvia, Lithuania and the Path to Independence* (New Haven: Yale University Press, 1993), p. 259.

30. "Sajudžio Centro Frakcijos įkurimas," memorandum by Rimvydas Valatka, a founding member of the Center Faction, written at my request in April 1991.

31. Author's interview with Čepaitis, published as "Ar reikalinga Kovo 11-tos Partija? Pokalbis su Virgilijum Čepaičiu," *Akiračiai,* 1990, no. 9.

32. Prunskiene published a series of memoirs recounting her public life: *Gintarines ledi išpažintis,* constituting issues no. 27–28 of the journal *Politika* (Vilnius, 1991); *Užkulisiai,* constituting issue no. 2 of *Politika,* 1992; *Leben für Litauen* (Berlin: Ullstein, 1992); and *Iššukis drakonui* (Kaunas: Europa, 1992). Compare the account of President George Bush's meeting with Prunskiene in May 1990 in Michael R. Beschloss and Strobe Talbott, *At the Highest Levels: The Inside Story of the End of the Cold War* (Boston: Little, Brown, 1993), pp. 206–207.

33. I published an account of these events as *Crisis in Lithuania, January 1991* (Chicago: Akiračiai, 1991). As I walked through the parliament on January 15, Antanas Terleckas stopped me to declare that Landsbergis was "irreplaceable." Prunskiene subsequently questioned whether there was a place for women in Lithuanian politics, but that issue goes beyond the bounds of this study. See her *Iššukis drakonui,* pp. 90–110.

34. On the Čepaitis affair, see the essays by Aleksandras Shtromas, Thomas Venclova, and Alfred E. Senn in *Akiračiai,* 1992, no. 2.

35. See his speech of January 3, 1993, reprinted in *The Baltic Observer,* January 15–21, 1993. Compare the evaluation of Landsbergis's term in office in Vincas Bartuševičius, "Entwicklungen in Litauen, 1990–1991," in *Jahrestagung 1991* (Lampertheim: Lihtauisches Kulturinstitut, 1992), pp. 68–70, praising Landsbergis's policy toward Russia, and p. 104, criticizing his domestic policy. On the election results, see also Lieven, *The Baltic Revolution,* pp. 266–270.

36. See the appeal of concerned American Lithuanians reprinted in *Akiračiai,* 1992, no. 10.

37. *Lietuvos aidas,* December 4, 1992.

38. Romualdas Ozolas, interview, January 12, 1993.

39. See Landsbergis's explanation of the relationship of individuals to institutions in his interview published in *Vilnius,* 1992, no. 3, p. 14: "One should in fact evaluate democracy in relation to the concrete situation—what sort of people and what are their interrelationships, how do they relate to the laws of the land—and the forms of administration and organization still really need improvement."

40. In December 1990 a visiting Lithuanian American noted, "My relatives were all former deportees. Now some of them supported Brazauskas, others Landsbergis. An argument developed over the economy, speculation, and who would best clean up the country." Liutas Mockunas, "Gruodžio mozaika," *Akiračiai,* 1991, no. 3.

41. I am indebted to my colleagues Andrejs Plakans of Iowa State University and Toivo Raun of Indiana University for their help in comparing the experiences of the three Baltic peoples.

Elite Transformation in Late-Soviet and Post-Soviet Transcaucasia, or What Happens When the Ruling Class Can't Rule?

Ronald Grigor Suny

Whether one adopts the language of the classical theorists of elites—Mosca, Pareto, Michels—or the rival conceptualizations of the Marxist tradition, it is difficult in the post-Soviet period to avoid the obvious: that political elites have been and still are an omnipresent part of the social structure of power. Whether we refer to the dominant political and economic actors in the Soviet Union and the post-Soviet republics as an "elite" or as a "ruling class," the terms should suggest not a tight unity among rulers but an appreciation of the heterogeneity and internal distinctions within any dominant group. The first assumption of this chapter is that as a ruling elite establishes and maintains its claim to rule, it acts much as one would expect a dominant class to act, constantly engaging in the difficult work of maintaining a degree of group identity and solidarity and struggling against the internal and external forces that threaten to break down its distinctiveness and undermine its right to rule. At the same time, rulership is seldom merely a matter of exercising power. Ultimately, it is about creating legitimate authority by creating a hegemonic political culture that legitimizes the ruling elite's or class's dominant position.

In each of the three Transcaucasian republics, old elites were at one time replaced at the top of the political structure by nationalist, anti-Communist counterelites. But, as in much of the former Soviet Union, the older political players managed to preserve considerable influence in the political structure and economy and even to return to power in some cases. The transformation of elites in the region was accompanied by more violence than in most of the former USSR, particularly in Georgia, where political disintegration and interethnic conflict resulted in civil war. Armenia experienced the most peaceful transfer of power and still enjoys the most stable democratic government, but in Azerbaijan transfers of power from the old elite to the nationalists and back again came only after brief armed struggles.

The End of Soviet Power

Soviet oligarchic rule effaced alternative political elites. Only the academic and literary intelligentsia remained somewhat autonomous in some republics. Once the Communist elite lost its ideological conviction, once its political will was weakened (from the top) during the Gorbachev revolution, the alternative elites that emerged proved to be extraordinarily weak and in most republics without broad social bases. One considerable source of strength was the ability of some intelligentsias to express their aspirations in the language of national revival or survival, but in many republics the old elites quickly attempted to appropriate the now-hegemonic discourse of nationalism.

Although it began as one more state-directed campaign to mobilize the population toward greater economic effort (*uskorenie,* or acceleration), the reform program of Mikhail Gorbachev from its inception invoked an explicit and radical critique of the relationship of the political elite to the people they ostensibly represented. Gorbachev's rhetoric of democracy and decentralization, along with the consequent fracturing of the Communist Party in the center and the peripheries into rival conservative and radical factions, opened a political space for nationalist counterelites and the massive nationalist movements that erupted, first with the Armenians, in early 1988. When political mobilization outstripped the glacial pace of economic development, the party lost the ideological conception of its right to rule (what Mosca called the "political formula"). The state withered, and the empire fell apart. "In contradiction to the image prevalent in the West at the time," as Judith Sue Kullberg noted, "the Party did not collapse due to popular pressure and mass political action; rather, the most striking feature of the story of the decline of the CPSU is the degree to which it consented to a reduced role and voluntarily gave up its control over both the political system and the society."[1]

Rather than claiming that the disintegration of the Soviet system was the inevitable, delayed effect of a wrongly conceived political project, I would argue that the Soviet Union suffered from its successes as well as its failures. Just as in nationality policy, where the contradictions of the Soviet system and its policies both created new, coherent nations within the pseudofederal structure of the USSR and undermined the sources of nationality and nationalism, so in the political sphere the very programs that created a more urban, educated, articulated, and articulate society eroded the need for a vanguard party monopolizing decisionmaking.[2] As Gorbachev must have eventually realized—and as the successor elites would discover—political elites may react to, initiate, shape or even inhibit larger historical processes, but they cannot control them. Political elites may make history but not just as they please.

However artificial some of the fifteen newly independent states might have been at their creation in the first decades of the twentieth century, they had become, through the years of Soviet power, something like nation-states. Almost all had majorities of the titular nationality (Kazakhstan was the single exception), and national Communist political elites remained in power in most of them, in one form or another. If we imagine a range of political regimes with varying degrees of old elite entrenchment and new elite stability, the fifteen republics are ranged as follows:

1. Turkmenistan and Uzbekistan: The old Communist elite remains in power and is largely uncontested.
2. Belarus, Moldova, and Kazakhstan: The old Communist elite continues in power but as a newly refurbished national elite.
3. Ukraine: The Communist elite remains in place but in a complex contestation for power with divided nationalist forces.
4. Azerbaijan and Tajikistan: The Communist elite has returned to power after defeating the emergent nationalist counterelite.
5. Kyrgyzstan and Russia: The Communist elite has been displaced by an elite committed to democratic reform and a market economy but remains well entrenched in secondary positions of power, political and economic.
6. Lithuania: The Communists have returned to power through free elections but in new social democratic garb.
7. Armenia, Estonia, and Latvia: Nationalist counterelites are in power with relatively unimportant Communist oppositions.
8. Georgia: Deeply divided counterelites and former Communists contend for power in a civil war complicated by interethnic hostilities.

Although the Transcaucasian republics fall at different spots in this list, they share certain commonalities. First, the ruling elites all have extremely weak social bases, experience internal fragmentation, and face extraordinary difficulties in forging support for the new regimes. Potentially powerful contenders for power are waiting in the wings: the Dashnaktsutiun (Armenian Revolutionary Federation) in Armenia; regional and nationalist forces in Azerbaijan; the followers of Zviad Gamsakhurdia and other factions in Georgia.

Second, in all three republics a deep and persistent substructure of regional and clan loyalties continues to be the touchstone of political identification and affiliation. Political, regional, familial, and even criminal mafias offer powerful resistance to sovereign law-based states. Displaced Communists remain the most coherent and unified presence, often well established in the governing structure of certain regions or institutions. One of the most powerful threats to the local nationalist government in Azerbaijan was the former chief of the Communist Party, Heidar Aliev, who had his own power base in the semiindependent Nakhichevan region and used his network of associates to return to power in June 1993.

Third, the Transcaucasian nationalist counterelites come from the same social background: academic and literary intellectuals (relatively cosmopolitan) outside the old power elite. They fit the stereotypic picture of a revolutionary elite— "overeducated outgroups" "whose capital is [their] knowledge."[3] They came to

power against the old ways of doing business, but once in power they accommodated the existing structures of power.

Finally, the project of state building and the building of authority (legitimated
power) for the new elites in all three republics goes on in conditions of extreme
physical difficulty, economic collapse, interrepublic and civil war, and blockade.

The similarities belie enormous differences among the three republics. To explain the winding paths into and out of power by the nationalists and former Communists, I consider the varying character, coherence, and content of the nationalist
discourses in the three republics, their inclusive or exclusive rhetorics; the ability
of nationalist counterelites to constitute themselves as an effective leadership and
control their mass following; and the flexibility (or intransigence) of the local
Communist elites. I argue that among the factors that lead to the successful reconstitution of a stable political elite are the availability of a political discourse that
binds the elite and a significant part of the population around shared cultural and
political goals and to which the elite can easily refer; the absence of interethnic
cleavages that have the potential of initiating and maintaining among the population a habit of violence; and the relative willingness of the old political elite to surrender power and accept the new rules of the political game.

Armenia

When perestroika provided an opening for pent-up political frustrations, the Armenian intelligentsia mobilized around three major issues: environmental pollution and the danger posed by the nuclear plant at Metsamor, near Erevan; the pe-
rennial issue of Karabakh; and the corruption and stagnation connected with the
long reign (1974–1988) of party chief Karen Demirchian.[4] At the same time, the
political leadership in Armenia was being undermined both from within and from
above. After the accession of Gorbachev, the central party press attacked the Armenian Communist Party (ACP) for corruption and favoritism.[5] Yet the ACP elite,
unified around Demirchian, managed to forestall reform of the party and the removal of Demirchian until the outbreak of the Karabakh movement in February
1988. Only then did the ACP, discredited in the eyes of much of the population,
rapidly lose authority to the growing movement in the streets.

After Demirchian fell in May, his successor, Suren Harutiunian (Arutiunian),
attempted to find common language with the national movement. But the Karabakh Committee, made up of nationalist intellectuals, many of them members of
the Communist Party, became more radical, calling for full democratization and
national sovereignty. Moscow's refusal to agree to the merger of Karabakh with
Armenia and its failure to deal firmly with the perpetrators of the Sumgait pogrom
by Azerbaijanis against Armenians contributed to the intransigence of the opposition.

Shortly after the earthquake of December 7, 1988, Soviet officials decided to
restore their authority by arresting the members of the Karabakh Committee. This

attempt to rule, in a sense, "without the nation" led to voters boycotting the general elections called by Gorbachev in March 1989 and to massive demonstrations in early May. Harutiunian's gestures to win over popular sentiment—recognizing a holiday on May 28, the day the nationalists had proclaimed Armenian independence in 1918, and accepting the tricolor flag of the independent republic—culminated in the release of the Karabakh Committee to the joyful greetings of demonstrators in Erevan.

The next five months (June–October 1989) were marked by a kind of condominium of the Communists and the Karabakh Committee. As uncomfortable allies, much like the popular fronts and communists in the Baltic republics, the competing Armenian elites actually made it possible for the popular nationalist movement to grow in a relatively free environment and for an eventual, peaceful transfer of power to ensue. In June the mushrooming unofficial organizations joined together to form the Pan-Armenian National Movement (Haiots Hamazgayin Sharzhum, HHSh), and the government gave them official recognition. The effective leader of the opposition, Levon Ter Petrosian, praised Harutiunian's defense of Armenian national interests at the Congress of People's Deputies and stated his belief that the interests of the ACP and the HHSh were converging.[6]

But by late fall 1989 the cooperative relationship had broken down. The benefits of moderation had been exhausted, as Moscow not only refused to cede Karabakh to Armenia but decided to return control of the region to Baku. The Karabakh movement accelerated its efforts toward democratization and independence. Under HHSh pressure, the Armenian Supreme Soviet revised the republic's constitution and gave itself the power to invalidate USSR laws.

Torn between the Kremlin's refusal to allow the merger of Karabakh with Armenia and the growing popular movement that would be satisfied with nothing less, Harutiunian resigned as first secretary of the ACP on April 6, 1990. The Communists, identified with the by then unpopular Gorbachev, with the refusal to allow Karabakh to join Armenia, and with a legacy of corruption and repression, had accumulated too many liabilities to govern effectively in Armenia. They fared poorly in the elections of spring and summer 1990, and the new Armenian parliament chose Ter Petrosian instead of the new Communist chief, Vladimir Movsesian, as its chairman.[7]

As it moved step by cautious step toward independence through 1990 and 1991, the Armenian national leadership loosened political and ideological ties with Moscow, all the while assiduously avoiding direct confrontation.[8] Its leading theorists rejected the traditional Russian orientation of the Armenian intelligentsia. In place of the long-held view that Armenia required Russian or Soviet protection against the danger of Pan-Turkism, the HHSh argued that Armenians must abandon their reliance on a "third force," rethink their traditional hostility toward and fear of the Turks, and create their own independent state now that the opportunity had arisen. These views echoed those long expressed by the leading diaspora party, the Dashnaktsutiun, though with significant differences.[9] Exhibiting caution and pragmatism, the HHSh noted that it was prepared to defer the question of Armenian lands in Turkey until the issue of full sovereignty and independence was resolved.

When the anti-Gorbachev plotters in August 1991 delivered the final blow to Soviet unity, Armenian voters struck out on their own political path. On September 20 they affirmed the commitment to independence in a referendum; on October 16 they elected Ter Petrosian president of the republic with an overwhelming 83 percent of the vote.[10] The Karabakh Committee had by fall 1991 been transformed into the popular government of an independent state with only a weak and divided opposition. Ideologically forged in the struggle for Karabakh, the movement had quickly developed into a successful movement against the mafialike party in Armenia.

The leaders of the post-Communist government in Armenia were the small circle of friends and colleagues who had graduated from the informal Karabakh Committee in 1988 and 1989 to become the core of a broad-based nationalist movement. Emblematic of their social origins in the academic intelligentsia was the newly elected president of Armenia, Levon Ter Petrosian, formerly a philologist who worked in the Matenadaran, the repository of medieval Armenian manuscripts in Erevan. Born in Aleppo, Syria, and brought to Armenia as a child, educated in the USSR, but always with that *aghber* sense of being different,[11] Ter Petrosian is a worldly, sophisticated, cosmopolitan intellectual who rose to influence because of his oratorical skills in mass meetings in 1988 and 1989. His greatest political quality seems to be balance and moderation—his ability to steer a course first away from Russia toward Turkey and back again while fending off advocates of a more militant stance toward the Karabakh problem. Ter Petrosian was open to bringing advisers from the diaspora, most notably Raffi Hovannisian, his first foreign minister, and Girair Libaridian, a close confidant. He proved willing to use the power of the state when he felt threatened by the Dashnak leadership and summarily exiled the chairman of the party from the republic. Yet he has maintained a firm commitment to a moderate democratic course, is free from narrow nationalism (his wife is Jewish), and lives in constant danger of being outflanked by more ardent "patriots."[12]

The national movement, which from its inception has employed a repertoire of symbols and cultural constructions immediately recognizable to large numbers of Armenians, was able both to mobilize large numbers of people in a single cause and to remain relatively united around its leadership. The leaders' strategy of gradualism and steady pressure rather than confrontation contributed to the peaceful and relatively violence-free transfer of power, though the absence of enduring interethnic conflicts within the republic was the most important factor freeing Armenians from a cycle of violence at home. The perceived danger of the Azerbaijanis worked also to unify much of the population around the emerging nationalist leadership. When the Karabakh conflict escalated into the killings at Sumgait and then into a blockade and open warfare, Armenians forcibly deported Azerbaijanis from the republic but with relatively little bloodshed.

In some ways the Armenian case parallels those in the Baltic regions, but in other ways it is quite different. As in Lithuania, so in Armenia the majority of the Communist Party chose the nation rather than the Soviet Union. Unlike in Latvia and Estonia, there were no so-called internationalist factions of Communists in Armenia to appeal to the forces of order in Moscow. The Armenian Communist Party, which worked with the nationalist movement for a time, resisted pressure from Moscow to take a harder line toward the Karabakh movement and eventually rejected the option of a coup against the elected majority in parliament, a choice that further contributed to the low level of internal violence.[13] Even though Armenia was the first of the Transcaucasian republics to form a non-Communist government, the nationalists deliberately adopted a strategy of working within the limits of the Soviet law of secession and thereby avoided much of the violence from the center that ensued in response to the more uncompromising push for independence, particularly in Lithuania and in Georgia.

In the first three and a half years after independence, the Ter Petrosian government displayed an enviable stability, despite the ongoing war in Karabakh and the growing opposition in parliament and society. The unity of the original band of nationalists who had led the Karabakh movement in Erevan splintered within the first year when key members broke with the government and formed opposition parties. Banditry and armed militias in the streets of the cities, along with the growth of independent centers of economic power, threatened the almost nonexistent state apparatus. Yet a series of victories in the Karabakh war, beginning in early 1993, and the expansion and stabilization of the front with a cease-fire in the spring of 1994, gave the Armenian government the breathing space it needed to bring civil order to its towns, lay the basis for a restoration of the economy, and win over foreign friends and aid. At the end of 1994, Ter Petrosian responded to the assassination of one of his former associates, Hambartsum Galstian, by cracking down hard on the Dashnaktsutiun, arresting its leaders and closing its newspapers. Though this breach of democratic practice shocked the diaspora and led to mild protests from the American government, the political crisis within the counterelite did not derail the most stable government in Transcaucasia from its steady consolidation of state authority.

Azerbaijan

The story of the emergence of the Azerbaijani nationalist elite differs from the Armenian experience, not least because the two nations were formed before and during the Soviet period in significantly different ways. Armenians in Transcaucasia were the most urban of the three major ethnic groups; they occupied positions of economic and political power in Tbilisi (Tiflis) and Baku, from which they would be largely displaced during the Soviet period. Yet even as Azerbaijanis and Georgians became the hegemonic nationality in political and intellectual life in their respective republics, they retained resentments against the Armenians. Armenians were disproportionately represented in the technical and other subelites, particularly in Azerbaijan. As Azerbaijanis moved into towns, suffering from the highest levels of unemployment in the Soviet Union and encountering a corrupt political elite of their own nationality, they directed much of their social and ethnic resentment toward the Armenian population of their own republic.

Whereas Armenians both in Karabakh and Armenia proper could refer to a clear sense of nationhood with a textual tradition of continuous existence and past statehood, the Azerbaijanis were more immediately a nation in the making. Specifically national traditions, as distinct from traditions shared by the larger Shia Muslim world, the Persian cultural milieu, or the Turkic-language community, were largely built during the Soviet period, as were a sense of shared history, a national (rather than regional or religious) identity, and a rootedness in a specific territory. Construction of a national tradition occurred in all the Soviet republics, and in each the titular nationality of the republic was privileged to the near exclusion of minority peoples.[14] Only with the outbreak of the Karabakh movement did the underlying sense of threat from Armenians coalesce with myriad other threats and anxieties to propel, first, small numbers of Azerbaijanis to take revenge on the Armenians of Sumgait for imagined injuries and, later, tens of thousands of others to join in massive demonstrations.

The ruling Communist elite in Azerbaijan has been the subject of several studies of the powerful interweaving of political and economic patron-client networks, or what is referred to in the vernacular as the "mafia."[15] After the ten-year reign of the incompetent and venal party first secretary, Veli Akhundov, Moscow decided in 1969 to appoint Heidar Aliev, the republic's KGB chairman, in order to revive the Azerbaijani economy and uproot the pervasive corruption within the ruling elite. New officials personally loyal to Aliev, drawn from his native region of Nakhichevan and from his associates in the security apparatus, were rapidly introduced into positions of power. But instead of fighting mafia rule in general, Aliev ended up replacing the old clientelistic network with one of his own. Ethnically homogeneous and ruthless, the Aliev elite was able to convince Moscow that it was competent in maintaining both political stability and a modicum of economic growth. In fact, the regime was falsifying results, repressing (sometimes killing) its critics, and lavishly enriching its favored members.[16]

Aliev left for Moscow in 1982, replaced by a loyal client, Kiamran Baghirov. Only with the ascent of Gorbachev and Aliev's dismissal from the Politburo in October 1987 was any serious attempt made to break up the Aliev machine. In May 1988, Baghirov was replaced by Abdulrahman Vazirov, who, like Harutiunian in Armenia, was from outside the republic (from the diplomatic corps). Like other Gorbachev appointments in national republics, Vazirov set out to purge the party apparatus of corrupt and time-serving officials, removing over forty district and city committee secretaries, cutting the number of central committee departments and secretaries, and reorganizing the party structure.[17] But Vazirov, who like all other post-Aliev Azerbaijani leaders had earlier been associated with Aliev, only superficially pushed the program of perestroika and the fight against the deep infrastructure of Azerbaijani politics. As in Armenia, the party entered the period of growing nationalism unsure of its mandate and its future role. Its traditional vanguard role was being undermined from both above and below; and with the erosion of a single, authoritative center as a source of authority and legitimation, the ruling elite faced a bitter choice between accommodation of the popular mood or harsh repression.

Vazirov did not so much face an aroused counterelite, as did Harutiunian in Armenia, as a restless population torn by social strains and agitated by fears of Armenian nationalism. Nearly a year of Armenian protests and demands for Karabakh mobilized nonelite Azerbaijanis to defend what they considered the territorial integrity of their republic. Crowds gathered outside Government House, 20,000 during the night, 500,000 during the day.[18] This disparate movement was led, at first, by workers and was peopled by Azerbaijani refugees from Armenia and migrants from the Azerbaijani countryside. A lathe operator, Neimat Panakhov, emerged as the major spokesman at mass rallies, expressing social as well as ethnic discontents and complaining that Azerbaijani workers were not given apartments when they relocated in the towns and were forced to live in dormitories. The targets of these resentments were the relatively privileged, the people of Baku—one slogan heard was "Baku bez bakintsev" (Baku without the Bakinians)—and Armenians.[19]

In June 1988, seven intellectuals, who earlier had formed a group within the research section of the Azerbaijani Academy of Sciences to support the goals of perestroika, wrote up a manifesto and created the Azerbaijan Popular Front (Azarbayjan Khalg Jabhasi, AKhJ). These cosmopolitan Baku intellectuals, said by some to speak better Russian than Azeri, were of a social democratic orientation, but they soon joined with other unofficial associations, broadening their base and program.[20] The AKhJ promoted the political and economic sovereignty of the republic of Azerbaijan within a democratic Soviet Union but was unable to reach the popular masses or control the opposition in the streets that exploded in November.

The Communist authorities refused to register the AKhJ as a legal organization and broke up its first congress by force. Meeting secretly, the AKhJ leaders organized a series of crippling strikes and a rail blockade of Armenia. Only in September did the Communist leaders reluctantly open negotiations with the front, eventually capitulating to the evident strength of the popular movement. On September 23, 1989, the Supreme Soviet of Azerbaijan recognized the sovereignty of the republic, and a few weeks later, the AKhJ was officially registered. In November, Moscow ended its direct control over Karabakh and ceded authority to Azerbaijan.

As in Armenia, the brief period of condominium lasted only a few months. Though there was regular consultation between the government and the AKhJ on the Karabakh issue, the question of democratic elections led to a split. The greater resistance by the Communists in Azerbaijan to power sharing with, let alone transfer of power to, the national movement contributed both to an escalation of internal violence and radicalization of the nationalist leadership. By mid-November 1989, protesters were tearing down the border posts separating Soviet Azerbaijan from Iranian Azerbaijan. Independent militants attacked party and police offices in the name of the AKhJ. Unable to follow the Armenian course by combining the goals of perestroika and national self-association, the Azerbaijani intelligentsia divided into more nationalistic and more democratic factions.[21] Paralyzed and divided, the AKhJ neither controlled its own membership nor had much influence on the crowds in the streets.

Suddenly, on January 13, 1990, as a quarter of a million Azerbaijanis listened to speeches in the central square in Baku, groups of young people broke away and began running through the city beating and killing ethnic Armenians. Two days later the Soviet government declared a state of emergency in Azerbaijan and launched a series of military maneuvers, first in Karabakh and then toward Baku. On January 20, as the AKhJ (loosely connected to an ad hoc National Defense Council) organized a haphazard defense of the city, the Soviet army stormed Baku, killing hundreds.[22] Most Armenians had already been evacuated, and the military's objective was clearly to restore the power of the Communist Party of Azerbaijan and remove the nationalist threat. Some 800 members of the AKhJ were arrested, and twelve regional organizations were closed.

"Reborn like a phoenix from the ashes of burnt party membership cards," the old Communist elite was able to restore its rule, if not its authority, thanks to the Soviet military.[23] Vazirov was replaced by Ayaz Niyaz Oghlu Mutalibov, the chairman of the Council of Ministers, who in May was selected president by the Supreme Soviet. For much of 1990 and 1991, a de facto alliance of convenience between Mutalibov and Gorbachev tilted Soviet policy in Transcaucasia toward Azerbaijan. Whereas Armenia was already committed to leaving the Soviet Union, rejecting Gorbachev's referendum, Mutalibov's government agreed to participate. In March 1991, 92 percent of those voting in Azerbaijan (75 percent of the electorate participated) endorsed preservation of the USSR.

Mutalibov's rule, however, could not depend on Soviet arms alone; at the same time as he contained the AKhJ, he sought to increase his popular support by prosecuting the war in Karabakh. Special military units, the OMON or Black Berets, were used to intimidate Armenians in and around Karabakh and drive them from the region.[24] In September 1990, the Communist Party won the largest numbers of votes in the Supreme Soviet elections with the AKhJ a distant second, but there was widespread feeling that the election results had been rigged.

The AKhJ, repressed and in disarray, was eventually allowed to operate legally. Its only hope for political relevance lay in its effective articulation of the nationalist, anti-Armenian discourse—what Mark Saroyan called the "Karabakh syndrome"—that had overwhelmed all other political discourses in Azerbaijan. After the Soviet invasion, the AKhJ came out in favor of full independence of Azerbaijan and the retention of Karabakh. The turn toward a more militant nationalism convinced some of the moderate elements within the AKhJ to leave it and join the small Azerbaijani Social Democratic Group.[25]

When the Azerbaijani president failed to condemn the August 1991 coup, demonstrations organized by the AKhJ called for his resignation. Mutalibov reacted quickly, resigning not as president but from his post as head of the local Communist Party. The next day he engineered a unanimous vote in the Supreme Soviet to "restore" the independence of Azerbaijan, and on September 8, he was elected president of the republic by popular vote. The AKhJ boycotted the election.

The fragility of political power in Azerbaijan and its contingent relationship with the war in Karabakh were vividly demonstrated in the six months from the coup in August to Mutalibov's resignation in early March 1992. In that half year, Mutalibov acted as if he were still a Communist first secretary, though now presenting himself as first representative of the nation. He set up a fifty-member National Council in which his supporters and the opposition sat in equal numbers, yet he operated independently of the council. Despite a unanimous rejection of membership in the new Commonwealth of Independent States by the council, in December 1991 Mutalibov signed the Alma-Ata agreement setting up the CIS. When news came of "massacres" by Armenians at Khodjaly, Mutalibov was forced to resign, but the new government was unable to bring stability to the country. The war in Karabakh went badly, as the Armenians took advantage of the political confusion in Baku. In rural districts armed men acting in the name of the AKhJ attempted to overthrow local authorities.[26]

Early in May, as violence nearing civil war engulfed the country, Mutalibov returned to the presidency, backed by his supporters in the streets and by a cowed parliament. The AKhJ reacted quickly, mobilizing tens of thousands of its own armed supporters around the parliament. Mutalibov fled to Moscow, and on May 16, the National Council formed a coalition government including members of the AKhJ in the powerful posts controlling police and security. New elections on June 6 confirmed Abulfaz Elchibey as president.

The new leader of Azerbaijan was a historian of the Orient, widely respected as a man of integrity and principle. His personal authority stemmed from his past as an implacable enemy of Moscow and his arrest in 1975 for "slandering" the Soviet state. Like other post-Mutalibov nationalist politicians in Baku, Elchibey was opposed to joining the CIS. His party was hostile to both Russia and Iran and oriented toward Kemalist Turkey, which he saw as the model democratic secular republic in the Muslim world.

The AKhJ was as divided in power as it had been in opposition. As the war in Karabakh dragged on without victory, the political mood grew ever more extreme. The instability of the regime was matched by the fragmentation in the country as a whole. At least four semiindependent, quasi-official militias roamed Azerbaijan. Dozens of well-organized, identifiable clans contended for influence, and powerful regional chieftains, like Heidar Aliev, who returned triumphantly from Moscow to his native Nakhichevan, thwarted the will of the Baku government.[27] In the unstable flux of Azerbaijani politics, oppositional figures like Neimat Panakhov and the National Independence Party leader, Etibar Mamedov, threatened the weak hold of the government.

The AKhJ government proved unable to demonstrate that it could effectively prosecute the war in Karabakh. By April 1993, Armenians had expanded the war from Karabakh to neighboring regions of Azerbaijan proper, and the crisis of a nation still in formation became even more acute. In June a military revolt led by Suret Huseinov drove Elchibey from Baku and brought Aliev to power. Azerbaijan's political orientation quickly shifted from reliance on Turkey to seeking aid and mediation from Russia. Aliev opened dialogue directly with the Karabakh Armenians and traveled to Moscow to meet with Boris Yeltsin and Ter Petrosian. Bolstered by yet another presidential election in October, in which he won the customary 90-plus percent of the vote, Aliev set out to stabilize his regime by removing the principal factor, the Karabakh conflict, that had undermined Azerbaijan's three previous governments. He broke with the more extreme nationalists and agreed to lead Azerbaijan into the CIS. As he reorientated Baku's policies away from Turkey back toward Russia, Aliev opened the way for Russia to gravitate away from its pro-Armenian stance. Although he was unable in the next year and a half to improve Azerbaijan's position at the front, Aliev managed to keep his domestic rivals, including Huseinov, from threatening his power and to interest foreign oil companies in a new deal to develop Caspian oil reserves. A cease-fire in the summer of 1994 raised fragile hopes of a negotiated settlement in the Karabakh war.

Despite the losses suffered in the Karabakh war, the Aliev government managed to consolidate its power, at least in the environs of Baku. In October 1994, Aliev beat back an attempted coup by his prime minister, Suret Huseinov, and declared a state of emergency that continued into the next year. The president used his powers to disarm militias loyal to the Popular Front, which retained significant support in Nakhichevan, but allowed demonstrations by a newly reconstituted Azerbaijani Communist Party. He renegotiated the oil concessions to Western companies and agreed to Russian and Iranian shares. After the "turn toward Turkey" under Elchibey, Aliev distanced his government somewhat from Ankara and drew closer to Moscow. But, sensitive to public opinion, he has steadfastly opposed the stationing of Russian troops in the republic. After the Russians launched their war against the Chechens in December, 1994, they closed the frontier with Azerbaijan, interrupting the republic's grain supplies, which come by rail through the North Caucasus, and creating bread shortages in several Azerbaijani towns and cities. Though it was far from a democratic government, Aliev's Azerbaijan had become a more stable state, riding the surface of a fragmented and dispirited society, by the spring of 1995.

Georgia

The cases of Armenia and Azerbaijan illustrate the differential effects of the flexibility or intransigence of the old ruling elite and the importance of the counterelite's ability to lead a mass movement. Georgia adds to these elements the salience of particular kinds of leaders and the specific appeals they use to secure influence and power. Although the Georgian story can be told in many different ways, the complex, intersecting, but divergent careers of two principal figures, Eduard Shevardnadze and Zviad Gamsakhurdia, reflect the contrasting rhetorical approaches to political struggle. In the multinational context of the Georgian republic, where ethnic Georgians made up a little over two-thirds of the population and where severe strains had alienated ethnic minorities from the dominant nationality throughout the Soviet period, leaders' rhetoric and symbolic choices could work to ameliorate these divisions in a unified struggle for independence and democracy or to reinforce and exacerbate the interethnic clevages within the republic.

Born in 1928 in the west Georgian village of Mamati, Eduard Shevardnadze grew up in a "large, friendly family" that tolerated intensely expressed, politically divergent views. In his memoirs, Shevardnadze recalled his family as "a kind of multiparty system." "Everyone around me spoke of class warfare and class enemies, and ... later in life, when a person was pointed out to me as a 'carrier of alien views,' I would remember my relatives and the people dear to me."[28]

In 1948, Shevardnadze joined the party and, after briefly studying medicine, accepted an appointment as political instructor in the Komsomol. He met his wife, Nanuli Tsagareishvili, in the last years of Stalin's life, ignoring warnings that it would be fatal to his career to marry a woman whose father had been executed as an "enemy of the people." Shevardnadze had powerful patrons, including Vasilii Mzhavanadze, the longtime head of the Georgian party appointed by Khrushchev, whom Shevardnadze described as "an exceptionally mild and trusting man."[29] He soon rose to be Georgian minister of internal affairs and from this post launched attacks on the rampant corruption and criminality in the republic. Finding favor with Brezhnev, he was chosen in September 1972 to succeed Mzhavanadze as first secretary of the Georgian party.

In his account, Shevardnadze emphasized how he was able to maneuver between the needs of the republic and the restrictive rules and directives from the center. His approach to the growing problem of nationalism in the republic was to intervene not with force but through negotiation and persuasion, as he did in the controversy in 1978 over the removal of the clause in the republic constitution that declared Georgian the official language of the republic. When Abkhaz demonstrators demanded secession from Georgia and merger with Russia, Shevardnadze once again opened a dialogue with the protesters.[30]

Shevardnadze's career reveals a man complexly formed by integrity and stubbornness, shrewd calculation of risk, and the ability to please his superiors. He knew the limits of what was possible within the system and yet often pushed right up against those limits without transgressing them. His campaigns against corruption were only partly successful, so deeply ingrained were the practices of the "second economy" in Georgian life. And for all his expressed humanism, Shevardnadze tolerated some of the worst police practices, including torture, in the Soviet Union.[31] As a post-Stalinist leader operating after the elimination of the worst excesses of the terror system, Shevardnadze both negotiated with representatives of dissident views in society and repressed the most intransigent in the extralegal dissident movement.[32]

Shortly after Shevardnadze became first secretary, a small group of intellectuals formed the Initiative Group for the Defense of Human Rights in Tbilisi. Among the founders of this embryonic dissident movement were Merab Kostava and Zviad Gamsakhurdia. The son of the most famous Georgian novelist of the twentieth century, Konstantine Gamsakhurdia, Zviad grew up a child of privilege and became a teacher of American literature at Tbilisi State University. As Shevardnadze hunted down corruption in the republic, Gamsakhurdia and his associates appealed to him to intensify the investigations that led to the wife of Mzhavanadze. Raising embarrassing issues of the systematic pillaging of Georgian religious treasures and the misfortunes of the Meskhetian Turks (Georgian Muslims exiled during Stalin's time), Gamsakhurdia and Kostava escalated their campaigns by making contact with Russian dissidents and the Western media. In 1975, about the time of his father's death, Zviad Gamsakhurdia began publishing a samizdat journal, *okros satsmisi* (Golden Fleece), and two years later he, Kostava, and Viktor Rtskhladze founded the Georgian Helsinki Watch Group.

The government cracked down in 1977, arresting Gamsakhurdia and Kostava and charging them with disseminating anti-Soviet propaganda. Sentenced to three years in prison and two in exile, Gamsakhurdia decided to recant his views on television in order to receive a pardon.[33] Kostava refused to capitulate, and Gamsakhurdia's authority as a dissident suffered for a time, although he reemerged briefly in 1981 during a campaign to protest restrictions on the Georgian language.

The Georgian Communist elite, both before, during, and after Shevardnadze's rule, was ethnically and personally cohesive and was able to withstand penetration by outside authorities. The solidarity of the elite had a complex ethnic coloration to it directed upward against Russians and downward against minority nationalities living in the republic—Armenians, Abkhaz, Ajars, Azerbaijanis, Osetins, and others. An "official" nationalism favoring Georgians over other peoples was tolerated, indeed encouraged by the Georgian leadership; even Shevardnadze, who periodically attacked "half-baked nationalism," accommodated himself to it. The illegal economic activities found in other parts of the Soviet Union took on a specifically ethnic tone and a systemic quality in Georgia. The center's policy of "indirect rule" permitted the local elite a degree of tolerance of deviant behavior. Close friendship and kinship ties within the elite reinforced the exclusionary character of politics in the republic—the sense of superiority of the titular nationality and inferiority of the non-Georgians.

During the early years of perestroika (1985–1988), Georgia was relatively quiet. Shevardnadze's successor, Jumber Patiashvili, was a somewhat conservative party leader who maintained a tight rein on dissent, attacked the church, and refused to engage in dialogue with the informal associations springing up in the republic.[34] But the Communist elite was caught between the policies of Gorbachev, who in 1986 and 1987 encouraged open critical expression by the non-party intelligentsia, and Georgia's own literary intelligentsia, which had long before become fervently nationalistic.[35] Not only were Georgian intellectuals dedicated to the preservation and dissemination of the Georgian language, but they also expressed a chauvinistic sense of Georgian superiority over non-Georgians in the republic.[36] The discourse of the nation, with its inherently anti-Communist and anti-Russian overtones, was appropriated so completely by the extraparty intellectuals that Communists and communism were easily constructed as alien to Georgianness.

Ecological, religious, and political issues combined by 1988 in a potent nationalist discourse that rapidly expanded the permissible bounds of glasnost. Yet, although overwhelmingly nationalist in a broad sense, the Georgian intelligentsia remained deeply divided in its attitudes toward the existing order and in its commitment to a radical move toward independence. The party and police attempted unsuccessfully to contain the movement, attacking Gamsakhurdia in the press and breaking up meetings and demonstrations on the anniversary of Georgian independence (May 26, 1988).

Events in neighboring Armenia and Azerbaijan stimulated the explosion of a new politics of ethnic conflict in Georgia. In June 1988, fifty-eight Abkhaz Communists sent a letter to the Nineteenth Party Conference in Moscow demanding the secession of Abkhazia from Georgia. The growing fear on the part of Georgians of an Abkhaz "Karabakh" in Georgia, combined with threatened changes in the USSR constitution that seemed to deny union republics the right to secession, led to massive demonstrations in Tbilisi in November.

Approximately 100,000 people defied the government's restrictions on demonstrations and marched through the streets carrying the red-black-and-white Georgian national flag and demanding an end to discrimination against Georgians by Abkhaz, Azerbaijanis, Ajars, and Osetins.[37] The government responded weakly to the growing oppositional mood by drafting laws on preservation of the Georgian language and historic landmarks and rejecting constitutional amendments that the crowd saw as infringements on Georgia's rights.[38]

The Abkhaz question, as well as the Ajar and the Osetin questions, distorted the issues of democratization and sovereignty put forth by the Georgian nationalist movements by confusing these issues with the issue of Georgian ethnic hegemony in the republic.[39] The problem of the non-Georgians, more than any other, resounded outside the Tbilisi intelligentsia and provided the dissident intellectual leaders with a mass following. Georgians made up 70 percent of the population of the republic as a whole, but non-Georgians were strategically located around the periphery. Although Abkhaz were a minority in Abkhazia (17 percent with 46 percent of the population Georgians), Osetins had a clear majority (66 percent) in the South Osetin Autonomous District. In each of the autonomous regions, the titular nationality had a dominant, though contested, political weight that was increasingly becoming intolerable to nationalist Georgians. To the non-Georgians, the republic fit the image drawn by Andrei Sakharov and others of Georgia as a "miniature empire." The Georgians' alarm was deepened not only by fears that nearly one-third of the republic's population could have potentially separatist agendas but also by anxiety about the chronically low birthrate for ethnic Georgians and the higher rates for non-Georgians.

Gaining a sense of its own power, the Georgian nationalist movement maintained its pressure after November through demonstrations and hunger strikes against the perceived Abkhaz threat. After a mass meeting of Abkhaz on March 18, 1989, called for separation of Abkhazia from Georgia, the protests escalated. Faced by growing crowds in the center of the capital and fearing for its survival, the Patiashvili government asked Moscow for permission to repress the demonstrators.[40] Early in the morning of April 9, 1989, Soviet troops wielding sharpened shovels and using toxic gas waded into the peaceful crowds in central Tbilisi. Nineteen people were killed, mostly women, and hundreds injured.

The Georgian national movement was further radicalized by the Tbilisi massacre. When Merab Kostava was killed in October 1989 in an automobile accident, Gamsakhurdia was left as the major figure in the movement.[41] His rhetoric included calls for "national wholeness" but left little room for compromise with or tolerance of alternative views. The more moderate groups—such as the Popular Front, the Rustaveli Society, and the Social Democratic Party—sought to lay the foundations for a multiparty system and agreed to participate in the parliamentary elections scheduled for March 1990. But it was the radicals, wanting no association with the "illegitimate" Communist regime, who determined the pace and shape of the movement.

Many of the dozens of organizations and self-styled parties—for example, the Society for National Justice, headed by Irakli Shengelaia; the Georgian National Democratic Party, headed by Giorgi Chanturia; the Society of St. Ilia the Righteous; the Monarchists; and the Republican Federative Party—refused to support the Popular Front because it worked within the existing system. When it appeared that most of the opposition would boycott the March Supreme Soviet elections, the Popular Front convinced the regime to postpone the elections until the fall. In late May 1990, the forces advocating the boycott brought together over 6,000 delegates for the first congress of the National Forum and overwhelmingly agreed to hold their own elections to a Georgian national congress that could then lead the country toward independence. On September 30, the elections were held, and the

National Independence Party, led by Erekle Tsereteli, emerged as the largest delegation with Chanturia's National Democrats second.[42]

Meanwhile, Gamsakhurdia, who was particularly hostile to Chanturia, had decided to work with those who agreed to participate in the elections to the Supreme Soviet. Opposing groups escalated the rhetoric, both against each other and against the non-Georgian minorities. Gamsakhurdia touched the underlying fears of Georgians that they were losing their hold over their own land by claiming that Azerbaijanis and Lezgins were illegally buying up property in eastern Georgia. His coalition—the Round Table—organized a rail blockade of the republic to force the government to accept a new electoral law stipulating that only parties operating through the whole territory of the republic could contest the elections. This law effectively disenfranchised the non-Georgians, whose parties were limited to specific regions.[43]

Gamsakhurdia both reflected the militance of many of the nationalists and inflamed it by his inflexible response to the non-Georgians, whom he accused of being stooges of Moscow. The national movement failed to develop a discourse of civil or human rights that expressed an unconditional right of national self-determination for its minorities. Instead, the non-Georgians were depicted as "foreigners," recent arrivals living on authentically Georgian land, and as more loyal to the imperial Russian power than to Georgia.[44]

Six nationalist blocs competed against the Communists in the parliamentary elections of October 28, 1990. Gamsakhurdia's Round Table coalition swept the elections with the Communists a distant second.[45] Elected chairman of the Supreme Soviet, Gamsakhurdia formed a non-Communist government headed by Tengiz Sigua.[46] As the Communists retired from power, the new government made clear its intention to lead Georgia toward full independence from the Soviet Union.[47]

In their new leader, Georgians had a charismatic but single-minded man. As one long-time observer of Gamsakhurdia noted:

Central to Gamsakhurdia's entire political career is his messianism—his mystic belief that he was divinely appointed by God to lead the Georgian people, and by extension, that Georgia has a divine mission to be a moral example to the rest of the world. Linked to this are his megalomania, his conviction that he is infallible—which didn't prevent him being alarmingly inconsistent—his paranoia (he appears to have been convinced that anyone who failed to agree with him, or failed to obey his orders, was an agent of Moscow charged with subverting Georgia's progress towards independence) and his intolerance, which has been described as not so much a character trait as a tactic.[48]

The euphoria of political renaissance was darkened by ominous shadows of not only interethnic warfare but also rival centers of power within the Georgian national movement and the growing authoritarianism and arbitrariness of the new leader of the republic.[49] Gamsakhurdia took control of the mass media and arrested both the leader of the Osetin resistance and his principal Georgian opponents, most notably Jaba Ioseliani, the commander of the paramilitary force *mkhedrioni*. Instead of local power being devolved to elected councils, Gamsakhurdia appointed regional prefects to carry out his policies. When the regional soviet of south Osetia decided to proclaim itself an autonomous republic, Gamsakhurdia declared publicly that "if [the Osetins] do not wish to live peacefully with us, then let them leave Georgia."[50] Within two weeks, 200 buses from Tbilisi drove toward Tskhinval to rally against the soviet's decision, and for twenty-four hours Osetins and Georgians faced each other with Ministry of Internal Affairs troops between them.

After a referendum in which almost 90 percent of the voters endorsed a "restoration of the state independence of Georgia," the formal declaration took place on the second anniversary of the Tbilisi killings, April 9, 1991.[51] A few days later, the parliament unanimously selected Gamsakhurdia president of the republic. And on the seventy-fourth anniversary of the first declaration of Georgian independence, May 26, 1991, voters overwhelmingly (86.5 percent of the ballots cast) chose Gamsakhurdia as Georgia's first popularly elected president.

Fearful of Communist designs on his republic, surrounded by armed men, his house guarded by vicious dogs, Gamsakhurdia saw enemies everywhere. A particular target of his wrath was Shevardnadze, whom, he said, had been falsely portrayed as a martyr to democracy. After Gamsakhurdia sent a telegram to Washington expressing regret about the Americans' choice of president, both the foreign minister, Giorgi Khoshtaria, and the prime minister, Tengiz Sigua, left the government. They were replaced by men whom many believed to have been close to the Georgian mafia, the complex network of entrepreneurs, politicians, and criminals that ran much of the second economy under the Soviets.

As the president moved steadily toward a more dictatorial posture, the opposition took advantage of Gamsakhurdia's failure to condemn resolutely the August 1991 coup against Gorbachev. Battle lines formed through the autumn, and compromise between two opposing coalitions within the nationalist movement proved impossible. On December 22, the president's opponents launched armed attacks on the parliament building in central Tbilisi, where Gamsakhurdia was holed up in a basement bunker. The "Soviet" army did not intervene—Georgia had rejected membership in the Commonwealth of Independent States—and dozens of people were killed as tanks roamed the streets. By January 2, 1992, the opposition had gained the upper hand, freed political prisoners, and set up a military council to replace the Gamsakhurdia government. When pro-president demonstrators rallied the next day, gunmen fired into the crowd killing two and wounding twenty-five. On January 6, Gamsakhurdia escaped from the parliament building and fled the country.[52]

In late February 1992, the Tbilisi nationalists invited Shevardnadze to return to Georgia, and within days of his arrival in early March, the former party chief was appointed chairman of the State Council. With no real power base of his own within Georgia, Shevardnadze had to form an alliance of convenience with the politicians—Ioseliani, Kitovani, and Sigua—who had invited him back to Georgia. His role was one of mediation and reconciliation, and his enormous international prestige contributed to the growing sense, both within the country and abroad, that he alone could bring peace to Georgia.

Though the painful fractures in the Georgian political elite in Tbilisi were not overcome by Shevardnadze's arrival, the principal source of political instability through 1992 and 1993 came from the Gamsakhurdia forces, mostly in western Georgia, and the renewed conflict in Abkhazia.

The anti-Gamsakhurdia coalition was as disunited as the nationalist movement from which it emerged. Kitovani and Ioseliani both had their own armed retinues, and yet neither of them could control their followers completely. The State Council sought to broaden its base and legitimize its rule by mounting a campaign to discredit Gamsakhurdia, who was depicted as a madman and a force of disintegration within Georgia, and by easing pressure on non-Georgians, freeing the press, registering political parties, and organizing elections to a new parliament. On October 11, 1992, the voters gave Shevardnadze the kind of mandate that a year and a half earlier they had given Gamsakhurdia: Of those voting (about 60 percent of the electorate participated), 89 percent voted for Shevardnadze as speaker.[53] His Peace Bloc (*mishvidoba*) won the largest number of votes of any party and took thirty-five seats in the new parliament; in second place was the October 11 Bloc, made up of moderate reformers from the Popular Front and other groups, with nineteen seats.[54] As in the Lithuanian elections about the same time, members of the former Communist elite reemerged into political life. Former party chief Jumber Patiashvili was elected from Mtskheta, the ancient Georgian capital, and other local bosses from Kutaisi, Kobi, and Telavi found seats in the new parliament, along with representatives of the non-Georgians.

The elections accomplished the first goal of Shevardnadze—to create a legitimate, inclusive organ of power in order to create a strong executive for Georgia. But, as in Azerbaijan, political stability was hostage to the internal ethnic war. In September 1993, Abkhaz nationalists abandoned a Russian-brokered cease-fire and took Sukhumi. At the same time, Gamsakhurdia's followers revived the war in western Georgia, driving back Shevardnadze's forces. Shevardnadze was forced to invite in Russian troops and agree to have Georgia enter the Commonwealth of Independent States, by then increasingly dominated by Yeltsin's Russia.

Although the ethnic, regional, ideological, and political divisions remained deep in Georgia, most of the Georgian political and intellectual elite recognized that Shevardnadze was the man most likely to bring about reconciliation of hitherto irreconcilable elements. Zviad Gamsakhurdia's mysterious death in December 1993 removed the main alternative to Shevardnadze for the moment, and the reentry of Russia into Transcaucasian politics also contributed to stabilization of the former party secretary's powers.

Shevardnadze's government suffered the loss of Abkhazia and the inability to negotiate a peaceful resolution of that crisis, the de facto separation of Osetia from the republic, widespread civil disorder and assassinations, and seemingly endless economic crisis. Yet the popularity of the president and the conviction that he alone can effect the end of the current disaster continued to rise. Georgia was a society deeply wounded by the interethnic and intra-Georgian conflicts already in their seventh year, and fatigue and despair were mitigated only slightly by the fragile hope that Shevardnadze, with his international prestige and mediation skills, could reunite the country. The Russian war in Chechnya rebounded to Tbilisi's benefit, for Dudaev and the Chechens had been allies of the rebel Abkhaz. Yeltsin and Shevardnadze's opposition to secession of ethnic regions coincided more exactly after December 1994, and the likelihood of Russian pressure on the Abkhaz leader, Vladimir Ardzinba, to come to terms with the Georgians increased. As he began his fourth year back in power, Shevardnadze still reigned over a fractious and splintered society, but at least some harbingers of political improvement had been sighted.

Conclusion

To explain the collapse of the Communist elites and the rocky roads to power of the new elites in Transcaucasia, I have emphasized several factors: the degree of unity and consensus achieved within the nationalist movements; the intransigence or flexibility of the ruling Communist elites; the nature of leadership in the nationalist movements; the nature of the various, competing nationalist discourses (inclusive, tolerant, and democratic or exclusivist, intolerant, and authoritarian); and the divisive factor of interethnic strife (largely absent in Armenia; thrust upon the Azerbaijanis by the Karabakh resistance; and fomented and encouraged by nationalist leaders in Georgia).

The relatively peaceful and democratic victory of the nationalists in Armenia was facilitated by the moderately flexible Communist elite, which by mid-1989 was already working with the nationalists. The homogeneous ethnic composition of the republic, which precluded internal ethnic problems (Azerbaijanis were quickly deported from the republic in late 1988 and early 1989), and the displacement of armed conflict outside the republic, to Karabakh, allowed Armenians to experience a relatively violence-free transition to democracy. The transformation of elites, finally, was lubricated by the ability of the nationalists to generate leadership and language that emphasized measured, pragmatic policies.

The delayed ascension to power of the Azerbaijani nationalists can be explained by the successful resistance of the Communist elite; its relative coherence and determination to hold on to its power; and the late formation, weak social base, and internal divisions of the nationalist elite. The inability of the nationalists to control effectively the autonomous mass movement, which expressed social as much as ethnic discontents, combined with the unpredictable and radicalizing factor of the Karabakh war to undermine the legitimacy of the old elite and open the way for the return of representative figures from the old regime. Azerbaijan's nationalist intellectuals suffered from the relative weakness of a widely accepted discourse of the nation and the absence of an overwhelming commitment to the nation-state of Azerbaijan that might have superseded local and clan loyalties.

The road to civil war in Georgia lay through the extremism of the nationalist leadership that emerged in the conflict with the Communists. The April killings radicalized the opposition and made accommodation with the Communists almost impossible, even as the latter attempted to find common ground. The multinationality of the Georgian republic became a source of conflict, in part because of the legacy of Georgian hegemonic and privileged rule, in part because so little effort was made to find an inclusivist rhetoric and program. Conflicts with the Abkhaz and Osetins created a cycle of violence that eventually enveloped the Georgian factions as well. When the divisiveness of Gamsakhurdia's policies and rhetoric reached into the very heart of the nationalist counterelite, leading politicians coalesced to overthrow the elected president and invite Shevardnadze, seen as a more conciliatory and prestigious figure, to reunify and pacify the fractured nation.

With the collapse of the Soviet Union and the simultaneous erasure of the "socialist choice," the new political game in town was nationalism. Only nation-based claims could compete in the new discursive and political environment for the available political and economic resources—for legitimacy and recognition by the great capitalist democracies and the multinational sources of funding, the International Monetary Fund and the World Bank. But in order for the claims of nationality to self-determination, sovereignty, and independent statehood to be fully acceptable to the international community, they had to be combined with the rhetoric and practice of democracy and a commitment to build a market system and to reject what was thought to be socialism. The difficulties in the short run in creating stable democratic states based on a dominant nationality were compounded by the deep and continuing weakening of state power, which was well under way under Gorbachev and only accelerated after him. Just as a rule of law seemed within reach, a new and pervasive lawlessness overwhelmed the means of enforcement. The successor states, particularly the least repressive ones, lost their monopoly over violence, as semiindependent militias (like *mkhedrioni* in Georgia), nationalist guerrillas (*fedayee* in Armenia), and remobilized Afghan veterans and mercenaries (in Azerbaijan) turned into independent, armed political actors. Over the whole process of state and market building hung the ever present threat of civil and interethnic war.

All of these elite transformations occurred in the broader Soviet, post-Soviet, and international contexts in which communism rapidly experienced an erosion of legitimacy and national self-determination, democracy, and market capitalism gained powerful, universal resonance. As the new elites in Transcaucasia attempt to gain legitimacy and longevity, as they try to turn themselves into new ruling classes, they may benefit from the warning expressed by Raymond Aron four decades ago:

A unified elite means the end of freedom. But when the groups of the elite are not only distinct but become a disunity, it means the end of the State. Freedom survives in those intermediate regions, which are continually threatened when there is moral unity of the elite, where men and groups preserve the secret of single and eternal wisdom and have learnt how to combine autonomy with cooperation.[55]

Notes

This chapter was completed with the research assistance of Lowell Barrington, who introduced me into the complexities of political elites and made suggestions to improve the argument. But even he could not overcome the foolishness of a historian treading into an alien discipline.

1. Judith Sue Kullberg, "The Origins of the Gorbachev Revolution: Industrialization, Social Structural Change, and Soviet Elite Value Transformation, 1917–1985" (Ph.D. dissertation, University of Michigan, 1992), p. 48. For fuller discussion, see pp. 163–187.

2. This is essentially the argument in Moshe Lewin, *The Gorbachev Phenomenon: A Historical Interpretation,* expanded ed. (Berkeley and Los Angeles: University of California Press, 1991); and in Ronald Grigor Suny, *The Revenge of the Past: Nationalism, Revolution, and the Collapse of the Soviet Union* (Stanford: Stanford University Press, 1993). Kullberg summed up this idea: "To a certain extent the Party's self-destruction in the perestroika period is a continuation, although expanded in size and compressed in time, of the long path the party had taken to self-elimination. Because its end goal was the modernization of society, which was seen as inextricably intertwined with the construction of socialism, it set about creating the social groups and organization of society that would eventually make it superfluous." Kullberg, "The Origins of the Gorbachev Revolution," pp. 412–413.

3. Robert D. Putnam, *The Comparative Study of Political Elites* (Englewood Cliffs, N.J.: Prentice-Hall, 1976), pp. 193–194; Harold Lasswell, Daniel Lerner, and C. Easton Rothwell, *The Comparative Study of Elites: An Introduction and Bibliography* (Stanford: Stanford University Press, 1952), p. 18.

4. Mountainous Karabakh, or Nagorno Karabakh (NKAO), was an autonomous region populated largely by Armenians within the Azerbaijan Soviet Republic. Armenians had opposed inclusion with Azerbaijan since incorporation in 1921, but the Soviet government had consistently rejected their appeals for merger with Armenia. Elizabeth Fuller, "Is Armenia on the Brink of an Ecological Disaster?" *Radio Liberty Research,* RL 307/86, August 5, 1986; "Armenian Authorities Appear to Yield to 'Ecological Lobby,'" ibid., RL 130/87, March 30, 1987; "Armenian Journalist Links Air Pollution and Infant Mortality," ibid., RL 275/87, July 14, 1987 (on Zori Balayan's article in *Literaturnaia gazeta,* no. 26, June 24, 1987); and "Mass Demonstration in Armenia Against Environmental Pollution," ibid., RL 421/87, October 18, 1987.

5. *Izvestiia,* January 6, 1988, p. 2; *Current Digest of the Soviet Press* (henceforth, *CDSP*) 40, 1, February 3, 1988, p. 17.

6. On the Karabakh movement and the struggle for Armenian independence, see Ronald Grigor Suny, *Looking Toward Ararat: Armenia in Modern History* (Bloomington: Indiana University Press, 1993), pp. 192–212, 231–246.

7. Soon afterward, the Armenian Communists regrouped at their Twenty-ninth Congress in November 1990. A group of delegates that favored a completely independent ACP left the congress after losing in a vote. S. K. Poghosyan was elected first secretary. On December 7 the party decided to remain within the CPSU and endorsed the move toward a market economy.

8. As early as January 1991, the Armenian parliament, led by the HHSh, decided not to participate in the referendum called by Gorbachev on the future of the Soviet Union. At the beginning of March the Armenian Supreme Soviet announced that the republic would hold its own referendum on September 21 to comply with the Soviet law on secession. Elizabeth Fuller, "The All-Union Referendum in the Transcaucasus," *Report on the USSR* 3, 13, March 29, 1991, p. 3.

9. See the parallel articles by Rafael Ishkhanian of the Karabakh Committee and Khajak Ter Grigorian of the Bureau of the Dashnaktsutiun in Gerard J. Libaridian, *Armenia at the Crossroads: Democracy and Nationhood in the Post-Soviet Era* (Watertown, Mass.: Blue Crane Books, 1991), pp. 9–38, 137–142. Both writers contrasted those Armenian heroes of the past who favored a Russian orientation (e.g., Israel Ori, Joseph Emin, Archbishop Hovsep Arghutian, Dr. Zavriev, General Antranik) unfavorably with those who proposed self-reliance (e.g., Davit Beg, Aram Manukian, Nzhdeh), though they did not use all the same examples.

10. Among the defeated candidates, the longtime militant Paruir Hairikian received 7.2 percent of the vote; Sos Sarksian, the Dashnak candidate, 4.3 percent; and the others—Zori Balayan, Raphael Ghazarian, and Ashod Navasartian—less than 0.5 percent each. *Armenian Mirror-Spectator,* October 26, 1991, pp. 1, 16.

11. *Aghber* is a western Armenian word for "brother" or "uncle," which was used pejoratively by Soviet Armenians for those immigrants who had "returned" to the homeland in the repatriation campaigns of the late 1940s.

12. Other leaders from the days of the Karabakh Committee include Ashot Manucharian, a vice principal of a secondary school, one of the most radically anti-Russian of the Karabakh movement's leaders, who became minister of the interior for a time; Samson Ghazarian, a schoolteacher in the same school, who later would join the Dashnaktsutiun; Hambartsum Galstian, a researcher in the Erevan city soviet's sociological research laboratory, who briefly served as mayor of Erevan; Rafael Kazarian, a physicist and corresponding member of the Armenian Academy of Sciences; Vano Siradeghian, a member of the Armenian Writers' Union, who later served as minister of the interior; Samvel Gevorkian, television commentator, who edited the HHSh newspaper *Haik;* Aleksan Hakopian, a researcher in the Institute of Oriental Studies of the Academy of Sciences, later editor of *Haik;* Vazgen Manukian, an instructor at Erevan State University, one of the most important theorists of the movement, who broke with Ter Petrosian to form the National Democratic Union only to return as acting defense minister; Babken Araktsian, department head at the university and later speaker of the parliament; David Vardanian, a senior researcher at the solid-state branch laboratory, now in opposition to Ter Petrosian; and Igor Muradian, a senior researcher at the Armenian Gosplan Economic Planning Research Institute.

13. From a conversation with a member of the Bureau of the Armenian Communist Party.

14. As Mark Saroyan argued, "The hegemony of the titular nationality was reproduced in all spheres of cultural practice, from the publishing of books, periodicals, and newspapers to the activities of theater and folkloric song and dance ensembles. ... Historiography was produced backwards from the current connection between nationality and territory, and, as a result, the officially canonized history of the titular nationality and that of the republic became virtually interchangeable." Saroyan, "Beyond the Nation-State: Culture and Ethnic Politics in Soviet Transcaucasia," *Soviet Union/Union Sovietique* 15, 1–2 (1988), p. 224.

15. For two overlapping but contrasting studies of the Aliev network, see John P. Willerton, *Patronage and Politics in the USSR* (Cambridge: Cambridge University Press, 1992), pp. 191–222; and Arkady Vaksberg, *The Soviet Mafia,* trans. John and Elizabeth Roberts (London: Widenfeld and Nicolson, 1991), pp. 170–204.

16. Arkady Vaksberg described the situation: "From the outside it looked like an uncompromising confrontation with the mafia. So one important point was omitted from the mass propaganda and also from the reports submitted to the Kremlin: the battle was not against the mafia but between one mafia and another. The overthrow of the first led to the enormous strengthening of the second." Vaksberg, *The Soviet Mafia,* p. 182.

17. Mark Saroyan, "The 'Karabakh Syndrome' and Azerbaijani Politics," *Problems of Communism* 39, 5 (September–October 1990), p. 19.

18. *Komsomolskaia pravda,* November 27, 1988, p. 2; *CDSP* 40, 48, December 28, 1988, p. 11.

19. *Krasnaia zvezda,* December 24, 1989; *CDSP* 40, 52, January 25, 1989, pp. 9–10. Panakhov managed to have an audience with the new party chief Vazirov and to convince him to release more than eighty apartments to workers. He was arrested in late December 1988.

20. The seven original members included Araz Alizade, Leila Iunusova, Salamov, Babaev, Kambarov, Hikmet Hajizade, and Tofik Gasimov. "The War Against the Azeri Popular Front: An Interview with Tofik Gasymov," *Uncaptive Minds* 3, 5 (14) (November–December 1990), p. 12.

21. Ibid. The leaders of the new group included Isa Gambarov, Naja Najafov, Vurvun Ajubov, Halakh Huseinov, and Abulfaz Aliev.

22. Among those on the five-member National Defense Council were Etibar Mamedov, Rakhim Gaziev, and the chair of the AKhJ, Abulfaz Aliev. The formation of the council had earlier been discussed by Mamedov and Gaziev with Vazirov. Ibid., p. 14.

23. *Rabochaia tribuna,* May 8, 1991; Elizabeth Fuller, "The Azerbaijani Presidential Election: A One-Horse Race," *Report on the USSR,* September 13, 1991, p. 13.

24. David E. Murphy, "Operation 'Ring': The Black Berets in Azerbaijan," *Journal of Soviet Military Studies* 5, 1 (March 1992), pp. 82.

25. *Bakinskii rabochii,* September 28, 1990; Fuller, "The Azerbaijani Presidential Election," p. 13. By fall, the Social Democrats could count about 2,000 members.

26. Elizabeth Fuller, "The Ongoing Political Struggle in Azerbaijan," *RFE/RL Research Report* 1, 18 (May 1, 1992); "Azerbaijan After the Presidential Elections," *RFE/RL Research Report* 1, 26 (June 26, 1992), pp. 1–2.

27. Elizabeth Fuller, "Azerbaijan: Geidar Aliev's Political Comeback," *RFE/RL Research Report* 2, 5 (January 29, 1993), pp. 6–11.

28. Eduard Shevardnadze, *The Future Belongs to Freedom,* trans. Catherine A. Fitzpatrick (London: Sinclair-Stevenson, 1991), p. 8.

29. Ibid., p. 28.

30. Ibid., p. 36.

31. These practices were guided by the head of the Georgian KGB, General Inauri, who stayed in his post from 1954 until late 1988.

32. As Shevardnadze explained: "I knew many of the people in the dissident movement in Georgia quite well. ... It was not within my power to protect the angry men and women who went beyond words to expose the system's faults and took steps that failed to conform to the Criminal Code.

"But there were hundreds of young people—students, scientists, and writers—whom I did manage to keep out of harm's way. We held open debates. Each of them fell under certain articles of the Criminal Code, which, however, were not invoked." Shevardnadze, *The Future Belongs to Freedom,* p. 37.

33. *New York Times,* May 20, 1978; *CDSP* 31, 27 (August 1, 1979), p. 20.

34. Stephen F. Jones, "Glasnost, Perestroika, and the Georgian Soviet Socialist Republic," *Armenian Review* 43, 2–3 (170–171) (Summer/Autumn 1990), p. 135; Elizabeth Fuller, "The Tenth Congress of the Georgian Union of Writers," *Radio Liberty Research,* RL 252/86, June 27, 1986, pp. 1–6.

35. For evidence of the growing nationalism in the Georgian intelligentsia, see Mark Kipnis, "The Georgian National Movement: Problems and Trends," *Crossroads* 1 (1978), pp. 193–215; Stephen F. Jones, "National Conflict at the Eighth All-Union Writers' Congress," *Nationalities Papers* 15, 1 (Spring 1987), pp. 7–21. Much of the material on Gamsakhurdia was gathered by Stephen Rapp.

36. *Kommunisti,* February 1, 1986; Elizabeth Fuller, "A Georgian-Armenian Literary Polemic," *Radio Liberty Research,* RL 375/86, September 24, 1986, pp. 1–4.

37. Banners called for Georgian sovereignty on a democratic basis, restoration of Georgian territories lost in the 1920s, and the end of KGB interference in the Georgian Orthodox Church.

38. *Kommunisti,* November 3, 1988; February 19, 1989; *Sakhalkho ganatleba,* February 15, 1989.

39. The Ajars are Muslim Georgians and have their own autonomous republic within Georgia, but Georgians insist that there are no important distinctions between Ajars and Georgians and in 1979 did not include a separate census category for Ajars. Frequent attacks on Islam in the Georgian press targeted Ajars but not the Azerbaijanis living in Georgia. Elizabeth Fuller, "Islam in Adzharia," *Radio Liberty Research,* RL 221/86, June 4, 1986, pp. 1–4; "The Georgian Press Again Attacks Islam," ibid., RL 81/87, February 24, 1987, pp. 1–4.

40. On the murky origins of the decision to suppress the Tbilisi demonstrations, see Egor Ligachev, *Tbilisskoe delo* (Moscow: Kodeks, 1991).

41. Elizabeth Fuller, "Merab Kostava: A Tribute," *Report on the USSR* 1, 43, October 27, 1989, pp. 19–20.

42. Elizabeth Fuller, "Georgian Movement for Democratization Jeopardized by Disunity," *Report on the USSR* 1, 36 (September 8, 1989), pp. 22–26; "Georgia Edges Towards Secession," *Report on the USSR* 2, 22, June 1, 1990, pp. 14–18; "Georgian Alternative Election Results Announced," ibid., 2, 43, October 26, 1990, pp. 23–24; "Georgia on the Eve of the Supreme Soviet Elections," ibid., 2, 45, November 9, 1990, pp. 18–21.

43. Within a month, the Supreme Soviet of Abkhazia declared itself a sovereign soviet socialist republic, and South Osetia declared itself an independent democratic Soviet republic.

44. See, for example, Giorgi Gachechiladze, "Ethnic Crisis in Georgia," *Georgian Messenger,* no. 2 (October 11–November 8, 1990), p. 3.

45. Fifty-one percent of the electorate participated in the September vote, and 68 percent in October. Out of 250 seats in the Supreme Soviet, the Round Table received 155 seats, the Communists 64, the Popular Front 12, and Democratic Georgia 4. The National Democrats, whose leader Chanturia was shot on the eve, boycotted the elections. Robert Parsons, "Turning Point in Georgia," *Soviet Analyst* 19, 18, September 12, 1990, pp. 3–5; "Nationalists Triumph in Georgian Elections," ibid., 19, 22, November 7, 1990, pp. 5–6; Daniel Abele, "A Restive Soviet Georgia Goes to the Polls," *New Outlook,* Fall 1990, pp. 38–43. Election results can be found in *Zaria vostoka,* November 9, 1990, p. 2; November 14, 1990, p. 2.

Probably because of Gamsakhurdia's preelection remarks proposing the abolition of Ajar autonomy, the Round Table won only 24 percent of the vote in Ajaria; the Communists won 56 percent. After the elections, Gamsakhurdia softened his position and said that abolition of Ajar autonomy would have to be initiated from the local population. Elizabeth Fuller, "Zviad Gamsakhurdia Proposes Abolition of Adzhar Autonomy," *Report on the USSR* 2, 48, November 30, 1990, pp. 13–14. A month after the elections, Avtandil Margiani replaced Gumbaridze as head of the Communist Party, and the party decided to secede from the CPSU. The Abkhaz and Osetin delegates to the party congress denounced this last move.

46. Sigua, born in 1934, was a metallurgical engineer and an active member of the nationalist movement during perestroika. In 1990, he was elected chairman of the Shota Rustaveli Society and was an important figure in the Round Table coalition.

47. On the elections and the views of the Communists and Round Table, see Lynn D. Nelson and Paata Amonashvili, "Voting and Political Attitudes in Soviet Georgia," *Soviet Studies* 44, 4 (1992), pp. 687–697. As might be expected, nationalism and a commitment to independence were widespread in Georgia; Communists tended to be less hostile to non-Georgian minorities than were members of the Round Table; Round Table adherents favored a shift to a market economy more than Communist supporters did, but in general the population was highly ambivalent about such a transition.

48. Elizabeth Fuller, "Geopolitics and the Gamsakhurdia Factor," paper delivered at American Association for the Advancement of Slavic Studies (AAASS) convention, Phoenix, November 19, 1992.

49. Elizabeth Fuller, "Spotlight on Georgia," *Report on the USSR* 3, 7, February 15, 1991, pp. 17–22; "Gamsakhurdia's First 100 Days," ibid., 3, 10, March 8, 1991, pp. 10–13.

50. *Zaria vostoka,* December 8, 1990.

51. Elizabeth Fuller, "How Wholehearted Is Support in Georgia for Independence?" *Report on the USSR* 3, 15, April 12, 1991, pp. 19–20; "Georgia Declares Independence," ibid., 3, 16, April 19, 1991, pp. 11–12.

52. Elizabeth Fuller, "Georgian President Flees After Opposition Seizes Power," *RFE/RL Research Report,* January 17, 1992, pp. 4–7.

53. Voting occurred only in ten electoral regions; in the nine districts of Abkhazia, South Osetia, and western Georgia (9 percent of the electorate), no voting took place. Elizabeth Fuller, "The Georgian Parliamentary Elections," *RFE/RE Research Report* 1, 47, November 27, 1992, pp. 1–4.

54. The Unity Bloc (a loose coalition of Afghan veterans, artists, and filmmakers) and Chanturia's National Democrats won 15 seats each. Former followers of Gamsakhurdia

who had broken with him in fall 1991 also won small representations: Charter-91, 9 seats; the monarchist Union of Georgian Traditionalists, 7 seats; the Merab Kostava Society, 7 seats. Among other parties were the Union for National Agreement and Revival, 5 seats; and the National Independence Party, 4 seats. The new parliament was largely a body made up of the scientific intelligentsia (72 of 150 members); the cultural intelligentsia (22); and "practical" intellectuals, like engineers or agronomists (20). About 10 deputies were former government officials, and another 10 were professionals, doctors, journalists, or businessmen. Darrell Slider, "The October 1992 Elections in Georgia," paper delivered at the AAASS, Phoenix, November 19, 1992.

55. Raymond Aron, "Social Structure and the Ruling Class," *British Journal of Sociology* 1, 2 (June 1950), p. 143.

CHAPTER 8

Nursultan Nazarbaev and the Balancing Act of State Building in Kazakhstan

Martha Brill Olcott

As even a brief biography will make clear, the career of Kazakhstan's first president is a Soviet success story. In another country, Nursultan Nazarbaev might well have remained what he was born, the son and grandson of cattle herders from a remote mountain village. Instead, because of Soviet education and experience as well as of his own talent and ambition, Nazarbaev has risen to attend the difficult birth of independence in a territory containing 16 million people, over lands stretching from China to the Caspian having agricultural, mineral, and petroleum potential sufficient to make Kazakhstan a giant of the twenty-first century. At the same time, Soviet legacy has left so many political, ethnic, and economic landmines strewn about Kazakhstan that Nazarbaev has not been able even to keep his society on the level at which it was at independence. Transformation of Kazakhstan from a post-Soviet administrative leftover into a true nation will require a series of political and economic miracles. What makes the process so engrossing to observe is that Nazarbaev is the man who may be able to work the necessary magic.

Preparing for Power

Nursultan Nazarbaev, son of Abis (and hence Abisevich or Abisuli), was born in 1940 in the village of Chemolgan, near the city of Alma-Ata (now Almaty), in what was then the Kazakh Soviet Socialist Republic of the USSR.[1] He was educated locally and in the Ukraine city of Dneprodzerzhinsk, where he completed a technical school in 1960. Upon graduation, he returned to Kazakhstan to work as a metallurgist in the Karaganda Metallurgical Combine in Temirtau.

It was in Temirtau that Nazarbaev became active in political organizations, first in the Komsomol and then in the local Communist Party. By 1979 he was second secretary of the Karaganda regional committee, from which post he was moved to Alma-Ata in 1980 to serve as secretary for industry on the republic's central committee. In 1984 Nazarbaev was appointed chairman of Kazakhstan's Council of Ministers, effectively the number two position in the republic after Dinmukhamed A. Kunaev, the republic's longtime Brezhnev-era leader.

When Mikhail Gorbachev finally forced Kunaev from office in December 1986, Nazarbaev presumably had hopes of succeeding to Kunaev's position, but Moscow appointed instead Gennadii Kolbin, a Russian who had no previous connection to Kazakhstan. This set off three days of rioting in Alma-Ata, December 16–18, 1986, the first major ethnic disturbance of a sort that soon was to become common throughout the USSR.

Kolbin returned to Moscow in June 1989 after riots in Novyi Uzen (a western Kazakhstan oil town), and Nazarbaev was appointed as his replacement, first as head of the Kazakhstan Communist Party and then, in September 1989, as chairman of the republic's Supreme Soviet. In accordance with Gorbachev's attempts to revivify the political structure of the USSR, in March 1990 Nazarbaev was elected president of the Kazakh SSR by the members of a newly elected, Communist Party–controlled parliament. On December 1, 1991, under the slogan of "Want a Flag for Kazakhstan? Cast Your Vote for Nursultan!" Nazarbaev was reconfirmed president by popular vote, of which he got nearly 98.8 percent (no second candidate was able to gather enough signatures to get his name on the ballot). On December 16, 1991, the fifth anniversary of the Alma-Ata riots, Nazarbaev declared Kazakhstan's independence.

Nazarbaev's Two Nationalities

Nazarbaev's upbringing was very Kazakh, but it could not be called traditional because by 1940 the age-old nomadic lifestyle of the Kazakhs had been shattered by tsarist and Soviet policies that between 1916 and 1935 had killed or forced into emigration more than 3 million Kazakhs, or nearly 70 percent of the population. However, unlike up to 40 percent of today's Kazakhs and most members of Kazakhstan's elite, Nazarbaev grew up fluent in his native language and aware of his people's past. Indeed, to Kazakhs and others who know the Kazakh system of clans and hordes (*zhus*), the friction between Kunaev and Nazarbaev that erupted in 1986 and continued in one form or another until Kunaev's death in 1993 is said to be fully explained by the fact that Kunaev was from the Great Horde[2] and Nazarbaev from the Small Horde.[3] Although he did not cite them in his autobiography, Nazarbaev indicated that he could name his "seven fathers," a basic constituent of Kazakh self-definition.

Nazarbaev has observed traditional rituals in his own family, marking his mother's death with a funeral that attendees claim would have honored the mother of a Kazakh prince. He has demonstrated on television and in public forums his ability to play the *dombra,* a Kazakh folk instrument, a skill in which he appears to take genuine pleasure. Certainly these accomplishments have given him an unquestioned Kazakh identity, which has been an important factor in the republic's politics.

In other regards Nazarbaev's biography is less typically Kazakh and more Soviet. For all its myriad faults, the Soviet system did provide rough but genuine ladders upward for ambitious, capable citizens, even those from remote cow-herding kolkhozes deep in Kazakhstan. Somewhat atypically for Kazakhs, who are badly underrepresented in the republic's industries, Nazarbaev chose not to remain a cowherd but went instead into metallurgical engineering after a brief flirtation with a desire to become a pilot.[4]

In addition to giving him perfect Russian language, Nazarbaev's education and manufacturing experience provided him the technical skills necessary to let him rise rapidly. The Karaganda region is the "other" Kazakhstan, heavily industrial, mineral-rich, and Russianized almost to the point of ethnic exclusivity. Although Nazarbaev's official "biography in interviews," *No Rightists nor Leftists,* suggests that he was an innovator throughout his career, his visible demeanor during the Brezhnev era was that of a loyal functionary. Indeed, in 1980, when he was made secretary of the Kazakhstan branch of the Communist Party, the party's elderly chief ideologist Mikhail Suslov claimed Nazarbaev as a protégé.[5]

Whatever his private feelings may have been as he worked in the party apparatus during the Brezhnev years, Nazarbaev was receiving solid training in the methods of party work, which entailed distrust of spontaneity and demanded rigorous hierarchical control. Nazarbaev's career also gave him an intimate understanding of Kazakhstan's economy, including its interdependence with the economies of the other Soviet republics.

Nazarbaev has spoken little of his reaction to Gorbachev's decision in December 1986 to force out Dinmukhamed Kunaev and replace him with Gennadii Kolbin. Kolbin, the party first secretary in the Russian province of Ulianovsk, not only was an ethnic Russian but also had no previous connection to Kazakhstan or Central Asia. The demographics and history of Kazakhstan make it possible to speculate that this appointment should have been a crisis for Nazarbaev, bringing into conflict elements of his identity that earlier would have worked harmoniously.

The vitriol the Gorbachev administration unleashed about the Brezhnev period has obscured the degree to which, for non-Russians, those decades permitted a limited sort of national renaissance. Perhaps because of his administrative experience in Kazakhstan and Moldavia (now Moldova), Brezhnev was sympathetic to non-Russian sensibilities in a way that Yurii Andropov and, even more so, Gorbachev were not. Under Brezhnev, non-Russians were able to gather considerable local power and to achieve genuine national prominence. Not only did the republic first secretaries have real latitude for creating native infrastructures,[6] but three of them who were from Turkic ethnic groups (Kunaev, Sharaf Rashidov of Uzbekistan, and Heidar Aliev of Azerbaijan) gained places on the party's Politburo. The ability to preserve large chunks of national identity as "traditional customs" let many non-Russians create dual patriotisms for themselves as members of their own ethnic entity and as "Soviets"; this permitted members of very different national communities to entertain more or less equal expectations of reaching positions of responsibility in the government and party.

As chairman of Kazakhstan's Council of Ministers and the second most prominent Kazakh in the party, Nazarbaev must have had expectations that he would be picked to replace Kunaev. Indeed, that may be one reason Nazarbaev was prominent in criticizing Kazakhstan and its leadership at the April 1985 plenum of the CPSU Central Committee and the May 1985 meeting of the Kazakhstan party Central Committee[7] that laid down the rationale for Kunaev's eventual dismissal. Nazarbaev's credentials for republic leadership were already superior to those of Gorbachev's appointees in Turkmenistan (Saparmurat Niiazov), Tajikistan (Kakhar Makhkamov), and Kirghizia (Absamat Masaliev), and his critiques of Kunaev during the period March 1985–December 1986 demonstrated the sort of reform-mindedness that should have made him a member of the Gorbachev-Ligachev-Ryzhkov reform team.

Gorbachev's decision to pass Nazarbaev over for a Russian from outside Kazakhstan broke the rules of Soviet society in a fundamental way, as the students who gathered on Alma-Ata's streets to protest had immediately realized. What may have seemed rational cadre politics in Moscow—a means of reducing local political influence and of increasing integration into the greater union—looked from Central Asia much more like Great Russian chauvinism. Indeed, even before Kolbin's appointment, the Gorbachev administration appeared the most Russo-centric in living memory. The high incidence of Slavs among the Gorbachev appointments, Raisa Gorbachev's increasingly highlighted patronage of cultural figures and of the Russian Orthodox Church, the equally obvious absence of non-Russians among the Gorbachevs' entourage, and the sharp diminution of non-Russian representation in the Politburo all made Kolbin's appointment look in Alma-Ata like a slap in the republic's face—a statement that Moscow no longer trusted Kazakhs even to pretend to run their own affairs.

Gorbachev had already forced out the longtime leaders of Turkmenistan, Kirghizia, and Tajikistan, accusing them of incompetence, cronyism, and malfeasance, and had overseen a purge of the party in Uzbekistan that replaced, for example, 143 of the 177 members of the republic's Central Committee and all but two of that body's bureau.[8] In Uzbekistan especially the purge looked ethnically motivated, with Yegor Ligachev making "Uzbek" a synonym for "corruption" in the nation's newspapers, and Moscow-dispatched police investigators using methods not seen since the 1930s to extract "confessions" and "resignations for reasons of health" from prominent Uzbek cadres. Uzbekistan's longtime leader, Rashidov, had died in 1983, but this spared him only replacement, not vilification. In what was seen as a deep, even sacrilegious insult by local populations throughout Central Asia, Rashidov's body was exhumed from its burial place of honor and exiled to an ordinary grave.

Although Nazarbaev later permitted himself to observe in an interview that during the Soviet era "there was in fact friendship [among peoples] but at the same time each people bore in its soul a repressed national pride" (which he saw as "the main cause of the collapse of the USSR as an empire"),[9] Nazarbaev's primary objection to Kolbin seems to have been functional: that the new first secretary was not able to introduce the reforms that Moscow was beginning to sanction. Nazarbaev was an early and enthusiastic supporter of Gorbachev who used his position as head of the Council of Ministers to lobby for better follow-through on Moscow's still tentative economic reforms. In his first interview in the central press, given in *Druzhba narodov* in 1987, Nazarbaev said, for example:

> In the countryside a great deal is changing for the better, but to be honest, the new economic methods are difficult to introduce, with many incidences of stagnation and formalism. Many administrators are proceeding along the tried-and-true paths of the past, and are put in their roles by force. Producers complain that creation of Gosagprom [the USSR State Committee for Agroindustry] hasn't removed all the problems, that producers still don't have any independence of action, that they are being checked not just on what they produce, but on every step of the process, as was always done in the past, which I see as caused by the fact that the cadres who are in charge in the villages have not been able to do their work as they ought.[10]

What Nazarbaev surely understood Kolbin's appointment to be, however, was a demonstration of Moscow's intention to reduce regional economic autonomy as a means to increase overall Soviet economic performance. From the perspective of the non-Russians, who perceived themselves as having suffered long years of economic exploitation mitigated only slightly by limited autonomy, this signified that Moscow would now be taking even more, and they would be receiving less. As head of Kazakhstan's government, Nazarbaev was in position to have a good idea of how much Kazakhstan was supplying to Moscow's coffers and how little the republic was receiving in return, particularly since he was spending as much as a third of the year traveling about the republic studying the various industries and enterprises on-site.[11]

In June 1989 some fruits of the new policies that directed more to Moscow and less to the republics became clear when ethnic rioting broke out between local Kazakhs and north Caucasian transient oil workers in Novyi Uzen (Mangyshlak). Moscow's past economic policies had imported a volatile mix of races to extract oil from the Mangyshlak Peninsula, but the new policies had abandoned them—and the Kazakhs upon whom they had been imposed—to hot, dry, hungry poverty. Although Kolbin had already been reported to be preparing for reassignment to Moscow, the Novyi Uzen riots hastened his departure. Three days after the conflict erupted, on June 22, 1989, Nursultan Nazarbaev was formally named to the post of first secretary of the Communist Party of Kazakhstan.

Nazarbaev Takes Command

Nazarbaev's role in the two years that remained of Soviet history is probably best understood as that of an economic manager who is attempting to make the most rational decisions he can in the best interests of the enterprise of which he is in charge, based on a shifting and expanding body of information. Terms like "reformer" and "counterreformer" do not apply, because Nazarbaev was both, strongly supporting Gorbachev yet at the same time fighting with increasing vigor for the right of his republic to benefit economically from the resources it was supplying to the center. As Nazarbaev asked rhetorically in his address to the Twenty-eighth Congress of the CPSU, "How can Kazakhstan help [in the restructuring of Soviet society] if 90 percent of its industry is controlled by agencies in Moscow?"[12] As Nazarbaev made plain in that same address, the problem facing the USSR was not one of ideology as much it was one of efficacy; programs were being proposed and abandoned with little consideration of whether they would actually work. As he said, "Two or three years ago we swore we would never consider a market economy. We were also adamantly against sovereignty of the republics. ... Today we are calling for a union of sovereign states."

The other theme Nazarbaev repeated endlessly in 1989 to 1991 was that whatever the injustices and stupidities of the system, the economies of the Soviet republics were too tightly interwoven to permit the republics to go it alone as independent entities. As he put it in his conclusion to an address delivered at a plenum of the Kazakhstan Central Committee in April 1991: "It is time, I think, that everyone understood that it is impossible to construct heaven in one region or in one republic. The only way we can leave this dead end is together."[13]

Nazarbaev's position appeared to fit in well with Gorbachev's attempts to retain control of ever increasing demands for regional sovereignty or even, in the case of the Baltic states, for outright separation. Nazarbaev's firm support of the major Gorbachev positions—all the more valuable because the endorsements were coming from a man whose career was identified with a republic and not with Moscow—guaranteed Nazarbaev rising prominence nationally and, after 1990, even internationally. Indeed, had the Union Treaty not collapsed as a result of the August 1991 coup, Gorbachev planned to name Nazarbaev to the post of union president.[14]

What the Gorbachev administration apparently did not realize, however, even though Nazarbaev had said as much at the June 1989 party congress,[15] was that Nazarbaev's support of Gorbachev's slogan "strong center and strong republics" was based much more on the second half of the phrase than on the first. Once elected first secretary, Nazarbaev moved steadily to bring the republic's administration under his control. Kolbin had not had great success in putting his own cadre infrastructure in place, which was one reason the Russian had had little effect on republic policy. Nazarbaev, by contrast, moved to heal rifts with other Kazakhstani officials that had been opened by his fight with Kunaev (including making peace with Kunaev himself in April 1991).[16] Perhaps even more important, Nazarbaev took increasing command of the administration of his republic, reorganizing the Council of Ministers and moving it under his direct control. In March 1990, following the example set by Gorbachev in Moscow, Nazarbaev converted his chairmanship of the Supreme Soviet to a presidency confirmed by parliamentary election.

As astute a politician as he is, it cannot have been lost on Nazarbaev that it was also his non-Russianness that made him so valuable to Gorbachev, not least as a counterweight—especially in the international arena—to separatist national leaders such as Lithuania's Vytautas Landsbergis. Nazarbaev was never a nationalist, but he was and remains a strong regionalist who understood that economic and political relations in the USSR worked to the advantage of Moscow and to the disadvantage of the various regions. As he pointed out angrily at the Fourth USSR Congress of People's Deputies, even had the changes of the new union configuration come about, the tax structure it brought with it would still have left Kazakhstan with a budget deficit of 11 billion rubles (in 1991 rubles) because Moscow was, for example, buying Kazakhstan's copper at 1,500 rubles per ton (1991 prices), then selling it on the world market at $3,500 per ton, almost 100 times as much. The republic, Nazarbaev said, had delivered nearly $2 billion worth of raw materials to Moscow, for which it had received nothing in return.[17]

Initially, the role Gorbachev was giving him of being spokesman for a multiethnic, regenerated union was not a difficult one for Nazarbaev to play, especially since his increased prominence allowed Nazarbaev to wring significant concessions for his republic out of Moscow. This showed especially clearly in his handling of the 1991 miners' strikes in Karaganda: Nazarbaev was able to convince miners to accept a four-month moratorium on threats to strike in exchange for his personal guarantee that he would force Gorbachev to grant the republic greater control of the income from the mines.[18] For all his personal identification with his own Kazakh people, Kazakhstan's president understood himself as a creation of the Soviet system and appreciated that his republic was a uniquely Soviet creation.

Nazarbaev and the Rise of Nationalism in Kazakhstan

All of the Soviet republics were peculiar hybrids of Stalinist politics and age-old ethnicity, but Kazakhstan might have been the most peculiar of all. At the time of independence, the population was about 40 percent Kazakh and 40 percent Russian; the remainder included about 100 other nationalities, enough of them Slavic or Russophone to make Slavs and Russian speakers the majority population. In the waning days of the Soviet era and the increasingly heated nationalist politics that marked them, the distinctions between nationalist and regionalist were increasingly difficult to differentiate. Nazarbaev understood that for all his success on the national level, his political base at home was changing, as Kazakhs began to assert demands not just for republic sovereignty but for ethnic sovereignty.

Kunaev had attempted, with some success, to create a regional identity for the people of his republic, so that one was a Kazakhstanets, a citizen of Kazakhstan, whether Russian or Kazakh. In ethnic terms, however, the December protests of 1986 would have confirmed for Nazarbaev that strong Kazakh nationalist sentiments lay beneath the surface in his republic, regardless of whether he experienced the events while leading a column of demonstrators, as claimed in his biography,[19] or, as a public protest in 1991 asserted was the real truth,[20] while watching from the windows of his office. Even Kolbin seemed to have some sense of the nationalist dimensions of those 1986 protests, to judge by such gestures as his promise to learn Kazakh or, more significant, to allow the posthumous rehabilitation of certain purged Kazakh national heroes.

Nazarbaev took office with public expectation, by ethnic Kazakhs at least, that he would do more. To a certain extent Nazarbaev satisfied nationalist expectation by sponsoring a corrective rewriting of history. As he put it to an interviewer, "A man who studies the history of his own people seriously and in depth, and then writes about the complex stages of their development honestly and without retouches, has the mark of 'nationalist' hung about his neck."[21] More important, Nazarbaev persuaded parliament to pass the September 1989 bill declaring the republic's official state language to be Kazakh, which had slipped into a steep decline under Soviet rule.

Although securing passage of the language law took considerable effort on Nazarbaev's part, the republic's small but growing group of Kazakh nationalists were dissatisfied because the same bill had also recognized Russian as the language of interethnic communication. Although the distinction was, as Nazarbaev pointed out, essentially meaningless,[22] Kazakh nationalists felt it was nevertheless too large a concession and a loophole that vitiated the purpose of the bill.

At the same time, the language bill made the Russian nationalists, also small in number and also growing, feel they were in danger of becoming second-class citizens after decades of being first among putative equals. Especially prominent among the protesters were the members of Cossack bands. Reappearing, complete with sabers, in the last Soviet years, the Cossacks claimed that their 400-year presence in areas now part of northern Kazakhstan made those territories and cities theirs.

By the end of the Soviet era, this simultaneous increase of both Kazakh and Russian nationalism was beginning to present Nazarbaev with a real dilemma of political identity, which in many important regards remains unsolved even today. The Gorbachev reforms had discredited the past practice of appointing political leadership, requiring instead that republic leaders affirm their positions with mandates achieved by local vote. The experience of Masaliev, Nazarbaev's colleague and neighbor, who in 1990 was defeated for Kyrgyzstan's presidency by darkhorse Askar Akaev, made clear that such mandates could not be taken for granted but had actually to be won.

Demographics and prevailing attitudes in Kazakhstan made politicking for such a mandate virtually a zero-sum affair. Russians and Kazakhs are differentiated in the republic by occupation and place of residence: The industrial north and east are indistinguishable from Russian Siberia, whereas the Kazakh south and west are much more Central Asian, resembling Uzbekistan more than they do Russia. Thus attempts to meet the demands of striking miners would seem to Kazakhs as favoring the Russians; attempts to increase the role of the Kazakh language in the republic seemed to Russians to be a Kazakh attempt to force them from the republic or at least to restrict their role in public life. As Nazarbaev succinctly put the same point: "Some people [in the republic] go around with placards saying 'Nazarbaev is a Cossack hetman' and others fear the law on languages like the plague."[23]

Even more complex is the fact that history has largely robbed the Kazakhs of cultural identity. Many do not know their own language or practice Islam; virtually none live as pastoral nomads, as their ancestors did, making it difficult to define precisely what a Kazakh "is." Nonetheless, that Kazakhs are not Russians is plain to both groups. This has created strong political pressure for "Kazakh-ness" to differentiate itself from "Russian-ness," particularly since the off-handedness with which Gorbachev and Yeltsin treated Nazarbaev made it clear that the Russians were continuing to view themselves as the senior people of the USSR. An especially egregious example for the Kazakhs was the discovery that Gorbachev had signed a deal with Chevron Oil to develop Kazakhstan's Tengiz fields but had not notified Nazarbaev of the fact until the final stages of negotiation.

Nevertheless, Nazarbaev understood that a monoethnic Kazakhstan was impossible, and thus he continued to work energetically for the Union Treaty Gorbachev had proposed. That treaty was never signed, preempted by the attempted coup of August 19–21, 1991. Coup leader Gennadii Yanaev's reference to Kazakhstan as a republic that needed no "state of emergency,"[24] as well as Nazarbaev's initial reaction to solely call for public calm, led to some speculation that Nazarbaev's precoup support for political change was more opportunistic than genuine. In fact, however, Nazarbaev's reaction was entirely consistent with his public stance throughout 1991.

Although Nazarbaev had generally good personal relations with Gorbachev, he several times had chided the Soviet president for poor administration. Nazarbaev had pointed out as early as January 1991 that the USSR had not been able even to adopt a budget for the current fiscal year.[25] Product of a system under which instability and unpredictability were deemed the greatest evils and small units could not be trusted to contribute to the whole without a strong central power to coordinate and motivate them, Nazarbaev would reasonably have waited to see whether the coup was going to restore a strong center that would hold the union together. It may be too that there was another, as yet undisclosed, dimension to Nazarbaev's silence, since Boris Yeltsin was Nazarbaev's guest in Alma-Ata on the eve of the attempted coup; indeed, Nazarbaev's hospitality delayed Yeltsin's departure for three hours, which both Yeltsin and Nazarbaev later claimed derailed a plan by coup leaders to sabotage the Russian president's plane.[26] Once it was clear that the coup was even more poorly managed than was Gorbachev's USSR, Nazarbaev made the logical choice of the lesser of two evils.

The strength of Nazarbaev's conviction that independence was economic suicide for the republics in general and Kazakhstan in particular showed in his continued support for Gorbachev through the fall of 1991. It was Nazarbaev who presented the hastily reworked version of a new union covenant to the hurriedly assembled USSR legislators in the days that followed the failed coup. The growing momentum for republic independence, however, made any sort of continuation of the union increasingly unlikely, no matter how the union might be reconstituted. Consequently, Nazarbaev also worked strenuously in the last three months of the union's existence to protect Kazakhstan's interests. Nazarbaev had resigned his party membership soon after the coup but did not follow Yeltsin's example of trying to uproot the party in entirety. Indeed, Nazarbaev allowed the Kazakhstan Communist Party to hold a scheduled congress.

Part of the reason for Nazarbaev's relative restraint was the need to secure administrative continuity, because he was making personnel shifts in his government in anticipation of the increased financial responsibility that sovereignty or independence would bring. In October 1991 Nazarbaev appointed a number of economists to his cabinet, including Erik Asanbaev as vice president, Uzakbai Karamanov (head of the Council of Ministers) as chairman of a new Council of Ministers, and Daulet Sembaev (former head of Nazarbaev's economic advisory council) as vice premier. All were Kazakhs, which made Nazarbaev's selection for prime minister all the more interesting; he named Sergei Tereshchenko, a Russo-Ukrainian agronomist who had been born in the Far East but had earned his degree in Chimkent where, among other things, he had mastered Kazakh. Nazarbaev also appointed the first of several foreign economic advisers, including Grigory Yavlinksy, one of the authors of the 500 Days plan of economic transformation Gorbachev had commissioned, then rejected. Despite what must have initially been a difficult personal relationship between the maverick Yeltsin and the consummate organization man Nazarbaev, the two presidents forged political alliances during the last half of 1991. Nazarbaev also got public commitments from both Yeltsin and his vice president, Aleksandr Rutskoi, that Russia's government would recognize the existing border between the USSR's two largest republics.[27]

Nazarbaev apparently was unaware that the presidents of the three Slavic republics were contemplating the dissolution of the Soviet Union,[28] but he attempted subsequently to soften the apparent Slavic rejection of the non-Slavs by saying that he was offered the chance to sign the agreement of December 8, 1991, but refused because he had not read the documents and had had no hand in preparing them.[29] According to sources close to him, though, Nazarbaev was stunned by what seemed to him an unthinkable turn of events.[30]

If he was surprised, Nazarbaev recovered quickly, first convening a meeting of the heads of the Central Asian republics to make the specter of a Turkestani union a credible answer to the threat of a Slavic union, and then securing the agreement of Yeltsin, Kravchuk, and Shushkevich that a different dissolution document would be drawn up, this time in Alma-Ata. That meeting was held on December 21, 1991, creating the Commonwealth of Independent States (CIS).

Once independence was inevitable and an accomplished fact, Nazarbaev's position in a sense became the obverse of what it had been before the dissolution when he had attempted to hold the union together. His primary task became to define and defend the interests of his new nation. At the same time, Nazarbaev understood the conundrum of Kazakhstan's independence very well—that his was a multinational state born into an increasingly nationalist world.

Nazarbaev and the Problems of State Building

As of late 1993, Nazarbaev was the most successful of all the CIS presidents in the creation of the institutions of a new state. Chief among these is Kazakhstan's post-Soviet constitution, which was actively debated throughout 1992 and signed into law on January 28, 1993. Although he faced some of the same resistance from his Communist-era Supreme Soviet as Yeltsin did from his in Russia, Nazarbaev was more successful in negotiating approval for what he calls a "strong presidential republic."[31] Although the constitution creates a national parliament and a system of lower-level bodies, the president is accorded the right to make virtually all appointments in the republic, from the chief executives responsible for implementation of policy down to the lowest level of government; this power effectively makes the entire government of the republic an extension of the president.[32]

It is important to point out that unlike the other strong presidents in Central Asia, Islam Karimov and Saparmurat Niiazov, Nazarbaev is not creating a cult of his own person. The constitution very clearly provides for mandatory succession by forbidding a president to serve more than two terms (although Nazarbaev would be very close to 70, the constitutionally required age of retirement, after the two consecutive five-year terms he can be presumed to be likely to win).

The sort of system the constitution mandates says a great deal about Nazarbaev's understanding of the function of government. To Nazarbaev, as to most people of Soviet heritage, government is not seen, as it generally is in the West, to be an institutionalized means of controlling and directing the competition among various economic and social interests; rather, government to them is a system for delivering to the greatest possible number of citizens the widest possible array of social benefits. Even though Nazarbaev observed caustically that the former USSR "raised 300 million people in the habit of living off someone else: just lie back, everybody will have all social guarantees,"[33] the constitution he forged for his new state generally accepts that citizens have considerable rights by fact of birth, which the state is obliged to supply. Among these are the right to work (Article 19), the right to vacation (Article 21), the right to housing (Article 22), the right to free medical care (Article 23), the right to free secondary, vocational, and higher education (Article 24), and the right to social provision in old age (Article 25).[34]

Because he accepts such large financial obligations as the legitimate function of the state, it is not surprising that Nazarbaev's presidential style has been largely managerial. Development of political culture has taken second place to economic development, for, as Nazarbaev put it: "In this vitally important sphere [of the economy] there is no room for an orgy of democracy."[35] It is indicative of Nazarbaev's understanding of the nature of democracy that although the constitution permits the formation of political parties, it also specifically forbids the president and vice president to "occupy posts in ... public associations." At the same time, Nazarbaev has understood the pitfalls of creating a political system based entirely upon one person.

Despite his conviction that "the stabilization of the economy and the transition to the market demand a categorical ban on any party, political, or ideological interference in this process,"[36] Nazarbaev began in early 1993 to create a Union of Unity and Progress for Kazakhstan, which he has agreed to head. Not legally a political party (in part because the constitution would then forbid Nazarbaev to hold office in it), this union seems to be intended to fill the function of the old Communist Party, although not to replace its ideology. That is, Nazarbaev is creating an entity larger than himself that will be able to demand the allegiance and, more important, the ethical behavior of its members.

In the international arena, Nazarbaev's policies have reflected a similar drive for balance, again for managerial reasons. Nazarbaev has repeatedly stated that Kazakhstan is neither Eastern nor Western, neither Islamic nor Christian, but rather is a bridge between both. Kazakhstan has joined neutral international bodies such as the United Nations, but was alone among the Central Asian states in initially accepting only observer status in the Muslim-dominated Economic Coordination Council. Nazarbaev has hosted visits by the Iranian foreign minister and president but did not, unlike his colleagues Karimov and Niiazov, make an immediate pilgrimage to Mecca; indeed, he has stressed his own atheism and ignorance of Islamic ritual although he did eventually become a *haji*.

The Development Potential of Kazakhstan

Nazarbaev's preferred focus on economic development is certainly justified by the magnitude of Kazakhstan's potential, which is large enough to allow the state to become a world economic power. The Tengiz fields alone, which Chevron is slated to codevelop over the next forty years, are thought to contain recoverable reserves of 25 billion barrels of oil, or about twice as much as is in the Alaskan North Slope. The republic currently produces 5 tons of gold a year and has proven reserves of at least 100 tons. In 1989 Kazakhstan produced 23.8 million tons of iron ore, 151,900 tons of manganese, 6.8 million tons of steel, and 5 million tons of ferrous metals. The republic also possesses commercial quantities of uranium, chrome, titanium, nickel, wolfram, molybdenum, bauxite, and copper. In agriculture, the republic's potential is almost as rich. In 1989 the republic produced 20.4 million tons of grain (and more than half again as much in the bumper year of 1992), 315,000 tons of cotton, 1.6 million tons of meat, 5.6 million tons of milk, and 1.1 million tons of wool.[37]

Even more important for the creation of the sort of state Nazarbaev envisions, he has long understood that economies that rely on supplying raw materials are in an inherently weak position because they sell nonrenewable resources at prices far lower than the cost of the goods manufactured from those raw materials, which the supplying country must then purchase. As early as 1989 Nazarbaev was calling this cycle "robbery in broad daylight"[38]—one reason the ambitious development plan he unveiled in May 1992 calls for the republic to make a rapid transition to a manufacturing economy. The timetable the plan envisions is, first, to stabilize and satisfy the consumer market by 1995; then to make the transition from supplier of raw materials to a primarily manufacturing and processing economy by 2005; and then, by 2010 to 2015, to take a position as a major manufacturing and exporting world economy as a nation that will enjoy a multiparty system with significant guarantees of democratic liberties and well-protected human rights.[39]

The Continuing Perils of Ethnicity

The economic plan concludes with what might be called a Nazarbaev credo: "This [plan] may be seen as a social contract, dictated by the times, between the government and the people." However, there is a significant qualifier: "providing that both parties fulfill as sacred their obligations pertaining to its realization." What Nazarbaev has increasingly discovered since independence is not only that "the people" have been reluctant to take up their part of the contract, but that the government cannot fulfill its part of the contract either, because, to a degree not matched in any of the other former Soviet states, Kazakhstan is really two nations of virtually equal size, each of which sees advances by the other as its own loss.

Ethnicity has added complex ramifications to virtually every policy the Nazarbaev government has attempted to introduce. The Kazakhs have almost no tradition of retail trade, so that the decision to sell shops and small services to individuals, as was begun in 1992, has meant that retail outlets pass from the control of the faceless, vaguely Kazakh state into the hands of individual Uzbeks, Koreans, Chechens, and Russians, to whom Kazakhs pay far higher prices than they did in the past. Traditional Kazakh pastoral agriculture requires large ranges of land for grazing, so that privatization of farms has meant that land and equipment have gone to Russians, Ukrainians, and Germans, who know how to farm smaller plots. The oil fields of Mangyshlak were worked by Azerbaijanis and north Caucasians, who will stand to benefit the most from an inflow of foreign capital as the oil industry is developed.

On the other side, the Nazarbaev government's active efforts to assist the Kazakh population—such as large grants of money and equipment to help settle actively recruited Kazakh immigrants from Mongolia, China, and elsewhere in the CIS (almost 58,000 people by 1992)[40] and the differential laws that give Kazakhs rights of dual citizenship or allow foreign Kazakhs to own property in the republic—create resentment among the non-Kazakhs. The visible enrichment of well-connected Kazakh administrators and their family members is another source of envious anger.

This resentment is strongest among the Russians, who live, for the most part, in European-style cities in the north and east with virtually no Kazakhs among them save for administrators appointed by officials in Almaty. Those Kazakhs who do live in the predominantly Russian areas tend to be Russianized, frequently have Russian or Slavic spouses, and often are unable themselves to read or speak Kazakh. The political allegiance of these Russian people, which was to the Soviet Union, has largely transferred to a loosely conceived "Mother Russia" in which they still feel as though they live.

Nazarbaev is unlikely ever to win real political allegiance from this population. He realizes that they are acquiescing to his leadership because he seems the fittest of all Kazakhs to rule them and because they believe their basic interests are being served. As soon as they decide that their interests are not being served, their loyalty will move elsewhere.

That has already been demonstrated in a number of struggles for local control in Russian-dominated areas, such as the Baikonur space complex or Karaganda, where Nazarbaev has had essentially to buy local cooperation by granting extraordinary degrees of local autonomy, or, as in the case of Baikonur, leasing entirely to Russia. In manufacturing and mining areas like Karaganda that has meant that (Russian-dominated) enterprises buy and sell abroad and keep proceeds in their (Russian-dominated) oblast rather than contribute to the budget of the (Kazakh-administered) state.

Faced with new requirements that they begin to learn Kazakh, that their sons serve in a Kazakhstan army and swear loyalty to Kazakhstan, that their children either demonstrate knowledge of Kazakh to be educated in state schools or pay hard currency to study in Moscow, and that they legally forswear Russian citizenship (the new constitution allows dual citizenship only for Kazakhs), some of Kazakhstan's Russians are beginning to move back to Russia (approximately 129,000 by mid-1992).[41] Far more of them, however, would like to see Russia move back to them—and many are waiting for Yeltsin or some other Russian figure to give a signal that they should agitate for this. The situation is further exacerbated by the flight of Russians from the other Central Asian republics (109,000 of whom took up residence in Kazakhstan in 1991)[42] and by the insistence of the Cossacks of Kazakhstan that they be granted the same rights of separate administration (including the right to form military units) as have been granted the Cossacks of Russia.

The Kazakhs in the republic are willing to give active allegiance to Nazarbaev but increasingly are demanding in return that their nation become more Kazakh. There is little overt public sentiment in favor of forcing the Russians out, but even the least nationalist of the Kazakh-dominated parties finds it reasonable that citizens of Kazakhstan be required to know the Kazakh language and swear allegiance to Kazakhstan. Even Nazarbaev has felt it necessary to take an unequivocal stance: "In the final quarter of the seventeenth century Kazakhs controlled virtually the entire territory of present-day Kazakhstan. This means that Kazakhstan in its present form is ... [the Kazakhs'] historical homeland."[43]

The Continuing Fact of Russia

Nazarbaev can ill afford to alienate his Russian population, and he knows it. Not only are there too many of them, but they provide most of the trained personnel necessary to keep the economy running even at its present rate, to say nothing of expanding. Equally important, Russia shares a 3,000-mile border with Kazakhstan and dominates its neighbor economically; 70 percent of Kazakhstan's economy either goes to or comes from Russia. This domination of Kazakhstan has shown especially clearly in three issues with which Nazarbaev has had to wrestle: the development of the Commonwealth of Independent States (CIS) as an entity and Kazakhstan's place within it; the problem of national currency; and development of the state infrastructure.

Nazarbaev was among the strongest advocates of a functioning CIS. He strongarmed (his characterization) the CIS presidents into accepting a unified interrepublic banking alliance in November 1992,[44] and he lobbied forcefully for continuation of a common, jointly directed defense establishment,[45] neither of which came into being. The failure of the CIS to develop into anything more than "a club of presidents," as he called it,[46] has clearly frustrated Nazarbaev, and by the end of 1992 he was asking, "Does the CIS even exist, or is this a trick, a huge deception of the people? As long as we have set ourselves afloat, we should be totally honest, and say let's part ... let's start living separately."[47]

Although the difficulties of "living separately" have been evident in several areas, the most dramatic and most destructive issue involved Nazarbaev's determination to remain within Russia's ruble zone. Despite his recognition that to have "only one ruble currency but ... twelve independent budgets ... is nonsense,"[48] Nazarbaev consistently resisted introduction of a separate currency for Kazakhstan (to be called the tenge) because he could see the obvious danger: Should the tenge prove stronger than the ruble, this could tempt the Siberian cities just over the border into irredentist adventures; should the ruble prove stronger than the tenge, it would be the Russian cities of Kazakhstan that could be tempted to secede.

The decision to remain linked to the ruble for so long had enormous economic impact on Kazakhstan. The freeing of Russian prices in January 1992 set off inflation in Kazakhstan, judged to be about 2,500 percent for 1993, that the state had no means of controlling, since Russia was the sole emission source of currency as well as the major supplier of goods; Kazakhstan was thus buying goods at new, inflated ruble prices while still supplying raw materials at old, preinflation prices. The institution of a clearinghouse system of "bookkeeping" rubles in January 1993, which was intended to speed settlement of interrepublic accounts, instead led to the creation of an enormous debt to Russia, acknowledged as 547.6 billion rubles.[49] When Moscow withdrew pre-1992 rubles in August 1993, the Yeltsin government refused to ship Kazakhstan new rubles until that debt was cleared in hard currency. Because it lacked new rubles, Kazakhstan had to keep the old rubles in circulation and thereby turned itself into the unwilling dumping ground for invalidated rubles, which flooded in from all over the CIS, exacerbating inflationary pressures; in September alone the Kazakhstan police intercepted 9 billion "out-dated" rubles.[50] Even so, political necessity still seemed to dictate that Kazakhstan remain within the ruble zone, and Nazarbaev thus accepted the stern new regulations Moscow imposed in August 1993 that required ruble-using nations to cede most budgetary and financial decisions to Russia. Only when Russia's conditions were further modified to require that ruble nations place large deposits of gold in Russian control as surety did Nazarbaev finally accept the inevitable and put the tenge into circulation in November 1993.

Part of the reason Nazarbaev clung so long to the ruble, even past the point at which in domestic politics his stance perhaps made him appear subservient to Russia, was his awareness that a separate currency would further complicate the herculean job of building an infrastructure for Kazakhstan. Nazarbaev inherited a state that had a badly underdeveloped and deteriorating system of roads, railroads, utilities, housing, and other facilities. Furthermore, tsarist and Soviet policies had deliberately designed the infrastructure so that Kazakhstan could serve as supplier of raw materials and consumer of Russian-made goods. The most glaring example of this is oil; despite Kazakhstan's vast resources, the state is a net importer of petroleum products. Not only are imports of gasoline and lubricants the single largest constituent of Kazakhstan's debt to Russia, but the need for them supplies Russia with a political tool, which it has already used at least once. In summer 1992, when Kazakhstan attempted to establish customs checks on its borders, Russia responded by halting all fuel shipments, thus bringing Kazakhstan's grain harvest to a halt. The checks were removed, and gas shipments resumed. Part of the necessity to import is geographical, for the population centers are in the east and the raw oil is thousands of miles away in the west; much more important, however, is that Kazakhstan has no refineries with the physical capability to process its own high-sulfur oil.

Solutions to this problem are also instructive of the dilemmas Nazarbaev faces. Contracts have been let to a Japanese firm to build a refinery in Aturau capable of processing Kazakhstan's oil, but it will be several years until that comes on line.

As important, acquiring the capital to build the refinery has meant that Kazakhstan has had to forfeit a portion of its potential income as the price of attracting foreign investment.

An even larger problem is what to do with that gasoline after it is refined or, during construction of the refinery, how to realize benefit from Kazakhstan's crude oil on a world market. Several proposals have been made, and certain contracts even have been let, but all of the possible solutions present Kazakhstan with potential problems. Transport through the south necessitates Iranian involvement, which sharply limits the number of possible Western or even Middle Eastern investors. Transport west involves not only the physically daunting barrier of the Caucasus but also the political instability of Georgia, Azerbaijan, and Armenia, all of which teeter on the edge of chaos and look likely to continue to do so. Transport east might be politically more agreeable, given Nazarbaev's general admiration for the Chinese model of development, but would require construction of a pipeline on a scale that would have seemed grandiose even in the Brezhnev era. This leaves only transport north through Russia, which is not only Kazakhstan's former master but a formidable economic rival as well.

Nazarbaev: The Father, But of What Country?

Nazarbaev in his economic plan noted grimly: "We can no longer continue in this situation, waiting in vain [for foreign development assistance]. The sole solution is obvious: it is necessary first and foremost to rely upon ourselves."[51] However, Kazakhstan requires far greater capital for the rapid development of its infrastructure than the nation can generate internally. Nazarbaev has encouraged the development of a Kazakhstani private sector and indeed has said that there is nothing evil in the differentiation of the state into rich and poor. It is difficult to believe, though, that the economist in Nazarbaev is pleased with the private sector that has emerged to date. As is true elsewhere in the CIS and the former Soviet bloc, the private sector that is flourishing in Kazakhstan is involved overwhelmingly in buying and selling, particularly of former state assets and commodities to which the sellers rarely have clear title; as Nazarbaev warned in 1992, "Criminal elements are becoming increasingly organized and persistent in their efforts to infiltrate entrepreneurial, financial, and banking activities and to use the state apparatus and law enforcement bodies for their own mercenary purposes."[52] In fact, the impoverishment of the greater part of the society (national income dropped 25.3 percent in 1992) and the general decline in productivity (in 1992 down 21.4 percent from 1991 when a 13 percent drop against 1990 was recorded across the USSR) suggest that rather than new wealth being created, the best that seems to be happening is that an existing pie is shrinking and being cut in different ways. The ongoing deterioration of the economy, the growing evidence of public-sector corruption, and the ever more obvious breakdown of public order are creating an atmosphere in which all groups feel themselves to be losing to the others.

If that trend continues, it is likely that Nazarbaev's attempts to meet the needs of his country's two nations are increasingly going to have to become efforts to preserve stability. The lesson all of Central Asia's leaders seem to have drawn from the civil war in Tajikistan is the high cost of instability, whatever its cause. In Nazarbaev's understanding of his duties as leader, preservation of public order will take primacy over defense of individual liberties, continuation of economic or political reforms, or creation of a civil society based upon laws.

That has increasingly been demonstrated since late 1993, when Nazarbaev dissolved the parliament that had been elected in 1990 under the Soviet-era constitution. The act of dissolution itself was of unclear legality, but Nazarbaev went ahead with it out of a perceived need to secure more manageable political backing. Elections to the 177 seats of the new Majlis were held in March 1994 under conditions that made it very difficult for nationalist candidates of any stripe to get on the ballot. Voting districts were also drawn in such a way as to create Kazakh pluralities wherever possible. Voting was conducted in such a way that observers from the CSCE were initially reluctant to certify that the process had been free and fair.

In the new parliament, 105 seats went to ethnic Kazakhs, and only 49 went to Russians; to most of the republic's Russians, this imbalance only increased the alienation they have already been made to feel by the fact that nearly 80 percent of Nazarbaev's appointments have gone to ethnic Kazakhs. Russian exclusion from the government was exacerbated even further in September 1994 when the government headed by Prime Minister Tereshchenko resigned, thus removing the last prominent non-Kazakh from the senior ranks of government.

Coming into almost immediate conflict with Nazarbaev, the new parliament lasted only one year. In early March 1995, the Constitutional Court upheld a suit by a disappointed Russian candidate, who argued that the parliament was illegal because both the drawing of voting districts and the method of voting itself had been unconstitutional. Nazarbaev vetoed the court's decision, only to be overruled by the court. On 11 March 1995, Nazarbaev dissolved Kazakhstan's first post-independence parliament, calling for new elections; in the interim, power is in his hands and those of Prime Minister Akizhan Kazhegeldin (appointed in September 1994). Led by Nazarbaev's ally-turned-rival Olzhas Suleimenov, about half the legislators made an unsuccessful attempt to establish an "alternative assembly."

Nazarbaev's dissolution of parliament is probably a sign of political weakness, not of strength. Awareness of his state's geopolitical and demographic vulnerabilities has consistently led Nazarbaev to seek ways in which to make Russia become the guarantor of Kazakhstan's continued existence. Through mid-1994, Nazarbaev tried to do so with some reshaped nonideological variant of the USSR, first through the CIS, and then, when it became clear that that body was failing, through his proposed Euro-Asian Union. This body, led by a Council of

Presidents and governed by a specially elected supranational parliament, would allow the republics to remain independent in name but would assign virtually all policymaking functions, including for defense and the economy, to the larger Union.[53]

The response of Russia and the other republics has been unenthusiastic, which suggests that the proposal is probably dead. Creation of the Interrepublic Economic Council, or IEC, the CIS's first formal institution, in which Russia allots itself 50 percent of the votes (with 80 percent necessary for a measure to pass), suggests that Russia is increasingly going to demand a position of regional dominance for itself. The same point seems clear from Russia's success at demanding a significant stake in previously negotiated oil deals in Azerbaijan and in its assertion of a right of veto over all Caspian oil deals.

Since the end of 1994, Nazarbaev seems to be fully aware that the fate of Kazakhstan will be decided in Moscow, just as the fates of a number of the other newly independent states have been. Events in 1993 offered the NIS presidents the lessons of Azerbaijan's president Abulfaz Elchibey and Georgia's Eduard Shevardnadze; both attempted to steer a path well clear of Russia, and both found sudden "wild wars" raging in their territory. Elchibey prudently vanished, but Shevardnadze chose, at first, to fight. In his vow to defend his cities to his death, Shevardnadze was for a brief moment the image of a hero, whose power derives from martyrdom but whose actions in their very futility define the meaning of a nation. In the final moments, however, he declined an ineffective martyrdom and chose inglorious reason instead, accepting Moscow's "assistance" at the cost of Georgia's last pretensions to independence.

Nazarbaev and Shevardnadze know one another well; it is safe to assume that Nazarbaev has pondered Shevardnadze's dilemma. Common sense would suggest that the logical response to continued Russian pressure on Kazakhstan will be continued acquiescence. Yeltsin's vivid demonstration in October 1993 of the willingness to use force even against his own parliament suggests how slender are the chances a Kazakhstani army would stand against the vast Russian army, even were it not for the additional fact that most of the officer corps and a certain part of the soldiers in that Kazakhstani force would be ethnic Russians and so at best of doubtful allegiance in a conflict with Russia.

However, Nazarbaev has stated a number of times that any attempt to redraw the borders of his nation will be a cause for war. This suggests that even Nazarbaev's sense of managerial efficacy has a limit. If events continue to make it ever more impossible for Nazarbaev to serve his country as a Kazakhstanets, then he too may one day face Shevardnadze's choice. Whether Nazarbaev will decide that day to be the Russified apparatchik his training made him or the Kazakh of his blood and ancestry is not clear. In either event the necessity to make that choice, if it comes, will fully justify Nazarbaev's prayer: "God grant that nobody will stir up Kazakhstan on ethnic grounds. That would be far worse even than Yugoslavia."[54]

Notes

1. *Kazakhstanskaia pravda,* April 25, 1990, p. 1.

2. D. Kunaev, *O moem vremeni* (Alma-Ata: RGZhI Douir, MP Yntymak, 1992), p. 10.

3. *Moskovskie novosti,* January 19, 1992, p. 1. However, it may be that this source is incorrect, as many claim that both Kunaev and Nazarbaev are from the Great Horde, though from different (and oftentimes) rival clans.

4. Nursultan Nazarbaev, interviewed by Mr. [sic] Jitnukhin, *Nursultan Nazarbaev: No Rightists nor Leftists* (Alma-Ata: Noy Publications, 1992), p. 21. Nazarbaev indicated that he withdrew his application to aviation school as a matter of filial duty, after his entire extended family gathered to consider the issue and then opposed his desire.

5. *Rossiikie vesti,* October 20, 1992, p. 2, as translated in *FBIS Daily Report Central Eurasia,* FBIS-USR-92-140, October 31, 1992, p. 84.

6. For an example, see James Critchlow, "Prelude to 'Independence': How the Uzbek Party Apparatus Broke Moscow's Grip on Elite Recruitment," in William Fierman, ed., *Soviet Central Asia: The Failed Transformation* (Boulder, Colo.: Westview Press, 1991), pp. 131–159.

7. Nazarbaev himself cited as the event most damaging to his relations with Kunaev a forty-minute critique he presented May 15, 1985, at a meeting of the republic's Central Committee. Nazarbaev, *No Rightists nor Leftists,* p. 82.

8. Donald S. Carlisle, "Power and Politics in Soviet Uzbekistan," in Fierman, *Soviet Central Asia,* p. 115.

9. *Argumenty i fakty,* no. 51–52, 1992, p. 1.

10. *Druzhba narodov,* no. 9, 1987, pp. 206–207.

11. *Ogonek,* no. 26, 1988, p. 11.

12. Nazarbaev, *No Rightists nor Leftists,* p. 132.

13. *Kazakhstanskaia pravda,* April 30, 1991, p. 1.

14. *Rossiiskie vesti,* October 20, 1992, p. 2, as translated in *FBIS Daily Report Central Eurasia,* FBIS-USR-92-140, October 31, 1992, p. 84. Other rumors were that Nazarbaev was slated for a vice presidency, presumably behind Gorbachev; still others were that he was to become prime minister.

15. Speech at Congress of People's Deputies, as translated in *FBIS Daily Report Soviet Union,* FBIS-SOV-89-104-S, June 1, 1989, p. 3.

16. *Komsomolskaia pravda,* April 13, 1991, p. 3.

17. Fourth Congress of USSR People's Deputies, as translated in *FBIS Daily Report Central Eurasia,* FBIS-SOV-91-007-S, January 10, 1991, p. 27–28.

18. *Radio Liberty Report on the USSR,* August 9, 1991, p. 13–14.

19. Nazarbaev, *No Rightists nor Leftists,* p. 105.

20. *Radio Liberty Report on the USSR,* November 1, 1991, p. 34.

21. *Ogonek,* no. 26, 1988, p. 11.

22. *Sovetskaia Rossiia,* October 18, 1989, p. 1.

23. *Kazakhstanskaia pravda,* November 23, 1991, p. 1.

24. *Radio Liberty Report on the USSR,* September 6, 1991, p. 43.

25. *Argumenty i fakty,* no. 9, 1991, p. 2.

26. Nazarbaev, *No Rightists nor Leftists,* p. 148.

27. The Yeltsin commitment was made on Moscow Radio, First Program, 1500 GMT (Greenwich mean time), August 29, 1991, as translated in *FBIS Daily Report Central Eurasia*, FBIS-SOV-91-169, August 30, 1991, p. 125; the Rutskoi commitment, delivered while the vice president was in Alma-Ata, was conveyed on the Vostok program, 1500 GMT, August 30, 1991, as translated in *FBIS Daily Report Central Eurasia*, FBIS-SOV-91-170, September 3, 1991, p. 112.

28. Interfax, 1640 GMT, December 9, 1991, as reported in *FBIS Daily Report Central Eurasia*, FBIS-SOV-91-237, December 10, 1991, p. 72.

29. *Argumenty i fakty*, no. 2, 1993, p. 2.

30. Interviews by author, March and May 1992.

31. *Ogni Alatau*, May 19, 1992, unpaginated insert.

32. Constitution of the Republic of Kazakhstan, adopted January 28, 1993.

33. All-Union Radio Network Maiak, 1610 GMT, November 26, 1991, as reported in *FBIS Daily Report Central Eurasia*, FBIS-SOV-91-229, November 27, 1991, p. 70.

34. Constitution of the Republic of Kazakhstan, adopted January 28, 1993.

35. *Trud*, May 14, 1992, p. 2.

36. Ibid.

37. Official figures put Kazakhstan's 1991 GNP at 77.4 billion rubles and projected a 1992 GNP of 74.5 billion rubles (in 1991 rubles, which were approximately 23 rubles/$1). However, Nazarbaev warned in his autobiography that "As a result [of Soviet accounting practices] we have absolutely no idea about our real gross national product." Nazarbaev, *No Rightists nor Leftists*, p. 77.

38. *Pravda*, December 15, 1989, p. 2.

39. *Ogni Alatau*, May 19, 1992.

40. *Ana-tili*, January 7, 1993, p. 4, as translated in *FBIS Daily Report Central Eurasia*, FBIS-USR-93-051, April 24, 1993, p. 81.

41. *Rossiiskaia gazeta*, June 3, 1992, p. 7.

42. *Argumenty i fakty*, no. 16, 1992, p. 6.

43. *Ogni Alatau*, May 19, 1992.

44. Moscow, Russian Television, 1900 GMT, November 19, 1992, as reported in *FBIS Daily Report Central Eurasia*, FBIS-SOV-92-226, November 23, 1992, p. 61.

45. *Nezavisimaia gazeta*, September 22, 1992, p. 3.

46. *Pravda*, December 10, 1992, p. 4.

47. *Argumenty i fakty*, no. 2, 1993, p. 2.

48. Moscow, Russian Television, 1900 GMT, November 19, 1992, as translated in *FBIS Daily Report Central Eurasia*, FBIS-SOV-92-226, November 23, 1992, p. 61.

49. *Kommersant*, August 6, 1993, p. 4.

50. *Izvestiia*, September 13, 1993, p. 4.

51. *Ogni Alatau*, May 19, 1992.

52. Alma-Ata, KAZTAG, 0825 GMT, October 26, 1992, as reported in *FBIS Daily Report Central Eurasia*, FBIS-SOV-92-208, October 27, 1992, p. 58. Nazarbaev's point and the problem in general of privatization of state property were summed up with particular force by Lev Timofeev in a 1993 article about Russia: "The greatest 'block of property' in the country is not private property and is not state property, but is rather the all-pervasive, immense, and unaccountable shadow property. This is property which on the one hand is impossible to describe as 'private property received by citizens from legal sources,' and on the other hand isn't state property. ... Russia is a land of shadow property. The major heri-

tage left to us by the communists is that we, Russia's citizens, know nothing about who is in charge of what in our country (or even who really controls our country). We know that everything of value has an owner somewhere, but who is that owner (stick your nose in and you'll get your head ripped off)? And what are the dimensions of that owner's holdings? We don't know. We don't know anything. All there are are shadows everywhere, so that it is impossible to make out where the real owners are, and who their real competitors are. This is not a country, but a theater of criminal shadows." *Izvestiia,* October 29, 1993, p. 4.

53. *Nezavisimaia gazeta,* June 8, 1994, p. 3.

54. *Kazakhstanskaia pravda,* November 23, 1991, p. 1.

CHAPTER 9

Islam Karimov and Uzbekistan: Back to the Future?

Donald S. Carlisle

Uzbekistan celebrated its political birth at Bukhara in February 1925 when the First Congress of the republic's Communist Party convened. The major external guest greeting those assembled was Mikhail Kalinin, the chairman of the Central Executive Committee of the Soviet Union, which was also a newcomer to statehood. He congratulated the crowd in the hall:

> Naturally, Uzbekistan must play a large role in Central Asia, a role one might even say of hegemony. This role must not be lost sight of, comrades. ... I consider this proper. Certainly Uzbekistan has available sufficiently large cultural forces. It has available great material possibilities, a large population; it has the most wealthy cities. I consider it a fully valid and natural desire to play first violin in Central Asia. But, if comrades want to play first violin, then it is reasonable that this be achieved in our Soviet Union only by increased labors, great generosity, huge work, and sacrifices for the neighboring republics which will come in contact with you. For when you are strong, because you are mighty, then from you will be demanded great compliance toward these republics. In a word, you must be related to them as Moscow is related to you.[1]

Prior to 1925 no unit comparable to Uzbekistan—officially constituted on ethnic grounds—had ever existed in Central Asia. Its appearance was the result of the "national delimitation," a complicated process begun in 1924 but traceable to an initial Moscow proposal in 1920. The redrawing of frontiers was followed by the appearance in December 1924 of Uzbekistan's first governing body, the Revkom (Revolutionary Committee), headed by Faizulla Khojaev.[2]

Locally, the instigators and major beneficiaries were the leaders of the Bukharan state. Prominent among them were Khojaev and his associates, only recently converted to communism and to alignment with Moscow. Their choice resulted in the disappearance from the map of the expansive Turkestan as well as the ancient principalities of Bukhara and Khiva; in their place appeared novel political formations such as Uzbekistan and Turkmenistan. In the course of the next fifteen years,

191

the relationship of the Central Asian republics to Moscow shifted decisively toward centralization and away from the looser arrangements envisioned by most "national" leaders when the USSR was established. The native Communists who had taken the national dispensation seriously and counted on continued power were liquidated by Stalin in 1937 and 1938.

In September 1991 Uzbekistan underwent a political rebirth, and the hope of self-determination surfaced again when it became an independent state in the wake of the failed Moscow putsch and the demise of the USSR. After joining the fledgling Commonwealth of Independent States, Uzbekistan was admitted to the United Nations in 1992 and recognized by major world powers.

The key figure in Uzbekistan's political life since 1989 has been its president, Islam Karimov. He is a controversial individual with a reputation as a temperamental leader who has presided over an increasingly authoritarian regime.[3] His dismal press clippings are in sharp contrast to those of the leaders of Kazakhstan and Kyrgyzstan, Nursultan Nazarbaev and Askar Akaev. Akaev, in particular, has been singled out for praise and has become a favorite in Washington for leading his country in a democratic direction.

Whatever the merits of the formulas for progress in adjacent states, it is as true today as in Kalinin's time that Uzbekistan cannot be ignored. Balanced judgment leads irresistibly to the conclusion that it occupies the pivotal position in Muslim Central Asia.[4] And Karimov has increasingly become the most important player as the consequences of the Tajik civil war have enveloped the region. Whether one likes him or not, it is necessary to come to terms with him.

Several points help establish perspective on Uzbekistan and its role in the region. First, it is axiomatic that in external relations it has entered a post-Soviet period, but in domestic life this has not yet occurred. The USSR as a formal structure has disappeared, but Soviet-type institutions remain largely intact on Uzbek soil. Long-standing patterns of rule and elite composition have not been revamped, although there is some change in both realms. Censorship and repression of dissent and opposition have resurfaced as part of Karimov's formula for authoritarian rule.[5]

Second, reports of the demise of the Soviet Union as a state entity, though true in a formal sense, may lead analysts to underestimate the retention and even the reassertion of informal controls and influences from the old imperial Soviet center. The unraveling of the Tajik political system beginning in February 1990 escalated in 1992 into a vicious civil war that threatened to spill over into Uzbekistan. The reaction to the violence in Tajikistan has halted, if not yet reversed, the decline in Moscow's influence in the region. Karimov has in this context become perhaps the pivotal figure in Central Asia, as he seeks to deflect the consequences of the Tajik disaster from his and others' borders. In the process, he has been forced to rely on the Russian military, to turn his back on Turkey and Iran, and to give signs of renewed deference to Moscow.

Background and Beginnings

An understanding of Uzbekistan's past is essential to assessment of current developments. There is every reason to believe that Kalinin's remarks in 1925 faithfully reflected the Kremlin's view of Uzbekistan's standing in Central Asia. Uzbekistan held center stage and its leaders were considered first among equals, if not, to use Stalinist parlance, the hegemon or "elder brother" regionally. But although Uzbekistan and its titular group, the Uzbeks, were paramount in Moscow eyes, they were not the only significant realities locally; there were other potent identities and allegiances that often superseded the nationality dimension so effectively propagandized in the years of Communist rule.

The salience and sustained vitality of loyalties other than national identity need to be considered. Use of a geopolitical focus shows that in the context of native politics, the label "Uzbek" and other ethnic concepts are often less useful than knowledge of attachment to place, roots in a region, or love of a locale.[6] After 1925, as before, the native populace by and large remained committed to traditional ways and memories and retained particularistic allegiances. Born and raised in the *mahallah,* the intimate neighborhood,[7] the masses identified with it and with family, tribe, friends, and clan. And it was not new Uzbekistan but old Bukhara, Samarkand, Khiva, and Kokand that brought to the Muslim mind memories of grandeur and glory.

In Uzbekistan a tightly integrated traditional society lived on into the Communist era and has continued into the present. Over the years it has proved resilient in the face of the threats to its integrity posed by modern life in general and the Soviet regime in particular. During these years the indigenous peoples—most of them ethnic Uzbeks but also Tajiks and other Asians—inhabited an updated version of the *mahallah.* This non-European world consisted of the natives' urban quarters and especially the rural *kishlaks* (villages) where the old ways were even more dominant.

There are moral and mental as well as political borders in Central Asia, the former often more important than the latter. Kith and kin, tribe and clan, not the artificial boundaries contrived by Soviet power, were the permanent and paramount realities. The nation and the nation-state, as well as everything associated in the modern mind with nationalism, were alien notions to the typical Turkic/Muslim inhabitant of the *mahallah.* True, he had a specific ethnic affiliation and this set him apart from other groups; to the outside observer, these ethnic formations might have appeared to provide the wherewithal for nations. But a *mahallah* uzbek or tajik was not an Uzbek or a Tajik in the modern nation-state sense.[8]

During the early years of the USSR, native Soviet politicians also viewed themselves as spokesmen for local realities and historical formations. This was certainly true of the two major figures of the 1920s and 1930s, Faizulla Khojaev and Akmal Ikramov, who led the republic's government and party, respectively.[9]

Khojaev was a Bukhara/Samarkand partisan who was instrumental in the machinations that brought about subdivision of Turkestan into national units. Although Bukhara was erased as such in 1925, its fate was not as disastrous as the map might suggest. What emerged as Uzbekistan could be viewed as a Greater Bukhara. Aside from a minor piece of territory in the west transferred to Turkmenistan, historical Bukhara reappeared as a larger and stronger unit augmented by land and peoples co-opted from defunct Turkestan and from what had been the Khivan khanate. And the new Uzbekistan was to be ruled by a Bukharan political elite.[10]

Stalin used Uzbekistan politicians—especially Ikramov and his Tashkent/Ferghana-based cadres—against the Bukhara/Samarkand cohort. Manipulation of local cleavages was a key to Moscow's game in the 1920s and 1930s. Ikramov would in turn be jettisoned by Stalin and replaced by Usman Yusupov and a more authentic Stalinist clique based in the Tashkent/Ferghana region. Khojaev and Ikramov were the only Central Asians singled out by Stalin to be defendants in the Moscow purge trials of the late 1930s and were killed shortly thereafter.

The Reign of Sharaf Rashidov

The changing of the guard brought an alteration in the class nature and the regional basis of the Uzbek political elite. Usman Yusupov was originally a poor peasant from the Ferghana valley who had matured in the Tashkent political machine. He had also served an apprenticeship in Moscow before being sent back to replace Ikramov upon his arrest in September 1937.

Shortly after Yusupov was appointed the USSR's minister of cotton production in 1950, the political baton was passed to a new echelon made up of individuals born after 1917 and trained under Soviet auspices and who came to maturity in the post-1937 Stalinist system. Yusupov's major successors were Nuritdin Mukhitdinov and Sharaf Rashidov, both born in 1917—the first at Tashkent and the second in the Samarkand region.[11]

It is ironic that a period that began in March 1959 with Rashidov edging into office by the skin of his teeth should have turned out so positively for him. Of all the candidates for first secretary of the Uzbekistan wing of the CPSU in 1959, he had the weakest credentials and commanded the least respect. Yet, once at the helm, he remained there for a quarter century, outlasting his opponents and defeating attempts to unseat him. Over ten years, he deposed all his enemies in the party and government apparatus and installed a following made up chiefly of outsiders to the Tashkent/Ferghana "clan" like himself.

The Rashidov era, which ended only with his death in October 1983, largely coincided with the Brezhnev era of stagnation in the USSR as a whole. An emphasis on stability and a distaste for change and reform were obvious traits of this period.

The Rashidov administration in Uzbekistan mirrored the Soviet center's conservative personality, its oligarchic politics, and its status quo policies. During this time the USSR functioned as a looser, less integrated edifice than before as the claims of unity were diluted and the pull of the imperial center was somewhat relaxed. In most republics, local party bosses functioned with an unprecedented degree of autonomy.

In Uzbekistan there surfaced a variant of communist feudalism or, to put it another way, an Uzbek version of Oriental Despotism, with Rashidov ruling as khan or emir and the CPSU bureau serving as a council of viziers. A great deal of power was also delegated to the party secretaries of the various provinces, who administered them much in the way begs (or beks) had ruled their dominions before the Russian conquest.[12]

The "Uzbek Affair" and De-Rashidovization

Yurii Andropov's accession to power in Moscow brought a preliminary attack on the Brezhnev legacy. Especially after Rashidov's death in 1983, a far-reaching purge was launched in Uzbekistan that lasted more than five years. Eventually the recentralization effort had to give way. Republic sovereignty was proclaimed in 1990, and "Uzbekization" was reestablished as postimperial practices and patterns took shape.

In the course of the purge, major reputations within and without Uzbekistan were destroyed. Most notable were those of Rashidov and his following. These developments came to be called throughout the USSR the "Uzbek affair." Because it was personalized and generalized to an entire ethnic group, the scandal came to have national overtones. This was deeply resented in the republic as a slur on the whole titular nationality.

The preparation for the purge began while Rashidov was still alive and may in fact have hastened his demise. It gathered momentum under his successor as first secretary, I. B. Usmankhodzhaev, especially after the June 1984 plenum of the Uzbekistan Central Committee, which Yegor Ligachev personally attended. In January 1986 it entered a new phase when Rashidov was publicly singled out as the main culprit. In 1987 and especially 1988, it reached a crescendo under the aegis of First Secretary Rafik Nishanov.

A shocking event—the riots in the Fergana valley in June 1989—helped turn around Moscow's stance toward Uzbekistan.[13] There followed the removal of Nishanov, the appointment of Karimov, and the exit of the Ligachev cadres. Within a year's time the anticorruption campaign was largely repudiated and new cadre policies were instituted. Totally unexpected but most significant were the intimations of Rashidov's rehabilitation by Karimov, the new first secretary of the local CPSU.

Enter Karimov

The tale of the emergence of Islam Karimov, replete in puzzling twists and turns, cannot be fathomed without a Kremlinological approach. Only by factoring in Soviet political culture and the purge of 1983–1988 is it possible to understand how he got to where he is today.

Nothing in Karimov's early life—he was born in 1938—or the bulk of his career suggested he was likely to climb to the top of the political pyramid. In the first phases of his career, Karimov was a rising economic technocrat, not a politically driven figure. He served for many years as a Gosplan official and eventually in 1986 became Uzbekistan's minister of finance. Thus he was not a typical member of the party inner circle. Before 1986 he had not held a party post and was never on a party bureau at any level or on the Uzbekistan Central Committee. Apparently he had not even attended a republic Communist Party congress until 1986.

As of December 1986 everything pointed to Karimov's continued prominence in a government post with little likelihood of further advancement. Ironically, his demotion that month to the distant and dismal terrain of Kashka-Daria, as party first secretary of the oblast, proved a precondition for his subsequent swift ascent. This form of political exile marked him as a man with a grievance against the Moscow-installed leadership and gave him experience in the CPSU elite, albeit in a backwater region.

Karimov's still mysterious elevation to Nishanov's post in June 1989 at first set limits on his independence. His lack of a personal political machine and his dependence on local politicians who supported his promotion and thought of him as their puppet prolonged and complicated his consolidation of power. This was the case even after he became president of Uzbekistan in March 1990, as he continued to owe much to the local forces that had aided his appointment. Throughout this time, he informally shared power with his old friend Shakarulla Mirsaidov, the leading Tashkent politician and an instrumental figure in his coming to power.[14]

Not until the aftermath of the August 1991 coup did Karimov defeat Mirsaidov and begin to draw power into his own hands. After his popular election as president of the republic in December 1991 and his installation in January 1992, he was reasonably secure and able to unveil his own policy agenda.

Unfortunately for Karimov and his more economic reform–minded allies, two developments in 1992 complicated matters mightily. The first was the student demonstrations in Tashkent in January 1992. These had lethal consequences and fueled an anti-Karimov opposition movement, which was in turn met by a police crackdown and rigorous repression of dissent.

The other turning point was an external event with ominous domestic and regional ramifications: the May 1992 upheaval in Dushanbe and the forced resignation of the president of Tajikistan, Rakhman Nabiev, that September.[15] Tajikistan's raging civil war and virtual disintegration reinforced authoritarian impulses in Uzbekistan. Arguing that the conflict could spill over into Uzbekistan, Karimov closed the borders with Tajikistan and cracked down with a vengeance on any trace of opposition at home.

The fear of a spread of Islamic fundamentalism, especially to Fergana, was Karimov's major justification for the crackdown that he continued through 1993. In the process, his economic reforms and other domestic initiatives were decisively set back, and a repressive mood reigned.

Karimov Consolidates Power

Karimov had to play major roles that must be filled generally for successful leadership outcomes. To be effective, aspiring leaders must come to terms with three endemic demands of a political system: maintaining, initiating, and protecting power.[16]

Karimov's responses to these needs were apparent in 1992. He did not always accord them equal priority, for increasingly he cast himself in the role of defender of the internal status quo. This self-selected mission was vividly illustrated on the massive billboard on the main avenue into Tashkent, which featured his remark writ large: "Stability is the treasure house of the Uzbek people and must be preserved."[17]

Politics and policies were intimately connected, and Karimov pursued the priority of cementing and expanding his personal dominance. This he viewed as the essential prerequisite of all other objectives. The policy mix pushed in 1992—augmented authoritarianism and limited economic reform—must be understood in this light.

Karimov's essential problem was outlined long ago by Machiavelli in *The Prince,* in which he advised insecure politicians newly arrived in power how to make themselves appear to be an "old prince." At one point Machiavelli listed the prerequisites of a consolidation of power in brutal and chaotic conditions like Renaissance Italy:

> to protect himself from his enemies, to win friends, to conquer either by force or by fraud, to make himself loved and feared by the people, to be followed and respected by his soldiers, to put to death those who can or may do him harm, to replace ancient traditions with new ones, to be severe and gracious, magnanimous and generous, to do away with unfaithful soldiers and to select new ones, to maintain the friendship of kings and princes in such a way that they must assist you gladly or offend you with caution.[18]

When this language is translated into the parlance of modern political science, it is obvious that Machiavelli was addressing how a leader could transform raw power into permanent authority and institutionalize his regime so as to give it legitimacy.

Karimov through 1993 displayed a determination to tackle this problem as he saw it. The clampdown within Uzbekistan had ramifications outside its borders. Foreign observers labeled the Karimov regime as repressive, and human rights violations were monitored, noted, and censured. U.S. officials took a dim view of Tashkent's tactics, and the diplomatic atmosphere was poisoned as a result.

The most pressing problem confronting Karimov in June 1989 had been the tension with Mirsaidov, who had helped bring Karimov back from exile and orchestrated his promotion to first secretary. As part of the deal that must have been struck, something like a dyarchy ensued. At first Mirsaidov served as prime minister, the key governmental post. When Karimov in March 1990 took on the post of president (like Gorbachev in Moscow), Mirsaidov became Uzbekistan's first vice president.

The impasse that followed over the next year was described to me by a reliable Uzbek source in summer 1991 as a struggle "between two bears that could not continue unresolved much longer." It appears that the August coup in Moscow helped break the deadlock in Uzbekistan. The conventional wisdom has had it that Uzbek authorities (Karimov included) immediately declared martial law and identified with the coup leaders, but there is a more complex assessment. Karimov had been on an official visit to India when the Moscow crisis broke. He returned home immediately, but there is reason to believe that the emergency measures imposed in Tashkent were independently taken—perhaps by Mirsaidov and his allies—before Karimov took charge. The failure of the coup thus weakened his enemies in the Tashkent establishment, not Karimov.

The subsequent rise in Karimov's fortunes and the decline in Mirsaidov's seem to corroborate this interpretation. Karimov was elected president in a contested ballot that gave him enhanced legitimacy.[19] He was now free from his previous "handlers" and able to move decisively against Mirsaidov. In January 1992 he downgraded the vice presidency, eventually abolishing the post. Mirsaidov, isolated, then resigned.

Demonstrations in Tashkent followed, ostensibly about economic conditions and price increases but likely related to Mirsaidov's demotion. There were several deaths during the riots; these events triggered Karimov's strike at dissent that figured so prominently in Uzbekistan's growing reputation for repression. But if my interpretation is correct, the crackdown had less to do with economic protests than with the succession struggle inside the Uzbek political elite. This explanation seems to have been missed by foreign observers, although it was clearly understood in Tashkent by everyone to whom I spoke.

In January 1992 Karimov also attempted to gain control over regional administrations by creating the office of *khokim,* or regional governor.[20] The *khokims* were superimposed on the oblast soviets and in function were the equivalent of the old oblast CPSU secretaries who had ruled the regions. The *khokimiate* (the *khokim* and his administration) was a new lever for Karimov at the local level. In Tashkent, meanwhile, he moved quickly to create a strong executive structure. It was the centerpiece of the new constitution for Uzbekistan that was publicized in autumn 1992 and approved on December 8.[21]

The Constitution and the Office of the President

The formal constitution did not merely codify Karimov's increasing preference for authoritarian rule. Its rapid preparation, discussion, and promulgation were meant to serve multiple purposes. The most important of these were linked to political and propagandistic needs, at home and abroad, as much as to legalistic considerations.

Two contending tasks had to be addressed through the text of the constitution. One was domestic-oriented, meant to produce a document that codified the concentration of power in the president's hands. The second was to create and publicize a legal framework congenial to Western constitutional experts and the politicians they advised. Pursuant to this, the final text contained a preamble and additional explicit provisions promising protection of human and civil rights and adherence to international law and UN standards.

The arrangements for governing the country are indeed present in the constitution but in camouflaged form. The constitution presents a tripartite division in which a separation of executive, legislative, and judicial branches approximates Western, especially U.S., patterns. The operation of the political system is in fact quite different. In place of the dispersal of power celebrated in the constitution, there is a concentration of power in the hands of the president and his main policy-making organ, the Office of the President. The operative pattern in relations among branches is not separation of power, let alone some sort of balance, but monopolization of power by the executive organs—in particular the presidency—with the legislative and judicial branches in effect subordinate to them.

In summary, the political arrangements by which Uzbekistan is governed remain highly centralized. The Cabinet of Ministers (the Council of Ministers of Soviet times) is placed within the direct jurisdiction of the president, who is formally designated chairman of the cabinet. A prime minister is in operational charge of the cabinet and is assisted by six deputy premiers who oversee a cluster of subordinate ministries and committees. In addition, there is within the cabinet the important post of first vice chairman, the direct representative of the president and the link between the cabinet and the president's office, the mainspring of the system.

The Office of the President is composed of six divisions, each headed by a state counselor (also known as an adviser to the president) who has an administrative staff. There are also other agencies in the president's office, but the six state counselors and their subordinates compose the inner sanctum of Karimov's political system.[22]

In many ways the Office of the President approximates in its relation to the president the role of the Secretariat vis-à-vis the former first secretary of the Communist Party. It occupies the same building, now sometimes called the Presidential Palace, that previously housed the party's headquarters.

The office is plainly designed to tower over all other government agencies and to supersede the officially distinct tripartite structure. It is composed of the president, his state secretary, and the immediate staff that serves him directly. Beneath it is a presidential bureaucracy with six branch departments for (1) personnel, (2) defense and legislative matters, (3) international affairs and foreign policy, (4) religion and societal affairs, (5) science and education, and (6) work among youth. A wide-ranging seventh division called operational and internal security has a roster of twenty-one. Departments range in size from twenty-five for defense and legislation to twelve for personnel, nine for international affairs, and five for religion and societal affairs.[23]

Past probings of Soviet Uzbekistan paid much attention to problems of Russification and Russianization. This led to stress on the relative weight of ethnic Russians and natives in key political bodies. Kremlinologists discovered a pattern in the distribution of posts: Uzbeks were allocated ceremonial or less influential positions; Russians or other outsiders directly controlled the most powerful posts or held backup positions to "shadow" native incumbents.[24] Developments during the Rashidov years indicated a change in that pattern and an increasing role for native personnel throughout the system. In the post-Soviet era, indications of relative Russian and Uzbek influence in the immediate power circle of the president are that very few Russians hold leading positions; in some departments, there are none. The largest Slavic contingent in 1993 served in the defense and legislation department, where they numbered five out of twenty-five. In the operational and internal security department, Russians held five of twenty-one staff positions listed.[25]

Rashidov and Tamerlane: Back to the Future

Perhaps the most startling aspect of Karimov's legitimation strategy has been his strong commitment to the rehabilitation of Sharaf Rashidov. There had been no love lost between Karimov and Nishanov, the orchestrator of de-Rashidovization and, incidentally, the author of Karimov's exile to Kashka-Daria. Soon after replacing Nishanov in 1989, Karimov began the process of reversing the results of Moscow's local purge, claiming that "hundreds, thousands" had been unjustly convicted. As noted, he also began to polish Rashidov's reputation.

In summer 1992 a concerted campaign was launched to return Rashidov to good graces. That November, his birthday was celebrated in lieu of the usual anniversary of the 1917 revolution. At a ceremony in Tashkent, a large statue of Rashidov was dedicated with pomp and circumstance at the spot where he was buried in 1983 and from which his body was disinterred when he was in dishonor. The nearby main thoroughfare, once called Lenin Prospect, was renamed for Rashidov.

Numerous press articles and pamphlets have since appeared seeking to refurbish his reputation and refute charges that "Rashidovism" was synonymous with corruption.[26] In fact, Rashidov, one of the rare Brezhnev-era luminaries returned to good favor, has been elevated to the pantheon of Uzbek national heroes. The two former leaders singled out for special praise by Karimov's regime are Tamerlane and Rashidov, and as part of the process, Uzbek historians are beginning to reevaluate the two men.

The reassessment of Rashidov has had systemic implications. It might also be read as fulfilling the maintaining and protecting functions discussed earlier. A message has been sent regarding Karimov's intentions for the future. Rashidov's rehabilitation is not just meant to do justice to a man whose service over many years to Uzbek interests is being extolled. More relevant politically is Karimov's attempt to enhance his personal authority by identifying his cause with that of a figure whom he believes was respected by the Uzbek masses and especially by local elites.

The concomitant campaign to resurrect the medieval conqueror Tamerlane as a figure of monumental proportions can also be read as an effort by the Karimov regime to acquire legitimacy by linking itself to a revered figure from a heroic time. Karimov, like most Uzbeks, has rejected the imperial patterns of the Soviet period. But emphasis on a native authoritarian tradition represented by Tamerlane has served present and future purposes.[27]

This has not meant that Karimov has targeted Europeans and the Russians as major villains. Quite the contrary. The exodus of Russians from the republic, which accelerated in 1989 and 1990, tapered off by 1992. Local Russians have certainly lost their privileged place so long sanctioned by tsarist and Soviet imperial practices. But the Karimov regime has reassured them as to a secure future in the multinational, secular Uzbekistan he envisages. As a secular nationalist, Karimov has held out his hand to these local Russians. They in turn seem to believe that the Uzbek former Communists offer them more hope than the radical young nationalists who call for more democracy but have been vocally anti-Russian, to say nothing of the Islamic fundamentalists who are feared by all nonnatives in the region. The Karimov government has unabashedly played up the Tajik disturbances and the danger of religious revivalism in Uzbekistan to buttress its support among Russians, especially in Tashkent, where they are so numerous.

Foreign Models and Foreign Policy Dilemmas

Not only are historical figures and previous patterns indigenous to the region in vogue. Karimov has also looked abroad to revive past relations with neighbors and kindred peoples and has established new connections with foreign states near and far. He was especially attracted to two countries in his initial travels, referring to their relevance for Uzbekistan's path of development. He repeatedly spoke favorably about Turkey and the "Turkish model," but it appears it was its Turkic character, economic success, and secular nature that proved most alluring. Turkey's turn toward political pluralism and democracy has been less attractive.[28] China also seems to have had a great impact on Karimov when he traveled there. Its capacity to sustain political authoritarianism while experimenting in the economic realm may be the unspoken model he has had in mind for Uzbekistan but has never been willing to articulate.

Negative models or experiences explicitly singled out by Uzbek commentators and repudiated should also be noted. As the Yeltsin regime came under attack because of precipitous economic reforms and faced challenges from the Russian parliament, Karimov's apologists pointed to the danger in too rapid a transition to democracy and the market system. Tajikistan's fate has also served as a negative example, providing guidelines as to what to avoid and contrasting sharply with the authoritarian solution imposed in Uzbekistan. To a secular nationalist and former Communist bureaucrat like Karimov, the alternative with least appeal has been the religious option. Especially unattractive has been the fundamentalist path, whether modeled on Iran, Saudi Arabia, or Pakistan. He seems to prefer close relations with India as opposed to links with Pakistan, whose geopolitical interest in Central Asia, especially in the wake of the Afghanistan war, seem suspect to him.

It is Iran's long-term ambitions that have been most feared by the Uzbekistan government, which believes that Iran's interest in Afghan affairs might expand into an effort to determine the fate of Tajikistan. Consequently, Karimov assiduously courted Turkey as a counterweight to Iran when he first ventured into international politics. Surely the 1993 visit of Turkey's minister of defense to Tashkent was not unrelated to volatile regional politics and uncertainties as to possible map-changing efforts by neighboring states. Tashkent has recently upgraded relations with Iran and seems to recognize that it is mainly through Teheran that it can manage to contain the interrelated Tajik and Afghan crises and also gain access to the Persian Gulf for trade with the outside world.

Karimov has viewed the need to ensure Tajikistan's territorial integrity as the core interest of Uzbekistan. In November 1992 he used his influence to restore to power the secular-oriented Tajik old guard, the former Communists, and sought to ensure a regime in Dushanbe opposed to fundamentalism. In this case his foreign policy objectives correlated exactly with his domestic priorities.

It has been a prime objective of Uzbekistan's foreign policy to enlist the forces of Russia, the CIS, or the former Soviet Central Asian republics as proxies to secure the border with Afghanistan and stabilize Tajikistan. Efforts to draw the United Nations and the United States into the task continued unabated for three years. Karimov's recent tilt to Moscow was partly a result of this failure and of the involvement of the United States in Uzbekistan's internal affairs (and its concomitant embrace of Kyrgyzstan and Kazakhstan). U.S. unwillingness to help the Uzbeks out of their economic and military difficulties removed leverage the United States might have had on Uzbek domestic affairs and helped Uzbekistan into Russia's arms.

Tajiks and Uzbeks

A word is in order about Tajikistan, the strife-torn post-Soviet republic next to Uzbekistan, whose history and recent experience offer an instructive contrast to Uzbekistan and whose crises have influenced Islam Karimov's thinking. The original settlers who spawned Central Asia's civilization were peoples whose descendants came to be called Tajiks and whose culture was largely Persian. Later, in the aftermath of the Arab conquest, the local culture was Islamized. There followed a difficult period when the hordes of Genghis Khan overran the region. This contributed to the image of harsh but not unjust autocratic rule as the ideal for political leaders. This model was to endure through the ages down to the Karimov regime.[29]

The zenith of Central Asian history was probably reached in the Chagatai period ushered in with the rule of Tamerlane in the late fourteenth century. He created an empire that encompassed Central Asia, extended to the present Middle East, and even reached the gates of Muscovy; its influence radiated out from Tamerlane's magnificent capital, Samarkand. The civilization's high point was achieved in the time of his successor, Ulugh-Beg. He was not as ruthless as his predecessor, and his reign ended abruptly in his betrayal by family and friends and murder.

In a sense, there were two patterns or variations bequeathed as to what constituted legitimate rule and just rulership; they were encapsulated in the competing images of these two quite different leaders. The harsh Tamerlane succeeded in creating an empire by destroying his enemies but provided the foundation for the cultural revival that followed. His more gentle successor, Ulugh-Beg, lacked the severity needed to rule that empire but created more than he destroyed and completed the construction of Samarkand, which remains the major legacy of the Chagatai period.

In the fifteenth century came a wave of nomadic Turkic invaders from the north, the Uzbeks, who overran the region and overturned the Chagatai dynasty. Eventually the Uzbeks adapted to the prevailing urban civilization and converted to Islam and a settled life; their rulers moved the capital to Bukhara where they created a center to rival Samarkand.

By the nineteenth century the age-old antagonism between Uzbeks and Tajiks had been muffled as the Tajiks adapted to their conquerors. They were on the way to being absorbed through a process of "Turkification." The "national delimitation" sponsored by the Soviets in the 1920s undercut this assimilation process. The Uzbeks were still singled out as the ethnic pivot around which Faizulla Khojaev and the Bukharans constructed their new state. They were of course intensely conscious of the "Tajik question." In fact, the Tajiks were one of the few favored ethnic categories constituting the primary national formations around which new units were to be constructed.

In 1924 the Tajiks were given a role and acquired a distinct jurisdiction—but not an independent territory—within Uzbekistan. The Uzbek lobby among the

Bukharans initially wanted to assign them the status of a mere oblast within the republic. This proposal was rejected, and the Tajiks were given an "autonomous republic" within Uzbekistan[30] and allocated a section of the Uzbekistan Communist Party equivalent to an oblast committee. Suddenly, in 1929, Tajikistan was established as a separate union republic of the USSR, equal in stature to Uzbekistan. One could make the case that this marked the beginning of a second phase of "national delimitation," solely based on Moscow's priorities, for it shrunk Uzbekistan and undercut the Bukharan politicians' grand design for dominating the southern part of Central Asia.

Civil War in Tajikistan

The Tajik civil war, a seminal event, is related to Moscow's earlier Afghan adventure and is inexplicable without it. The still unresolved conflict in Tajikistan and the regional power realignment it has precipitated have forced the Central Asian states, with Uzbekistan in the lead, to focus on state security issues and reaffirm their interests in common with Russia. The war has accelerated the emergence of Uzbekistan as the paramount state in the region and brought Russia's return as a Central Asian player, if not yet again the regional great power.

Moscow's earlier failure in Afghanistan contributed to the development of centrifugal forces that gathered momentum throughout the USSR. One of the consequences was that as the center contracted and lost control over the periphery, the idea of a smaller or truncated Russia surfaced. Some Moscow leaders began to contemplate a restrained view of their Central Asian presence. The Commonwealth of Independent States created in December 1991 was at best a weak confederation, not an authentic federation and not comparable in scope and power to the defunct Soviet Union.

In May 1992, just after the fall of Kabul, the ongoing political strife in Tajikistan exploded into major armed conflict. By September the power struggle had escalated into a full-fledged civil war. *Moscow News* described the war in early November: "Central Asia has not only broken the monopoly of the Transcaucasus on lengthy armed conflicts but also shown that the tragic 'records' of Caucasian wars may be beaten. ... In battles lasting from October 20 to 28 more people were killed in Kurgan-Tiube region alone than in all the armed conflicts on USSR territory from 1987 to 1991."[31] It is possible that 40,000 to 50,000 were killed within the span of a few months. The refugees created numbered well over 100,000, and many thousands were so fearful that they fled across the border to Afghanistan for safety.

The turmoil in Tajikistan and Russia's intervention in alliance with Uzbekistan has arrested the contraction of Russian regional power that followed the debacle in Afghanistan and the collapse of the USSR. Although Central Asia's relation to Moscow will not likely again approximate its colonial subordination of over one hundred years, the Tajik situation is surely a watershed.

Tajikistan has a complicated topography and social structure. Mountains cover more than 90 percent of its territory, and it has an extensive border with Afghanistan. Eastern Tajikistan, or the Pamirs region, makes up about one-half of the country and is truly a distinct area. To understand Tajikistan's local patriotism and personal allegiances, it is dangerous to rely on the notion of the nation and nationalism:

> The official ethnic categories ... correspond only partially to people's actual identities. Some groups of "Tajiks" have distinctive cultural features. The autonomous region (oblast) of Gorno-Badakhshan is home to a sub-nationality, the mountain Tajiks or Pamiris (after the Pamir mountains which are their home). The Pamiris speak languages related to Persian but distinct from Tajik. Unlike other Tajiks, who are Sunni Muslims, they follow the Ismaili sect of Islam. ... As Ismailis are generally minorities among other Muslims, they have tended to support secular politics, as the Pamiris have in Tajikistan. In addition, many of those classified as Tajiks in the southern province of Quarghan Teppa (Kurgan Tiube) consider themselves to be Arabs by descent, though members of this traditionally nomadic group speak Tajik.[32]

Tajikistan's numerous natural divisions make a geopolitical approach especially relevant there. The western half of the country can be divided on a horizontal axis with a high range of mountains separating the north from the central and southern regions. The terrain to the south borders Afghanistan where there are extensive Tajik (and Uzbek) minorities. South Tajikistan itself should also be subdivided into at least two distinct parts: the Kulab and Kurgan-Tiube regions. In the far north, beyond the mountains and distant from the capital, Dushanbe, is a distinct compact area with Leninabad/Khojent and Kanibadam its major urban centers. This district was originally included in Uzbekistan in 1925. In 1929, as something of a punishment to the Uzbek authorities, the Khojent region was detached and transferred to Tajik jurisdiction.

What must be understood is that Soviet Tajikistan, like Uzbekistan, was never an integrated, modern state uniting a single self-conscious nationality. It was a fragile composite of regions, cobbled together because of local political ambitions. It was never a reflection of an expressed national will of its peoples—who were never, needless to say, consulted about their preferences. Its ruling elite reflected regional cleavages that existed below the surface of the superficial national veneer.

Tajikistan's northern region, Leninabad/Khojent, the most highly developed area and closely linked to Uzbekistan, dominated the republic's politics and provided the country with its top politicians before the 1930s purges. After 1938 there was a short hiatus in which outsiders were in control,[33] but by 1946 the Leninabad/Khojent cadres were in command again. They remained so until September 1992, when President Nabiev was removed and again newcomers—this time from the south and the Pamirs—took over. The ousted northerners were considered beholden to Moscow and Tashkent. Those trying to discredit Nabiev among his compatriots argued he was an Uzbek in disguise.[34]

In some ways, the war was a rebellion of south Tajikistan against the more prosperous north. In this explanation, "A split occurred between the residents of the comparatively well-off northern city of Leninabad, bordering on Uzbekistan, and the Pamir and Gharm highlands where the living standard is much lower."[35] The notion of a revolt against the domination of the Leninabad elite and its Uzbek supporters in the south draws attention to the regional bases of the conflict and helps transcend the juxtaposition of democrats/Islamicists (the so-called opposition) and Communists to give a more nuanced analysis.

By fall 1992 the opposition forces had won and the Communist establishment based in Leninabad/Khojent was overthrown. This triggered a reaction among people from Kulab and from Uzbek communities in Tajikistan against the new rulers and thus accelerated the savage civil war. The intervention of Russia and Uzbekistan in winter 1992 tilted the scales, bringing about the restoration of the status quo ante and ensuring the opposition's defeat.[36]

Today, however, a conflict among the victors threatens political stability. The Kulabi dominate Dushanbe politics and have refused to defer to the Leninabad/Khojent clan. The dispute was personified in a struggle between the Kulab representative, Imomali Rakhmonov, who was in effect head of state, and Prime Minister Abdumalik Abdullodzhanov, his bitter foe and the spokesman for the Khojent region. In December 1993 the prime minister was removed and named ambassador to Russia. As the controversy heated up, there were rumors that northern Tajikistan asked to be absorbed by Uzbekistan, which would turn the clock back to 1929. Karimov rejected the petition. Uzbekistan's primary interest in solidifying its existing territorial and ethnic arrangements counseled against what might have been a logical but untimely solution. Of course, Tashkent may simply prefer to achieve this objective indirectly without running the risks that a formal territorial absorption would generate.

Uzbekistan and the Future of Central Asia

Consider the different domestic directions available to the Central Asian countries. The proclamation of sovereignty and independence underlines the nation-state face of the former Soviet republics. Each seems oriented on a national axis with nationalism as the natural ideology. There are, however, broader forces to be considered before division into competing national states can be certified as final.

At least two considerations caution against the conclusion that the nation-state form and nationalist ideology are the wave of the future in Central Asia. First, within each state the national integration expected of an authentic nation-state is lacking. The configuration of national units like Uzbekistan or Tajikistan was artificial, concocted only in the 1920s and stifled during the succeeding years as they became subordinate provinces of the Soviet empire. In addition, there are subrepublic realms where real loyalties are still rooted; this provides additional identities to those of Uzbek and Tajik. These internal cleavages make regional and local realities often more salient than the political units cavalierly carved out under Stalinist aegis.

In addition to internal divisions and subnational cleavages, there are transnational allegiances that cut across national identity. Uzbekistan has at least five major internal geopolitical regions. Tajikistan's complexity yields at least a threefold axis: Northern Tajikistan is more closely linked on virtually every score with Uzbekistan than with the republic's southern and eastern areas; in the south, Tajiks have more in common with ethnic compatriots in Afghanistan than with those to the north of the mountain spine dividing the country; in the east is the high Pamirs region inhabited by the mountain Tajiks who have major differences with their ethnic kin in the valleys.

Cleavage exists also between Uzbek communities in south Tajikistan and the local Tajiks. Diverse tribe and clan loyalties and different location combine to create divergent identities and conflicting allegiances. These facts are the key to the Tajik civil war.

In Kazakhstan the basic but unofficial division between a Russian north and a native south is an overriding fact. And within the Kazakh ethnic group itself there are recognized relationships of superior and inferior based on supposed lineages and descent from the various hordes. Kyrgyzstan, too, has a fundamental internal split between northern and southern regions as well as the tribal differences to be found everywhere. Besides the divisions within particular national groups, there must be considered conflicts between the major nationalities within particular states and between the states as well. There are major problems of ethnic minorities—for instance, the Tajiks in Uzbekistan, the Uzbeks in Tajikistan and Kyrgyzstan, and, of course, the Russians everywhere.

These realities make it difficult to credit the notion of an Uzbek or Tajik "national interest" beyond the bare minimum needed to ensure the internal integrity of the state and to secure its borders. Nationalism and nation-state perspectives pale in significance against the mosaic of subnational and transnational realities—not to mention emerging religious allegiances and long-standing cultural cleavages.

Competing with the official nation-state framework and the continuing vitality of subnational patriotism is an inclusive Central Asian perspective. This draws attention to a Pan-Turkic identity with the potential to draw many of the diverse peoples together. Regional differences and mounting economic difficulties encountered in the post-Soviet period conceal an ongoing search for what they share in common. The presidents and governing elites have made numerous efforts since 1991 to promote mutually advantageous solutions to regional problems. But it is true that so far little has been accomplished in translating the soaring rhetoric into real endeavors.

Given the dialectics of CIS politics, the Central Asian states would seem to have an objective interest in coordinating their actions so as to present the Slavic states and Russia above all with a common front. Indeed, they have the lesson from the Stalinist and Soviet periods of Moscow keeping Central Asia divided to serve its interests.

But there are obstacles to cooperation within the CIS and against Russia. Increased unity and less political independence threatens some states more than others. In the southern tier, there is a general fear that Uzbekistan would acquire leverage over the rest. The Tajiks, as a non-Turkic people, on principle hold back. Turkmenistan fears the Uzbeks' dynamism and their potential demographic dominance. The Kazakh-Uzbek competition is centuries old, and their leaders, Nazarbaev and Karimov, are intensely jealous of each other.

Developments over the course of 1993 sorted out some of the uncertainties and accelerated events in a direction that brought deepened involvement of Russia in Central Asia and increased the power and status of Uzbekistan and its leader, Karimov. In January 1993 the leaders of the five states proclaimed a mutual commitment to an entity called Central Asia, and some steps were taken to institute relations on a regional basis. Later in the year, Kazakhstan and Uzbekistan committed themselves to an economic common market. Russia's deepening involvement in Tajikistan, which all agree is necessary, may have persuaded some former antagonists that increased Turkic unity is needed in response.[37]

If steps taken to seal the Afghan border are successful, and if some sort of stability within Tajikistan is established, a semblance of normality may return to the region. But what is normal in Central Asia, and what does such stability imply for the future? In the southern-tier states (Turkmenistan, Uzbekistan, and Tajikistan), authoritarian regimes are likely to be around for some time to come. It appears that for Central Asia to achieve the promise of pluralism, reform will have to be implemented in the economic realm before prospects for political democratization become real.

The increased regional role of Uzbekistan threatens to produce a reaction from the other states, which hesitate to risk steps toward regional unity because of fear of Uzbek hegemony. However, Russia's increased presence contributes to unity. The outcome will depend on whether Central Asian elites fear Uzbekistan or Russia more.

There is mounting evidence that Iran is intent on businesslike relations with Russia; this factor will help stabilize the southern borders if incursions into Tajikistan from Afghanistan can be rebuffed. As to new trouble spots, the ethnically mixed Fergana valley is the area most likely to explode in the future. Central Asian leaders must anticipate this and recognize that problems there, along with the water issue and the crisis of the Aral Sea, which has been drying up because of diversion of river waters to cotton irrigation, have to be addressed collectively in the near future.

Karimov and Uzbekistan in Transition

Islam Karimov is a transitional leader, but so in a certain sense are all leaders. In some constitutional democracies, a power transfer is mandated by law. In the United States, no president can serve more than two terms; some incumbents are granted no more than one four-year term, as the Carter and Bush administrations learned. Karimov has been the elected president of Uzbekistan for a short time and has had but a brief moment to put his stamp on his country.

Karimov faced two crises in 1992: student demonstrations domestically and the raging Tajik conflict regionally. Combined, these two emergencies deepened the regime's authoritarian tendencies and reinforced its repressive character. The repercussions of these two crises undercut and obscured the reform-oriented side of Karimov's initial economic agenda. His need to solidify relations with the local elites counseled rehabilitation of Tamerlane and Rashidov. But time and again through these years he has emphasized the need for economic change and backed market-oriented measures.[38] True, his regime refuses to apply this principle extensively to the countryside, arguing that water, the scarcest local resource, cannot be privatized. Nonetheless, there have been stirrings of economic change.

A deputy prime minister commented to me that Uzbeks are natural merchants and have the necessary talents for a market economy "in their blood." He added that the West should not underestimate mercantile possibilities or forget that the fabled Silk Route ran through Samarkand and other towns of present-day Uzbekistan. Indeed, it might be argued that economic problems are the least of Karimov's worries in the long run. Yet, although prospects are good, the catastrophic consequences of cotton monoculture and the still-unfolding Aral Sea disaster loom large over the near horizon.

In political matters, Karimov's preoccupation with consolidation of personal power and the construction of a strong presidency have left him little time to consider long-term arrangements and the possibility of a transition to something other than authoritarianism.[39] The constitution pays lip service to Western constitutional ideals, but these are not applied in practice. The office of vice president was abolished in 1992, and its closest surrogate as a power position, the post of state secretary, is a creature of the president and its occupant serves at his pleasure. There is no individual primed to succeed the president should disaster strike.[40] Nor is there a procedure in place whereby alternative leadership would be presented, tested, and approved or rejected. The Karimov regime was to hold elections in late 1994. Should they prove to be competitive contests, some optimism about Uzbekistan's political future may be warranted.

Reliance on the device of plebiscites, provided for in the constitution but not yet utilized, may be Karimov's way of concocting a direct connection with the masses and testing public opinion. But an authentic multiparty system and electoral politics seem years away. Karimov has provided evidence that market conditions and some degree of privatization are on his agenda—that the future devolution of some economic power and the creation of a private sector are possibilities. But he seems to have no interest in a parallel evolution toward political democracy. The repressive politics of his administration are not, to say the least, conducive to pluralism; the stifling of dissent undermines the possibility of the tolerance and diversity required if a civic polity is to emerge in the future.

But there are liberals—if not full-fledged democrats—in Karimov's entourage. Some Western-oriented figures occupy high posts in the administration, and although they make the case for authoritarianism today, they seem uneasy with the prospects it portends for the day after tomorrow. The new state university that opened in Tashkent in January 1993 on the president's personal initiative is meant to train diplomats, journalists, and public administrators in the ways of the West.[41] International standards for teaching and training were to be adopted. Western textbooks and teachers and the exchange of faculty and students will no doubt contribute to creating cadres who recognize the relevance of democratic political patterns as well as the usefulness of the West's economic models.

The transition to democracy in Karimov's Uzbekistan has been postponed—given local conditions, perhaps this is justified—but prudent leaders must recognize that it cannot be avoided indefinitely.[42] Either the regime itself will control the parameters of change by beginning a political as well as an economic transition, or it will be supplanted by figures with a radical past- or future-oriented agenda in mind.

Notes

1. M. I. Kalinin, *Izbrannye proizvedeniya,* Tom I (1917–1925), Moskva, 1960, p. 630.

2. For a detailed discussion of Uzbekistan's origin, see Donald S. Carlisle, "Soviet Uzbekistan: State and Nation in Historical Perspective" in Beatrice F. Manz, ed., *Soviet Central Asia in Historical Perspective* (Boulder, Colo.: Westview Press, 1994).

3. For his September 1993 initial trip to the United States to address the United Nations, Karimov had a special public relations package prepared and distributed. It included a large foreign trade book and a glossy brochure on the president and his policies. I am told Karimov played a role in composing and editing the biography; this gives the text an autobiographical character. It includes this passage about the president in which Karimov is effectively describing himself: "The star of Islom Karimov rose up rapidly and brightly on Uzbekistan's political arena. There was hardly anyone up to the middle of the 80's who could assume that a regular expert of the State Planning Commission—efficient and knowledgeable (although inconvenient at times, since he could unhesitantly tell his opinions to his boss's face)—that this somewhat sharp-tempered man would become the most powerful generator of the Republic's political and economic independence. Moreover, not only the author of the then seemingly chimerical idea, but also an outstanding organizer of its practical realization." The book and brochure were printed in Germany. See *Business Guide: Uzbekistan, from the Heart of Central Asia to the World* (p. 248), and *President of Uzbekistan* (p. 12), excerpt cited is on p. 2.

The trip to the United States was a political failure because Karimov had been seeking for some time a meeting with President Clinton. The U.S. position on Uzbekistan's human rights record made such a meeting impossible. I met with President Karimov for two and a half hours in Tashkent on August 23, 1994. His observations were comparable to his remarks in an earlier interview: "We favor an American presence in Uzbekistan and Central Asia as a guarantor of our democratic development, but you've got to help us rather than assume moralistic poses. We will build democratic institutions—but keeping in mind our own special circumstances. Do you think it was possible to create other political parties in a state long dominated by the Communist Party? We aligned ourselves by the stars atop the Kremlin, and you suddenly expect us to have a democratic state in only two years? Why should this issue become a stumbling block in relations with Uzbekistan?" *Time,* July 25, 1994, p. 43.

For a chronicle of the repression of dissent and a discussion of specific cases, see Helsinki Watch, *Human Rights in Uzbekistan,* May 1993.

4. Uzbekistan is situated in the heart of Central Asia and contains all major cities—Samarkand, Bukhara, Khiva, and Kokand—that were the historical cultural centers. The other Central Asian states have large cities—Almaty, Bishkek, Ashkhabad—but they are largely creatures of the Russian period. Tashkent, Uzbekistan's capital, also fits into this mold.

Uzbekistan comprises 447,200 square kilometers (approximately the size of California) and has over 22 million inhabitants. Its population far exceeds that of any of its neighbors in the southern tier of Central Asian states—Turkmenistan, Tajikistan, and Kyrgyzstan. To the north is Kazakhstan, a huge unit that dwarfs Uzbekistan in size but has a population of only 15 million, of whom 38 percent are Russian. Kazakhstan is a special case and not a part of Central Asia proper; it should be viewed as a Eurasian state with a longtime—and possibly permanent—subordination to Russia.

5. Karimov laid out his perspective in a number of programmatic speeches: on the occasion of the November 1991 First Congress of the People's Democratic Party (the renamed Communist Party); in July 1992 in an address to the Supreme Soviet (with remarks on dissent and Tajikistan); and again in December 1993 when the new constitution was presented to that body for its approval. For the texts of Karimov's speeches, see *Pravda Vostoka,* November 2, 1991, pp. 1–2, and July 4, 1992, pp. 1–3. For his remarks at the time of the constitution's approval, see *Narodnoe slovo,* December 9, 1992, pp. 1–3. A comprehensive statement of Karimov's views on the economy and other matters can be found in I. A. Karimov, *Uzbekistan—sobstvennaia model' perekhoda na rynochnye otnosheniia* (Bishkek: Kyrgyzstan, 1994).

6. For the application of a geopolitical paradigm, see Donald S. Carlisle, "The Uzbek Power Elite: Politburo and Secretariat (1938–83)," *Central Asian Survey,* vol. 5, no. 3/4 (1986), esp. pp. 91–96. I stressed the need for a regional framework ten years earlier in "Uzbekistan and the Uzbeks," in Zev Katz, Rosemary Rogers, and Frederic Harned, eds., *Handbook of Major Soviet Nationalities* (New York: Free Press, 1975), pp. 283–284. A similar prism was used (under the title "Regional Heterogenity") by Edward Allworth in the last chapter of his book *The Modern Uzbeks, from the Fourteenth Century to the Present* (Stanford: Hoover Institution Press, 1990), pp. 325–329. Much recent literature on the civil war in Tajikistan uses a regional paradigm like the one I applied to Uzbekistan. For instance, see Oliver Roy, *The Civil War in Tajikistan: Causes and Implications* (Washington, D.C.: U.S. Institute of Peace, 1993).

7. This term (in Russian, *makhallya*) refers to the nuclei of local life—its native neighborhoods or wards. Russian and Western literature hardly mentioned it or directly addressed the fundamental role of these building blocks of native identity. Recently, and for the first time to my knowledge, the *mahallah* was highlighted in Sergei P. Poliakov's *Everyday Islam,* edited with an introduction by Martha Brill Olcott (New York and London: M. E. Sharpe, 1992), pp. 76–80.

8. In labeling ethnic cohorts, I have sometimes used lowercase as opposed to capital letters (i.e., uzbek versus Uzbek and tajik versus Tajik); this is to drive home the distinction between prenational group identities and nationality in a homogeneous nation-state. There is also a third type of identity: the ideal of ethnicity diluted in a multinational setting and superseded by supranational state citizenship. Multinational states of this sort have come on hard times; witness the fate of the Soviet Union, Yugoslavia, and Czechoslovakia. Even the United States—a geopolitical state, never a nation-state—is threatened; its ideology and integration have been eroded by claims for supranational, prenational, postnational, and nonnational identities.

9. For a discussion of Khojaev and Ikramov (as well as Usman Yusupov), see Donald S. Carlisle, "Modernization, Generations, and the Uzbek Soviet Intelligentsia" in Paul Cocks, Robert V. Daniels, and Nancy Whittier Heer, eds., *The Dynamics of Soviet Politics* (Cambridge: Harvard University Press, 1976), pp. 242–248; and Donald S. Carlisle, "K istorii destalinizatsii v Uzbekistane" in *Obozrenie,* No. 2, 1982.

10. Consult Carlisle, "Soviet Uzbekistan."

11. Mukhitdinov's and Rashidov's careers are documented in detail in Carlisle, "The Uzbek Power Elite," pp. 104–118.

12. The Rashidov period is analyzed in my "Uzbekistan and the Uzbeks," *Problems of Communism,* September-October 1991, pp. 28–33.

13. The attacks in Fergana on Meskhetian Turks—who had been exiled from the Caucasus at the end of World War II—resulted in 112 deaths. Many Turks had to be airlifted out of the region. The Fergana valley was probably the most densely populated region of the former USSR. The demographic explosion there resulted in a plentiful and restive youth cohort. Economic and social grievances were multiple, and unemployment had been rising prior to the riots. These combustible elements were waiting to be torched by an incident or accident—perhaps by a political provocation—but no one knows for certain who or what actually triggered it.

14. Tashkent and the Tashkent region occupy a special place as a virtually autonomous city-state within Uzbekistan. A gigantic area with a population of well over 2 million, it is an island of separateness—in many ways an alien entity identified with a foreign culture. It is not just a Russian center; it is a cosmopolitan city. There are of course native Tashkenters, but these Uzbeks have been set apart from others. They provided Moscow with its most reliable cadres during Communist rule.

Recent references to a "Tashkent mafia" reflect the centrality of the city's elite; Rashidov accommodated to these facts of life and ruled with the Tashkent elite, not against the region and certainly not over it. Shakarulla Mirsaidov was born in 1938 in Tashkent; he personifes the Tashkenter as ambitious politician. He came to know Karimov when both were officials in the Ministry of Finance. His career led him to the chief post in Tashkent's government. Mirsaidov was the main figure in the local elite securing Karimov's promotion from an obscure oblast post to Nishanov's position.

15. The best overview of the Tajik catastrophe is provided in O. Roy, *The Civil War in Tajikistan.*

16. Political leadership is exercised in three distinguishable contexts: (1) system genesis; (2) system maintenance; and if maintenance fails, (3) system degeneration. "Leaders are power holders, but they are also power spenders and power makers," observed C. J. Friedrich. "There appears to be three primary roles of leadership, namely initiating, maintaining, and protecting leadership to which correspond characteristic behaviors of the followers: imitating, obeying, and acclaiming." Carl Joachim Friedrich, *Man and His Government* (New York: McGraw-Hill, 1963), pp. 170–179.

17. During trips to Uzbekistan in late 1992 and early 1993, I observed this sign and other evidence of Karimov giving priority to maintenance of the status quo as opposed to striking out in novel directions. His innovations had to do with securing the present and recapturing the past rather than exploring the future. In foreign policy, however, Karimov was initially no prisoner of the past and sought to establish close relations with Turkey, China, South Korea, the United States, Israel, Germany, and the United Nations.

18. Niccolo Machiavelli, *The Prince,* Oxford University Press, New York, 1984. My contention that Machiavelli's analysis was relevant to Karimov's predicament was reinforced when in October 1992 I happened on a recently published edition of *The Prince* in several Tashkent bookstores. See Nikkolo Makiavelli, *Gosudar'* (Moskva: Izdatelstva Planeta, 1990), p. 90. It cost five rubles and was published in Russian in a 500,000-copy printing.

19. Karimov ran against the candidate of Erk (which broke from Birlik, the mainstream opposition movement), S. Madaminov, a writer known as Mukhammad Solikh. The president won 86 percent against Solikh's 12.7 percent. By all accounts it was a fair election, and monitors did not report major irregularities. This was the first contested election in Central Asia. Although Karimov as the incumbent had assets denied Solikh and received better media coverage, results by region testify to the authentic character of the process. In Kashka-Daria, where Karimov once was obkom secretary, his unpopularity was reflected in Solikh's 19.3 percent of the vote. In Khorezm, Karimov's native territory, Solikh won 58.5 percent of the electorate. In the unstable Fergana valley, dissatisfaction there led to 10, 11, and 8 percent of the vote in key oblasts being registered against Karimov. A simultaneous referendum on Uzbekistan's independence was supported by 98.2 percent of the electorate. All the data—including the embarrassing results in Khorezm and Kashka-Daria—were reported on the front page of *Pravda Vostoka,* January 1, 1992.

20. In some cases the *khokim* was a former state or party official in the oblast who was transferred from one key post to another. This was the case in Bukhara where Yadgarov, who headed the oblast Soviet, became *khokim.* In the Novoi oblast the new *khokim,* A. A. Aidarkulov—a Kazakh, not an Uzbek—had been chairman of the Syr-Daria *oblispolkom.* In the unruly Namangan oblast, the new *khokim,* Burgutali Rapigiliev, had previously been chief of the Papsk *raisoviet.* See *Pravda Vostoka,* January 29, 1992, p. 1.

21. For text of the constitution see *Pravda Vostoka,* December 8, 1992.

22. While in Tashkent in October 1992, I was fortunate to obtain copies of the telephone directory of top goverment officials and a similar list of the personnel in the Office of the President. These are unpublished sources. My analysis of the political elite's composition is based on these documents.

23. Ibid.

24. Treatment of the "rules of the game" in Soviet colonial staffing practices is provided in Michael Rywkin, *Russia in Central Asia* (New York: Collier Books, 1963), esp. chs. 7, 8.

25. Calculated from lists of officials provided in the telephone directory of the Office of the President.

26. Karimov began to rehabilitate Rashidov almost immediately, but a full-fledged campaign got under way only in May 1992. (See the front-page announcement of the plan to celebrate the seventy-fifth anniversary of Rashidov's birth and the commission established for that purpose in *Pravda Vostoka,* June 11, 1992.) For the two-part article triggering the celebration, see P. Safarov, "Triumf i bol'," *Pravda Vostoka,* October 29 and 30, 1992, p. 2. On November 5, virtually the whole issue was devoted to Rashidov; his picture appeared on the front page. Karimov led the unveiling of a bust of Rashidov in Dzhizak, his hometown, and gave a speech entitled, "Plamennoe serdtse syna naroda" (The burning heart of the son of the people). See *Pravda Vostoka,* November 10, 1992.

27. During the Soviet years, Tamerlane (Timur) was under a cloud. I recall an Uzbek, who had named his son Timur, asking why Russians could honor Ivan the Terrible and Peter the Great, but Uzbeks were not allowed to celebrate Tamerlane's exploits. Today a main avenue in Tashkent, once named for Engels, is called Amir Timur. A calendar for 1993 featured Tamerlane as its major figure, and a local magazine included the caption "'Tamerlane'—Ten Years Mature" and this notice: "Cognac 'Tamerlane' has now been made in Uzbekistan. ... The oak wood for special staves for the wine vats, which adds the inexpressible vanilla flavor to cognac, was shipped from the Ukraine and France. The makers of the cognac believe the 'Tamerlane' may rival the famous French 'Napoleon.'" *Uzbekiston-Contact,* nos. 10–12, 1992.

28. A special brochure prepared by the president's press service was printed in early 1992. It was a compilation of laws, decrees (*ukazy*), agreements, and documents chronicling Uzbekistan's first months of independence and emphasizing Karimov's role. Highlighted were his activities prior to and after the December elections as well as his travels abroad, especially to Turkey. See Prezident Respubliki Uzbekistan, *Press-Byulleten'* No. 4, Tashkent, 1992, pp. 78 (600-copy printing).

29. For a learned but idiosyncratic treatment of the cultural heritage, see Allworth, *The Modern Uzbeks.*

30. The major analysis of Tajikistan's history and politics is Teresa Rakowska-Harmstone, *Russia and Nationalism in Central Asia* (Baltimore and London: Johns Hopkins University Press, 1970). However, this valuable study does not treat the origins of Tajikistan and its relationship to Uzbekistan.

31. *Moscow News,* no. 45, November 8–15, 1992, p. 1.

32. Barnet Rubin, "The Fragmentation of Tajikistan," unpublished manuscript. Professor Rubin is a member of Columbia University's Political Science Department and heads its program on Central Asia.

33. The first leaders of Tajikistan were politicians from Bukhara, A. Mukhitdinov and N. Makhsum. In fall 1929 Khodzhibaev—a Fergana valley native—arrived in Stalinabad from Tashkent to replace Mukhitdinov. He and Makhsum were removed in a December 1933 purge and disappeared. The new leaders were S. Shotomir, a Pamiri, and A. Rakhimbaev, who was born in Khojent and spent the previous ten years in Moscow. In fall 1937 all of the Tajik leadership was removed and Russians temporarily came center stage. In 1946 Bobodzhan Gafurov, who was from Khojent/Leninabad, became party chief, a post

he held until 1955 when he transferred to Moscow to become editor of the journal *Narody Azii i Africa.* After Gafurov the party leader was always from Leninabad.

34. The identical ploy was used in Uzbekistan where Rashidov's opponents sought to discredit him by claiming he was a Tajik. The same tactics have been employed against Karimov, although there is some substance to the charge because his mother was Tajik.

35. Arkady Dubnow, "The Tajik Calamity," *New Times,* no. 6 (June 1993), p. 10.

36. Bess Brown, "Central Asian States Seek Russian Help," *RFE/RL Research Report,* vol. 3, no. 25 (June 18, 1993).

37. One would think that the December 1993 Russian election would contribute to Central Asian solidarity. In late January 1994 the leaders of Kazakhstan, Turkmenistan, and Uzbekistan gathered at the World Economic Forum in Davos, Switzerland. They were asked to comment on the election. "This mood which is emerging in Russia is something which represents a danger to Uzbekistan," Karimov observed at a press conference, adding: "It's not Zhirinovsky, the individual, who's at the center of our attention; we're more concerned about the people who voted for him." Quoted in *Boston Sunday Globe,* January 30, 1994, p. 10.

My extended discussion with President Karimov on August 23, 1994, left me with the impression that he believes Russia intends to turn Tajikistan into the first post-USSR satellite. He suspects that Russia is engaged in a subtle diplomatic game with Iran. Perhaps, he intimated, the Russians and Iranians think that the competing interests of their countries can be reconciled by trade-offs involving Turkmenistan and Tajikistan. This of course would require their isolating Uzbekistan regionally. Other Karimov remarks were comparable to those cited in an interview with an American magazine, where he observed: "Zhirinovsky only says in public what's on the minds of many politicians and government officials in Russia. What really concerns me is that Zhirinovsky meets no [official] opposition, nobody opposes him in the legislative branch. I have asked Yeltsin to take a stand against these xenophobic and anti-Semitic statements. I must know where the state stands on this issue. Zhirinovsky's maniacal concepts reflect, in fact, the traditional goal of Russian imperialists to reach the Indian Ocean. As far as they are concerned, we're just some gray mass that happens to be in their way and has no value of its own." *Time,* July 25, 1994, p. 43.

38. A little-appreciated aspect of the politics of privatization is that the regime's slow pace reflects not only bureaucratic reluctance to relinquish state control to the private sector but also fear as to which private sector will be strengthened. Given the pervasive role of the "shadow economy," the Karimov regime believes its opponents will buy up the resources. Thus those strengthened by privatization are likely to be local mafias; the Tashkent establishment, which Karimov has yet to break politically, would be strengthened by devolution of economic power. For a general discussion of corruption and the shadow economy in past years, see T. Gdlyan and E. Dodopev, *Mafiya: Vremen bezzakoniya* (Erevan, 1991), p. 158.

39. Karimov learned too well from the threat posed by an ambitious figure, Mirsaidov, located too close to power. He therefore abolished the office of vice president in January 1992. The president thus has no logical replacement or political heir; there is a cumbersome process in the constitution to be triggered should he die. In removing the potential for a successor who might threaten him, Karimov has increased the problem of succession for the system as a whole.

40. Several talented individuals have achieved prominence in Karimov's immediate circle. But he apparently prefers around him apolitical technocrats; he transfers or removes others. He seems to fear individuals who prove to be independent, who have acquired too much stature, or who in his view are politically ambitious. In the short term this may be a prudent tactic; it is a formula for disaster in the long run because no politician is indispensable.

41. A September 1992 presidential decree called for the new University of World Economy and Diplomacy to open in Tashkent by January 1993. Its importance was reflected not just in Karimov's direct involvement but in the fact that his close adviser, Saidmukhtar Saidkasimov, was named its rector. Evidence of its priority was the premises allotted to it: the quarters of the former Communist Party's Higher Party School, the best facilities available in Uzbekistan. Placed in charge was Mansur Rakhmankulov, a young, well-connected former Komsomol official who was given carte blanche to staff the university and acquire a student body; he was able to requisition whatever was needed to meet the deadline.

It is clear that the university was given a cadre mission similar to the task of the institution previously housed on its premises: to turn out economists, diplomats, and journalists to satisfy the regime's need for loyal personnel and in the process to train a younger generation and retrain older officials.

42. The most relevant study suggesting options available and avenues to follow is Samuel Huntington, *The Third Wave: Democratization in the Late Twentieth Century* (Norman and London: University of Oklahoma Press, 1991).

CHAPTER 10

Leadership in Uzbekistan and Kazakhstan: The Views of the Led

Nancy Lubin

In the halting move toward democratic reform in Central Asia, popular attitudes toward leadership play an increasingly important role. The orientation of the region's population toward different systems of government and democratic reform, the traits that are most sought in a leader, and the legitimacy that leaders hold in the population's eyes all affect the way and the degree to which democratic and market reforms may or may not be initiated or take hold.

As a small step toward understanding some of these popular views, and under the auspices of the U.S. Institute of Peace and with the Expert Center in Central Asia, I conducted a representative public opinion survey in June and July 1993 among 2,066 respondents in Uzbekistan and Kazakhstan—countries that together comprise almost three-quarters of Central Asia's population and about 80 percent of its land mass. The distribution of respondents by age, sex, nationality, urban or rural area, place of habitation (oblast), level of education, and profession closely follows census data in most respects (see Table 10.1). The poll was conducted face-to-face in one of four languages: Uzbek, Kazakh, Russian, and Karakalpak.

By themselves, the survey responses do not paint a definitive picture of the views of Uzbekistan's or Kazakhstan's citizens. Responses were undoubtedly influenced, for example, by the prevailing party line, by fear, or by a likely desire among many respondents to give a "right" answer—an answer the respondent believed the interviewer would like to hear rather than his or her personal opinion. As with other types of research, the survey was also undoubtedly influenced by outside events and local media coverage at the time the survey was conducted. In some instances, the results may have been overtaken by events. And survey research generally, as any other type of research, is plagued by a host of other uncertainties and inexactitudes.

The effect of these problems in the survey, however, may have been less than anticipated. First, for several questions, it was unclear what the proper answer or party line was at the time the survey was taken regarding such issues as Islam, leadership, and corruption and organized crime. The survey questionnaire, moreover, was designed to minimize these problems by including a good deal of overlap (asking the same type of question several times in different contexts and in dif-

217

TABLE 10.1   Comparison of Overall Population Distribution and the Survey Sample in Kazakhstan and Uzbekistan (in percent except in line one)

		Kazakhstan			Uzbekistan	
	Year	Official Data	Survey	Year	Official Data	Survey
Total	1990	16,464,464	801	1991	20,613,123	1,266
Male	1990	48.43	47.8	1991	49.44	52.70
Female	1990	51.57	52.2	1991	50.56	47.30
Urban	1990	57.11	52.30	1991	40.14	66.70
Rural	1990	42.89	47.70	1991	59.86	33.30
Age 18–29	1991	33.50	27.00	1991	21.58	28.00
Age 30–39	1991	24.00	26.50	1991	12.90	29.90
Age 40–49	1991	14.00	19.60	1991	5.96	18.20
Age 50–59	1991	13.70	14.20	1991	5.98	11.90
Age 60 +	1991	14.60	11.40	1991	6.45	11.90
Higher education	1991	13.00	20.10	1991	9.17	21.30
Secondary education	1991	64.00	59.90	1991	57.70	62.80
Unfinished secondary education	1991	23.00	18.10	1991	33.13	14.60
Titular nationality	1991	41.00	42.90	1991	71.39	70.40
Russian	1991	36.00	31.70	1991	8.35	10.50
Other	1991	23.00	25.40	1991	20.26	19.10

ferent ways) and by focusing as much on the behavior of respondents as on their attitudes. My personal observations (in rural and urban areas of the Ferghana valley and Tashkent oblast) and observations by survey takers (throughout Uzbekistan and Kazakhstan), both during the survey and since its administration, suggest that respondents were more forthcoming and honest about their answers than one might have expected and that fundamental patterns were probably not distorted in a major way.

The data, their limitations aside, provide useful insight on attitudes and values among Uzbekistan's and Kazakhstan's populations, matters that are not easily assessed using other methodologies. The following are some of the results regarding attitudes toward democratic reform and leadership. The quest for political stability and economic improvement tends to dominate the respondents' views, but the overall picture is of a region characterized by confusion and contradiction.

Attitudes Toward Democracy and Economic Reform

Popular attitudes toward different government systems, democratization, and economic reform provide a backdrop against which Central Asians tend to evaluate leadership and demonstrate perhaps the greatest contradictions and challenges. Previous surveys in Uzbekistan and Kazakhstan have demonstrated relatively widespread support for democratic reform among these populations. Although "democracy" has become a catchword used by leaders and the general population

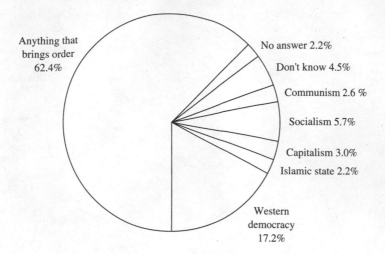

Anything that
brings order
62.4%

No answer 2.2%

Don't know 4.5%

Communism 2.6 %

Socialism 5.7%

Capitalism 3.0%
Islamic state 2.2%

Western
democracy
17.2%

FIGURE 10.1   Best Political System for Kazakhstan

alike throughout Central Asia, issues of stability, law and order, and how to reduce the enormous economic hardship citizens face today are far greater priorities than the construction of any particular government system. With no history of democratic rule in their countries, citizens perceive democracy, at best, as an ideal for some distant future, not the best system to help resolve Uzbekistan's or Kazakhstan's problems today. Notions of what "democracy" even is are tenuous, superficial, and contradictory.

When asked, for example, which political system would best promote the resolution of Uzbekistan's or Kazakhstan's problems, slightly over half of all respondents in Uzbekistan and almost two-thirds of Kazakhstani respondents supported "any system, as long as there is order" (Figures 10.1 and 10.2). The proportion of Central Asians and Slavs, male and females, and different age groups did not differ greatly on this answer. About one-eighth of all respondents in Uzbekistan (about 10 percent of all Central Asians and 25 percent of all Slavs) selected a Western-style democracy—only slightly higher than the number of respondents who chose an Islamic state (about 11 percent of all Central Asians but only 2 percent of all Slavs). Roughly 17 percent of Kazakhstani respondents (16 percent of the Kazakhs and 17 percent of the Russians) selected a Western-style democracy. Only 2 percent of Kazakhstani respondents selected an Islamic state.

Those who supported democracy (hereafter, democrats) also displayed contradictory sentiments. As a rule, for example, the democrats in Uzbekistan expressed a high degree of support and confidence in the government of President Islam Karimov. Such support for an incumbent leader is typical of their culture, but in this case the president is widely viewed as heading one of the least democratic of the governments that have emerged since the disintegration of the USSR. The

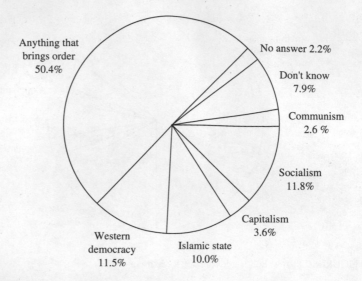

FIGURE 10.2   Best Political System for Uzbekistan

democrats were mixed in their views regarding opposition parties; almost half of the respondents who supported democracy in Uzbekistan and about 30 percent in Kazakhstan also believed that opposition groups should be limited or banned. Almost 60 percent of Kazakhstani democrats believed that opposition parties should be given full freedom in Kazakhstan; approximately 30 percent of those who supported democracy in Uzbekistan believed likewise. Interestingly, Central Asians were more inclined to want to give full freedom to opposition parties than Slavs were.

Contradictions were widely evident. In Kazakhstan, for example, respondents from the Almaty and northern Kazakhstan regions showed the greatest support not only for democracy (41 percent and 29 percent respectively) but also for socialism and communism (24 percent in northern Kazakhstan). In Uzbekistan, support for democracy was uniformly weak but was relatively stronger in Tashkent, Samarkand, and Khorezm.

Contradictory responses were not limited, of course, to democracy: Of the 12 percent of Uzbekistani respondents who called for an Islamic state, only 17 percent felt it was important in their voting decision for the politician even to be a Muslim. Instead, as with other groups, the most important traits were that the politician be honest and decent (68 percent) and be an experienced leader (49 percent). Also more important than religious affiliation were that the politician defend the poor (24 percent); understand people well (23 percent); and bring law and order (19 percent). In addition, almost all respondents supported President Karimov, despite the fact that Karimov has been quite vocal in his opposition to the establishment of an Islamic state.

TABLE 10.2   Importance of Various Measures to Achieve Normal Living Conditions in Uzbekistan (in percent)

	Important	Not Very Important	Unimportant/ Undesirable	Don't Know/ Difficult to Say/ No Answer
Strengthen order and discipline	91.2	7.6	0.9	0.2
Guarantee free speech and press	47.5	35.5	11.9	5.1
Strengthen independence of Uzbekistan	84.2	11.3	2.7	1.8
Strengthen unity within CIS	62.0	23.4	8.2	6.5
Attraction of foreign capital	34.7	30.6	20.7	14.0
State control over prices	89.0	6.4	3.1	1.5
Protection of environment	80.8	15.3	1.6	2.2
Fight against speculation	83.4	10.5	5.0	1.1
Right of individual to own, buy, and sell land	40.1	29.2	18.7	12.0

In terms of priorities, among all respondents, the heavy focus on order at the expense of democratic freedom emerged from other questions as well. When respondents were asked the extent to which a list of problems were important, not very important, totally unimportant, or undesirable, the problem most often selected as important—by roughly 90 percent of respondents in both countries—was strengthening social order and discipline (Tables 10.2 and 10.3). In both countries, responses were roughly the same by nationality. (Respondents were allowed to select up to three problems.) Over 70 percent of the sample in both countries also considered the following problems to be among the most important: establishing government control over prices; securing the independence of Uzbekistan or Kazakhstan; fighting speculation; and protecting the environment.

On the other hand, the responses indicated less support for elements fundamental to a democracy—free speech, freedom of the press, pluralism, and tolerance of other political views. In the same question, for example, less than 40 percent of all respondents in Kazakhstan and less than half of all respondents (47 percent) in Uzbekistan believed that securing free press and free speech was important (Tables 10.2 and 10.3). More than one-third of all respondents in both countries deemed these elements not very important; over one-tenth in Uzbekistan and almost 15 percent in Kazakhstan said they were unimportant; and about 2 percent of Uzbekistani and 4 percent of Kazakhstani respondents stated that a free press and free speech were undesirable. (Respondents in each category did not differ greatly by nationality, although surprisingly, slightly more Russians stated that these rights were unimportant.)

The same held for economic reform in terms of similar questions and contradictions reflected in survey responses. Economic problems clearly were among

TABLE 10.3   Importance of Various Measures to Achieve Normal Living Conditions in Kazakhstan (in percent)

	Important	Not Very Important	Unimportant/ Undesirable	Don't Know/ Difficult to Say/ No Answer
Strengthen order and discipline	87.5	5.6	2.5	4.3
Guarantee free speech and press	39.6	33.1	17.6	9.8
Strengthen independence of Kazakhstan	73.7	12.9	5.4	8.0
Strengthen unity within CIS	64.7	14.9	7.9	12.5
Attraction of foreign capital	31.5	25.2	27.4	16.0
State control over prices	76.2	11.0	6.2	6.6
Protection of environment	81.3	9.2	1.6	7.9
Fight against speculation	71.9	1.6	8.0	7.5
Right of individual to own, buy, and sell land	45.3	16.6	24.4	13.8

the greatest concerns of all respondents. When asked to select the most important current problems, respondents ranked economic problems uniformly on top, with 29 percent in Uzbekistan and 24 percent in Kazakhstan naming high prices as the greatest problem that must be resolved in their country, and 23 and 16 percent naming unemployment. Both of these figures were slightly higher among Uzbek respondents, although in Kazakhstan there was no difference by nationality. In light of the economic upheavals that have affected both countries since this survey was conducted, one can only assume that these concerns have intensified.

Although "market reform" has become a favored phrase throughout Central Asia, many citizens have only seen their quality of life decline since economic reform became a government slogan, and they feel that severe economic problems loom large. When asked, for example, if they had gained or lost from the economic reforms begun in Uzbekistan, only about one-tenth of all respondents said they had gained, but four times as many (close to two-fifths of all respondents) said they had lost (Table 10.4). The situation was more glaring in Kazakhstan: Only 7 percent believed they had gained from economic reform; almost half (45 percent) said they had lost. Forty-four percent of respondents said they had stayed roughly the same. Among ethnic Russians, more than half said they had lost, but only 5 percent believed they had gained.

None of these results should be surprising in countries that have a long history and tradition of authoritarianism, colonial rule, and economic hardship. But they do reflect on how Central Asia's population views its leaders and future. Most important to the survey respondents were questions of maintaining order and stability in the wake of the chaos of political and economic disruption throughout the former Soviet Union. It is perhaps largely because of this attitude that Karimov's

TABLE 10.4   Effects on Respondents of Economic Reform in Uzbekistan and Kazakhstan (in percent)

	Gained	Neither Gained nor Lost	Lost	Don't Know/ Difficult to Say
Kazakhstan				
Total	7.3	42.7	45.3	4.6
Kazakh/Central Asian	7.5	46.7	42.0	4.6
Russian/Slavic	6.2	36.5	53.5	3.7
Uzbekistan				
Total	10.6	43.8	36.7	7.9
Uzbek/Central Asian	11.4	43.9	36.4	8.3
Russian/Slavic	5.7	42.6	49.6	2.1

Note: The choices in the question were as follows: definitely gained; sooner gained than lost; neither gained nor lost; sooner lost than gained; definitely lost; don't know/difficult to answer; no answer.

strategy of casting himself in the role of defender of stability and security (described by Donald Carlisle in Chapter 9) has proved to be so effective. The yearning for more political stability and less economic hardship pervades every aspect of life in Central Asia, including how citizens view the leadership challenges ahead of them.

Views Toward Leadership

Leadership Traits

Survey respondents seemed to judge leaders more on their ability to bring order and stability to government and to reduce economic hardship than on other factors. When asked what needs a political leader must answer, and what key traits a political leader must have to win their votes, respondents overwhelmingly named three traits as most important (Table 10.5): that a prospective leader be honest and upright (60 percent of respondents from both countries); be able to bring order to the government (59 percent of Kazakhstani and 42 percent of Uzbekistani respondents); and understand economics (44 percent of Kazakhstani and 35 percent of Uzbekistani respondents). These were the top priorities for Russians and Central Asians alike.[1]

These were also the main priorities among the self-proclaimed democrats, although this group differed somewhat by nationality. In Uzbekistan, well over half of the Central Asian respondents said that the candidate should be honest and decent, 40 percent that he or she should understand economics, and one-third that he or she should bring law and order. (About one-fourth of the Uzbeks believed it was important that the leader know their customs and be of their nationality, as compared to very few of the Slavs.) Two-thirds of Slavic democrats said the leader

TABLE 10.5   Traits Needed by a Leader to Gain Vote (in percent)

	Uzbekistan	Kazakhstan
Be a countryman	7.3	3.2
Be honest/decent	60.4	59.4
Be of same clan, tribe	3.1	2.4
Be of same nationality	12.3	10.5
Be of same religion	8.4	2.1
Know customs of people	17.8	14.0
Be an experienced leader	27.3	22.1
Understand economics well	35.3	44.2
Be democratic	10.5	12.1
Be highly educated, intelligent	13.8	16.4
Understand people well	19.4	14.1
Defend the poor	25.3	17.1
Be able to bring order in the government	41.6	58.9
Don't know/difficult to answer	0.5	1.5
No answer	0.5	2.4

should be honest and decent and understand economics, and roughly two-fifths said he or she should be a democrat and bring law and order.

In general, the role of nationality, clan, and religion as criteria for selecting a leader was lower for respondents as a whole, although this has likely risen since the survey. Roughly 20 percent of the Central Asians in both countries (including 22 percent of the Kazakhs and 16 percent of the Uzbeks) believed it important for the leader to be of their nationality, and a similar number of Central Asians believed the leader should know the people's traditions and customs. This response among the indigenous nationalities perhaps stemmed from their assumption that their leaders will be of the same nationality in any event. Among Uzbekistani respondents, the role of tribe and religion was strongest in Karakalpakstan, and nationality was strongest in Khorezm and Namangan. In Kazakhstan, interestingly, the role of nationality was highest in the heavily Russian oblast of Semipalatinsk.

The President

The desire for strong leadership was reflected in the widespread support accorded Presidents Karimov and Nazarbaev. Over 80 percent of respondents in each country believed the president wielded a great deal of power and influence and supported reform.

For example, when asked to estimate the amount of real power and influence particular people or organizations wielded in Uzbekistan, 86 percent of respondents said the president of Uzbekistan wielded unlimited power (Table 10.6). On a scale of 1 through 9 (1 representing virtually no power, 9 signifying unlimited power), 95 percent ranked the president's power between 7 and 9. Only 2 percent of respondents believed that Karimov's power was either in the middle ground or nonexistent. President Nazarbaev's rankings were slightly lower in the survey

TABLE 10.6   Perceptions of Locus of Power in Uzbekistan

	Has No Power 1	2–3	4–6	7–8	Has Unlimited Power 9	Don't Know	No Answer
Oblast leaders	25	27	226	336	523	109	8
(khokimy)	2.0%	2.2%	18.0%	26.8%	41.7%	8.7%	0.6%
Raiou and city leaders	34	44	306	310	435	114	9
	2.7%	3.5%	24.4%	24.8%	34.7%	9.1%	0.7%
President of the re-	9	2	14	122	1075	24	6
public	0.7%	0.2%	1.1%	9.7%	85.9%	1.9%	0.5%
Local soviets	80	128	338	210	321	154	14
	6.4%	10.3%	27.1%	16.9%	25.8%	12.4%	1.1%
The mafia	304	62	172	147	195	331	28
	24.5%	5.0%	13.9%	11.9%	15.7%	26.7%	2.3%
Supreme Soviet	28	21	139	365	549	128	36
	2.2%	1.7%	11.0%	28.8%	43.4%	10.1%	2.8%
Cabinet of ministers	14	14	113	418	553	121	33
	1.1%	1.1%	9.0%	33.1%	43.7%	9.6%	2.6%
People's Democratic	149	145	284	144	201	297	25
Party	12.0%	11.6%	22.8%	11.6%	16.1%	23.9%	2.0%
Muslim clergy	210	136	315	212	119	233	17
	16.9%	11.0%	25.4%	17.1%	9.6%	18.8%	1.4%
Army	116	80	255	275	272	221	19
	9.4%	6.5%	20.6%	22.2%	22.0%	17.9%	1.5%
SNB (formerly KGB)	77	51	224	269	285	297	30
	6.2%	4.1%	18.2%	21.8%	23.1%	24.1%	2.4%

(Table 10.7) but still reflected a perception of extensive power: Nearly 83 percent of respondents placed him between 7 and 9 on the scale; a higher proportion (one-eighth) than in the Uzbekistan survey did not know or did not answer.

Likewise, more than 80 percent of the Uzbekistani respondents and about three-fourths of the Kazakhstani respondents stated that their respective president was greatly facilitating the development of democracy and market reform. On another scale of 1 to 9 (1 signifying that the leader or organization was preventing market reforms, 9 that the leader or group was greatly facilitating market reforms), 80 percent of Uzbekistani respondents gave President Karimov a 9. He was ranked between 7 and 9 by 90 percent (including 79 percent of Russians); 85 percent of Kazakhstani respondents gave Nazarbaev that ranking.

Karimov's popularity was high among all groups in Uzbekistan relative to other Central Asian and world leaders; the same was true for Nazarbaev's popularity in Kazakhstan. From a list of fourteen past and present leaders of Central Asia, Russia, and the West, respondents were asked to select the three whom they most respected as government leaders (Tables 10.8 and 10.9). Among Uzbekistani respondents, 52 percent put President Karimov in first place, Vladimir Ilyich Lenin second (15.5 percent), and Nursultan Nazarbaev, the president of neighboring Ka-

TABLE 10.7   Perceptions of Locus of Power in Kazakhstan

	Has No Power 1	2–3	4–6	7–8	Has Unlimited Power 9	Don't Know	No Answer
Oblast leaders (akimy)	23	29	146	269	215	62	50
	2.9%	3.7%	18.4%	33.9%	27.1%	7.8%	6.3%
Raion and city leaders	26	49	191	261	148	62	57
	3.3%	6.2%	24.1%	32.9%	18.6%	7.8%	7.2%
President of the republic	10	6	28	153	501	38	58
	1.3%	0.8%	3.5%	19.3%	63.1%	4.8%	7.3%
Local soviets	91	129	250	125	73	66	60
	11.5%	16.2%	31.5%	15.7%	9.2%	8.3%	7.6%
The mafia	52	36	117	168	208	156	57
	6.5%	4.5%	14.7%	21.2%	26.2%	19.6%	7.2%
Supreme Soviet	20	23	114	313	193	67	71
	2.5%	2.9%	14.3%	39%	24.1%	8.4%	8.9%
Cabinet of ministers	14	21	102	357	151	85	71
	1.7%	2.6%	12.7%	44.6%	18.9%	10.6%	8.9%
Socialist Party	202	88	82	28	10	314	70
	25.4%	11.1%	10.3%	3.5%	1.3%	39.5%	8.8%
Muslim clergy	119	125	194	53	34	205	64
	15.0%	15.7%	24.4%	6.7%	4.3%	25.8%	8.1%
Army	74	93	200	166	52	146	63
	9.3%	11.7%	25.2%	20.9%	6.5%	18.4%	7.9%
SNB (formerly KGB)	29	35	143	224	73	206	84
	3.7%	4.4%	18.0%	28.2%	9.2%	25.9%	10.6%

zakhstan, third (7 percent); only 0.4 percent selected President Askar Akaev of Kyrgyzstan. As for leaders beyond Central Asia's borders, almost 4 percent picked Boris Yeltsin, and slightly over 1 percent selected Bill Clinton.

In Kazakhstan, almost half (48 percent) selected Nazarbaev as first choice with Lenin again the next most popular leader (15 percent). The next largest group of respondents named Kunaev and Stalin as their most respected leaders (4.5 percent in each case). Only around 2 percent of Kazakhstani respondents selected President Karimov as their most respected leader—slightly less than those who selected Gorbachev, Yeltsin, and Brezhnev but more than those who selected Presidents Akaev and Niiazov.

The top three choices in Uzbekistan for first place were relatively similar between Uzbeks and Russians. Among respondents of both nationality groups, Karimov was selected as first choice, although by 56 percent of Uzbek respondents and only 39 percent of Russian respondents. Among Russians and Uzbeks alike, Lenin received about 15 percent of the vote. Only the third choice differed dramatically: Twenty percent of Russians put Nazarbaev in first place, whereas the next high for Uzbeks was 7.7 percent for Sharaf Rashidov, former party boss of Uzbekistan.

TABLE 10.8   Views of Political Leaders: Uzbekistani Respondents (in percent)

	Most Respected	Second Most Respected	Third Most Respected	Most Disliked
Gorbachev	3.7	3.2	9.8	44.7
Yeltsin	2.6	5.9	11.5	13.2
Lenin	15.5	5.7	5.1	2.3
Nazarbaev	7.1	21.7	15.7	0.3
Karimov	52.1	20.2	8.9	0.4
Rashidov	6.4	18.8	8.4	0.6
Clinton	1.1	1.6	4.5	0.1
Akaev	0.4	3.2	4.3	1.4
Niiazov	2.2	4.0	6.8	0.1
Brezhnev	2.5	4.8	7.5	2.1
Stalin	3.2	3.5	4.4	7.2
Bush	0.6	0.9	1.8	0.3
Khomeini	0.2	0.2	0.6	1.7
Hussein	0.2	1.1	2.3	7.7
Don't know	1.7	4.7	7.8	16.9
No answer	0.3	0.4	0.5	1.2

In all cases, with the exception of Lenin, few respondents found favorites out-side of Central Asia. In Uzbekistan, less than 5 percent of Russian respondents se-lected Boris Yeltsin, less than 5 percent, Gorbachev, and almost 4 percent of the Russians picked Bill Clinton (versus less than 1 percent of the Uzbeks). The same individuals were predominant in the second and third choices, except that Boris Yeltsin became more popular, with 11 percent of respondents choosing him as third choice.

When respondents were asked to name from among the same choices the lead-ers they most disliked, the highest proportions of respondents in both countries named Mikhail Gorbachev (36 percent of all Kazakhstani respondents and 45 per-cent of all Uzbekistani respondents) and Boris Yeltsin (12–13 percent in both countries) (Tables 10.8 and 10.9). In both surveys, Joseph Stalin and Sadam Hus-sein were next on the list (in Kazakhstan, Stalin received the same percentage as Yeltsin). None of the other choices in either country received more than 3 percent of the vote.

Views of Other Leaders

However genuine, the high level of confidence expressed in Presidents Karimov and Nazarbaev was not accorded to lower-level leaders. Despite the stated support for their presidents, three-quarters of Kazakhstani respondents and roughly half of Uzbekistan's respondents believed that their country's current government as a whole was either not doing very much or was doing nothing at all to ease the life of its citizens. Whereas well over three-quarters of respondents in each country said their president was significantly facilitating market reform, only one-eighth of

TABLE 10.9   Views of Political Leaders: Kazakhstani Respondents (in percent)

	Most Respected	Second Most Respected	Third Most Respected	Most Disliked
Gorbachev	2.7	5.2	6.5	36.2
Yeltsin	2.9	8.1	9.9	12.4
Lenin	14.9	5.9	6.7	1.4
Nazarbaev	47.6	15.1	10.1	0.0
Karimov	2.4	7.6	4.9	0.2
D. Kunaev	4.5	11.1	5.4	0.2
Clinton	1.0	4.4	3.6	1.4
Akaev	0.7	5.9	7.0	0.1
Niiazov	0.7	2.0	1.9	0.1
Brezhnev	3.5	5.7	5.4	1.9
Stalin	4.5	4.2	2.5	12.5
Bush	2.0	3.0	4.1	0.4
Khomeini	0.2	0.5	0.6	0.9
Hussein	0.9	0.6	0.9	8.1
Don't know	4.5	10.7	18.9	11.7
No answer	7.0	9.9	11.7	12.5

Kazakhstani respondents and about one-third of Uzbekistani respondents believed oblast and raion leaders were doing so.[2]

In Kazakhstan, there was little difference between Central Asians and Slavs in their views. In Uzbekistan, Central Asian respondents demonstrated somewhat more support for the government than did Slavs. But among both groups, leadership support seemed to decline the farther removed officials were from the president's shadow. Whereas close to 60 percent of Central Asians believed that the government was doing everything possible to ease the life of its citizens, only 43 percent of Russians and Slavs did. But among both nationality groups, support was much weaker for all levels of government than it was for Karimov.

This picture was mirrored in perceptions of actual power wielded (Tables 10.6 and 10.7). In each country, the Supreme Soviet and cabinet of ministers were viewed as enjoying the most power and influence after the president: Around three-fourths of all Uzbekistani respondents and almost two-thirds of Kazakhstani respondents put these two government bodies between 7 and 9 on the nine-point scale. Almost on the same level in both countries were the oblast leaders; the raion and city leaders were viewed as enjoying slightly less power; local soviets were viewed as wielding little power and influence, if any at all.

The Muslim clergy were perceived as among the least powerful actors on the political stage. In Uzbekistan, where they were viewed as stronger than in Kazakhstan, only 9 percent of respondents ranked the Muslim clergy as having unlimited power, and only about one-fourth of respondents placed them between 7 and 9 on the scale. About the same proportion ranked them between 1 and 3, and 17 percent of respondents stated the clergy had absolutely no real power or influence. Interestingly, Russians and Slavs seemed to ascribe more power to the Islamic clergy than Uzbeks and Central Asians did.

The army and SNB (former KGB) were viewed as still exerting a good deal of power and influence. This was true especially in Uzbekistan, where almost one-quarter of respondents believed both the army and SNB exerted unlimited power, and about 45 percent placed them between 7 and 9 on the scale. In both cases, Central Asians tended to ascribe more power to the military and the SNB than Slavs did. In Kazakhstan, these numbers were lower with the power of the SNB and the army perceived as below that of all government bodies except the local soviets.

Although answers fluctuated widely by question, the western areas of both countries seemed to be among the most disaffected regions. In Kazakhstan, Aturau and both northern and southern Kazakhstan appeared to be most disaffected. Most respondents here believed the government was doing little to improve the lives of its citizens, and few people in these oblates believed the government was promoting democracy. Semipalatinsk was especially disenchanted with its local leadership. The most disaffected regions in Uzbekistan appeared to be Karakalpakstan, followed by Syrdarinskaia oblast and Tashkent.

Political parties were viewed as having little effective power or influence, especially opposition party leaders and especially in Uzbekistan. Opposition leaders Mohammed Pulatov and Mohammed Solih had most support in Navoi and Khorezm, and Solih had a good deal of support in Namangan, but their support was still relatively low. About 16 percent of respondents in Uzbekistan ascribed a good deal of power to the People's Democratic Party (the party seen as having the most power in the survey); this was about the same amount of power as ascribed to the mafia (Table 10.6).

This response highlights one of the most striking features of the power equation: the amount of power and influence ascribed to the so-called mafia. The power of the mafia, which encompasses a vague notion of groups and government leaders involved in criminal activities and corruption, was viewed as especially high in Kazakhstan (Table 10.7). Whereas almost two-thirds of all respondents believed Nazarbaev wielded unlimited power, the groups perceived as next most powerful (i.e., they received a score of 9 from more than one-quarter of respondents) were oblast leaders and the mafia. Only then came the parliament, cabinet of ministers, and raion and city leaders.

Role of Political Corruption

Perceptions of corruption, abuse of power, and organized crime played a major role in shaping respondents' views toward lower-level officials in both Uzbekistan and Kazakhstan.

It goes without saying that corruption has long been a way of life in both countries. Indeed, it has become such an integral and accepted part of Uzbekistan's economy that it is no longer considered a "second" economy there; rather, many believe it *is* the economy. But perceptions of widespread corruption in government in the face of growing economic hardship for the population as a whole have affected the degree of legitimacy accorded local leaders more than before.

This was certainly reflected in the survey. About 70 percent of respondents in Kazakhstan and two-thirds in Uzbekistan believed that it was virtually impossible to get anything done in a timely way without paying a bribe. When respondents were asked whether they agreed with the statement that "without bribes it is impossible to resolve any question in a timely way," only 14 percent responded that they disagreed more than they agreed, and only 13 percent were in total disagreement. These responses were roughly similar along nationality lines, although a higher proportion of Russians felt bribes were critical to resolving anything than did Uzbeks.

When asked to assess whether a list of individuals and organizations were, as a rule, either themselves members of the mafia, tied to the mafia, not tied to the mafia, or had no relations whatsoever with the mafia, over 60 percent of Kazakhstani respondents and close to half of all respondents in Uzbekistan said that, as a rule, highly placed government workers and officials were either themselves members of the mafia or tied to the mafia (Figure 10.3). In both countries, a slightly higher proportion of Slavs than Central Asians felt this way, but the belief was widespread. Less than 18 percent of Kazakhstani respondents said that, as a rule, highly placed officials were not tied to the mafia or had no relations with the mafia, and only about one-fifth did not know or found it difficult to answer. There was little variation by gender or age.

When asked at another point in the survey how frequently bribery was found in different levels of government—whether it was found often, sometimes, rarely, or not at all—almost half of all respondents found it difficult to answer or gave no answer. Among those who did answer, almost three-fifths of all Kazakhstani respondents and 40 percent of all Uzbekistani respondents said bribery was found often or sometimes in the government. About three-fourths of Kazakhstani respondents and over half of Uzbekistani respondents said it was found often or sometimes in the *khokimiaty*. In both cases, Russian respondents said bribery occurred with more frequency than their Uzbek or Kazakh counterparts did. For example, almost 30 percent of all Russians in Uzbekistan versus 23 percent of Uzbeks said that bribery occurred frequently or sometimes in the government, and 47 percent of Russians versus 25 percent of Uzbeks said it occurred in the *khokimiaty*.

Role of Ethnic and National Identity

The role of ethnic and national identity in assessing leadership questions is complex. Although ethnic identity was not named as one of the most important traits a politician should have to receive support, it played a critical role, according to respondents, at a more personal level. A desire not to work or be neighbors with

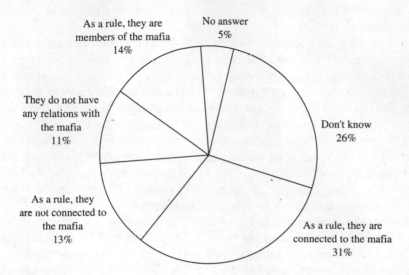

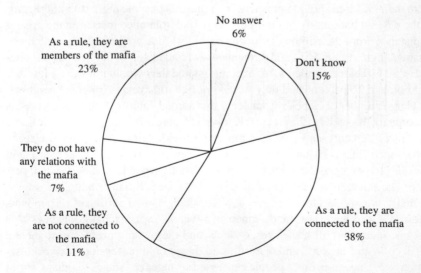

FIGURE 10.3 Perceptions of Involvement in Mafia Activity by High-Level Government Officials

other ethnic groups—let alone to have them as family members—was strong in both countries. Prejudice seemed to be especially high against Jews and Armenians and was as high among the self-proclaimed democrats as among respondents as a whole.

For example, when respondents were asked whom they would like to have as a son- or daughter-in-law, a neighbor, and a colleague at work, most respondents—and especially Central Asian respondents—tended to have strong preferences and biases. In both surveys, over 90 percent of Uzbek and Kazakh respondents said they would like their son or daughter to marry someone of the same nationality; about 10 percent said they would like their son or daughter to marry a Russian; only 4 or 5 percent said it did not matter what nationality the individual was. Between half and two-thirds of all Russian respondents (with a higher percentage in Uzbekistan) said they would like to have a Russian as a son- or daughter-in-law; about 13 percent said an Uzbek; 10 percent said a Kazakh; about one-quarter of the Russians in both countries said nationality did not matter.

When asked whom they would not want to see as a son- or daughter-in-law, Central Asians likewise had strong feelings. Most unfavored in both countries were Jews and Armenians. They were followed by a number of Central Asian ethnic groups as well as Russians. More than 35 percent of all respondents named Russians, Uighurs, and Uzbeks as undesirable sons- or daughters-in-law. More than one-fifth of the Uzbeks named Russians, Kyrgyz, and Kazakhs as undesirable. Only 4 percent of the Uzbeks said they did not have strong feelings about whom their children should not marry. Respondents became more tolerant regarding the desired nationality of their neighbors (i.e., tolerance increased the greater the distance from their immediate personal lives), but prejudice and intolerance remained high. Again, Jews and Armenians were at the top of the list. Almost one-third of all Uzbek respondents, for example, stated they would not want a Jew as a neighbor, and 26 percent said they would not like to have an Armenian neighbor. But a large number of Uzbek respondents also named Tatars (19 percent), Koreans (15 percent), Kazakhs (12 percent), Kyrgyz (11 percent), Tajiks (8 percent), and Russians (7 percent); and a large number of Kazakh respondents named Uzbeks (14 percent), Tatars (20 percent), Koreans (19 percent), Uighurs (17 percent), and Russians (10 percent). Only 9 percent of the Uzbek respondents and about 20 percent of Kazakh respondents said it made no difference who their neighbor was.

Finally, with regard to colleagues at work, again, a good portion of respondents preferred not to have Jews and Armenians even as professional colleagues. Almost one-quarter of all Uzbek respondents said they would prefer not to have a Jewish colleague at work, and one-fifth said they would prefer not to have an Armenian one. But again, more people expressed stronger resistance to other Central Asian and non-Russian nationalities than to Russians. Over 10 percent of Kazakhs said they would prefer not to have a colleague who was Uzbek (11 percent), Tatar (13 percent), Korean (11 percent), or Uighur (11 percent), whereas 6 percent said they would prefer not to have a Russian colleague. Many Uzbeks preferred not to have a Kyrgyz, Tajik, Tatar, Kazakh, or Korean coworker. Only 10 percent of the Uzbeks versus 26 percent of the Russians said it made no difference.

These patterns were similar among the younger generations and more highly educated portions of the sample, who proved to be no more tolerant than their older or less-educated counterparts. Indeed, generally they were less tolerant.

These patterns were also similar among the self-proclaimed democrats in both countries. In Uzbekistan, for example, well over 40 percent of those respondents supporting democracy also said they would not want a Jew or an Armenian as a son- or daughter-in-law; close to one-third would not want a Tatar or Korean; over one-fifth would not want a Tajik or Kyrgyz; 18 percent would not want a Russian. Only 14 percent said the nationality of their son- or daughter-in-law did not matter to them.

Likewise, about one-third of those supporting democracy in Uzbekistan said they would not want a Jew or an Armenian as a neighbor; many did not want their neighbor to be a Tajik, Tatar, Korean, or Kyrgyz; only 20 percent said the nationality of their neighbor made little difference to them. One-fourth of Uzbekistani democrats did not want to have a Jewish or an Armenian colleague at work; almost the same proportion expressed no preference; between 10 and 20 percent would not want a Tatar or Kyrgyz colleague at work.

These data, then, provide an ambiguous picture of the role of ethnic and national identity in political as well as personal views of the survey respondents. Ethnic and national divisions run deep and will likely have an enormous influence on Uzbekistan's and Kazakhstan's paths to reform and the legitimacy of their respective leaderships.

Conclusion

Although this survey was but a snapshot in time, subsequent visits to Central Asia throughout 1994 suggested that the views outlined here remained strong in Uzbekistan and Kazakhstan. Presidents Nazarbaev and Karimov appeared to enjoy at least outward support as strong leaders who were striving to bring order, stability, and economic growth to their countries. Many of the problems in these countries were consistently blamed on the *chinovniki* and lower-level officials. Corruption in government had become a major theme, openly discussed in the press at least in Kazakhstan and viewed as perhaps the most formidable brake on reform.

The survey suggested that on the surface, both leaders were viewed as maintaining order, and there were no obvious alternatives to challenge their power. But it also suggested that much of the legitimacy of these leaders would depend on the severity of any further economic deterioration and continued perceived abuses of power.

Notes

This chapter is an expanded version of a paper (*Central Asians Take Stock: Reform, Corruption and Identity, 1995*) produced while I was a fellow at the U.S. Institute of Peace. I gratefully acknowledge the institute's support and assistance. I also greatly appreciate the support of the National Council for Soviet and East European Research for much of the background research and the excellent research assistance of John Loncle.

1. These three categories were named as the most important by Central Asians and Slavs alike. Other important traits for Uzbeks were that the leader show interest toward the poor (29 percent); have good leadership experience (27 percent); know Uzbek traditions and customs (20 percent); and be of the same nationality (16 percent). For Russians, the most important categories were that the leader have good leadership experience (24 percent); be highly educated and intelligent (23 percent); be able to sort people out well (18 percent); and be democratic (17 percent). Interestingly, 11 percent of the 18–29 age group said the candidate should be of the respondent's religion—a relatively small proportion but a higher proportion than found in any other age or nationality group.

2. Whereas 80 percent of Uzbekistani respondents said that President Karimov was significantly facilitating market reform, little over half (54 percent) placed the cabinet of ministers in the same category, and only 36 percent placed oblast and raion leaders in the same category.

CHAPTER 11

Conclusion

Robert C. Tucker

A reader of the studies brought together in this book will hardly be left in doubt about the contention in the Introduction that leadership is a significant factor in the study of politics in the final phase of the Soviet era and in the Soviet successor states afterward.

The chapter contributors have shown that political leaders, starting with Mikhail Gorbachev as a would-be reformer who came to power in 1985, played history-making parts (contrary to Gorbachev's and many others' intentions) in bringing about the breakup of the Soviet Union. They have demonstrated how leaders in various Soviet republics, and first of all Russia, took advantage of opportunities during perestroika to move out in new ways toward the independent statehood for their republics that came about at the close of 1991. Although these leaders acted under the influence and pressure of emerging sociopolitical movements for change in at least some of these republics, their roles as leaders in the processes of change also were factors.

After the demise of Soviet statehood, forces developed in some of the successor republics that set limits to the capacity of the new national leaders to influence events as they had been doing up to that point. Not simply the key leaders but, as some of the studies in this collection show, elites as a whole became major actors in the political as well as economic and social processes of the new states. Such especially was the case in those successor states—notably Russia, Ukraine, Belarus, and the three Baltic states, and to a lesser extent Kazakhstan—where institutions of democratic rule emerged and free (or more or less free) elections took place. In some, on the other hand, especially Uzbekistan under Karimov and Turkmenistan under Niiazov, harsh forms of dictatorial rule came to the fore. Finally, forces of war, separatism, and chaos took over to such an extent in some of the successor states—Tajikistan and the three Transcaucasian republics of Georgia, Armenia, and Azerbaijan—that political leadership simply floundered in the face of them.

During the Soviet era, the fifteen nominally sovereign union republics of the USSR were factually ruled as provinces under the prevailing party-state political system. Consequently, the very phrase "successor states" must be used with caution, for the building of post-Soviet forms of statehood, or nation-statehood, has been and remains a centrally important task for leadership in them—and one that cannot be accomplished without popular support. In one of the successor states, Belarus, leadership by early 1994 had entered into a monetary union with Russia and more or less given up the project of independent nation-statehood; it seemed headed toward some form of merger with the Russian Federation.

In some others, including the Baltic states (especially Latvia and Estonia), strong tendencies toward ethnocratic rule on behalf of the titular nationality have manifested themselves, and in this respect we see a leader like President Nursultan Nazarbaev of Kazakhstan engaging in a "balancing act of state building," as Martha Brill Olcott puts it in Chapter 8. Where ethnocratic tendencies have been strong, resulting discrimination against members of the 25-million-strong ethnically Russian diaspora in the states of the "near abroad" has motivated many to migrate to a Russia ill prepared to house and find livable conditions for them. The numbers of such migrants now run into the millions, and Russian experts on the process estimate that from 2 million to 4 million will have come into Russia from the near abroad in 1994 alone.[1]

In the case of Russia, which remains the world's largest country with one-eighth of the earth's territory and a population of 150 million, leadership confronts the formidable challenge of forging a nondiscriminatory nation-state in place of what for centuries, including in the Soviet period, has been a Russian empire. Russia has significant ethnic minorities—they are 17 percent of its population—but the largest challenge involves policy toward the other Soviet successor states. The ruling Russian elite is apparently divided on this issue between two approaches. On the one hand are elites who would proclaim a Russian "Monroe Doctrine" as cover for a policy of restoration of Russian imperial domination of the other successor states. On the other are those who would encourage and facilitate economic, cultural, and political reintegrative tendencies only insofar as the non-Russian successor states freely opt for them, an approach that points the way toward a Eurasian version of the project of a united Europe.

Along with the task of building post-Soviet forms of nation-statehood, the leaders of the successor states have had to confront the problem of systemic change in their economies and polities. In this respect, national leadership in some of the successor states, including Ukraine and Belarus, has proved conservative, which has resulted in deepening of economic hardship and social problems. In others, among them the Baltic countries, Kazakhstan, and Kyrgyzstan, leaders have promoted movement toward market economies. And in Russia itself the leadership that came to power with Yeltsin in 1991 began with what was intended as a revolutionary break with the Soviet economic system and resultant rapid movement toward a Western-style market economy and a democratic polity. By mid-1994, however, the outcome was being described by some knowledgeable Russian commentators as "*nomenklatura* capitalism" along with "*nomenklatura* democracy,"[2] meaning that an elite still heavily dominated by holdovers from communist rule was securely in charge in a Yeltsin-led Russia with a still huge governmental bureaucracy and still weak central and local legislative institutions.

Study of leadership in the post-Soviet states shows that despite the change-directed efforts of most of the transitional leaders, these successor states were by mid-1994 truly post-Soviet in a formal sense only. The end of the Soviet Union as a state formation and of communism as a state ideology with its supporting party institutions did not mean the end of the long-ingrained patterns of thought and conduct that formed in their entirety the political culture of Soviet Russia. The tenacity of that political culture is due in part to the fact that various elements of the centuries-old political culture of tsarism—including bureaucratic rule and the corruption typical of it, autocracy and the people's acceptance of it, and so on—took on new life during the Soviet period, especially during the three decades of Stalin's rule. Despite the early post-1991 efforts of Yeltsin and other leaders toward a radical break with the Russian Soviet past, the overcoming of the political culture of that past is bound to be a matter not of years but of a generation or more.

The national leaders examined in this book have been, in their diverse ways, leaders in and for transition from the Soviet period to a post-Soviet future for their countries. These leaders are themselves transitional figures, and a number of them—the late Zviad Gamsakhurdia of Georgia, Abulfaz Elchibey of Azerbaijan, Vytautas Landsbergis of Lithuania, Stanislav Shushkevich of Belarus, Ruslan Khasbulatov of Russia, and Leonid Kravchuk of Ukraine—have already transited out of leading positions for one reason or another. As of late 1994, others seem to be approaching the end of their time in power. And Yeltsin, who may or may not run again for the Russian presidency in the election planned for 1996, is no longer the charismatic (that is, savior) leader that he was for millions of Russians early in his presidency. What made him that was not only his heroic behavior atop a tank during the attempted putsch of August 1991 but still more the fact that he embodied the hopes of multitudes of the people for exit from the rigors of Soviet life into a "civilized society" of plenty such as exists in most Western countries. Because of the hardships of the years of transition, which brought high inflation, deep poverty for many, the threat of massive unemployment, and the dangers of life in crime-infested cities, Yeltsin by 1994 no longer embodied the promise of a better life and had lost his charisma in the eyes of a wide section of the populace.

These considerations suggest that we may do well to conclude with some thoughts about future directions for study. The following observations refer especially to the study of leaders and leadership in the Russian Federation but, mutatis mutandis, may have relevance to others of the successor states.

First, more attention to the study of elites (represented, for example, in Chapter 2 by David Lane and Chapter 7 by Ronald Suny) will be needed along with continuing study of individual leaders and of the governmental, parliamentary, and other institutions in which political and other kinds of leadership show themselves. In Russia, a process of elite transformation that began in the late 1980s continues now in the mid-1990s. A survey by the Russian Academy of Sciences' Institute of Sociology showed that as of mid-1994 new people (meaning people who did not belong to the Soviet-period *nomenklatura*) accounted for 25 percent of government members, 40 percent of parliament, 17 percent of the regional elite, and 42 percent of the elite members of the fifty or so extant Russian political parties; and that women made up no more than 2.9 percent of the government elite and were not represented at all in the rising business elite.[3] Such studies, along with analysis of changing elite attitudes and outlooks, are very much in order.

Second, a very special focus for needed study is the Russian intellectual elite, historically the "intelligentsia." The Soviet period was notable for the large size of and wealth of resources expended on an intellectual elite whose mission was to serve the state in science and all other fields, including history and the other humanities and social sciences. When we consider the crucial part played by elements of the intelligentsia in the final Soviet decades in generating the international and other forms of "new thinking" that underlay the Gorbachev regime's subsequent reform efforts and that helped bring about the end of the Cold War, the importance of further study of the changing intellectual elite becomes obvious. Whether Russia in the coming years and decades will retain or lose the conceptually minded, historically knowledgeable, and critically thinking intelligentsia that has played so potent a part in its history is a serious question with implications that go beyond the internal life of the Russian Federation. Worrisome in this regard is that in recent years the intellectual elite employed in the institutes of the Russian Academy of Sciences has come on economic hard times, a factor that has led many younger members of it to join or seek to join the brain drain to the West.

Third, further study of individual leaders at the national level will need to focus more attention on the younger figures, now in their forties, who are set to take over in top positions within the coming few years as the cohort of leaders mainly discussed in this book moves out. In the Russian Federation, four individuals in their forties have already announced interest in running for president in the elections scheduled in 1996. They are economic reformer Grigory Yavlinsky, forty-two; Vladimir Zhirinovsky, forty-eight; former vice president Aleksandr Rutskoi, forty-seven; and the former head of Yeltsin's Security Council, Yurii Skokov, forty-five, who is presently chairman of the Federation of Manufacturers and could well become Yeltsin's new premier in the rumored event of Premier Viktor Chernomyrdin's early resignation. Still other younger leaders are Yeltsin's former acting premier and subsequently the leader of the Russia's Choice electoral bloc, Yegor Gaidar; Vice Premier Sergei Shakhrai; and former Finance Minister Boris Fedorov, now a deputy in the State Duma and a brilliant, principled reformer with democratic convictions. Comparable younger figures may emerge in leadership roles in other Soviet successor states in the not distant future, and they merit careful study.

Fourth, regional elites and individual leaders, especially but by no means exclusively in huge Russia, are worthy of greater research attention than they have yet received. Already such regional leaders as the reformist governor of Nizhnii Novgorod oblast, Boris Nemtsov, and the more conservative, technocratic mayor of Moscow, Yurii Luzhkov, have made their appearance as nationally influential figures. If Russia emerges from its new Time of Troubles without the restoration of a highly authoritarian and centralized administrative-command system, leadership at the regional level will become increasingly important in the country's affairs and figure as a major subject of study. Even if recentralization occurs, regional elites may well be a significant recruitment pool for a reinvigorated national leadership.

Finally, the study of leadership in the context of historical models and experiences is in order. A number of chapters in this book point to the rediscovery of—and in some instances the actual invention of—national traditions of political organization and leadership. In the Baltic states, where there is a substantial memory of democratic—as well as nondemocratic—government between the world wars, embrace of the past is one of a number of factors leading to a rapid progression away from the authoritarian Soviet archetype. In other cases, however, such as Uzbekistan, the national tradition as interpreted by the current leadership has much in common with Communist Party rule, and it remains to be seen how much if any independent effect historical pre-Soviet models will have.

In the case of Russia, one must ask whether a restoration on the historical autocratic model is in the offing. If, as suggested earlier, elements of tsarist Russian political culture rose again in the Soviet period with help from leaders such as Stalin, then we must be prepared for the possibility of a comparable revival in the post-Soviet period, albeit no doubt under non-Communist ideological auspices. It is significant in this connection that two of the four previously mentioned individuals in their forties who have announced presidential ambitions, Zhirinovsky and Rutskoi, are leaders of strongly oppositional cast and virulently Russian nationalist outlook.

Zhirinovsky has openly espoused the goal of recreating a dictatorial, imperial, and expansionist Russian state. Rutskoi, since his release from prison following the parliament-granted amnesty in February 1994, has set about the effort to found a mass nationalist opposition movement under the name of Derzhava (State or Power). Others prominent in the so-called irreconcilable opposition include Sergei Baburin, Gennadii Ziuganov, Aleksandr Nevzorov, Aleksandr Prokhanov, Valentin Chikin, and Viktor Anpilov. These and other like figures may usefully be studied in the frame of sociopolitical movements and of their ideologies ranging from ultranationalism to outright fascism.

In conclusion, a few words may be in order about leadership by the Gulag survivor and writer Aleksandr Solzhenitsyn, who in mid-1994 ended his twenty-year exile abroad by returning to his native soil via Vladivostok and a month-long railway journey with many stops en route to Moscow. At chosen main stops along the way, he would meet with governors of regions and address large throngs of provincial Russians who gathered to welcome him home, making clear his view that the resurrection of Russia as a great country, and its establishment at long last as a land of popular rule, should begin there in the regions rather than in the capital. Russians will not see democracy, he told the welcoming crowd in Irkutsk, "so long as we do not start building a territorial democracy of small expanses, starting with villages, districts, and towns." An accompanying Russian journalist compared his "hard work" along the way with a U.S. president's election campaign.[4] And although he disclaimed intention of seeking political office, he forthrightly spoke out—as he had in his 1990 tract *How We Should Reconstruct Russia*—as an informal national figure performing the tasks of a political leader by diagnosing Russia's contemporary situation, prescribing ways of overcoming the crisis, and mobilizing support for movement in the prescribed direction. In doing all this, he dramatized the role that leadership, including informal leadership, has sought to play and at times has succeeded in playing in the history of Russia and its neighbors.

At the invitation of the State Duma, Solzhenitsyn addressed this body on October 28, 1994, in his capacity as an informal national leader back in Moscow. Declaring that market economics cannot create a new state order and the moral foundations of society, he called the free-market-oriented Russian policy course "the most distorted, the most painful, the most absurd" way out of communism and observed that Russia is now an oligarchy rather than a democracy. Apart from advocating the development of an effective system of local and provincial institutions of self-government, as well as a union of the three Slavic successor states and Kazakhstan, however, he had little to offer in the way of a positive program.

Perhaps what this symbolizes is the colossal size and complexity of the problems confronting Russia and the other successor states and the limits of even the most well-intentioned leadership in taking their measure and finding successful solutions. As of early 1995, the troubled times in that sixth of the world were not over.

Notes

1. *Rossiia,* May 18–24, 1994, p. 4.
2. Yurii Burtin and Grigorii Vodolazov, *Nezavisimaia gazeta,* June 2, 1994, p. 5.
3. *Izvestiia,* May 18, 1994, p. 2.
4. *Literaturnaia gazeta,* June 15, 1994, p. 3.

About the Book and Editors

Leadership, a mainstay of Soviet political studies, has been a much-neglected subject since the collapse of the Soviet regime. However, developments in post-Soviet affairs show that leadership still matters greatly, even as democratization in many states has opened up the political process to wider circles of the population.

This volume explores new developments and old continuities in elite politics in the Russian Federation and other post-Soviet states during the period of transition and consolidation. The contributing authors analyze the significance of personal character and values, of changing leadership roles and institutions, and of cultural and historical traditions for the functioning and effectiveness of the new governments and their top leaders.

Timothy J. Colton is professor of government and director of the Russian Research Center at Harvard University. **Robert C. Tucker** is professor of politics, emeritus, at Princeton University.

About the Contributors

Yitzhak M. Brudny is assistant professor of political science at Yale University. He is the author of *Reinventing Russia: Russian Nationalist Intellectuals and the Soviet State, 1953–1991*; his other publications appeared in *Studies in Comparative Communism, Soviet Economy,* and *Post-Soviet Affairs.* He is also a member of the Editorial Committee of *Comparative Politics.*

Donald S. Carlisle is professor of political science at Boston College, where he is also associate director of its Center for Russia, East Europe, and Asia. Since 1968 Professor Carlisle has been a Fellow of the Russian Research Center at Harvard University. For several years he has served as a United Nations consultant on Central Asia. Professor Carlisle is the author of studies of Soviet and Russian domestic and foreign policy and has published many works on Central Asia. He traveled to Uzbekistan for the first time in 1963 and has made numerous visits since then, including two trips in 1993.

Timothy J. Colton is Morris and Anna Feldberg Professor of Government and Russian Studies and Director of the Russian Research Center at Harvard University. He is the author of several works on Soviet and Russian politics, including *Commissars, Commanders, and Civilian Authority* and *Moscow: Governing the Socialist Metropolis* (forthcoming, 1995). He is currently engaged in a study of the Russian parliamentary elections of 1993.

David Lane has taught at the Universities of Essex and Birmingham where, until 1990, he was professor of sociology. He is currently Reader in Sociology and Fellow of Emmanuel College, Cambridge University. He has been a visiting professor at Cornell University and a Visiting Scholar at the Russian Research Center, Harvard University. He has written extensively on socialism, social stratification, and political power. His recent books include *Soviet Society Under Perestroika* (1990, 2d ed. 1991) and *Russia in Flux* (1993). Supported by the British Economic and Social Research Council, he is currently researching the structure and composition of elites in the former USSR and contemporary Russia.

Nancy Lubin is currently president of JNA Associates, Inc., and adjunct professor at both Carnegie Mellon and Georgetown Universities, after several years as an associate professor at Carnegie Mellon. She was also a project director and the Sovietologist at the Congressional Office of Technology Assessment, and a Fellow at both the Woodrow Wilson Center for International Scholars and the U.S. Institute of Peace. She has lived in and traveled to Central Asia for almost two decades. Dr. Lubin is the author of *Labour and Nationality in Soviet Central Asia: An Uneasy Compromise,* as well as numerous articles and congressional studies.

Alexander J. Motyl is an adjunct professor of political science and associate director of the Harriman Institute at Columbia University. His teaching and research interests include post-Soviet politics, theory and methodology, empires, revolutions, and nationalism. He is the author of *Dilemmas of Independence: Ukraine after Totalitarianism; Thinking Theoretically About Soviet Nationalities; The Post-Soviet Nations; Sovietology, Rationality, Nationality;* and *Coming to Grips with Nationalism in the USSR.*

Martha Brill Olcott is professor of political science at Colgate University and a senior fellow at the Foreign Policy Research Institute in Philadelphia, Pennsylvania. She is the author of *The Kazakhs* (1987), and is now completing *Central Asia in Modern Times.*

Alfred Erich Senn is professor of history at the University of Wisconsin at Madison. He has written extensively on Lithuanian and East European history and culture. His recent books include *Mikalojus Konstantinas Ciurlionis: Music of the Spheres* (1986) and *Lithuania Awakening* (1990).

Ronald Grigor Suny is the Alex Manoogian Professor of Modern Armenian History at the University of Michigan and the author of *The Baku Commune, 1917–1918: Class and Nationality in the Russian Revolution; The Making of the Georgian Nation; Looking Toward Ararat: Armenia in Modern History;* and *The Revenge of the Past: Nationalism, Revolution, and the Collapse of the Soviet Union.* He is the editor of *The Russian Revolution and the Bolshevik Victory: Visions and Revisions; Party, State, and Society in the Russian Civil War;* and *Making Workers Soviet: Power, Class, and Identity.*

Robert C. Tucker is emeritus professor of politics at Princeton University. He has published widely, most recently *Political Culture and Leadership in Soviet Russia: From Lenin to Gorbachev* and *Stalin in Power: The Revolution from Above, 1928–1941.*

Index

Grishin, Viktor, 52
Griškevičius, Petras, 124
Gromov, Boris, 81
Gylys, Povilas, 135

Haiots Hamazgayin Sharzhum. *See* Pan-Armenian National Movement
Hairikian, Paruir, 163(n10)
Hajizade, Hikmet, 164(n20)
Hakopian, Aleksan, 163(n12)
Harutiunian, Suren, 144, 145, 149
HHSh. *See* Pan-Armenian National Movement
Hitler-Stalin Pact, 6–7, 8
Hovannisian, Raffi, 146
How We Should Reconstruct Russia (Solzhenitsyn), 240
Hurenko, Stanislav, 109
Huseinov, Halakh, 164(n21)
Huseinov, Suret, 152
Hussein, Sadam, 227

IEC. *See* Interrepublic Economic Council
Ikramov, Akmal, 193, 194
Imperial Russia. *See* Tsarist Russia
Inauri, 165(n31)
Independence Party (Lithuania), 132
India, 202
Inflation, 11–12, 61, 183–184
Initiative Group for the Defense of Human Rights (Georgia), 154
Intelligentsia, 35, 40, 43, 142, 238
  Armenia, 144, 146
  Georgia, 155, 167(n54)
  Lithuania, 127, 128, 131
  and Yeltsin, 56–57, 65, 72(n29)
International Monetary Fund, 161
International political system, 32, 33, 43, 45, 46
Interregional Deputies' Group, 56–57
Interrepublic Economic Council (IEC), 187
Ioseliani, Jaba, 158, 159
Iran, 151, 180, 202, 208, 215(n37)
Isakov, Vladimir, 2, 15, 18, 26
Iunusova, Leila, 164(n20)
Ivan the Terrible, 5

Ivashko, Volodymyr, 109
Izvestiia, 26, 88–89

Jermalavičius, Juozas, 127, 138(n17)
Juzeliunas, Julius, 128

Kalinin, Mikhail, 191, 193
Kalmykia, 18, 21
Kambarov, 164(n20)
Karabakh. *See* Armenia; Azerbaijan; Nagorno-Karabakh (NKAO) conflict
Karabakh Committee (Armenia), 144–145, 146, 163(n12)
Karamanov, Uzakbai, 178
Karelian Republic, 20
Karimov, Islam
  authoritarianism, 10, 25, 179, 192, 197, 198, 211(n5), 235
  background of, 196
  as defender of tradition, 58, 197, 200–201, 213(n17), 214(nn 26, 27)
  and economic reform, 209–210, 215(n38), 234(n2)
  and foreign policy, 201–202, 213(n17)
  and Islam, 180
  and Kazakhstan, 208
  and Mirsaidov, 196, 198, 212(n14), 215(n39)
  on December 1993 Russian elections, 215(n37)
  power consolidation, 197–199, 209, 213(nn 19, 20), 215(n39), 216(n40)
  public opinion, 219, 220, 222–223, 224, 225, 226, 234(n2)
  and Tajikistan, 206, 215(n34)
  and United States, 210–211(n3)
  See also Uzbekistan
Kazakhstan, 143, 169–187
  constitution, 179–180
  economy, 173, 180–181, 183–186, 189(n37), 235, 236
  and Gorbachev regime, 170, 171, 172–175, 176, 177, 188(n14)
  independence, 170
  instability in, 185–187
  Kolbin appointment, 170, 171, 172–173
  nationalism in, 175–179

Sigua, Tengiz, 157, 158, 159, 166(n46)
Silaev, Ivan, 67, 81
Siradeghian, Vano, 163(n12)
Skokov, Yurii, 37, 67, 74(n62), 238
Skuodis, Vytautas, 125, 137–138(n7)
Sladkevicius, Vincentas Cardinal, 131
Šleževičius, Adolfas, 135
Smith, Hendrick, 126
Sniečkus, Antanas, 124
Sobchak, Anatolii, 15, 23
Sobolevskii, Andrei, 20
Social Democratic Party (Georgia), 156
Socialist Party of Ukraine, 105
Society for National Justice (Georgia), 156
Society of St. Ilia the Righteous (Georgia), 156
Solih, Mohammed, 229
Solikh, Mukhammad, 213(n19)
Solzhenitsyn, Aleksandr, 239–240
Songaila, Ringaudas, 124, 126, 127
South Osetia, 158, 165(n43)
Soviet dissolution, 7–8, 13–14
  historical continuity of, 5–9, 25–26
  and Kazakhstan, 178–179
  Khasbulatov and Rutskoi roles in, 75, 76, 83
  Minsk accords, 8, 58, 76, 83, 93
  and system successes, 142, 162(n2)
  See also specific topics
Soviet political culture
  and elites, 142
  "equilibrium of lies" in, 53, 71(n16)
  leadership in, 2
  and republics, 13, 235–236
  and Russian president-parliament conflict, 16, 17
  successes of, 142, 162(n2)
  and tsarist political culture, 6–7, 239
  See also Soviet dissolution; specific topics
Soviet political culture survival, 9–10, 16, 237
  Georgia, 154, 165(nn 31, 32)
  Lithuania, 123, 129
  Transcaucasian republics, 141, 159

Uzbekistan, 192, 197, 211(n5), 213(n17), 239
  and Yeltsin, 26, 53, 56, 62–63, 73(n45)
Stalin, Joseph V., 6–7, 111, 194, 227, 239
START I. See Strategic Arms Reduction Treaty
State Council (Russian Federation), 66, 67
State Duma (Russian Federation), 22, 23–24, 26, 96
Sterligov, Aleksandr, 15
Strategic Arms Reduction Treaty (START I), 117
Sukhanov, Lev, 55, 57, 62, 72(n29)
Suleimenov, Olzhas, 186
Supreme Consultative and Coordinating Council, 65, 74(n63)
Supreme Soviet (Russian Federation), 15, 85–86, 99(n33). See also Russian president-parliament conflict
Supreme Soviet (USSR), 83
Suslov, Mikhail, 124, 171
Svarinskas, Monsignor Alfonsas, 131, 138(n22)

Table of Ranks, 6
Tajik civil war, 8, 10, 25, 192, 235
  and Uzbekistan, 192, 196–197, 202, 204–206, 215(n34)
Tajikistan, 172, 203–204, 214–215(n33)
  elites in, 143
  and Russian Federation, 204, 206, 208, 215(n37)
  See also Tajik civil war
Tamerlane, 201, 203, 214(n27)
Tatarstan, 20–21
Tautininkai. See Nationalists (Lithuania)
Tereshchenko, Sergei, 178
Terleckas, Antanas, 129, 139(n33)
Ter Petrosian, Levon, 145, 146, 147, 163(nn 11, 12)
Thatcher, Margaret, 32, 47(n5)
There Is Such a State-Ukraine (Kravchuk), 115–116
Timofeev, Lev, 189–190(n52)
Timur. See Tamerlane
Transcaucasian republics
  elites in, 141, 143–144, 160–162